*Identity, Culture, and Politics
in the Basque Diaspora*

The Basque Series

GLORIA P. TOTORICAGÜENA

Identity, Culture, and Politics in the Basque Diaspora

University of Nevada Press
Reno & Las Vegas

The Basque Series
Series Editor: William A. Douglass

University of Nevada Press,
Reno, Nevada 89557 USA
Copyright © 2004 by
the University of Nevada Press
Unless otherwise noted, photographs by
Gloria P. Totoricagüena
All rights reserved
Manufactured in the
United States of America
The paper used in this book meets the
requirements of American National Standard
for Information Sciences—Permanence of
Paper for Printed Library Materials, ANSI/
NISO Z39.48-1992 (R2002). Binding materials
were selected for strength and durability.

Library of Congress
Cataloging-in-Publication Data
Totoricagüena, Gloria P. (Gloria Pilar), 1961–
Identity, culture, and politics in the Basque
diaspora / Gloria P. Totoricagüena.— 1st ed.
p. cm. — (The Basque series)
Includes bibliographical references and
index.
ISBN 0-87417-547-x (hardcover : alk. paper)
ISBN-13: 978-0-87417-547-9
1. Basques—Ethnic identity. 2. Basques—
Foreign countries. 3. Nationalism—Spain—
País Vasco. 4. País Vasco (Spain)—Politics and
government—20th century. I. Title.
II. Series.
DP302.B55 T67 2004
305.89'992—dc21   2003011147

University of Nevada Press
Paperback Edition, 2015
23 22 21 20 19 18 17 16 15
5 4 3 2 1
ISBN-13: 978-0-87417-976-7 (pbk.: alk. paper)

We left the Basque Country for political reasons. One of our daughters
is in prison as a convicted ETA sympathizer, and another daughter decided
to stay in Donostia, so we go home often. Brussels is close,
and it is easy to keep up with the events in Euskadi.
We will go back someday after she is released.
I will not live in a country where my daughter is in a cage.
—Emigrant to Belgium

I don't ever remember a time when I didn't know I was Basque.
Although my parents didn't speak to me in Basque, my mother spoke to
her mother in Basque. My grandparents came to the U.S. from
Ibarranguelua and wanted to forget the old country. They couldn't. I was
born in the U.S. and thought I could be like the Americans. I can't.
—Second-generation, born in the United States

Well, you see, I was a sugarcane cutter. It is not a prestigious job
like my grandfather had in Zornotza where he owned a sawmill.
But times were hard in the Sixties, and I needed to find work.
Because I took my wife from her family and our homeland, I have tried
to recover that part of Euskal Herria by helping to organize the Basque
club of Sydney. We imagine that we are still in Zornotza
and recreate the fiestas every year. My son knows his history
and I hope will teach it to his children.
—Emigrant to Australia

Fifth-generation Uruguayan! Can you imagine that I just visited my
family's farmhouse near Donibane Garazi for the first time? I wept.
I wept for all that I have missed. For what my parents and grandparents
never knew. All of my ancestors in Uruguay died without knowing,
without feeling, without smelling, without completing.
Can you imagine that I have just visited my family's farmhouse?
—Fifth-generation, born in Uruguay

Contents

List of Illustrations	ix
List of Maps, Tables, and Figures	x
Acknowledgments	xi
Introduction	xiii

Chapter One
    Ethnicity, Ethnic Identity Persistence, and Diaspora   1

Chapter Two
    Basque Country History, the Development of Basque Nationalism, and Contemporary Homeland Identity   19

Chapter Three
    The Formation of the Basque Diaspora   55

Chapter Four
    Ethnonationalism and Political Attitudes in the Diaspora   81

Chapter Five
    Basque Ethnicity Affirmation and Maintenance   120

Chapter Six
    Basque Government–Diaspora Relations   155

Chapter Seven
    Amaia: An Interconnected Disconnectedness   192

    Notes   209
    Glossary   213
    Sources   217
    Index   255

Illustrations

PHOTOGRAPHS
(*following page 80*)

Typical dress at the end of the 1800s in the Basque Country
Unloading coal at the Sendeja Street dock, Bilbao, ca. 1893
Dining hall for recent immigrants to Montevideo, Uruguay, ca. late 1800s
Uruguayan Basques, ca. late 1800s
The Totorica Sheep Company in Grandview, Idaho, 1935
Basques in Ingham, North Queensland, Australia
Argentine National Basque Week parade, Mar del Plata, 1986
The Gure Txoko Basque Club members in Sydney, Australia, 1997
Miren Garagarza Pérez and Jon Ander Bilbao, Melbourne, Australia, 1997
Basque parent and child, Mar del Plata, 1986
The second home of the Laurak Bat Basque society, Buenos Aires, Argentina
The Laurak Bat Mixed Choir, Buenos Aires, Argentina, 1915
The Emakume Abertzale Batza and Basque Country delegation, Buenos Aires, Argentina, 1939
Oinkari Basque Dancers in Boise, Idaho, July 2001
The Biotzetik Basque Choir, Boise, Idaho, 2000
Txantxangorriak musical group of Boise, Idaho, 2001
Nere Inda, Boise students, and visiting Basque Government officials, 2002
Mus players at Euskal Etxea, Lima, Peru, 1996
Basque-language classes in Montevideo, Uruguay, 1986
Father Jean Pierre Cachenaut, 1985
The Emakume Abertzale Batza of Rosario, Argentina, 1996
Basque dancers, Rosario, Argentina, 1996
Txistulariak from Argentina, 1996
Basque Museum and Cultural Center gift shop, Boise, Idaho
Pelotariak Julianón, Oriñuela, Moro, Bilbao, and Aguirrezabal, Sydney, Australia
Basques from Sydney, Australia
Delegates to the 1999 Second World Congress of Basque Collectivities
Delegates to the 1999 Second World Congress of Basque Collectivities
Basque youth in the Gaztemundu 2001 program

Idaho Secretary of State Pete Cenarrusa in Boise, Idaho, and
representatives of the city council of Gernika-Lumo, 2000

The Gaztemundu 2000 participants from Lima, Peru, with Lehendakari
Ibarretxe

The delegation of the Basque Autonomous Community to the European
Union, Brussels, Belgium, 1996

MAPS

2.1 The seven regions of the Basque Country and its political divisions	21
6.1 Officially registered Basque centers around the world, 2003	158

FIGURES

6.1 Diaspora Policy Creation and Implementation	167
6.2 Foreign-Policy Responsibilities of the Basque Autonomous Government	183

TABLES

4.1 Homeland Political Party Preference	86
4.2 Preference for Basque Cultural Events over Political Events	102
4.3 Host-Country Political Party Affiliation	103
4.4 Participation in Host-Country Political Movements	105
4.5 Most Desirable Future for the Seven Basque Provinces	106
4.6 Political Violence Effectiveness for Achieving Autonomy	108
4.7 Basque Ancestry Necessary for Basqueness	111
4.8 Basque-Language Knowledge Necessary for Basqueness	112
5.1 Language Knowledge, Usage, and Literacy by Host Country and By Age	135
5.2 Favorable and Unfavorable Treatment Because of Basque Ethnicity	152
6.1 Possible Voting Blocs for Advisory Council Assessor Representation	168
6.2 Basque Autonomous Government Appropriations to Diaspora Communities	180
6.3 Diaspora Voting in the 1990, 1994, 1998, and 2001 Parliamentary Elections	189

Acknowledgments

I gratefully acknowledge several scholars whose guidance helped me produce this publication. Professor Brendan O'Leary, the London School of Economics and Political Science, supervised this work in its original form as a PhD thesis. Professor Gregorio Monreal Zia, Universidad Pública de Navarra, finetuned the data regarding Basque Country history. José C. Moya, University of California–Los Angeles; Sebastian Balfour, London School of Economics; and Alfonso Pérez-Agote, University of the Basque Country, also added valuable improvements. The meticulous editing of Margaret Fisher Dalrymple, University of Nevada Press, facilitated my adjustments for the final publication and corrected and enhanced the entire composition. Many thanks also to Razmik Panossian, London School of Economics, and to mentor Professor Gregory A. Raymond, Boise State University, and his nearly twenty years of inspiration and faith in my academic abilities. Fellowships from the American Association of University Women, Euskal Fundazioa, Federación de Entidades Vasco Argentinas, Idaho Humanities Council, and Eusko Jaurlaritza contributed to the financial requirements of my international travel.

Four years of research involving travel in eight countries provided numerous debts of gratitude to many new friends. *Eskerrik asko bihotzetik* to those Basques who opened their homes and personal lives to me for interviews that often asked them to revisit painful memories. Their courage to survive, accept, and supersede their circumstances exemplifies the meaning of endurance and spirit and is indeed humbling. Sincere appreciation goes to Felipe Muguerza and Miren Arozarena in Argentina for generously aiding the re-creation of my fieldwork after my luggage was stolen—including laptop computer, all backup disks, completed questionnaires, and taped interviews. It would have been easy to quit without their advocacy. To Gurutz Iguain, Carlota Oyarbide, Deli Ahuntchain, and Alberto Irigoyen for facilitating fieldwork, travel, and interviews; many Basque dinners; and an ever-open door in Uruguay—*mila esker*. Thanks to German Garbizu, Ion Guarotxena, Víctor Ortuzar, and Raúl Noblecilla in Peru, my stay in Lima was academically and personally rewarding. In Australia, Joe and Jenny Goicoechea, José and Dolores Mendiolea Larrazabal, Mary Bengoa Arrate, Nekane Kandino, Miren Garagarza, Carlos Orúe and Miren Sanz, and Mari Asun Salazar all demonstrated an unbelievable solidarity with my project—commandeering living rooms and marshaling interview schedules.

In Belgium, Ibon Mendibelzua helped organize questionnaire and interview details, and Enrike Pagoaga offered his home, office, and kitchen table for endless conversations.

My fieldwork in the United States really began more than twenty years ago when, as a teenage Basque dancer, our troupe traveled around the West meeting other Basques whom I found had the same double identity as I did. Two decades of Basque festivals, conferences, and serving as a representative to Basque organizations have kept my antennae tuned to definitions of Basqueness. Thank you to former North American Basque Organizations (NABO) presidents Bob Echeverria and Steve Mendive for document sharing and many good laughs about the stamina and iron will of Basque women. Thanks also to Iñaki Aguirre Arizmendi and Josu Legarreta, director of relations for Basque collectivities of the Basque Autonomous Government, for providing much data and time for several interviews.

Earning the PhD and writing this book have required much dedication and sacrifice from my family and myself. We have endured my travels to London and throughout Argentina, Uruguay, Peru, Australia, Belgium, the Basque Country, and the West of the United States; stolen luggage and data; health traumas; and the trials of adolescence. During the path of this research there have been births and deaths and numerous spiritual renewals in my "Totoricagüena Tribe" of parents, Mari Carmen and Teodoro; and siblings, Dolores, Tony, Carmen, Rosa Mari, Ted, and Teresa; and their families (who for various reasons are also the authors of this work). We are reinforced by our common family values of unconditional love, respect, pride, loyalty, and responsibility to each other and to our joint futures. I dedicate this book to my parents, whose experiences from the bombing of Gernika and Franco dictatorship and lives as Basques in the United States planted the curiosity for this research, and my family and daughter Amaia Pilar, whose love, commitment, and patience enabled its realization.

Introduction

In November 1995, Vitoria-Gasteiz, the capital city of the Basque Autonomous Community in Spain, hosted the First World Congress of Basque Collectivities. The fourteen different countries sending delegates ranged from Canada, with a few thousand Basques and one formal organization, to Argentina, which boasted ninety separate Basque organizations and numerous smaller social clubs. Delegates had been elected or appointed by their organizations to travel to the Basque Country—*Euskal Herria* in the Basque language—to help the Basque Autonomous Government formulate policy regarding Basques in the diaspora.

Curiously, these Basques had more in common than not. Comments from interviews regarding Basque identity maintenance revealed very similar responses whether from fourth-generation Uruguayans, fifth-generation Argentineans, first-generation Australians, or second-generation Belgians: "We are Basques who live outside the homeland, but that does not make us any less Basque."

Until this congress, these people had not met each other, nor had any of these organizations ever interacted institutionally, with the exception of Argentina with Uruguay. If generally accepted theories of acculturation and assimilation would be considered, these Basques should have all been very distinct from each other because of the influence of the host society to which their ancestors had emigrated. By the fifth generation, they should exhibit characteristics common to the new society. Why then was there so much homogeneity and consensus in their views toward ethnonationalism and ethnic identity maintenance when their host societies are so different from one another? This book aims to answer this puzzling question and to describe diaspora Basques individually and collectively with regard to their persistent connection to Basque ethnic identity and to their transnational diaspora linkages.

The phenomenon of ethnic identity emerges where the fields of anthropology, sociology, political science, and psychology converge. The contemporary escalation of ethnonationalism and ethnicity as determining factors in political conflict demands urgent scrutiny, investigation, and analysis. The definition of ethnic identity, as I shall demonstrate, is not stagnant, and in the case of the Basques it is being constructed among this population as political, economic, technological, and human-geography factors take on new significance.

And this identity construction prompts a number of questions: In what ways is the concept of ethnic identity transformed when the definition is created and established outside the homeland of the ethnic group? What effect does a host society have on an immigrant's self-identification with his ancestors, with their myths and history of origin, with homeland events, and with the traditional culture? Since a formerly accepted definition of a Basque was a person born in the Basque Country, of Basque ancestry, who spoke the Basque language, can a person who has none of these attributes be, or become, Basque? Today, many of the hundreds of thousands of Basques who left the homeland for economic opportunities or for political exile and their descendants, who currently outnumber the population of the Basque Country itself, are answering "yes."

The diaspora represents the extraterritoriality of Basqueness. I will investigate what constitutes Basque identity in the diaspora if it is no longer defined and described by territory, language, or ancestry, as it was traditionally. For those living outside the homeland and in the diaspora, it is beneficial to modify the criteria for inclusion, since most of them have only one of three of these attributes, that of ancestry. The ancestry of many is also mixed, as they are fourth- and fifth-generation in their host countries and their ancestors have intermarried with other ethnic groups. My investigation was prompted by curiosity about why Basque identity persists for these people, and what it is about being Basque, and the characteristics and behaviors of Basque people, that allow this culture to endure and not only to maintain itself but recently to demonstrate an actual growth in interest about it—and how this interest is related to the process of globalization. I also search for evidence of instrumental reasons and benefits derived by creating and maintaining transnational links with the homeland and with other Basque-diaspora communities.

These themes can be examined by comparing Basques of different generations in different host societies. How have the factors of generation and host country affected identity maintenance in each country? This study will examine self-identifying Basques who are, or previously have been, members of a Basque organization in their communities in Argentina, Uruguay, Peru, the United States, Australia, and Belgium. Each group has a different time period and circumstance for emigration out of Euskal Herria, with Peru and Argentina being the earliest and Belgium the most recent. Most emigrants left the homeland in search of economic opportunities and/or for political exile. Over the centuries, they departed from each of the seven provinces on both sides of the Spanish-French international border, speaking Spanish, French, and a variety of dialects of Basque. Regardless of their local diversity, they united in their new countries to form Basque institutions with similar goals of maintaining their traditions and ethnic identity, and of nurturing the music, dance, poetry, cuisine, history, sports, language, and religious practices of their ancestors' homeland. These are not reproductions of homeland religious or cultural institutions or networks as seen in other diaspora communities, but immigrant-specific and, later, ethnicity-maintenance organizations.

Rationale for This Study

Past research on Basques in the diaspora has focused on institutions and descriptions of communal structures and their activities (Cava Mesa 1996; Escobedo Mansilla et al. 1996); on histories of immigrants and their participation in the development of local economies (Pérez-Agote et al. 1997; Galíndez 1984; Douglass and Bilbao 1975), on the Basque government-in-exile during the dictatorship of General Francisco Franco and on subsequent political exiles (Amezaga Clark 1991; San Sebastián 1991; Anasagasti 1988; Beltza 1977); and on biographies of Basque personalities who climbed the economic and social ladders in their respective countries of settlement (Azcona Pastor 1992; Pildain 1984; Decroos 1983). This is the first published study of contemporary Basque diaspora identity and Basque ethnonationalism in the diaspora, and the first comparison of Basque diaspora communities and their structure, goals, activities, programs for culture maintenance, and future plans. There is a vacuum in studies of Basque diaspora communities and their relations with homeland institutions, both public and private. There are no publications regarding the current Basque government's attempts to create business and political ties in the host societies using the prestige and status of the immigrant Basque organizations to open these designated doors. There are no works describing or analyzing the effects of globalization on Basque ethnic identity outside the homeland.

This work, then, is original in its contributions to ethnic studies and is the first comparison of Basque communities in the diaspora. Benefiting from historical analysis of Basques in the Americas from the fifteenth to mid-twentieth centuries (Douglass and Bilbao 1975; Azcona Pastor 1992; Bilbao Azkarreta 1992; Alvarez Gila 1996; Pérez-Agote et al. 1997) and their tendencies to group together and form associations, this project builds on those foundations and extends into contemporary research in anthropology, nationalism, and ethnicity and diaspora studies. Although there are academic theses and some published materials dealing with the history of Basque emigration to Argentina, Uruguay, Peru, and the United States that are extremely beneficial, there are only a few descriptive studies of Basques in Australia (Douglass 1996; Orúe 1996), and nothing for Belgium, except for an excellent study of war evacuees and orphans cared for there during and after the Spanish Civil War (Legarreta 1984). I have created my primary-source information from additional research and interviews in both countries.

The fields of immigration research, ethnic identity persistence, and diaspora-homeland relations are underdeveloped yet emerging academic topics. There is ample description referring to certain groups in certain countries—for example, the Jewish, Greek, and Armenian diasporas, the Irish in the United States, Greeks in Australia, and Italians in Argentina—but theories of explaining and testing the salience of ethnicity outside the homeland are lacking. This book examines the fundamental concepts and theories concerning personal and social identity for immigrants and creates a map of possible directions for understanding and explaining diasporas and the transnational ethnic identity persistence of Basques in their various host societies.

In the following chapters, I shall investigate several anomalies and factors regarding ethnic identity maintenance in the Basque diaspora. Is it possible that despite geographic and generational differences, the core elements of Basque ethnic identity in these six countries are defined in a constant manner? Do the differences between the host countries and the differences between recent and older immigrants impact the outcomes? Are there similarities in the patterns of development of Basque ethnic institutions, although they are located in various host countries and the generations creating the institutions reflect different eras of immigration?

Do these self-defining Basque populations actually constitute a diaspora? I shall show that Basque collectivities in these six countries tend to describe themselves in diasporic terms and fit the diaspora categorization of political scientists and sociologists, and that population specifically defined by Robin Cohen:

> (1) dispersal from an original homeland, often traumatically; (2) alternatively, the expansion from a homeland in search of work, in pursuit of trade or to further colonial ambitions; (3) a collective memory and myth about the homeland; (4) an idealization of the supposed ancestral homeland; (5) a return movement; (6) a strong ethnic group consciousness sustained over a long time; (7) a troubled relationship with host societies; (8) a sense of solidarity with co-ethnic members in other countries; and (9) the possibility of a distinctive creative, enriching life in tolerant host countries (Cohen, *Global Diasporas*, 180).

These overseas Basques imagine themselves as connected to the homeland and to each other. I suggest that chain migration and constant interaction with the homeland through transnational ties have strengthened this consciousness in diaspora Basque centers.

I shall argue that a resurgence in Basque ethnic identity salience is related to globalization but is not a partner in a causal relationship or a defensive reaction to it. The tools of global communications are being embraced and utilized by the homeland and by the diaspora to educate and to intercommunicate. Although global technology networks are perceived as positive media for creating interest in and for the maintenance and enhancement of Basque diaspora ethnic identity, do they merely fortify and simplify transnationalism, an already existing phenomenon in these communities? Does gender affect Basque ethnic identity maintenance or the definition of Basqueness itself? Is there any difference in how males and females perceive and understand the act of immigration and the process of acculturation? I shall demonstrate the respondents? statistical similarities and differences from anonymous questionnaire data, and the variances from in-depth personal interviews.

Homeland definitions of nationalism and Basqueness have in recent years progressed to a more civic and inclusive nationalism, while diaspora definitions lag behind, tending to follow the traditional late-nineteenth-century conservatism of the father of Basque nationalism, Sabino Arana y Goiri, whose definitions were linked to exclusive race, language, and religion. I propose that as communications and transnational links are intensified and accelerated with the process of globalization, diaspora definitions of Basqueness will more closely mirror those in the Basque Country for Basques who participate in their ethnic institutions.

Organization of This Work

In order to fortify an understanding of the phenomena in this investigation, I shall review several of the well-known interpretations of ethnicity and ethnic identity maintenance and persistence, as well as some theories of the nature of diasporas. Unlike many other group memberships, ethnicity is oriented toward the past and the history and origin of the family, group, and nation. Ethnic identity and diasporic imagination combine the past with one's present and future selves.

To understand the Basque collective past, real and imagined, I summarize Basque history as written by Basques and non-Basques, and the importance of the old foral laws and the concept of collective nobility that are elements of homeland and diaspora identity. I shall trace Basque nationalist rhetoric from the 1700s to Sabino Arana y Goiri's pronouncements of the late 1800s and early 1900s, continuing through the establishment of the Basque Nationalist Party (PNV) and the *Euskadi eta Askatasuna* (ETA—Basque Homeland and Liberty) organization, to contemporary homeland and diaspora definitions and attitudes toward Basque nationalism. The Basques' own perceptions of their history are essential to understanding their myth of a collective past and diaspora consciousness.

I discuss the formation of Basque communities abroad by focusing on four stages: Basques as an element in the Spanish colonization of Latin America; the impact of the Carlist Wars and primogeniture inheritance systems; the Spanish Civil War and exiles from the Franco dictatorship; and the current temporary migration of young educated professionals.

Basque immigrants' political attitudes toward homeland politics are demonstrated in several tables. I include the results of interviews and questionnaire responses revealing attitudes toward separatism and independence movements; homeland and host-country political partisanship; the immigrants' political mobilization as communities; and the exclusivity and, more recently, inclusivity of their definitions of Basque identity. Survey results will demonstrate the degree to which these Basque diaspora communities are politically or culturally defined, and whether or not there are differences based on variables of generation, geography, or gender.

I also analyze the maintenance of Basque cultural traditions in these communities, Basque language preservation, the effects of globalization and the Internet in "downloading identity," ties to Euskal Herria, and institutional connections between Basques through their ethnic Basque centers. I also delve into the idea of a Basque sisterhood and search for gender similarities in migration experiences. The daily ethnic socialization process and aspects of "mundane" and "banal" Basque ethnonationalism are explored when I examine home decoration and personal adornment used by Basques in these six countries.

This work ends with an interpretation of the development of homeland-diaspora personal and institutional networks, explaining the "Law of Relations with the Basque Collectivities in the Exterior" and its fundamental importance to future relations between and among the Basques worldwide. Spanish constitutional and Basque statutory law and policy-making for the diaspora are detailed with regard to congresses of Basque diaspora collectivities, Basque government grant subsidies, diaspora rights and benefits including voting, and the extension of Basque media to diaspora communities.

Concluding observations compare my analysis of the Basque diaspora to that of other diasporas and present my suggestions for future research in transnational identity, diaspora communities, and the relationships both have with the process and effects of globalization.

Choosing the Right Words

In the complex reality of the Basque Country, there are Spanish names for Basque places and Basque names for Spanish places, to say nothing of the North, which is bestowed with the equivalent puzzle in French. How one determines the correct name for an appropriate place depends much on one's own identity and political opinions. In an attempt to demonstrate neutrality, I shall when possible utilize English terminology and language. Where there is no separate English-language term, I shall utilize the standardized Batua Basque language and the official toponyms decreed by the Resolution of 17 December 2001, which lists the official place names and spellings selected by the municipal councils themselves (*Boletín Oficial del País Vasco,* No. 1, 2 January 2002, with the latest update from 30 September 2002). The legislative branches of Bizkaia (1986) and Gipuzkoa (1990) voted to use the Basque orthography as the official form in their provinces, and Álava voted to use *Álava* as the official spelling of the province for materials published in Spanish and *Araba* for materials published in Basque. I therefore use *Araba, Bizkaia,* and *Gipuzkoa* when referring to these areas. For this work, I utilize the current geopolitical boundaries as stipulated in the Spanish Constitution of 1978, the Statutes of Autonomy of Euskadi of 1979, and the Statutes of Autonomy of Navarre of 1979, and by the French department of Pyrénées-Atlantiques. Pyrénées-Atlantiques encompasses the Basque provinces of Lapurdi (Labourd), Behe Nafarroa (Basse Navarre), and Zuberoa (Soule). Euskadi is the political name for the politically and economically autonomous region of Spain that includes the provinces of Araba, Bizkaia, and Gipuzkoa; and Nafarroa is the separate autonomous province of Navarre. The glossary provides the Spanish or French equivalent for the names of Basque towns.

In the traditional Basque language, there are various spellings and entire words that differ depending on regional variations. I shall apply the standardized Basque language, known as Batua (one or united), which is the official version of the Basque Autonomous Government, the Basque public media, and the Basque Language Academy. Especially important are uses of *Basque Country* and *Euskal Herria,* by which I mean all seven provinces described above; *Euskadi,* which denotes only the three provinces of Araba, Bizkaia, and Gipuzkoa; and *Nafarroa,* which includes only the lands in today's Spain that made up the historical Kingdom of Navarre and today is ruled by its own Statutes of Autonomy.

*Identity, Culture, and Politics
in the Basque Diaspora*

Chapter One

Ethnicity, Ethnic Identity Persistence, and Diaspora

What exactly is meant by "ethnic identity," and what is "ethnicity"? Is it the language one speaks and the civic territory in which one lives? In the case of the Basques, ancestry plays a crucial role in this determination. My research asked self-defining Basques these very questions: What does it take to be a Basque? Who is considered a Basque and who is not? What characteristics must one have to be a Basque, regardless of where one lives?

Prospecting in the literature of anthropology, psychology, sociology, and social-psychology reveals a rich body of theories, approaches, and arguments concerning personal and social identity creation and maintenance. Fredrik Barth's writings are especially helpful commencing points when specifically attempting to understand and explain ethnic identity. Using Naroll's 1964 anthropological definition, Barth designates an ethnic group as a population that:

1. Is largely biologically self-perpetuating;
2. Shares fundamental cultural values, realized in overt cultural unity in cultural forms;
3. Makes up a field of communication and interaction;
4. Has a membership that identifies itself, and is identified by others, as constituting a category distinguishable from other categories of the same order. (Barth 1969, 10)

Barth's arguments assert that clear boundaries persist and are maintained despite changing participation and membership in the groups; important social relations are maintained across boundaries; cultural differences can persist despite interethnic contact and interdependence; and ethnic groups are categories of ascription and identification by the persons themselves (Barth 1969). This describes the particular Basque populations that I sampled in each host country.

Theories of Ethnic Identity and Ethnicity

PRIMORDIALISM

The natural, affective attachments of identity are called primordialism, a concept first introduced by Shils (1957; quoted in Scott 1990) when examining the effect of "primordial qualities" on social interaction. According to Shils, race and ethnicity are seen as primary sources of loyalty and the essence of the manner in which people group themselves. The primordial perspective focuses attention on the great emotional strength of ethnic bonds because primordial "givens" are not seen to change. Subsequently, da Silva (1975) argues that the continued vitality of Basque nationalism is a result of this emotional power of the Basques' group identity. Primordialists generally argue that ethnic identity is a function of strong emotional ties based upon common descent and the distinctive past of a group.

Greeley (1974), Isaacs (1975), and Connor (1978) broadly presume the importance of primordial loyalties and the human primal need to belong. The current tide of ethnonationalism sweeping the world demonstrates that an "intuitive bond felt toward an informal and unstructured subdivision of mankind is far more profound and potent than are the ties that bind them to the formal legalistic state structure in which they find themselves" (Connor 1978, 377). This could describe the loyalty of diaspora Basques to their Basque culture and identity over time and distance, even though they are a part of a "formal legalistic state structure" elsewhere.

The application of Shils's concept is expanded by Clifford Geertz (1973) beyond kinship to larger-scale groups based on territory, religion, language, and other customs. These attachments are the "givens" of the human condition, rooted in the nonrational foundations of the personality, and provide a basis for affinity with others from the same background. In a more controversial usage, Pierre van den Berghe (1981; 1996, 62) connects primordial ethnic feelings to sociobiology, which rests on genetic tendencies derived from the kinship process, and the practice of "in-group amity and out-group enmity." The attachments forming the core of ethnicity are then biological and genetic in nature, making the argument that ethnicity is based upon descent. Paul Brass (Hutchinson and Smith, eds., 1994, 85) reduces primordialist assertions to the core features that ethnic groups are based on distinctive cultures, origin myths, or patterns of exchange with other groups, and persist through time.

The primordial approach to Basque identity would refute the idea that identity is fluid, rational, or calculated. This approach seeks a psychological or biological explanation for the behavioral phenomenon of continued ethnic solidarity and ethnic identity persistence. It focuses on the important emotional strength of ethnic bonds that persist over time in radically different environments and adds a historical dimension by highlighting a group's distinctive past. Research aimed at this area has shown that some ethnic attachments persist for hundreds of years and in certain cases override loyalties to other significant groups, such as religious affiliations or economic ties. Spicer (1971) observed that Basque ethnic populations have demonstrated a remarkable capacity to adapt to new environments, which has enabled them to maintain their traditional cultural systems. This could help us understand Basque identity persistence in the diaspora five and six generations after emigration.

However, scholars have hastened to dismantle this hypothesis. Why, some ask, is it that some Basques in some communities have these primordial attachments and others do not? If they are natural, biological, and genetic, everyone should experience these feelings, should they not? Why have some Basques dropped their ethnic identity when emigrating and established themselves as Argentineans, or Belgians, or Australians? Why would many Basques in Euskal Herria identify themselves as Spanish or French and not Basque? Identities are subject to change; people change religious beliefs, learn new languages, leave their homelands and settle elsewhere. If ethnic identity is founded on beliefs and practices shared through time, what about new identities that are constructed or reconstructed, or have undergone transformations and adaptations? Primordial sentiments would be fixed and static, would they not? Perhaps it would be more beneficial and enlightening for us to examine ethnic identity in different situations.

CIRCUMSTANTIALIST, MOBILIZATIONIST, AND INSTRUMENTALIST APPROACHES TO ETHNICITY

In refining these ideas of choosing identities, some sociologists argue that ethnic identity is amenable to fluctuations (Matsuo 1922, 507) and that ethnicity involves a great deal of choice, as demonstrated in Waters's research on European ethnics in the United States (M. Waters 1990). Scott argues that primordial sentiments have to be elicited by some experience, thus they are tied to circumstances (Scott 1990, as quoted in Eller and Coughlan 1993, 48). Circumstantialists suggest that ethnic identities have a social source and are not natural givens from birth.

Lyman and Douglass (1973) argued originally that ethnic group boundaries are not only selected and permeable but that people use ethnicity differently in varying situations. The "us" and the "them" change according to circumstances, and different identities are called upon according to their appropriateness for each situation. What is "appropriate" may also be whatever is instrumental in achieving a goal or specific objective. In the early stages of Basque immigration to Argentina, Uruguay, and the United States, Basques were likely to help other Basques setting up bakeries, working in tanning operations, buying livestock and land, dairying, or in a few other pursuits, which meant that this ethnic group, like others, evolved with certain labor specialties. If members of an ethnic group tend to be relatively homogeneous with respect to occupation and residence when they settle in a new host society, they are affected in much the same way by government actions and policies. Ethnic groups are therefore likely to become interest groups, and this fact breathes new life into Old World social groups and identities (Glazer and Moynihan 1970, Olzak 1983). In societies lacking sharp class divisions, ethnicity may tend to be underscored for social-class positioning and then becomes the "appropriate" instrument used to obtain government resources and benefits or a positive social status and identity in the community.

Theorists who adopt this viewpoint agree on at least one essential feature: renewed ethnic tensions and conflict are not only the result of a primordial need to belong but are the "conscious efforts of individuals and groups mobilizing ethnic symbols in order to obtain access to social, political, and material resources" (McKay 1982, 399). Glazer and Moynihan write about the "strategic efficacy of ethnicity"; van den Berghe (1978) claims that the use of ethnic symbols for gaining access to economic and political resources is an "ethnic game" played in nearly all multiethnic societies; and Bernard (1971, quoted in McKay 1982) and Henry (1976, quoted in ibid.) argue that ethnic identities and ideologies are maintained and highlighted in order to influence political and social policies, though ethnic identity is situationally variable and involves both revivals and creative constructions (Nagel 1994). However, the public profile and degree of participation in politics that ethnic groups achieve in their host countries is related to the wider questions of assimilation and integration and is tied to the "host country's legal, political, administrative and cultural-ideological apparatus" (Tölölyan 1996, 20). The rational-choice account of ethnic identity persistence focuses on group loyalty and the congruence of self-interest and group identification as well as on the costs and benefits of ethnic identity maintenance as opposed to total assimilation (Hardin 1995; Congleton 1995; Hechter 1996). Survey data presented here will investigate correlations between self-interest and the maintenance of Basque ethnic identity.

The fact that a group has common interests does not mean it will mobilize as an interest group. Explanations dealing exclusively with political and economic factors "underrate" the emotional power of ethnic bonds and "exaggerate" the influence of materialism on human behavior (Connor 1972; Epstein 1978). Indeed, instrumentalist (strategic) and primordialist (cultural) approaches need not be mutually exclusive (A. D. Smith 1984, 285). The fact that some ethnic groups pursue domestic and transnational political and economic interests does not mean that all ethnic groups have identical actions, and the groups that do pursue resources and certain policy outcomes are not *ipso facto* political interest groups.

What will we find in each of the six selected countries? Belgium, Australia, and the United States have established societies without sharp class divisions, and they also have democratic governments where party competition and interest-group activity is allowed and encouraged, yet Basques in these countries do not see their ethnicity as an instrument for gaining political power, resources, or benefits.[1] Only 1.9 percent of the total respondents have received any sort of special government benefit by maintaining their Basque identity, and a mere 6.4 percent believed that Basques, collectively or *because of their ethnic identification,* could influence their own host-country politics. Comparing these survey answers will begin to focus this picture of Basque diaspora ethnicity as primordial, circumstantial, instrumental, or something else.

Ethnic Identity Persistence

ASSIMILATION, ACCULTURATION, AND SYMBOLIC ETHNICITY

Researchers of culture have generally assumed that direct and continuous contact between groups of different cultures leads to a decrease in the differences among them. The minority culture might add a little to the dominant one, but eventually it would take on the majority's characteristics and become assimilated, losing its separate identity and becoming merely another element in the majority culture. Sandberg (1974) named this the "straight-line theory" of acculturation and assimilation. Each native-born generation acculturates further and further and raises its socioeconomic status vis-à-vis the previous one, reflecting the upward economic and social mobility of succeeding generations until they are an indistinguishable part of the host society. Although this theory has been valid for various immigrant populations in many different host-country settings (Alba 1990; M. Waters 1990; Jupp and Kabala 1993; Okamura 1998; Gjerde 1997; Nagel 1995), there have been several criticisms of it. I shall examine it in the context of Basque immigrants and their descendants in these communities.

Herbert J. Gans (1992, 175) believes a more apt term for the process of assimilation and acculturation may be the "bumpy-line theory." The graph line may not always decline into a final and complete assimilation, and it is possible, and he believes likely, that ethnic groups reach a plateau after several generations in which they continue to categorize themselves as members of an ethnic group but mainly participate in familial and leisure-time ethnicity. He has termed this phenomenon "symbolic ethnicity" (Gans 1979). Others have more precisely categorized ethnic persistence distinguishing "assimilation," meaning total submersion within the dominant society's culture, from "integration," denoting participation in the culture of the dominant host society while still maintaining a separate ethnic self-identity (Berry and Annis 1988, 45; Berry 1992).

In his original article in *Ethnic and Racial Studies* (1979), Gans argued that symbolic ethnicity and the consumption and use of ethnic symbols were intended mainly for the purpose of feeling or being identified with a particular ethnicity, whether or not the ethnics participated in an existing ethnic organization or its economic activities, or actually practiced an ongoing ethnic culture. Therefore, the assimilation process might continue, but the ethnic identity could still be a very prevalent part of the psychological make-up of the person. He argued that "symbolic ethnicity would persist at least through the fifth and sixth generation in America" (Gans 1979, 15).

But what factors determine if a person's ethnic identity is "symbolic"? If "symbolic" is defined as that which represents something else, what is the something else? Something more "real"? Who and what determine whether a person's ethnicity is "real" or only represents something real and is instead "symbolic"? Gans wrote in 1994 that he was trying to make empirical observations and was not suggesting that contemporary ethnicity was "unauthentic, unserious, meaningless," or not real. He considers symbolic ethnicity equivalent to leisure-time ethnicity. I continue to raise the same questions about the perceived importance or triviality of "leisure-time" or "symbolic" ethnicity. Many understand them both as diminutive and as making ethnicity inconsequential for later generations—thus the importance of the survey results and interviews in this research. How do these Basques *themselves* perceive their individual ethnic identity?

I also question Gans's assumptions that erosion continues, on the whole voluntarily, because old traditional cultures and groups no longer seem relevant to people trying to make their way in a new host society. He believes that for young people especially, immersion in their new country's culture is easier and more socially rewarding than "paying obeisance to an old culture that had little meaning for them, mainly to please their parents and grandparents" (Gans 1994, 579). Though in Australia the Sydney and Melbourne organizations are weakening, as are a few others in these countries, I discovered that since 1985 Basques in every country surveyed have created or reestablished Basque-interest organizations: 48 in Argentine (some new, some reestablished); 10 in the United States (all new); 6 in Uruguay (all new); 1 in Australia (new, currently organizing); and 1 reestablished in Belgium. In 2002, there were 137 Basque organizations around the world that have officially registered with the government of the Basque Autonomous Community.

The increasing interest in ethnicity manifestation is not only from elderly or first-generation Basques. As I said above, each of the countries in this study, except for Peru, has a demonstrated growth in the establishment of Basque institutions, which include members of all ages, with various activities for differing interests. This is not a result of new emigration out of the Basque Country. If the number of organizations is growing—and in several, memberships are increasing—I would argue that we are experiencing the opposite of the assimilationist effect and that perhaps globalization is facilitating avenues for reconstructing and maintaining transnational ethnic identity.

Related to this reconsideration of ethnicity is Marcus Lee Hansen's ([1937] 1990) "third-generation return hypothesis," which explained that the first generation in the host society, the emigrants themselves, established ethnic organizations, churches, perhaps schools and other institutions, and promoted some sense of cultural continuity. These institutions were the repositories of their homeland cultures, symbols, and languages. Their children's generation then revolted against their emigrant parents' life-styles and—wanting to fit in and be like their peers in the society—purposefully cast off their parents' beliefs and customs, including ethnic and religious affiliations. The grandchildren, having no reason to feel inferior and already fitting into the society, felt a need to belong to something and found ethnic uniqueness especially appealing. These third-generation individuals then sought their ethnic identity, which fulfilled their need to belong and be recognized as part of a group. Perhaps this explanation would be useful in explaining the increase in the number of people recently joining Basque clubs and establishing new ones—if they are generally third-generation. However, not only do the newcomers represent all generations, but in these Basque organizations there does not seem to have been a decrease of second-generation participants. Responses in the surveys from questions asking whether or not previous-generation family members had participated in Basque activities confirm this assumption.

In Anny Bakalian's investigation of the ethnic identity of Armenian immigrants in the United States (1993), she describes assimilation as a dynamic process that may be reversed. She proposes that the processes of assimilation and maintenance of identity go hand in hand because Armenianness changes in form and function. She utilizes Gans's concept to describe "symbolic Armenianness as voluntary, rational, and situational, in contrast to the traditional Armenianness of the emigrant generation, which is ascribed, unconscious, and compulsive" (Bakalian 1993, 6). Her aim is not to measure how similar to other immigrant groups the Armenians in the United States are but to measure their departures from traditional Armenian value systems, behavioral forms, and life-styles. I believe Bakalian's approach creates a more interesting question and focus. Adopting this application, my study does not converge on sociological or psychological reasons for assimilation, though they are essential to understanding the overall picture regarding persistence of ethnicity in the diaspora. Rather, I shall center on how and why these Basques who have not taken on a singularly host-country identity continue to define and identify themselves transnationally with both the homeland and their host society, and how they define who, and what, is Basque.

I shall examine Gans's suggestions of looking to "old culture" and traditions as a means of measuring ethnic identity. If a person living in Euskal Herria drives a Japanese Toyota Celica to his work at Fraunhofer Gesellschaft, cooks a frozen Italian lasagna in a microwave for dinner, and relaxes at night watching Hollywood-produced movies and listening to an Irish U2 CD, does that mean this person is not Basque? He is not practicing the "old culture" of his grandparents nor living the way in which they did, so is he only "symbolically" Basque because he does not live the way his grandparents did? What would one need to do, think, and feel to be a "real" Basque?

This line of reasoning supposes that there is no contemporary homeland culture, that culture is stagnant in the home country of the immigrants, frozen in a certain time period. Of course contemporary Basque culture is not the culture of the grandparents—neither is Argentine culture that of Argentinean grandparents. Perhaps "symbolic ethnicity" and symbolic culture are practiced in every society and might be better termed historical ethnicity, or historical culture. Ethnic groups have shared memories of ancestors in their own historical context, and the reproduction of those historical traditions, myths, and memories is indeed symbolic of the times they represent. In that vein, recreating a folk dance in traditional costume is symbolic and representative of how the ancestors used to dress and celebrate special occasions, so "symbolic ethnicity," it would have to be argued, is also practiced in the homeland. "Symbolic ethnicity" could also be more acceptable to students of diaspora ethnicity if it meant that the diaspora communities reproduce the culture of the homeland in their own ways, and that this symbolizes the homeland culture to them. Nevertheless, this would be an erroneous interpretation of Gans's concept. Perhaps it would be more accurate to think of Basque ethnic identity as an optional identity that varies widely in intensity from symbolic ethnicity to ethnic fundamentalism.

SOCIAL IDENTITY THEORY

An alternative sociological conception of ethnic identity comes from Henri Tajfel's "social identity theory," which concerns the perception that individuals have of themselves in comparison to others in the society (Tajfel 1978, 1981, 1982; Tajfel and Turner 1979; Abrams and Hogg 1988). The comparison becomes increasingly salient when people compare themselves to other individuals, looking for positive distinctiveness, and more specifically, when people compare their own group to other groups, again looking for the same positive distinctiveness.

If individuals have an upward directional drive and compare themselves to others who are similar to or slightly better than they are, it follows that a person would maintain his ethnic identity and maintain his group affiliation in order to augment his comparative social status. My aim is to look at the prestige given to Basque immigrants in Argentina, Uruguay, Peru, Australia, the United States, and increasingly in Belgium, and to determine if this is a significant factor in explaining Basque identity maintenance. Social identity theory provides additional descriptive and explanatory measures for the persistence of identifying with an ethnic group, and, as chapter 5 shows, survey respondents, from a low 59 percent in Belgium to the high of 90 percent in the United States, perceive Basques to have a positive social status in their host countries.

Edward Spicer's "oppositional" approach to explaining ethnic solidarity and persistence is also valuable for understanding the persistence of diaspora populations. He synthesizes the primordialist approach described above with the "circumstantial" hypothesis. As long as there is some sort of "other" or "opposition," there is reason for unity and an "us." The opposition process frequently produces intense collective consciousness and a high degree of internal solidarity. Spicer (1971, 795–99) uses the concept of the persistent identity system to refer to ethnic groups that have demonstrated their abilities to survive over long periods in different cultural settings—thus the primordial approach. He cites the Basques, Jews, Irish, Catalans, Maya, and Navajo as examples of groups that share characteristics of primordial attachments that are called into importance and utilized to create group solidarity. This group solidarity persists as long as the "opposition" establishes the need for a reaction from the "us."

For most Basque nationalists, the opposing "other" since the mid-nineteenth century and especially after the 1930s has been the Spanish central government, especially the Franco dictatorship. Basques in the diaspora, often influenced by Civil War exiles, have followed the homeland reaction to the "opposition." Franco died, however, and there is now a form of federal democracy in Spain granting autonomy to the three provinces of Araba, Bizkaia, and Gipuzkoa, named together as Euskadi, and to Nafarroa separately. Who or what is the current "opposition"? For many political exiles in this study, the "opposition" will remain the Spanish state until the Basque Country is entirely independent, and they do not trust the central government in Madrid. Several interviewees in Uruguay, the United States, and Belgium believed that the Spanish government has treaties or executive agreements with their respective host countries to monitor Basque individuals and institutional activities for future civil and criminal prosecution.

Definitions, Elements, and Theories of Diaspora

In the emerging field of diaspora studies, there exists a need for additional empirical research and theoretical consideration of the specific phenomenon of ethnonational diasporas. The essential questions of diaspora are *when* and *why* individuals and small groups of immigrants decide to stay in their host country, maintain or revive their historic ethnicity, and form diasporic communities that preserve ties with their homelands. This ability to establish and maintain international networks is related to ethnic identity maintenance and diasporic consciousness. Diasporic communities are at the same time local and international forms of social organization. To investigate the Basque diasporic populations, it is imperative to understand the daily lives of Basque political exiles and economic immigrants, analyze local community Basque centers specifically organized by ethnic immigrants, and track the links developed with their host societies and with their homeland. The different Basque diasporic groups preserve their ethnic identities by considering and "imagining" themselves as a part of a global Basque ethnic community.

Contemporary growth in worldwide international migration begs the question of whether or not ethnic groups will eventually assimilate completely into their new host states' culture, life-style, religion, and traditions, or will continue to safeguard their own ethnic identity and basically lead two lives, one in the privacy of their own homes with family ethnic traditions, and another separate public life outside the home that reflects the common culture of the host-country environment but is influenced by their own ethnicity. Basque migrants have selected both paths. Many have assimilated and incorporated the host culture or a different aspect of identity and no longer define themselves as Basque. Others have preserved and/or reconstructed a Basque identity, and continue, even after five or six generations, to define themselves as Basques and to maintain ties to the homeland. Results of interviews and questionnaires demonstrate that this choice is not dependent on time or generation, because there are examples of sixth-generation Basques in Uruguay and Argentina who continue to identify themselves as Basque, and there are also abundant examples of a "return to ethnicity" in each generation.

DIASPORA? IMMIGRANT COMMUNITY? POLITICAL AND ECONOMIC EXILES?

How should ethnic populations be defined and categorized, and by what criteria? In arguing that Basque collectivities outside the homeland constitute diasporas, I shall utilize Robin Cohen's definition of the concept of diaspora (see above).

Each of these points is discussed and utilized to categorize these Basque populations as indeed diaspora. Basques in all six countries, whether voluntary economic immigrants or forced political exiles, have established political and social organizations. These communities permanently reside in their host countries, though they individually and institutionally maintain personal and informational exchanges with others in the Basque Country. They demonstrate solidarity with fellow Basques through social, political, and economic activities—as, for example, in the United States, where many Democratic Basque voters stated in my interviews that they cross party lines to vote for Basque Republican candidates. Questionnaires and interviews demonstrate a dual loyalty to both host country and Euskal Herria. Eighty-three percent of the 832 questionnaire respondents defined themselves as hybrid Basque–host-country or host-country–Basque, and a few from Belgium added "Basque-European," leaving only 17 percent identifying themselves singly as one or the other—either "Basque," or "Argentine," "Uruguayan," "Peruvian," etc. In the conjuncture Basque–host-country, the hyphen marks a nonhierarchic union.

Cohen's model imposes a diaspora status on populations that meet these criteria, though perhaps the individuals do not identify themselves as "transnational" or "diaspora." This is often the case with this study's participants, who may not utilize the terminology of diaspora, and a few of whom demonstrate an aversion to the term and its negative connotation of banishment and punishment connected with Jews. However, their behavior, attitudes, and feelings described in the coming chapters do place them in this academic category of diaspora and as transnational actors.

Individuals may have ties and identity claims that are not limited to one single political space in terms of territory. One's presence inside a particular territorial boundary does not restrict one from engaging in transnational relations. Benedict Anderson describes diaspora politics as a "radically unaccountable form of politics" and diasporas as participating in "long distance" and "e-mail nationalism" (Anderson 1991, 327). For example, the Basque Nationalist Party, the Euskal Herritarrok Party, and the Udalbiltza organization of municipal mayors from all seven provinces all sent regular e-mail messages to diaspora Basque centers and to delegates who attended the World Congress of Basque Collectivities in 1999, attempting to inform and influence the diaspora vote for the May 2001 elections in Euskadi.

However, diasporas often do not have politics compatible with the ruling homeland elite, and they sometimes even lobby against their homeland governments, as United States Filipinos did against Marcos and United States Cubans against Castro. Although some diasporas wish to be politically effective at gaining attention for their cause or recognition for their homeland, Basques' political attitudes and activities are usually much more *ethno*nationalist—focusing on cultural and not political goals—as I shall demonstrate in chapter 4. I illustrate how political developments in the Basque Country since the death of Franco have affected diaspora Basque ethnonationalism, political attitudes, partisan opinions, and globalized networks of communications, keeping in mind that "people's relationship to the past is continually and doubly influenced by developments in the host country and in the homeland, and especially so where conditions in the homeland have become uncertain" (Hall 1990, 222–37; Winland 1995, 5). Desires for autonomy inside Spain and France, separatism from both, and independent statehood are canvassed from the survey data of the 832 responses.

In the discipline of diaspora studies, there is a gray area in the categorization of individuals, whether a person is a guest worker, asylum seeker, refugee, international migrant, or permanent migrant, and when that person becomes part of a permanent diaspora. Each host-country setting varies, as do the persons who migrate and their political, economic, and personal reasons for migrating. In Brussels, for example, are employees of the Basque Autonomous Government Delegation and European Union professionals part of the Basque diaspora in Belgium? They affirm that they are not because they will be eventually returning to the Basque Country. However, they influence other Basques in Belgium and participate in Basque cultural activities, and they fill the role of agents in chain migration and transnationalism. They share language, current news, values, opinions, customs, and traditions that are real and not mythical, fantasized, or nostalgic memories of their homeland. A few of these Eurocrats have married Belgians or other Europeans and are living permanently in Brussels. In this case, would they be considered a part of the diaspora? There is no satisfactory demarcation for the point at which one is a permanent part of this category. Each person defines for himself whether he is "in" or "out" of the group. Perhaps one should apply individual- and collective-choice models to this issue in the life of immigrants. The element of choice by individuals and by groups has been neglected in past studies of Basque identity, as have the varieties of Basque identity and the differing degrees of saliency and participation, from staunch ethnic fundamentalists to people whose only overt Basque connection is attendance at the annual Aberri Eguna (Day of the Homeland) festival—a connection similar to that of "Christmas Catholics."

Although Western democracies currently exhibit relatively favorable climates for multiculturalism, each host society has problems with small groups of xenophobes expressing anti-immigrant ideologies and behaviors. For example, in Australia and the United States, maintaining Basque ethnic identity is generally viewed positively when it does not conflict with Anglo-Saxon Christian values. Because Basques have no physically differentiating characteristics identifiable from other white Europeans, they do not experience the racial discrimination so prevalent in European-settler societies. In Australia, white European ethnic identities are celebrated by the society, though not necessarily those of Aboriginal peoples or the many varied Asian communities in that country. Basques in Sydney, Melbourne, and North Queensland tend to feel that they have been socially accepted with a semipositive status because of their excellent work reputations with non-Basque employers.

Recent Basque immigrants to these states no longer perceive a necessity to rapidly adapt and conform to the norms of the host society, although learning the host-country language for employment is an exception. Basques from the Spanish provinces emigrating to South America already speak Spanish, and Basques from the North emigrating to Belgium already speak French, but Basques from either region would need to learn a new language if selecting Australia or the United States as their destination. There is very little new Basque immigration in any of the six countries studied, excluding Belgium, and most diaspora Basques are second- and third-generation, or more, speak the host-country language, and have been raised and educated in the host-country environment. They are not choosing to maintain their ethnicity for economic benefits, nor are they making political demands for special recognition or treatment in any of these countries. Ethnicity maintenance in the Basque diasporic communities follows sociological and psychological arguments of belonging, self-fulfillment, and positive social status in daily life.

TRANSNATIONALISM AND GLOBALIZATION

Neither globalization nor transnationalism is a new phenomenon. I will utilize *globalization* to refer to the social, political, and economic interconnectedness of the world and the development of networks of interaction and exchange. Contemporary effects of technology have accelerated and deepened these webs. The concept of transnational identity matches well with diaspora consciousness and has been aptly defined as:

> The ability to add identities rather than being forced to substitute one for another; multiple identities and "cross-pressures" to enhance rather than inhibit one's options; to anchor one's uniqueness in the complex constellation of communities to which one chooses to make a commitment; the opportunity to be different people in different settings—these implications of communities in the unbundled world appear to be mutually reinforcing elements of a broad syndrome which fits our current self-image as autonomous individuals and stands in marked contrast to older notions of rank, status, and duty within an overarching community which claims all our loyalties ... each individual is, in effect, a community of the communities individually accepted or chosen. (Elkins 1997, 150)

Interviewees' narratives of feeling "just as much Peruvian as Basque and vice versa" also fit the description given by Featherstone, that transnationalism "is the capacity to shift the frame, and move between varying range of foci, the capacity to handle a range of symbolic material out of which various identities can be formed and reformed in different situations, which is relevant in the contemporary global situation.... There has been an extension of cultural repertoires and an enhancement in the resourcefulness of groups to create new symbolic modes of affiliation and belonging" (Featherstone 1995, 110).

We shall see that the effects of globalization on transnationalism and diasporas "disrupt the spatial-temporal units of analysis" (Lavie and Swedenburg 1996, 14). Basques are physically connected to the host countries where they currently live, and emotionally and psychologically connected to ancestral homelands. This is a transnational identity. "When I am in Xiberoa, I miss the excitement of San Francisco. I miss my family and friends. When I am in the U.S., I miss the socializing, the smells of foods, the mountains, and people strolling every night" (second-generation, United States). The boundaries of diaspora identity are imagined, just as the diaspora identity is itself imagined.

Transnationalism broadly refers to multiple ties and interactions linking people or institutions across the borders of states (Vertovec 1999, 447). Transnationalism is also described as "the formation of social, political, and economic relationships among migrants that span several societies" and people whose "networks, activities and patterns of life encompass both their host and home societies" (Basch, Glick Schiller, Szanton Blanc 1994, 1). New technologies, especially telecommunications, foment transnational ties with increasing speed. Despite great distances and lengthy time periods of immigration, transnational ties in the Basque communities have been intensified with the globalization of communications. For example, in May 2001 Basques gathered at the Laurak Bat Center in Buenos Aires to watch Basque parliamentary-election results live on Euskal Irrati Telebista (Basque Television) cable, while others participated in live electronic election chatrooms. The frequency of communication and contact among the diaspora communities and between the diaspora and the Basque Country, I argue, will continue to increase. Political scientists suggest that the world is witnessing a slow emergence of interstate societies. I propose that the Basque diaspora is one such community.

Transnationalism is related to globalization and a real or perceived intensification of planetary interconnectedness. Globalization has been defined as "a process (or set of processes) which embodies a transformation in the spatial organization of social relations and transactions—assessed in terms of their extensity, intensity, velocity and impact—generating transcontinental or interregional flows and networks of activity, interaction and the exercise of power" (Held et al. 1999, 16).

This process is difficult to demonstrate with quantitative evidence because it also entails qualitative shifts that affect the nature of societies and the outlook of individuals toward themselves, their societies, and their world. In all six countries, interviewees' statements regarding their feelings of connectedness to, and identification with, Basques around the world give an indication of the growing "extensity" and "impact" of globalization processes in the Basque diaspora. The flow of e-mail and the exchanges of information by newsletters, bulletins, and visits of Basques from one community to another have mushroomed. At the 2000 Jaialdi International Festival in Boise, Idaho, attending Basques included people from Canada, Mexico, Peru, Argentina, Uruguay, Australia, and hundreds from the Basque Country.

Contemporary patterns of globalization manifest a distinctive historical form that is a product of a unique conjuncture of social, political, economic, and technological forces, and particular forms of globalization may differ according to historical era. In their research on discrete historical epochs of globalization, Held et al. argue that contemporary global infrastructures of culture and communication have contributed to "the development and entrenchment of diasporic cultures and communities" (Held et al. 1999, 370). Globalization is *aterritorial* because it involves a complex deterritorialization and reterritorialization of political and economic power (ibid., 28) and, for the Basques in this study, a shift in their evolving ethnic identity paradigm. The processes of the current form of globalization facilitate transnationalism in the Basque diaspora by aiding the creation and maintenance of communications among Basque collectivities and with Euskal Herria. Diaspora identity bridges this gap between local and global identities. However, although globalization and diasporization are separate phenomena with no necessarily *causal* connections, Basque ethnic identity maintenance and diaspora "extensity" are facilitated by the latest processes of globalization.

"OUR IDENTITY IS AT ONCE PLURAL AND PARTIAL"

As Salman Rushdie stated in *Imaginary Homelands,* diaspora communities have actually created their own self-consciousness as a collectivity and fashioned a group identity out of their shared experiences of exile, immigration, and life in their new host societies. They also react and evolve, transforming and mutating according to outside influences. Cohen suggests that "diasporas can be constituted by acts of the imagination" (Cohen 1996, 516). A diaspora can be held together and recreated through a shared experience, such as ethnogenesis—a process whereby immigrants practice a transfigured cultural identity creating a sort of hybrid culture, or synthesis, from the ancestral culture and that of the new host environment. This provides a link from the homeland to the new country for recent emigrants and ties from the new society to the homeland for later generations. Ethnicity and ethnic identity are not merely behavioral but also incorporate deeper, more profound attitudes, feelings, and psychological outlooks, as well as networks that are preserved similarly in these communities.

I shall demonstrate that Basque migration is not a one-time event from place A to place B. Locations are linked by the flows and returns of people, resources, and remittances, New World and Old World life-styles, and by economic and political relations between the Basque Country and the host countries. Basque immigration is time- and circumstance-specific, but in each of these cases chain-migration theory advances the understanding of how immigrants continued to follow their cues for ethnic identity from a continuous trickle of relatives and fellow villagers arriving from the homeland. The chain-migration phenomenon resulted from the desire to avoid uncertainty and to move from a known place to a known person. By moving to a location with family or friendship contacts, Basques left their homeland with a hope of finding work and economic viability. Chain migration also meant that Basques were likely to settle in a limited number of places in these host countries. If these more-recent arrivals were relatively young, they were role models for diaspora youth of what Basques in Euskal Herria were currently like. They provided a reason for diaspora youth to learn and practice the Basque language and a reminder that Basque culture is not only that of the fishing villages and farmsteads but includes Basque punk-rock music, computer software in Basque, and Basque home pages on the Internet. Though very few people are leaving Euskal Herria today, new immigrants in the host societies have updated the Basque emigrant communities' idealized memories of 1920s to 1960s farms and hamlets in the Pyrenees to the new millennium's contemporary reality. Most significantly, they marry into the diaspora Basque community and often speak Basque to their children, creating incentives for others to learn or maintain the language; they implant, permeate, and inspire again the maintenance of ethnic tradition; and in the perception of some, they add "authenticity" and "potency" to Basque center activities and functions. They also continue the transnational aspect of the Basque community by adding new networks. The question, of course, is whether they constitute sufficient critical mass to effect a cultural staying power over the long term.

Basque political scientist Gurutz Jáuregui Bereciartu (1986; interview 1998) argues that the upsurge in ethnonationalism and returns to ethnicity by Basques in Euskal Herria and around the world are actually protests against the depersonalized postmodern technocratic world. It could be that those who fear the future and the social trends they are witnessing are turning to the past for comfort and identity, recognition, and self-actualization.

Manuel Castells points to nationalism and the resurgence of ethnic identity as products of conflicting trends of globalization, the information-technology revolution, and the restructuring of capitalism, all creating a network society, versus expressions of collective identity that challenge modernization in favor of local and communal identity and cultural distinctiveness (1997, 1). He argues that many people are choosing to move from the unknown future to the known and understood traditional past. However, this does not explain the consistent and persistent maintenance of Basque ethnicity over five centuries of emigrants prior to this age of globalization and modernization. Basque transnationalism is not new, though the methods of maintaining these networks and identities are influenced by the globalization of communications.

THE POLITICIZATION OF THE BASQUE DIASPORA

Utilizing print media as an example of communications, Gellner (1983) and Anderson (1991) regard print culture that interconnects people over space and time as a crucial factor in the construction of nationalism. The possibility of a nation depends on the book and the newspaper and on a literate reading public able to read the publications and imagine themselves as part of a larger community. In chapter 5, I shall demonstrate readership of newspapers and magazines concerned with Basque Country topics and the importance of the Basque government publication for the diaspora, *Euskal Etxeak* (Basque Centers), which seems to serve as "print culture" in the construction of a Basque diaspora mentality and in enhancing the imagination of these Basques as being part of a larger diaspora Basque community.

The increased frequency and volume of contact between diaspora communities and the Basque Autonomous Government could result in either conflict or increased commitment. Diasporas may be a foreign policy or economic asset that home governments are eager to exploit (Esman 1984, 345). I shall examine the general idea of the "triadic relationship" (Sheffer 1986; Safran 1991; A. D. Smith 1995, 16) between the diaspora community, its homeland, and its host country in these Basque communities as the economic and business *institutos* and *fundaciones* created by the Basque Autonomous Government multiply and intensify their political activities in the host countries of these Basque immigrants, and I shall illustrate how the Basque Autonomous Government is successfully using the diaspora to pursue its own external economic goals with the establishment of the institutes and foundations described in chapter 6.

I shall demonstrate that the Basque Autonomous Government has never had reason to interfere in any host country to protect its diaspora population, thus evading political conflicts between homeland and host countries. While Basques have had access to the democratic "opportunity structure" (Esman 1984, 338) in each of the countries studied, except Peru, to organize and promote their domestic and international interests, they have not often utilized this opportunity except when mobilizing to aid political exiles of the Spanish Civil War and to protest the Franco court's handling of the Burgos Trials of ETA suspects in 1970. Isolated political activism by individual initiative in attempts to influence political and economic policy-making in the homeland before, during, or after the Franco dictatorship has occurred infrequently.

Though some diasporas attempt to determine political outcomes in their homelands and to influence the making of domestic and foreign policy, there is no evidence of this in the contemporary Basque case, beyond the few individuals who participate in Basque Country elections. Milton Esman's conclusions that ethnic solidarities become internationally significant by way of transnational economic and political networks (Esman 1995, 114) pertains to the Basques' case in that these solidarities are significant to them, though not necessarily to the international economic system. What is salient in categorizing the Basque phenomenon as a diaspora is the consistent commitment to maintaining ties—sentimental, economic, political, religious, and kinship—with the homeland.

The Basque diaspora communities may prove to be effective and significant non-state actors proceeding on behalf of their homeland government, institutions, and businesses. Though the role can be evaluated for its importance, the "unofficial ambassador" status will be influential in the cases analyzed here. However, I shall also show that diaspora communities do not operate as monolithic blocs of ethnic or political consciousness and that there are personal conflicts and individual agendas that interfere with the effective administration of grants, and with economic and political ties between and among the diaspora and homeland populations.

Chapter Two

Basque Country History, the Development of Basque Nationalism, and Contemporary Homeland Identity

An ethnic group's own history, both real and romanticized, is an active force in determining its present behavior and attitudes. In this chapter, I shall summarize the basic outline of Basque history, pointing out those elements that have most influenced the perceptions of Basques in the diaspora. It is obvious that the collective memory of diaspora populations represents a certain idealized past. The story includes Basque history and anthropology from the last two millennia; Basque dispersion through five centuries of emigration out of Euskal Herria; the consolidation of Spain as a political entity and the ensuing battles for Basque autonomy; contemporary Basque ethnonationalism as manifested during the Spanish Civil War and the subsequent Franco dictatorship; and finally the situation in the Basque Country today and the actuality of homeland Basque ethnic identity.

The Golden Age of the Basques

THE BASQUES

Basques in the diaspora communities tend to idealize their homeland as a pristine niche. The physical borders of Euskal Herria have helped to shelter it from invasion and infiltration by other cultures and military forces as well as provided a gateway to the rest of the world. Its major physical border is the sea, a factor that has played an important role in the history of Basque emigration and has fostered the relative ease of mobility for the population. The Pyrenees' imposing peaks have until recently created communication barriers between the Basques themselves, because the mountains separate the northern and southern provinces. The summit of the range also created a political barrier as the international border between France and Spain.

The Basque Country is small in both territory and population. The total population (which has the lowest per-capita birthrate in the European Union) is nearly three million. In today's political terminology, when Basques refer to "the North"—Iparralde—they are referring to the three provinces that are in France, "to the north" of what many Basques consider an artificial political border. "The South"—Hegoalde—denotes all four provinces that lie in Spain. These provinces are administratively differentiated in the current Spanish state created by the Constitution of 1978. The Statutes of Autonomy passed in the 1979 referenda established that together Bizkaia, Gipuzkoa, and Araba make up the Basque Autonomous Community of Euskadi. Nafarroa, or Navarre, has its own separate autonomous statutes negotiated between the *Diputación* of Nafarroa (executive branch) and the central government in Madrid, and it also has a permanent right to join the Basque Autonomous Community. These divisions are a part of today's political reality and have caused identity divisions among the Basque population in the homeland and in the diaspora as well. For example, Argentinean Basques established the Laurac Bat (which literally means "the four are one," referring to the four Spanish provinces) in 1877, a Navarrese center in 1895, and a French Basque center in 1895.

Homeland and diaspora Basques refer to themselves as *Euskaldunak* or "speakers of Euskera," the Basque language. However, in the diaspora, one does not have to speak the language to be defined as Euskaldunak; one must merely have Basque ancestry. This primal identifying factor invokes one of the strongest indicators of Basque cultural uniqueness, the language.[1] Despite five centuries of speculation by linguists and philologists concerning possible relationships between Basque and other languages, no studies have indicated a conclusive relationship between Basque and any other language (Michelena 1985; Tovar 1957; Collins 1986, 8–12). This makes Euskera unique among Western and Central European languages and is often pointed out by diaspora Basques as a sign of difference and prestige. However, defining "Basque people" as "those who speak Basque" becomes problematic in that so many of those who live in Euskal Herria no longer utilize Euskera regularly. The Basque language was prohibited as a means of communication during the Franco years (1939–75), and it had already been lost in many of the hispanicized urban centers in the 1800s. Although language has played a relative role in the definition of ethnic identity, diaspora and homeland Basques continue to utilize Euskera as one of the unifying factors of "Basqueness" because it was a common element of their ancestors.

Claims to physiognomic distinctiveness are not unique to Basques, but among the Basques certain features in physiological makeup point to uniqueness and are utilized in nationalist rhetoric. Basques differ from the surrounding populations in their blood types; for example, they manifest the highest rate in any European population of the blood type O and the lowest occurrence of blood type B. They also have the highest occurrence of any population in

Map 2.1. The seven regions of the Basque Country and its political divisions of Euskadi, the Basque Autonomous Community; Nafarroa, the historic foral community of Navarre; and Iparralde, the northern regions in the French state.

the world of the Rh-negative factor (Cavalli-Sforza and Cavalli-Sforza 1995; Collins 1986, 4–8). This evidence suggests that the Basque people have remained, over a long period of time, a small and isolated breeding population (Irujo e Irujo interview 1997; Mar-Molinero and Smith 1996, 8). These factors are salient because of their perceived importance to Basques themselves. They are elements used to argue that Basques are linguistically and biologically distinct from any other population and are therefore deserving of political recognition and status. This was an opinion held by the majority of the diaspora Basques in each country interviewed for this book. Fact or myth, perception becomes reality, and these physiological factors are often utilized to rationalize difference and self-categorization by diaspora Basques.

Basque collective myth includes the possibility of a history that stretches back to cave populations and continuous human occupation of Euskal Herria since the Stone Age (Caro Baroja 1998). Some authorities suggest that the Basques are direct descendants of the cave painters who created the sites at Lascaux and Santimamiñe. Skeptics, however, place the modern Basques in the Pyrenees from approximately 5,000 to 3,000 B.C. Even with this most conservative interpretation, Basques are placed in the western Pyrenees well before the invasions of the Indo-European–speaking tribes into Western Europe in the second millennium B.C. In each diaspora community, there were interviewees who believed there was archaeological evidence that *proved* that the Basques are lineal descendants of Cro-Magnon men.

What is certain is that there are no recorded histories or information describing the Basques specifically until the Romans entered the Iberian Peninsula and wrote that the Basque population was organized into small tribal units inhabiting the valleys of the western Pyrenees (and beyond, according to later linguistic studies). These people originally did not form a single civic unit and spoke a variety of tribal dialects of Euskera whose diversity persists to the present day. Although until recently Basques have believed otherwise, the latest scientific research demonstrates that the Basque territory was indeed subject to Roman administrative, political, and military domain until approximately the fourth century A.D. Other questions arise regarding the linguistic and cultural Romanization of the existing populations. It seems that the agricultural mentality of the colonizers led to the fertile lowlands near the rivers experiencing more intense Roman cultural impact than did the more mountainous and forested areas (Sayas Abengoechea 1999). Christianity was introduced into the Basque region during Roman times, but it scarcely spread beyond the southern fringes of lower Araba and Navarre.

The debut of the Basques as a separate entity in the history of Western Europe follows the fall of the Roman Empire and the establishment of the Germanic kingdoms in Western Europe. The era's chronicles describe the Basques' staunch resistance to the Visigothic powers in Toledo and the attempts at assimilation by the Franks from the north (Sayas Abengoechea 1999). The perseverance of early Basque resistance through the seventh and eighth centuries indicates that some kind of civic cooperation may have been established among these tribes. The reality of their resistance to conquest and assimilation had an enormous effect on the political philosophy of the Basques at the end of the Middle Ages and during the following centuries.

THE EMERGENCE OF SPAIN

Contemporary Spain arose from an unstable alliance of independent Christian kingdoms defending themselves against Islamic invaders. During the eighth century, the independent and Christian populations in the northern sections of the peninsula began to coalesce around regional nuclei determined by three main factors: geography, ethnic identity, and prevailing politico-military pressures. Hence, the historic Spanish kingdoms did not have their roots in Roman or Visigothic origins but in the defensive reaction against Muslims in the early Middle Ages that led to the process of regaining lands. Unlike León, Aragon, and Catalonia, Castile had no previous political existence and was basically a product of the long *Reconquista* (718–1492). In the diaspora communities, several interviewees remarked on this phase of history and on how the perception that the Basques have never been dominated by others is important to their identity. Though only a few were familiar with detailed historical facts, many perceive this time period as the beginning of the unification of Basques, and they perpetuate this myth in their communities abroad.

Historians write that by the eighth century Basques in the area of Pamplona constituted a kingdom, which by the twelfth century—as a result of gradually allying themselves with other lands free of Muslim occupation (as were Bizkaia, Gipuzkoa, and Araba)—became known as the Kingdom of Navarre (Lacarra 1972). For the next century, all of the Basque-inhabited territory south of the Pyrenees recognized a single Basque political sovereignty for the first and last time in its history thus far. Though remote in time, this period of political unification has had a significant impact in the development of Basque nationalism in the homeland and in the diaspora.

These centuries of political unification ended in 1200, when the three western Basque territories were militarily occupied by Alfonso VIII of Castile. From this point on, their development was tied to the powerful Kingdom of Castile, into which their incorporation was interpreted as a bilateral pact, with liberties protected as the status quo. Gradually, the self-government of Basque communities grew, as recorded in the *fueros*, or local laws.

As a result of Basque political thought and collaboration since the Middle Ages, Basques emphasize that the three western territories' association with

Castile was conditional on the crown's recognition of the *fueros*, which were the Basque customs, traditions, local laws, and citizen rights, and on the autonomy of each province. The legal and administrative structures of the historic Basque districts were based upon an elaborate series of foral laws, which originated in two different ways: one by recognition of Basque customs as laws, and the other through specific agreements with the Crown of Castile that the Basques demanded in order to protect their civil and economic rights and privileges, local governing rights, and civic responsibilities.

By the beginning of the modern age, Araba, Bizkaia, and Gipuzkoa possessed their own political system inside the Kingdom of Castile. There was universal nobility—a custom by which all Basques were pronounced as noble by virtue of having been born in the Basque territories or to a Basque family outside the region—personal and procedural or due-process liberties, commercial freedoms, and exemptions from conscripted military service and from taxes. Municipal governments enjoyed autonomy, as did the legislative bodies of the General Assemblies and the *Diputaciones*. This political arrangement was protected by the mechanisms in which the foral authorities evaluated and accepted, or rejected, provisions and orders submitted by the Crown (Monreal Zia interview, 2001).

Homeland and diaspora Basques underscore the fact that the Basque provinces retained their *fueros* and exemptions from crown regulations longer than any other region—a fact used in today's arguments for self-governance. The *fueros* played a role in establishing regional identities reaching beyond that of connection with village or town. The Basques set themselves apart from the Castilian population and control because of this separate political structure, reinforced by their linguistic and ethno-cultural uniqueness. Simultaneously, because of excess population in the Basque region, Basques undertook significant migrations, repopulating areas of Castile taken from the Moors and also serving important functions in the Castilian bureaucracy.

The Basque region entered advanced development during the twelfth through fifteenth centuries with the growth of maritime and commercial activities. Bizkaian and Gipuzkoan seaports participated in cooperative associations with non-Basque towns, with commercial interests in Belgium and coastal towns along the North Sea, and in whaling in the North Atlantic. Later, during the fourteenth and fifteenth centuries, using their independent diplomatic status, they signed naval pacts with the English Crown. The fifteenth century was another period of notable economic development, especially for Bizkaia and Gipuzkoa. The Bay of Biscay, and particularly Bizkaian shipping, dominated the peninsula's trade with northern ports in Europe. Basque merchants and seamen served as the middlemen and as freighters for Castilian wool while simultaneously developing their own fishing and whaling industries. Their maritime expertise was especially necessary for New World exploration, while at home in the interior of the Basque Country the production of iron expanded and these operations moved into the river valleys for easier transport (Suárez Fernández 1959; J. A. García de Cortázar et al. 1979).

Though the peninsula had been divided between the five Christian kingdoms of Castile-León, Portugal, Aragon, Catalonia, and Navarre since the Middle Ages, between 1479 and 1512 all but one were united under the Trastamara-Habsburg Dynasty, which created the Spanish monarchy. The Spanish Habsburg state of the sixteenth and seventeenth centuries was a pluralistic royal confederation composed of the Kingdom of Castile and the three separate Basque provinces of Bizkaia, Araba, and Gipuzkoa that were associated with it; the Kingdoms of Aragon, Navarre, and Valencia; and the principalities of Catalonia and of the Balearic Islands. Portugal was united later, in 1580.

The colonization of the Americas was mainly a function of the Kingdom of Castile-León, which greatly advantaged the Basques because of the legal exclusion of the other kingdoms. The 1512 conquest of the Kingdom of Navarre and its incorporation into the political superstructure of Castile-León granted the Navarrese the same privileges. Most attention was turned to the New World and the opportunities and problems presented by its administration. The royal central authority organized and administered colonization efforts. The Basque Country was oriented toward the Americas in providing maritime expertise in shipbuilding and navigation, and a Basque bureaucratic bourgeoisie developed within the organs of the central government and in colonial administrative posts.

The sixteenth century was a period of continually expanding economy and social change in the Basque provinces. Bizkaia and Gipuzkoa were the two juridically freest and most egalitarian areas in all of Spain. Throughout most of Castile, the peasantry was crushed by taxes and by the social and economic predominance of the aristocracy, whereas in Bizkaia (1526) and Gipuzkoa (1610) the struggle for equality had been won with royal recognition of the "noble" status of all their native inhabitants. Every person would enjoy equality before the law and freedom from most common taxes (Kamen 1983, 226). In Araba and Navarre, different communities were protected by their different *fueros*, and some had already established collective nobility for their residents. Other towns and villages continued this process of emancipation and social mobility through the seventeenth century.

The integration of the Basques into the Spanish monarchy entered a crisis at the beginning of the eighteenth century with a change of dynasty. With the accession of Felipe V, the Bourbons consolidated the Spanish Crown and, following French tradition, unified it by dismantling the confederal structure. They implanted a centralized state system with a single Cortes and ministers whose powers extended over all territories. Nevertheless, there remained an exception to the unification: the four Basque provinces. The *fueros* of these four territories remained valid and were enforced. This maintained the political differentiation of "Vasconia" but simultaneously ushered in a period of tension between the administrations of Araba, Bizkaia, Gipuzkoa, and Navarre with the monarchy in Madrid.

The Basque presence in Madrid and the American colonies continued to be significant in the eighteenth century. The creation of the Gipuzkoan Company of Caracas demonstrated the great Basque mercantile society involved in the colonization of Venezuela, and the Consulate of Bilbao produced the Ordinances that served as the model for commercial trade in Spain and in the Americas. The cultural influence of the Basques in the colonial diaspora extended throughout the new territories. The Royal Basque Society of the Friends of the Basque Country, initiated in 1765, had members throughout the Spanish empire and a branch in Madrid.

In 1808, the influence of elite Basques in the New World was also pointed out to the French. Napoleon had gained control of the Iberian Peninsula that year and, having received the abdicated powers of Carlos IV and Fernando VII to create a new dynasty, decided to endow Spain with a new constitution. Napoleon planned to submit the text and amendments to a meeting of the Assembly of Notables in Baiona, or Bayonne. The attending representatives of the Basques reminded the French Emperor that the four Basque provinces in Spain already had their own constitutions and therefore should be exempt from the new charter. The Basque officials argued various points justifying their exemption. One stands out particularly: they reminded Napoleon that Basques from the four provinces in question controlled the colonial administration in the New World, and that these people could be decisive in the emancipation and independence of the American territories should Napoleon deprive their homeland of its original historical constitutions, or *fueros* (Monreal Zia interview 2000).

The eighteenth century produced a new interest in Basque historiography, particularly in Bizkaia and Gipuzkoa. Resistance to pressures from Madrid, together with concerns about preserving Basque identity in a more complex and demanding world, resulted in the expansion of myths about Basque history and the preservation of Basque ethnic and civic identity. The origins of the Basque people were contemplated, and mythical connections to biblical personages as direct ancestors were sustained. Basque grammar books were also first published in the 1700s. Despite Basque initiative in several aspects of Spain's industrial progress, the structure of Basque society was in general little altered by the end of the eighteenth century and beginning of the nineteenth.

Basques that I interviewed often mentioned that "the Basque Country has been the Basque Country longer than Spain has been Spain," defining themselves in opposition to Spain and somehow trying to increase their legitimacy or authenticity vis-à-vis the Spanish kingdom/state. The collective understanding of history in the diaspora is that for more than a millennium Basques demonstrated an ability to accept technical improvements and modernization in commerce and maritime activities without altering the foundations of their own culture. Advances had already been made in terms of local freedoms, relative civic liberties, legal equality, and widespread property distribution. However, Basque religious values were more conservative than in other parts of Spain and France. The paradox of the Basque Country was that it was one of the most progressive, while concurrently most conservative, areas in all of Western Europe.

THE "NORTH" AND THE "SOUTH"

Though the Euskera-speaking populations on both sides of the Pyrenees had not recently formed a single independent political system, the emerging modern centralized state system had the effect of severing the southern and northern regions more effectively than geography did. After their final incorporation into the French monarchy in the fifteenth and sixteenth centuries, the northern Basque provinces retained their local privileges and governmental structures to almost as great a degree as did the southern four. All three had representative assemblies, elected town mayors, and enjoyed the codified *fors,* or *fueros,* of customary laws and citizen privileges. For Basques from Iparralde, the notion of a common history through self-government and representative politics is also strong, and diasporan Basques see this as a tie connecting north and south.

The 1512 Spanish-French border that divided the Kingdom of Navarre caused a separation of the Basque Country that has remained until today. The division into "Iparralde" and "Hegoalde" created an indelible mental categorization of the North and the South being split permanently and irrevocably. Until recently, the nationalist conception and these terms were not utilized, and Basques in France were referred to as "French" and Basques in Spain as "Spanish." It is true that there is still an extensive kinship network that straddles both sides of this political line, and there was, and is, a tendency for many Basques to see their common interests as conflicting with those of Madrid and Paris (Letamendia 1997; Jacob 1994). However, there is no doubt that the Spanish-French division weakened Basque cultural homogeneity. Each division, north and south, has been exposed to centuries of official "nation-building." Everything from Basque vocabulary loan words from Spanish or French to the actual pronunciation of *Euskera,* to the school systems and political socialization, the patterns of bureaucracy and governmental administration, forms of democracies and differing dictatorships, Spanish and French colonial legacies, and wars have differently affected and influenced the mentalities and realities of Iparralde and Hegoalde. In general, the French government has historically paid little attention to the Basque region, deeming it a slight, remote, and backward area. In total contrast to the prominent role that Basques played in Spanish affairs, northern Basques were inconspicuous in the state affairs of France.

The North is also one of the most depressed areas in France. Other than a thriving summer tourist season, small agricultural production continues as the economic mainstay of the population. The three provinces of Iparralde receive more from French government subsidies than they pay in taxes. The typical settlement of the inland region is a peasant village whose major economic activity derives from a mixed farming economy. A vision of whitewashed stone homesteads with red-tiled roofs in lush green mountains and valleys remains in the mental picture of diaspora Basques who have never traveled to the homeland. Postcards, picture books, and tourist information propagate this representation for both sides of the Pyrenees.

In contrast, Hegoalde, especially the industrial zones of Bizkaia and Gipuzkoa, constitutes one of the most dynamic sectors in all of Spain. Historically, it has been the focus of shipbuilding and maritime commerce, iron mining, steel processing, and manufacturing. After the Spanish Civil War (1936–39), industry began to penetrate the inner countryside, converting former agricultural towns into secondary manufacturing centers of sewing machines, small armaments, cutlery, clothing, household appliances, cement, tires, furniture, and other products. Today, the Vitoria-Gasteiz, Donostia-San Sebastián, and Zamudio (Bilbao) areas include mini "Silicon Valleys" of high-technology research, such as the Sener aerospace engineering company and various computer industries. The Basque provinces enjoyed the highest per-capita income of any region of the Iberian Peninsula until the 1990s, when they were surpassed by Catalonia's economic development.

THE FUEROS: A POWERFUL SOURCE OF SEPARATE IDENTITY

For centuries, the Basque provinces maintained exclusively separate legal codes and created their own autonomous political institutions. This arrangement granted formal recognition to their autonomy under the Castilian Crown. Importantly for Basques, the separate regions were regarded as having a contractual rather than a subordinate position vis-à-vis the central royal authority. Castilian royal rule remained indirect, though the monarch did enjoy certain limited direct powers. Unlike Cantabria, Asturias, and Galicia, which formed part of Castile, and unlike the areas newly conquered from the Arabs (Extremadura and Andalusia), the Basques retained sufficient autonomy to give themselves political leverage in dealings with the monarchy. Diaspora interviewees repeated the idea that the Basques were not subjects of Castile but rather citizens of a land that had accepted the king of Castile as its sovereign. This is a crucial distinction to today's Basques because it meant that, historically, Basque loyalties went first to their own villages and provinces, then second to the king of Castile, contingent upon the monarch's continued respect for local autonomy and tradition as written into the local *fueros*. Nationalists stress this "independence," as do the diaspora populations, when describing their own history.[2]

Spanish nationalists claim that the *fueros* were privileges granted by the monarchy, and therefore rescindable, whereas Basque nationalists argue that these rights were not granted by the king but were based upon Basque legal traditions dating to early medieval times. Under the *fueros*, the popular assemblies, or *biltzarrak*, were granted legislative authority, and the kings and lords were subject to their laws. Although both church leaders and lords were excluded from legislative debate and deliberations, upon accession to the throne the political sovereign was required to appear before the assemblies to swear to respect their authority. Among the rights guaranteed to citizens by the 1452 *Fuero Viejo de Vizcaya* (Bizkaia) were: the freedom of every Bizkaian to engage in commerce; rights of due process in all legal proceedings; ownership of land in Bizkaia reserved for Bizkaians; exemption from taxes on maritime activity; and exemption from obligatory military service outside the Basque territory.

Another important aspect of distinction between regions in Spain was the concept of universal nobility, which can be traced to 1053 and the Valley of the Roncal in Navarre. In the Basque provinces, there was a legislated collective nobility—all were considered "noble." Thus, any citizen of the Basque region, regardless of his origins, could aspire to noble privileges and offices, a fact that would later greatly affect relations between Basques and non-Basques in the New World. Of course, nobility did not mean that all were able to exercise the powers of the wealthy, but collective nobility was often cited by the Basques in support of their claims for independence or for unique status within the Spanish state. While collective nobility affirmed equality between Basques, it also functioned to exclude outsiders and to reinforce the concept of "we Basques." In addition, universal nobility served to create a barrier against the excesses of the Castilian aristocracy and—significantly—facilitated emigration to the Spanish colonial empire in the New World.

Basques in the three French provinces also utilized the *fors* as their political and social organization. As early as 1311, the provinces of Lapurdi (Labourd) and Zuberoa (Soule) received assurances from first English and then French kings that their special rights and exemptions from taxes would be upheld. The content of these royal charters and of customary and, later, written laws was different for each province and coexisted with local norms. As in Spain, the *fors* regulated economic and social life as well as political representation and economic obligations to the monarchy (Jacob 1994, 8).

Termination of provincial privileges and *fors* in the French Basque territories resulted from the August 1789 debates in the National Assembly that brought an end to the *ancien régime*. The 1790 incorporation of the French Basque provinces with Béarn in the new department of Basses-Pyrénées proved detrimental to Basque language, culture, and the maintenance of traditional political structures, as pressures for cultural assimilation increased. Jacob argues that the French Revolution "did real violence to Basque institutions and social values. Despite its fraternal intentions, the Revolution served to destroy a highly participatory Basque political culture through abolition of the *fors* and suppression of the Labourdin Bilçar and the Estates of Navarre and Soule" (Jacob 1994, 37).

The Development of Basque Nationalism

The emergence and ideological characteristics of Basque nationalism in nineteenth- and twentieth-century Spain are a dramatic expression of the conflict between modernity and tradition. For four centuries, Basques occupied a position of importance within both the Old World and the New World Spanish bureaucracy that was out of proportion to their numbers in the state's population. The Basque provinces also enjoyed a privileged status within the Spanish state, as guaranteed by the *fueros*. They were arguably economically more developed than the center, Madrid, and were the industrial capital of Spain. The significance of colonization for Spain should be kept in mind because during the period that Spain ruled its multicultural empire, ethnic pluralism within its own metropolitan boundaries was much less visible and less important. With the collapse of the Spanish empire in the 1898 "Disaster"—defeat in the Spanish-American War and the liberation or occupation by the U.S. of overseas territories—all attention would be concentrated on the population within Spain's own borders. However, Spanish nation-building often resulted in defensive reactions from some in the regions (Mar-Molinero and Smith 1996, 8; Balfour 1995, 109).

THE FOUNDATIONS OF BASQUE ETHNONATIONALISM

A superficial reading of Basque nationalism would begin in the late 1800s with the writings of its founder, Sabino Arana y Goiri, whose picture is prominently displayed in several of the Basque cultural centers in the United States, Argentina, and Uruguay. However, because longevity seems to lend authenticity and legitimacy for Basque nationalists, investigations of Arana y Goiri's antecedents have identified several predecessors promoting the ideas of a "Basque nation" and territorial independence. More than a century before Arana's publications, the Jesuit Manuel de Larramendi, a Basque political ideologist (1690–1766), had approached the idea of government by the people, the legitimacy of power deriving from the people, and the people's right to determine their own destiny. Monreal Zia writes that "Larramendi is aware that the community or identity of Basques is a phenomenon better manifested outside of the country," since Larramendi knew the 1609 works of Echave in Mexico. He adds that "the pan-Basque vision of Larramendi, founded on common language, consists of all of the territories, including Navarre and the French territories" (Monreal Zia 1992, 110–11). Larramendi also attributed assigning political rights to cultural nations (ibid., 130). Larramendi defined the first political project for a separate Basque state with its own legal system, a classical Greek form of confederation that could develop either into a republic or an elected monarchy, with the election of a king rotating between the seven provinces. Though unpublished until the nineteenth century, Larramendi's works suggested a Basque state independent of France and Spain, a "United Provinces of the Pyrenees."

The 1765 Real Sociedad Bascongada de los Amigos del País (Royal Society of the Friends of the Basque Country) dedicated itself to instilling a love of the Basque Country, preserving ethnic ties, and increasing political unity between the three southern provinces. These Basque elites were also interested in fostering communication and instilling a knowledge of Basque topics and information regarding Basques outside of Euskal Herria, exemplifying an inclusive group mentality. They demonstrated one of the first concrete examples of institutionalized Basque transnationalism and diaspora consciousness. Between 1776 and 1804, one-fourth of the seminarians at the Sociedad's Seminary of Bergara were sons of members from New Spain, Cuba, the Viceroyalty of Peru, Venezuela, Rio de la Plata (later Argentina and Uruguay), Colombia, and Puerto Rico (Bilbao Azkarreta 1992, 182), whose contributions most likely contributed to a transnational "Basqueness" at the institution. The Sociedad's publication *Extractos* included articles about its Basque brotherhood and its special unity with the Royal Congregation of Saint Ignatius in Madrid, as well as news of diaspora membership. By 1787, New World membership numbers equaled membership in Spain, including 530 members from New Spain; by 1790, there were 121 members in Peru, and dozens more in the other Spanish colonies.

At home, a new era of Spanish politics led to an additional spark of Basque ethnic unity with the death of King Fernando VII in 1833 and the subsequent outbreak of the First Carlist War. The issue at stake was the succession to the Spanish throne, which law mandated would go to the eldest legitimate child whether male or female—in this case, the three-year-old Princess Isabel. Fernando's younger brother, Carlos, argued that the crown should follow a male-only lineage, making him the new sovereign. Carlos, a traditional, piously clerical individual, wanted to restore conservativism and especially Catholicism to Spanish institutions, reversing the liberal path of constitutional monarchy, individualism, and capitalism fostered by his late brother. The first official group to announce its support for Carlos was a group from Bizkaia that favored the religious focus and believed that the foral liberties were more likely to be preserved by a traditionalist monarchy. Small bands of Carlists formed throughout the Basque territories. Although the larger towns favored Isabel and the liberals, the majority of the Basque population was rural and favored the Carlists and a return to religiosity, the distinct *fueros* system, and Basque traditionalism.

The paradox of the support for Carlism's divine monarchy comes from the fact that church and state were more separated in the Basque areas than anywhere else in Spain. Clerics there had never been allowed to hold political office. However, the assault of liberal anticlerics roused more intense opposition in the Basque Country than elsewhere because it was perceived as part of a general attack against the institutions and values of the local society. Historians argue that Basque Carlists were not fighting to uphold the monarchists or aristocratic privileges, but rather for their own rights, values, and way of life as Basques. In 1834, the Regency Council noted that, by that time, the war had become a national one for the four provinces (Barahona 1989; Payne 1975, 44). A Basque writer from the northern province of Zuberoa, Joseph Augustín Chaho, interpreted the basic motivations in his publications in 1837, positing a common identity among all Basques on both sides of the Pyrenees. He interpreted Basque support for Carlism as based on the defense of Basque liberties, which he deemed the freest and most egalitarian constitutional system in the world. Chaho concluded that the political problem of the Basque region would never be solved unless the Basques were fully allowed to affirm their separate identity (Jacob 1994, 37–38). Eventually, internal ideological divisions among the Carlists, Carlos's own indecisive leadership, and general exhaustion took their toll. In 1839, the Carlist General Maroto and the Liberal General Espartero agreed to the Compromise of Bergara, whereby the Carlist forces were to lay down their arms in exchange for the retention of the Basque *fueros*.

Following the First Carlist War, the mid-nineteenth century was a time of discovery of regional cultures. The European Romantic stress on the cultural *Volkgeist* affected new historiography in the Basque region, and by 1864 Basque parliamentary representatives were referring to their kinspeople as a separate "nationality," drawing heated rebukes from the prime minister that there was only one nationality in Spain. Spanish political state-building had proved to be more successful than Spanish ethnic nation-building.

A new monarchist regime was introduced in Spain in 1868, and a new wave of anticlericalism, together with the expansion of liberalism and further measures of centralization, produced a reactive revival of Carlism. The second major Carlist civil war (1873–76) resulted in defeat of the Carlist cause. The three western Basque provinces had their autonomous *fueros* revoked, and Navarre retained only some of its administrative and fiscal autonomy as contracted with the Spanish state in 1841. This difference in treatment accentuated what during the next two generations would become a growing difference between Navarre and the more united and interdependent provinces of Araba, Bizkaia, and Gipuzkoa. A century later, this different treatment would be repeated by the Spanish central government when it negotiated the Statutes of Autonomy separately for Nafarroa in 1981–82 and Euskadi in 1979, creating a third "partition" of Euskal Herria. In the diaspora, many Basques perceived this as an example of Spain's "divide and conquer" strategy.

The Basque Association of Navarre was created in 1878 and exhibited a cultural and historicist, not separatist, nationalism. Though the Association never gelled electorally, it reflected another form of nationalism based on culture and history, and more flexible in its attitude toward the state. Fidel de Sagarminaga y Epalza (1830–94) also advocated the unification of Alava, Bizkaia, Gipuzkoa, and Navarre as the home of the prehistoric Basque-Navarrese people, remaining as part of the Spanish state. He believed the new Spanish American republics' Basque populations served as good examples where "the emblem of the LAURAC-BAT reunited in one single family those of the vascongadas and of Navarre" (Monreal Zia, forthcoming 2003). In the 1880s in Araba and Navarre, general economic and social stagnation led to emigration in the aftermath of the Second Carlist War. In contrast, Bizkaia and Gipuzkoa developed the bases of modern industrial economies. Bizkaia, with its iron-producing economy, and the port of Bilbao especially, was becoming highly differentiated structurally from the rest of Spain. This process of development had placed a heavy strain on Bizkaian society, threatening traditional values and identity. Basque capitalism was oriented toward Spanish markets, and the economic distance between the capitalists and the more traditional society was great (Diez Medrano 1994, 559). There was only a very small local bourgeoisie, and the wealthiest Basque capitalist families were incorporated into the Spanish power elite. At this time, the people who tended to emigrate were those from rural areas looking for work, trade, and economic opportunity, and they transported their rural life-style and traditions to the host communities in which they settled, mainly in Argentina and Uruguay. These are the collective images that have been inherited by later generations in the diaspora, rather than images derived from an urbanizing Euskal Herria.

The process of economic and social modernization was a challenge to Basque rural identity, institutions, and values. For the first time, there was large-scale non-Basque immigration into the area, especially into Bizkaia, and an increased social atomization of Basque society. Traditionalism, coupled with the onset of full-scale industrialization, required drastic social adjustment to adapt to the new modern circumstances. In the homeland, it was within this environment of a rapidly changing and industrializing Bizkaia, added to the long history of autonomy, wars, and demands for separate status, that the traditional Basque nationalism of Sabino Arana y Goiri emerged.

SABINO ARANA Y GOIRI AND TRADITIONAL BASQUE NATIONALISM

Sabino Arana y Goiri, recognized by Basques around the world as the founder of modern Basque nationalism, was a product of both traditionalism and industrialism. Sabino's older brother, Luis, actually deserves recognition for the beginnings of modern Basque nationalism. It was Luis who consolidated the idea that Basques were intrinsically different from Spaniards and that it would be necessary to secede from Spain and France in order to achieve the kind of traditional society that had been prevalent in Bizkaia for centuries. Luis Arana argued that Carlism should not be the main focus for the political future because, realistically, the Basques had nothing in common with the rest of Spain, which had usurped the government and rights of Bizkaia. Total independence should be the goal for Basques.

An Arana family move to Barcelona for Sabino's studies coincided with the climax of a cultural renaissance in Catalonia. New publications in the Catalan language, including the first daily newspaper in Catalan, were produced in the time of the "gold fever" of economic prosperity between 1876 and 1886. Cultural societies were born, and there followed an explosion of cultural, linguistic, and literary activities, which also took political form. The argument was made that Catalanism was based on a distinct regional culture and society whose psychology and values differed from the rest of Spain. This movement, among other European movements, served as an indirect stimulus to Arana y Goiri's doctrine of Bizkaian-Basque nationalism, and in 1885 Sabino devoted himself entirely to Basque studies.

He returned to Bilbao in 1888 and developed an ideology and a movement of Bizkaianism that ultimately became Basque nationalism and the platform of the Basque Nationalist Party (Partido Nacionalista Vasco—PNV). His profound belief in Catholicism affected his founding of this nationalism on the "salvation of Euzkadi." Some of his articles were signed with "We are for Euzkadi and Euzkadi is for God." He also used "God and the Old Law," a mutation of the Carlist "Dios y Fueros." He announced his intention to form a political movement that would work to restore Bizkaia to its original state of independence and liberty. None of the new literature and historiography in the Basque provinces at the time had proposed anything so radical.

In the late 1880s and early 1890s, Bilbao was a city in transformation. The population tripled between 1876 and 1890, and the province of Bizkaia was the most densely populated in all of Spain. Industrialization demanded an ever-growing cheap labor force greatly in excess of what the Basque region could provide. Hence, there followed a vast inflow of non-Basque immigrants from the impoverished rural regions of Spain. The new industrial society emerged with vigor, and socialism gained followers, especially among the working class. However, Arana's concept of a Basque nation was based to a large degree on the Romantic roots in vogue when he had studied in Barcelona. According to the Romantics, nations had existed forever and were a natural phenomenon, based on ethnicity and ethnic interests more salient than coalitions rooted in class interests. Every nation had the right to form a state.

By 1894, the Aranas' political ideas were widely known in the homeland and in the diaspora, as printed in Basque newspapers in Argentina. Sabino Arana had extended the definition of his Basque nation to include all seven provinces and promoted the idea of an independent confederation of Basque states that would be named *Euzkadi*, the place of the Basque race (*Euskadi* in today's standardized Basque). The first PNV Center, which was to serve as a meeting place for the first Bizkaianist political party, opened the same year, and the *ikurriña*—the Basque flag designed by the Arana brothers—was raised. Although between 1893 and 1898 the movement to develop an effective strategy for creating this independent confederacy did not realize any success, it stimulated discussion and debate, which resulted in the formation of additional Basque nationalist groups in the homeland and in the diaspora that followed similar ideologies.

For Basque Country and diaspora Aranists, Spain was a corrupt entity, and the Basque language, Euskera, would serve as a wall, a weapon, to contain the Spanish invasion and contagion. The loss of Euskera was in direct proportion to the advance of the Castilian language and the customs of the Spanish invader (Corcuera Atienza 1979). The concept of Basque nationality, for Arana, was realized by a traditionalist path, whereby Basqueness was defined as antiliberal and antisocialist. Liberalism was equated with atheism, although other nationalists preferred to eliminate Arana's many references to Rome and the idea that the goal of Basque nationalism would be to Christianize the Basque people.

According to Arana, race was the principal defining element of a nation. He promoted endogamy among Basques and the expulsion of non-Basques from the Basque territories. Race was a God-given condition that could never be achieved by an outsider. Membership was determined by birth, and continued inclusion was achieved through the moral action of language, character, and following traditional values. Race also brought political loyalty and a natural right to self-government. It demanded cohesion and collective action against outsiders and outside threats. Biological kinship meant that a Basque was always a Basque and a Spaniard always a Spaniard. Though this ideology generally survives today in the Basque centers abroad, responses from diaspora interviewees demonstrate that currently prevailing attitudes accept that a Catalan descendant might be able to "become Basque" after living in the Basque Country for several generations and learning the Basque language, but that it is a doubtful possibility for someone from Madrid.[3] Diaspora interviewees' definitions of "Basqueness" tended to be wrapped in ancestral terms, with participants often proud to state the surnames of "all-Basque" relatives. Biological credentials were essential to Arana. Proof of Basqueness would come in a person's surnames, and someone who did not speak Basque would still be Basque if he had Basque surnames in his line of ascendants. Surnames took on an overwhelming importance, especially when so much of the population of the Basque provinces did not at that time speak Basque. The surname also served as a marker of "insider" and "outsider" to categorize immigrants.[4]

Unlike other European nationalists of his time, Arana did not regard territoriality as an essential or constant feature of the nation. He wrote, "The patria is measured by race, history, law, customs, character, and language.... our *Euskeria* would still be *Euskeria* if it were moved to an island in the Pacific" (Arana, as cited in Heiberg 1989, 52). In the following chapters, we shall see that many respondents in personal interviews determine that a Basque is a Basque no matter where that person may physically happen to be, because being Basque is a biological, genetic, and spiritual identity. One does not have to be born in, or live in, the Basque Country to be Basque. One must have Basque ancestry to be Basque.

The preservation of language carried similar importance. Arana wanted to use the language to stop the invasion of immigrants who "contaminated and diluted" the Basque race and purity of language. He was opposed to contemporary philologists who were admitting that Basque was useless as an educated language; indeed, Euskera's disappearance in urban areas was generally accepted by the Basque bourgeoisie of the time. Because of this decline, Arana blamed the natives more than the foreigners for the situation of the language. "*Euskera* is dying. It is true. The foreigner is not killing it. The Basques themselves are killing it" (Arana y Goiri 1965, 2, 379). Euskera was seen by many urban Basques as a language of the unsophisticated peasantry and of very low status, whereas Spanish was the language of culture and refinement and of the educated urban populations. Many emigrant interviewees agreed with this perception and divulged that upon reaching their new host societies they had made no effort to teach their children Basque because of its assumed uselessness at the time of their migration.

By the beginning of the twentieth century, the Basque literary movement was following the renaissance of culture and was stimulating the nationalist movement as well. Euskera was purged of its Spanish letters, along with entire words that were labeled as alien influences on Basque culture. Literature praising the traditional rural peasantry as the focus of liberty, moral purity, and true Basque values was presented by Trueba, Chaho, Yparraguirre, Campión, and Askue. In 1898, others such as Unamuno, Maeztu, and Pío Baroja wrote about the ideal, harmonious, moral nature of Basque traditional life, as opposed to the contaminated misery of industrialized society. Though not all readers agreed, each also wrote about the opposition between the Basques and the Spanish as fundamental. The Spanish were depicted as threatening corrupters of the pure Basque traditional values and life-style. These writers were quoted in the diaspora press (San Sebastián 1991; Amezaga Clark 1991), adding to the idealized perception of the homeland among diaspora Basques.

For Arana nationalists, the Basque people represented tradition, precapitalist society, egalitarianism and democracy, peace and social order, Catholicism, and spiritual rectitude. The anti-Basque movement represented modernization, industrial society, hierarchies and authoritarianism, violence and disruption, anticlericalism, and spiritual corruption. Basques therefore were obligated to defend the nation from such a threat. To do so, one had to become an *abertzale*, a patriot, which granted the status of insider. Patriotism was an obligation, and Basques who were not patriots were just as deplorable as the Spanish.

BUILDING NATIONALIST COALITIONS

Post-Arana nationalism was divided into many camps, including the religious Aranists, the linguistic Aranists, the political independentists led by brother Luis Arana, as well as those following Elias Gallastegui and the Marxist-humanist workers. Basque capitalism emerged as one of the main beneficiaries of Spain's military neutrality during World War I, and there were also capitalist Basque nationalists. Now more than ever, the Basque economy was directly linked to Spain's, and by 1917, moderate nationalists had dropped the rhetoric of separatism and substituted the vocabulary of regionalism. Various leaders saw no contradiction in overlapping Spanish civil and Basque ethnic identities.

The PNV continued working to establish an infrastructure of support throughout the Basque Country by creating the political party club as the focal point for information and activity organization. A nationalist labor union formed in 1911 restricted membership to Basques only and gave the PNV a degree of working-class support. The conversion of large numbers of lower clergy to the nationalists also affected mass support because of the close connections between the Church and Basque local life and customs. One group of Basque priests founded an association aimed at giving religious education in Euskera. It was the precursor to the *ikastola* (Basque-language school) movement that would give the Basques their own educational system. Women formed a special group of nationalists with their own organization inside the PNV, the *Emakume Abertzale Batza* (EAB, Association of Patriotic Women), which also organized in the diaspora and still survives as a group in Rosario, Argentina. Emigrants who departed in the first decades of the century transferred this familiarity with the PNV and its politics to their new Basque communities in the diaspora, as seen in published articles and meetings held in diaspora Basque centers (San Sebastián 1991; Bilbao Azkarreta 1992).

In 1923, Miguel Primo de Rivera staged a coup in Madrid establishing a military dictatorship for the remainder of the decade. Non-Spanish nationalism in all forms was suppressed, and many Basque nationalists were imprisoned or exiled, fleeing to Mexico, Venezuela, Chile, Argentina, and Uruguay. The PNV leadership shelved its demands for independence and instead struggled to obtain a statute of autonomy similar to that of Catalonia. During the Second Republic (1931–36), Basque nationalists demanded and worked almost exclusively for that Statute of Autonomy. By 1936, Basque nationalism had become the most powerful political force in Bizkaia and Gipuzkoa by attracting support from both the traditionalists and the local bourgeoisie for a conservative middle-class program aimed at establishing a society of small-scale industrial and agricultural producers in which religious principles would inform most aspects of life. Electoral results and outcomes of the referenda for the approval of the drafts of the Statutes of Autonomy demonstrate that there was no great support in Araba or in Navarre. The Statutes were first presented to the Spanish Parliament in 1931, and by October 1936 the Parliament had approved a fourth draft, which did not include Navarre. However, by this time the Spanish Civil War had begun.

There never was a homogeneous Basque nationalism. The differences were various, including rural versus urban, protraditional society versus promodernization, industrial versus agricultural interests, liberal versus Carlist, and autonomists versus separatists. However, nothing succeeds in unifying a people quite like fighting a common enemy, and the stronger the enemy, the stronger the reaction.

Basque Nationalism and Ethnic Identity in the Franco Years

The greatest number of diaspora Basques who are living emigrants left the Basque Country in the 1930s, immediately before, during, or after the Spanish

Civil War. Their perceptions of what they lived through, passed on to their children and grandchildren, have prominently influenced the diaspora communities that received this phase of Basque emigration. Though the emigrants may not recall the historical facts correctly, what is pertinent are the emotions, attitudes, and opinions that correlate with diaspora rhetoric of "traumatic dispersal," "collective memory of ills to the Basque population," "solidarity with co-ethnics in the homeland and in the diaspora," "a return movement—both real and mythical," "an enriched ethnic life in the host society," and a maintenance of links with the homeland.

THE SPANISH CIVIL WAR: BURNING MEMORIES

The revolt of the Spanish army was not unexpected. Support for a fascist coup against the Second Republic was solicited as early as 1932, and in March 1934 Spanish monarchists visited Mussolini to seek backing from the Italian government. Once the civil war commenced, Italy immediately sent men, air power, and a billion lira (N. MacDonald 1987, 36); additionally, the German Condor Legion was used for air raids and in the destruction of Durango, Gernika, Santander, and Bilbao. The United Kingdom, France, and the United States declared neutrality and gave no aid to the elected government of the Republic, necessitating reliance on munitions purchased from the Soviet Union. Diaspora Basques recalled how they sent financial aid home to their families, and in the majority of communities in Argentina, Uruguay, and the United States interviewees could recall at least a few men from their areas who had returned to Euskal Herria to fight with the Republicans.

The top PNV leaders denounced the military's revolt and interference in an elected constitutional government, and their pronouncements depicted the struggle as one between civil rights and fascism, republic and monarchy. Basque nationalist leadership declared that "its principles led it to come down on the side of civil rights and the Republic in consonance with the democratic and republican regime of our people during its centuries of liberty" (Payne 1975, 163). However, this civil war was not only a delineated conflict between two political ideas; it was also a civil war between Basques in the four provinces. In Navarre, army rebels of General Mola were aided by former Carlists after he declared that the remaining foral privileges in the province would be completely upheld. The PNV leadership in Navarre issued its own declaration of support, saying that it would not endorse or support the Republican government. In Araba, there was support for both sides, but the military insurgents seized control of the capital, Vitoria-Gasteiz, and sent troops to close the Basque nationalists' offices in the area. PNV leaders were arrested and forced to write declarations urging Basque nationalists to support the military takeover. A few months later, in Navarre, General Mola dissolved the Basque nationalist organizations. On certain issues, Basque nationalists had much in common with the Spanish nationalists of Mola and Franco, sharing their strong ties to Catholicism and their emphasis on social order, discipline, and traditional values.

On 1 October 1936, the Spanish Republican Parliament approved the Basque autonomy statute, which established an autonomous regional government for the three provinces of Araba, Bizkaia, and Gipuzkoa, although all that remained free at this point was Bizkaia and a section of Gipuzkoa. The president of the new Basque government was elected by municipal councils, and the unanimous choice was José Antonio de Aguirre y Lecube. Basque nationalists were divided in support of the autonomy statute, and many perceived it as a sell-out to the Spanish government because of the lack of total independence. When Aguirre swore his oath of office under the traditional Tree of Gernika, as Basque representatives of fueroist governments had done for centuries before him, many onlookers jeered and protested for independence. The same day, Luis Arana y Goiri officially resigned from the PNV in repudiation of its compromising of nationalist principles and objectives (Payne 1975, 179).

The war in the north of Spain entailed Basque nationalists and leftist supporters fighting other Basques, Spaniards, Germans, and Italians. On 26 April 1937, the most famous incident of the war occurred with the saturation bombing and partial razing of the historic foral center of Gernika. Worldwide condemnation of the bombing of civilians, and subsequently Pablo Picasso's painting *Guernica*, demonstrated the horrors suffered in this war. Because the entire town of Gernika was destroyed, except for the church, the parliament building, and the Tree of Gernika where representatives had met for almost one thousand years, Basques have promulgated as a part of the common history and Basque myth that the symbolism of Basque nationalism, history, and identity can never be eliminated. Tree of Gernika symbols, posters, paintings, and sculptures decorate diaspora Basque centers and homes, and numerous discussions of Gernika during my interviews uncovered a diaspora faith that "God saved the Tree of Gernika to show the world that as the Tree of Gernika lives, so shall the Basques" (Anacabe Franzoia interview, U.S.A., 1998).

An estimated 30,000 children were evacuated from Bizkaia to refugee camps in safer locations in Iparralde and to other parts of France, England, Belgium, the Soviet Union, Switzerland, Denmark, Mexico, and Cuba. Many were orphans, or soon to become orphans, and, having no families to which to return, many remained in their host countries. Others, upon returning to the Basque Country after the war's end, found their families the targets of persecution by Franco's government and escaped Euskal Herria as political exiles (Legarreta 1984).[5] The end of military struggle for the Basque nationalists came with the fall of Bilbao on 19 June 1937, leaving nearly all of Bizkaia now in the hands of the Spanish Nationalists. The Spanish Republic finally collapsed in 1939 after an estimated 600,000 deaths, thousands more left homeless, about 150,000 exiled, and the majority on both sides economically, psychologically, and emotionally devastated. Defeat halted the growing institutionalization of the Basque nationalist movement but failed to eradicate nationalist sentiments. On the contrary, for many, Basque nationalism intensified because of their suffering and losses.

SPANISH NATION-BUILDING À LA FRANCO

The collective memory of victimization during the Franco dictatorship is shared by the diaspora with their homeland co-ethnics. Whether or not they personally experienced it, respondents in all six host communities offered remarkably similar narratives of the Franco era. Occupation forces descended upon the Basque Country determined to erase all signs of a distinctive Basque culture and any remnants of Basque nationalism. The anti-Basque nationalist purge extended from schools and churches to businesses and factories. Properties of Basque nationalists were confiscated, teachers and civil servants were fired and replaced, and Basque priests suffered imprisonment, deportation, and execution. Because Basque nationalism relied so heavily on the linguistic identification of race, culture, and nation, Madrid placed a special emphasis on the destruction of this aspect of non-Spanish behavior. The most damaging to Basque culture was the outlawing of the use of the language as a functioning means of communication. Euskera was prohibited in all public places and even for a conversation on the streets. All Basque-language newspapers, magazines, and radio programs were banned. However, the grandparents' generation still included Basque monolinguals, so therefore behind closed doors Basque was still spoken or whispered.

Basques, as well as Catalonians and Galicians, were required to "become" Spanish. The Basque language was removed from school curricula and from the streets. The names of newborns recorded in the civil registry had to be Spanish, not Basque, and the spelling of Basque surnames was hispanicized. Names of towns were changed to Spanish spellings, streets and plazas were renamed to honor Spanish Nationalist war heroes. Cemetery tombstone names were erased and in some cases re-engraved with the Spanish equivalents. Masses were allowed in Spanish only, and non-Basque clergy were brought in to administer to the now Spanish-speaking Basque Catholics. Non-Basque teachers were brought in from the south of Spain to instruct the now Spanish-speaking Basque children. Most noticeably, Bizkaian and Gipuzkoan security forces, the *miqueletes*, disappeared and non-Basque Guardia Civil—military civil guards—were imposed in the provinces for policing the population. Civil liberties were nonexistent.

After the conclusion of the Civil War in 1939, Franco promulgated the infamous "Law on Political Responsibilities," which made it a crime for anyone over the age of fourteen (1) to have "helped to undermine public order" at any time since 1 October 1934; (2) "to have impeded the Spanish Nationalist movement" even by being passive at any time after the beginning day of the war; or (3) to have belonged at any time to any leftist political parties, to any regional nationalist parties, to the Liberal Party, or to a Masonic lodge (Clark 1979, 82). Anyone convicted of any of these crimes could have all properties confiscated, be deprived of his nationality, be deported to Africa, or be sentenced to a prison term. Trials were conducted by mixed military-Falangist tribunals, and there was no right to appeal.

In the fifteen years after the end of the Spanish Civil War and the exile or imprisonment of most of the Basque nationalist leaders, a durable Basque resistance emerged in spite of Franco's efforts to hispanicize the Basque population. The Basque government-in-exile installed in Paris was supported by a sympathetic French government and by the Basque diaspora. The oppressive measures utilized to make Spaniards out of Basques backfired, instead galvanizing anti-Spanish sentiments in Euskal Herria. Iparralde Basques were especially helpful during the Civil War and became essential to the underground resistance and movement of arms and people into and out of Spain. Because of the French government's unofficial blind-eye policy, Iparralde became a safe haven for numerous Basque activists and exiles, whose first stop before embarking for the Americas, the Philippines, or Australia was usually a Basque family in the North.

Basque resistance in Spain emerged in the mid-1940s with the creation in Baiona of the Basque Consultative Council, which represented all of the Basque political parties and included delegates from the trade and labor unions in the Basque provinces. The council was responsible for ensuring that the Basque government-in-exile in Paris would remain in close contact with the main forces and current events in the Basque Country, for coordinating resistance and anti-Franco activities in all seven provinces, and for coordinating the activities of the resistance with the political strategy of the government-in-exile. The PNV created the Basque Resistance Committee in the early 1940s, which operated primarily on the Spanish side of the border but also coordinated anti-Franco activities in France and England. The Basque Resistance Committee was also active in the overall World War II effort against Nazi Germany. The American Consulate in Bilbao directed Allied intelligence-gathering operations conducted in part by the Committee. Diaspora communities in Mexico and Argentina published newspapers and information bulletins that were distributed in Euskal Herria, and clandestine radio broadcasts were transmitted to the south of the Basque Country from Iparralde, and later from Caracas,

Venezuela, for thirteen years (Beltza 1977; Amezaga Clark 1991; Galíndez 1984).

Meanwhile, the Basque bourgeoisie, never separatist nationalists, had continued its association with the Spanish system, and the economic elite enjoyed preferential treatment within Franco's designed economy. The underground PNV reinforced its reputation as a parliamentarian and Christian Democratic party of the middle class, and it continued to define itself within the Spanish state. For many followers of the PNV at this time, a goal of outright independence had decades ago been exchanged publicly for autonomy within the state. The PNV even disassociated itself from nationalist movements in Iparralde (Jacob 1994). The prewar rifts and divisions between nationalists—temporarily fused by the war effort—surfaced again.

BASQUE NATIONALIST UNDERGROUND RESISTANCE

During the 1950s and 1960s, nationalist feelings remained strong among the same groups as previously: farmers, peasants, white-collar workers of the lower-middle class, shopkeepers and small entrepreneurs, and a few skilled urban workers. During this time, the young liberal clergy and the Basque intelligentsia also became the most dissident sectors of the society, partly in response to the slow but steady growth of secularism in what had been potently Catholic territory. Growing modernization also stimulated growing crises of identity and values. All of these factors, added to the repression of Basque culture, language, and traditions, fueled an explosion of frustrations that are still being vented today.

Basque underground resistance at this time produced the same cleavages in the nationalist movement that had prevailed before the Civil War and the Franco repressions. Some Basques saw this struggle as a political and partisan one; for them, the focus was the Basque Nationalist Party. Others saw economic questions as of higher importance and joined the struggle through membership in one of the trade or labor Basque unions. Still others defined the resistance as a fight for cultural identity and preservation of the language, focusing their efforts on the clandestine *ikastola*, the Basque schools movement, and pressuring the Spanish government to allow the use of Euskera in public. Later, in the 1950s and 1960s, some members of the Basque underground resistance, tired of waiting for the Basque government-in-exile to take decisive action, declared war on Spain, the Spanish language, and capitalism as well.

The more cautious and conservative PNV repelled many young people who called for political violence in response to Franco's state violence. The PNV was more concerned with long-range plans for maintaining contact with all anti-Franco forces and preparing the groundwork for the emergence of democracy in Spain once Franco died. Theirs was a defensive strategy, to wait it out and work with Madrid and within a democratic Spanish government. The activities of the PNV reflected its passive form of political struggle. The party's energy and resources went to organize the diaspora efforts and the Basque government-in-exile, to establish ties to other underground anti-Franco groups in Spain, and to raise money to support resistance activities. Diaspora communities received personal information from their family members, but the older communities in Argentina and Uruguay relied more on Basque government interpretations of desired future goals. The preference for the PNV continues in the diaspora today, as demonstrated in chapter 4.

Homeland dissent was expressed by those who believed that Basques should act to obtain their independence without reference to what was happening in Madrid. They argued that no Spanish government would ever be willing to release the Basque provinces to form their own state, so the sooner the process began, the sooner it would be completed. Voices began to complain that the government-in-exile did not truly represent all Basques and had never been ratified by a popular vote. Many believed that confrontational politics would be more effective than working through established political channels.

EUSKADI ETA ASKATASUNA

In the 1950s, clandestine groups of students began meeting to write and publish magazines and newspapers, distribute Basque diaspora publications coming from Argentina, Venezuela, and Mexico, and discuss examples of European contemporary political writings. Eventually, in Bilbao, they formed a secret organization called *Ekin*, which in Basque means "to act." The participants in Ekin were frustrated with the PNV's lack of commitment to preserve Euskera, which was being sidelined in the list of priorities. Student leader José Luis Álvarez Emparanza, known by the political pseudonym "Txillardegui," argued that Euskera was on the verge of extinction not only because of the massive immigration of Spaniards into the Basque Country but because of the laziness of those who knew it and did not use it to communicate. Members of Ekin announced that a true Basque patriot should not be content until an independent state of all seven provinces was realized. Most of the older, established Basque nationalist leaders found such ideas utopian and feared that such expectations would alienate potential allies in Spain, France, and elsewhere. In 1959, Txillardegui and other youth leaders decided to separate from the PNV, creating the independent group *Euskadi 'ta Askatasuna* (ETA, Basque Homeland and Liberty).

Because of ongoing police repression and its inability to organize and spread information publicly, from the beginning ETA lacked a centralized system of authority. Local groups often acted independently of each other, and there was a general lack of coordination of activity. There was also no coordinated effort to educate the diaspora or to utilize its potential for the homeland struggle, so the organized diaspora continued to take its cues from the PNV. In the early 1960s, ETA activity consisted mainly of educating new *etarras*, as members were called, preparing ETA activists, and studying the works of Arana and Elias Gallastegui. Representatives agreed that ETA was a "Basque Revolutionary Movement of National Liberation" and not a political party, and that it would dedicate itself to securing political and cultural liberty for Basques in all seven provinces, and to changing the existing society. It would promote mass propaganda, labor activism, internal publications, paramilitary preparation, grassroots agitation, and popular demonstrations (Pagoaga Gallastegui interview, Belgium, 1997).

In its "Statement of Principles," ETA proposed the creation of an independent, democratically elected political order for the region, not dominated by any one party but by the people at large. Basques would enjoy internationally recognized human rights, such as freedom of speech, press, religion, and assembly, which were not a part of the society Franco allowed. Unions would have constitutionally protected rights, as would ethnic and linguistic minorities. The political framework would be decentralized, with as much power as possible reserved for municipalities. Although there was ambivalence about government planning and centralized power regarding the economy, the *etarras* advocated a modified market economy in which personal wealth and income inequality would be limited. Various sectors and resources would be government-owned or -managed, and workers' cooperatives would be encouraged (Zirakzadeh 1991, 152). Methods of achieving this Basque state were vague at this point; there was much disagreement among ETA planners between following Ghandi's nonviolent-resistance movement, Julen Madariaga's calculated use of defensive violence, offensive tactics and declarations of war, and all varieties of combinations.

The Basque economy continued to expand, and soon the memberships of ETA and labor unions overlapped. Because of constant arrests, imprisonments, and exile to France and Belgium, the less-experienced labor-oriented activists soon inherited control of the leadership offices. Now, university-educated urbanites together with the new directors who had inherited control of ETA entertained joining their forces with immigrant workers and advancing proletarian demands while simultaneously pushing for Basque self-determination in an independent state. The themes of cultural and ethnic oppression were superseded by complaints of economic exploitation. Publications concerning traditions, values, and language were replaced with those referring to the proletariat, the misery of factory production, class struggle, and the destruction of the roots of capitalism. ETA leaders read and studied Europe's New Left theoreticians, who argued for a novel way of thinking about social revolution, deducing that socialism would not come from a dramatic economic collapse, nor from a coup, which the international community would not allow. Instead, workers would gradually gain control over society through patient labor activity and local policy-making centers. Other strategists referred to inspiring anticolonial struggles and wished to adapt the contemporary liberation-movement models of Franz Fanon (*The Wretched of the Earth* was required reading for the organization), Ernesto "Che" Guevara, and Mao Tse-tung. They believed that action, not the hibernation of the PNV, would bring about change.

Federico Krutwig, using the political pseudonym Fernando Sarrailh de Ihartza, declared in the publication *Vasconia* that violence could be effectively used to set off widespread popular mobilizations against a government (Sarrailh de Ihartza 1964). Proposing the positive correlation between state violence and popular violence, Krutwig saw an accelerating spiral of violence between Basque protestors and the Guardia Civil leading to greater popular anger and militancy to the point of revolution. Krutwig's arguments detailed how a guerrilla movement should operate against a government, becoming a primer for ETA guerrilla warfare. If during the first half of the decade ETA's energies and resources were devoted primarily to cultural activism, the second half of the 1960s could be exemplified by the following statement published in the ETA newsletter *Zutik* (Arise): "Violence is necessary—a contagious, destructive violence that supports our struggle, a good struggle, one that the Israelis, Congolese, and Algerians have taught us" (Zirakzadeh 1991, 162).

Opposition to the focus on labor and to strategies of violence mounted. Txillardegui and other senior ETA members, many of whom were in exile in Belgium, France, and several Latin American countries, packed a Fifth Assembly meeting and overthrew the labor leadership, expelling them from ETA. The original ETA became known as ETA-V, because of the significance of the Fifth Assembly, while the expelled New Left members and followers formed an ETA-*berri*, literally the "New ETA."[6] The fragmentation confused Basques in Euskal Herria and those in the diaspora, who were being asked to support the Basque government-in-exile, ETA, ETA-V, and ETA-*berri*. ETA split from the PNV, and subsequent divisions within ETA confounded an already extremely fragmented nationalist movement. In Euskal Herria, ETA participants from all the various groups continued to disagree about objectives and the methods for achieving such objectives, and they formed additional detached groups that promoted different paths to different goals for the Basque Country. The original objectives of Txillardegui's ETA—territorial independence and cultural revitalization—were now hardly recognizable and were greatly misunderstood in the diaspora.

A SHIFT TO ARMED STRUGGLE

When Basque nationalism slowly resurfaced in the 1960s, its ideology had shifted dramatically. Previously, the nationalists had declared socialism and socialists to be anti-Christ and anti-Basque. However, the young nationalists who emerged with ETA proclaimed themselves to be socialists as well as nationalists, and many were members of the Catholic clergy. This conversion was inspired in part by student demonstrations and movements elsewhere in Europe, Vatican II proclamations and changes in Church relations with oppressed peoples, and Third World anticolonial and anti-imperialism struggles. The importance of Basque culture had replaced Basque race, and Basque socialism had replaced Basque Catholicism. Gradually, an agreement emerged to justify a right to self-determination and therefore an inherent right to sovereignty—that only Basques could and should rule Basques.

What had not been altered was the significance of being *abertzale*, or patriotic, to be a "good" or "true" Basque according to ETA sympathizers. Only a nationalist could be an *abertzale*, and hence only an *abertzale* could be a nationalist. Basque society became polarized into *abertzales* and *españolistas*, one was either Basque or anti-Basque. "Anti-Basques" included the Spanish police, the Guardia Civil, the Communist and Socialist parties in Euskadi, and ancestrally Basque people who were not nationalists, especially Basque industrialists, who had suffered tremendously at the hands of ETA, with kidnappings, extortion payments, and assassinations.

In 1968, Melitón Manzanas, a Spanish police commissioner with a reputation as a torturer, was assassinated, and ETA participants were fingered as the main suspects. The Spanish government imposed a state of exception and over two thousand Basques were arrested, with many beaten and tortured for information. Sixteen nationalists (two of whom were priests, and others admitted *etarras* and ETA sympathizers) were charged with the killing, though all pleaded innocent. Conviction was to result in capital punishment. Burgos, outside of the Basque provinces, was chosen for the military tribunal site. Foreign journalists reported repeated violations of international human rights conventions and principles of due process, and described in detail the suspects' descriptions of police torture. Diaspora communities mobilized in rare collective political action and attempted to influence their host-country governments' foreign policy with Spain. Readers around the world reacted in shock and solidarity for the suspects, out of either identification with an ethnic minority and opposition to discrimination, or from class consciousness and support for fellow workers. Within Euskal Herria, the unanticipated outpouring of international attention and support reinforced the commitment of activists within the ETA movement and catapulted other supporters into action for the first time. Six defendants were found guilty, but after an intercession by the pope

Franco granted stays of execution, reprieves, and lesser prison sentences to the others. Although in the aftermath of the Manzanas killing ETA had been decimated by arrests and flights from the homeland, now hundreds of new recruits were ready to fill the vacancies. Worldwide attention to the plight of the Basques as an oppressed people lent credence and justification for ETA's actions for the first time, and Basques in diaspora communities began to appreciate ETA activities as previously they had not. A recurring theme in my interviews in all six countries was that though respondents may not support current ETA operations, they had favored Franco-era ETA activities as necessary defensive reactions to state terrorism. They used the Burgos Trials as one more example of the repeated victimization by Spanish political powers.

Prior to Franco's death in 1975, and conforming to Krutwig's spiral theory of violence, ETA unleashed a wave of violent political protest unlike anything ever experienced before in the Basque Country. Armed robberies, bombings of personal, commercial, and military properties, kidnappings, and assassinations were defended as necessary acts against the region's symbols of capitalist wealth. The kidnapping of industrialist Lorenzo Zabala in 1972 was perplexing, because he was ethnically and linguistically Basque. ETA-V argued that the kidnapping demonstrated how ETA's armed struggle and the demands of striking workers could be combined for success. A new justification for violence was put forth: intense differences of opinion among government officials concerning responses to ETA violence would bring down the coalitions of moderate reformers and hard-core Francoists (Zirakzadeh 1991, 186).

Contrary to expectations, there did not seem to be any fissures or doubts about another harsh crack-down by the Guardia Civil when ETA assassinated Franco's political successor, Admiral Luís Carrero Blanco, by bombing his car sky high in 1973. Another series of arrests, beatings, and tortures of suspected ETA sympathizers and labor dissidents, together with a mass exodus into exile in France, Belgium, and Venezuela, left organized Basque nationalist groups in the four southern provinces devoid of senior leadership. More in-fighting regarding the lack of communication and approval of acts to be undertaken, doubts about aligning with non-Basque labor groups, and immediate plans for action after Franco's imminent death further divided the already fragmented Basque nationalists. The labeling of *etarras* now would include ETA-Politic-Militar, referring to those who favored subordinating violent military action to the political task of mobilizing nonelites, and ETA-Militar, or those who believed that ETA's most important goal should be to continue the armed struggle and strategy in accordance with the spiral theory of violence. Military operations were out of control, and there was no oversight or communications between field organizers (Karmelo Landa interview, Euskadi, 1996; Pagoaga Gallastegui interview, Belgium, 1997). Operations backfired, and instead of inspiring popular action they repelled many people by the use of terror against other Basques. Former ETA members and sympathizers watched from Euskal Herria and from exile as Basque nationalists became each other's worst enemies.

Franco's widely celebrated death in November 1975[7] did nothing to change ETA activities immediately. State violence and repression triggered more Basque violent reaction. Although murders carried out by ETA units had never exceeded seventeen per year between 1968 and 1977, in *each* of the years 1978, 1979, and 1980, over sixty-five killings were attributed to ETA groups (Clark 1984, 133). The spiral theory of violence was accurate for ETA and Spanish state actions, but a popular uprising against the regime never materialized. The very opposite attitude seemed to have affected most in the middle and upper classes, and the lower working class was tiring of bearing the brunt of state repression. They believed that ETA tactics had been unsuccessful in igniting popular revolution, and they anticipated that with a new prime minister and king, improvements should be on the way. They had waited forty years, so what would five or six more matter?

Spanish President Adolfo Suárez established a representative body, the Basque General Council, to facilitate the expected limited transfer of powers from Madrid to the Basque region. All political groups, unions, and other sectors of Basque society demanded inclusion in the Basque General Council or to be heard by it. Exhausted by government repression and arrests, frustrated by the failure of the spiral theory of violence and the inability to ignite popular resistance, and subject to the increasingly strong disfavor of the public and other Basque nationalist groups, most units of ETA-Político-Militar dissolved in the 1980s, leaving only a small sector of ETA-Militar still engaged in armed struggle. Former participants decided to utilize nonviolent means and new legal opportunities presented in the increasingly democratic institutions of the Autonomous Community. A number of ETA leaders also endorsed the idea of negotiating immediately while there was still something to negotiate, before a new French government policy of cooperation with the Spanish wiped out their safe houses, weapons, and money in France. A new coalition of former and current *etarras* and their sympathizers developed, calling itself *Herri Batasuna* (HB, One United People or One United Land). It was a loose coalition that agreed to promote what is known as the KAS Alternative (*Koordinadora Abertzale Sozialista*, Democratic Alternative for the Basque Country), which demanded immediate withdrawal of Spanish police forces from the Basque provinces, release of all Basque political prisoners, and political independence for the four Basque provinces. The Herri Batasuna coalition refused to participate in the newly developed political institutions. With the legalization of political parties and unions, and with limited autonomy and self-governance granted by the Spanish government to the Basque regions, the KAS Alternative lost importance to other nationalists who were willing to play by the rules of the new constitution.

In the summer of 1979, the Suárez government proposed an autonomy statute allowing the provinces of Araba, Bizkaia, and Gipuzkoa to establish a regional parliament with limited fiscal, educational, and a few other policy-making rights, and to allow the Basque provinces their own police force. Many citizens vividly remember the parades of the initial *Ertzaintza* (Basque police) before cheering and emotional crowds throughout the four provinces. Navarre negotiated a separate autonomy apart from the other three, which are now politically known as Euskadi, the Basque Autonomous Community. The PNV and *Euskadiko Ezkerra* (Basque Left) endorsed the proposal and urged Basque citizens to approve it through the referendum process. Herri Batasuna opposed the statute and favored abstention, complaining that the powers granted were too limited; that Navarre had been separated on purpose, to divide the power of the Basques, and should be included with the other three; and that demands for removing the Spanish military police and granting amnesty to political prisoners had not been addressed. The voter turnout was 57 percent, and 94.6 percent voted in favor of the proposed statute. The referendum passed.

Contemporary Basque Identity in Euskal Herria

Since 1980, the southern four provinces of the Basque Country have lived through tremendous political, economic, and social changes. They have established their own autonomous governments and institutions, and parallel to this political consolidation they have experienced a transformation in the economy. The centuries-old traditional economy of agriculture, iron, and steel, which formerly produced mainly for the internal markets of Spain, has now stepped up to meet the demands of the European Union and its Common Market. The Basques have reorganized and modernized rapidly in order to respond to the competitive requirements of an increasingly open economic and civil society, and each of these factors has affected contemporary Basque identity in the homeland and relations with Basques abroad.

Commencing after 1978, the Spanish central government set about writing a new constitution, creating from the fifty provinces seventeen new autonomous regions with separate and different powers devolved to each. The powers granted to the Basque Autonomous Community, Euskadi (Araba, Bizkaia, Gipuzkoa), are not the same as those granted to the separate Foral Community of Nafarroa. The Statute of Autonomy for Euskadi, also known as the Statute of Gernika, ratifies political, social, and economic relations between the Basque Autonomous Community and the Spanish state administration. The Basque government has executive and legislative powers, including the essential control over taxation. The greater part of tax resources are gathered by the institutions of the provincial *Diputationes,* or executive branches, not the central Spanish government. The Statute of Autonomy gives the Basque government control over all matters that concern the Basque police force, management and development of education and health care, extensive responsibilities in the fields of infrastructure and public works in general, culture, agriculture, industry, and social welfare.

The Basque legislative branch is made up of seventy-five deputies, twenty-five from each province, and its seat is in Vitoria-Gasteiz, the capital city of Araba, chosen to increase the incorporation of Arabans, who have historically been the least nationalist of Basques. Basque nationalist parties combined receive a majority of the votes cast, as was the case again in the 2001 regional parliamentary elections. However, there are eight or nine parties and coalition groups that present candidates in each election, so no single political party has ever reached a 50-percent majority of the electorate. The PNV set a historic record when it earned 42.7 percent of the 2001 vote. The fragmentation continues in the party system, exemplified by the breaking away of the *Eusko Alkartasuna* (Basque Solidarity Party) from the PNV in 1989. Some coalitions last for only one election, and even they may break up while in office.

The support that ETA once enjoyed has decreased, and its political arm, *Euskal Herritarrok,* the new name of the Herri Batasuna, won only 10.1 percent of the vote for the regional parliament in 2001. In 1988, all six major Basque regional parties, except Herri Batasuna, signed an antiterrorism pact designed to isolate and reduce the influence of ETA. This agreement, *El Pacto de Ajuria Enea,* named after the presidential palace in Vitoria-Gasteiz, was also taken to the World Congress of Basque Collectivities in the Diaspora, which met in Bahia Blanca, Argentina, in 1989. Delegates from the world's Basque centers also signaled their support for it, with abstentions from the United States, Uruguay, and Basque centers within Spain that are not in the Basque provinces.

The new Spanish constitution of 1978 states that Euskera and Spanish will share official-language status in Euskadi and Nafarroa, and that all inhabitants have the right to know and use both languages. This establishes a legal framework for bilingualism, though not an actual bilingual society. Many students utilize Euskera in the classroom, but once on the streets with friends or at home with parents who may not speak Basque, they are likely to utilize Spanish. Because the Basque tradition is to be accommodating to all, if one member of a group does not know Basque, the others will all speak Spanish, instead of that one person being expected to learn and use Basque (Tejerina Montaña 1992). There is also the situation of many Basque dialects being spoken in the general society, while the Basque being learned in classrooms is the new

Standardized Basque, or Batua. Some students learn Batua in school and then upon returning home speak the local dialect with family and friends. The hope is that in future generations, all schoolchildren will have studied the same Batua Basque and will be able to communicate with each other easily. Basque television, radio, and print media also use Batua as a means of communication. Road signs, advertising, and all government documentation utilize the standardized Batua Basque. For many people, the use of Basque is most important to stimulate patriotic consciousness (Pérez-Agote 1987, 26).

Basques in the diaspora who are learning Euskera are studying Batua, even though their parents and other older members of their Basque communities speak regional dialects. When these new Basque speakers travel to the Basque Country, they are often disappointed to hear so much Spanish being spoken. These diaspora Basques have become examples to Basques living in Euskal Herria of how a "true" Basque should speak. The homeland media are quite happy to report examples of diaspora Basques who have maintained their language skills, and to demonstrate examples of new Basque speakers with the added commentary, "Shouldn't we be ashamed to live in the Basque Country and not utilize our Basque when there are thousands of Basques in other parts of the world trying to learn and practice it to maintain their identity?" (Aranburu Iturbe interview, Euskal Irrati Telebista, 1997).

Language continues to be a very important factor in Basque identity, especially for the younger generations who have every opportunity to learn it at school. The Civil War generation and Basques born afterward were prohibited by the Franco government from learning and using Euskera outside their homes, and hence there is a generation gap in the knowledge and use of Basque. The significant influx of non-Basque–speaking families from other areas of Spain into the four provinces also negatively impacted the use of Euskera. Therefore, in today's grandparent and grandchildren generations, many speak Basque as mother tongue or have learned it at school, whereas the middle generation of today's parents is likely to speak Basque only if they heard it at home while growing up, but they are typically illiterate. Their refusal to take advantage of free evening language classes offered in all cities and almost all towns is seen by many Basque nationalists as reflecting a lack of interest in Basque culture, as well as categorizing them as not being Basque patriots. The term *abertzale* is still reserved for those who are active and vocal about maintaining Basque culture, history, and traditions. It also means that politically such a person would support Basque, not Spanish, political parties. For some, *abertzale* means a person who favors political separation from Spain and France and total independence for the seven provinces of the Basque homeland. In public-opinion polls taken in the Basque Autonomous Community, results demonstrate that a person who is considered *abertzale* is "more" Basque than those who are not *abertzale* (Ramirez Goicoechea 1991, 113). Change has been slow to come to the definitions and marking factors of "Basqueness"; it is also important to point out the continuation of a "Spanish" identity for many Basques in the four southern Basque provinces.

What has changed is the shifting emphasis from a racial to a linguistic and territorial definition of Basque identity. Basque nationalist literature has become more inclusive and is now accepting as Basque those who live and work in the Basque Country, learn Euskera, and identify themselves with Basque culture, traditions, and values. In Ramirez Goicoechea's 1991 survey of Basque ethnic-identity definitions among youth in a Gipuzkoan area, 70 percent of the respondents listed as the most important marker of "being Basque" following "the Basque customs and [being] interested in the events of the Basque Country." Following this, "those who speak Basque" (27.35 percent) and "those who were born in the Basque Country" (21.08 percent) are the most important indicators of who is "more Basque." Her research demonstrates that these categories are the most inclusive and that "being Basque" can be a matter of behavior and of choice. Respondents selected "following Basque customs" as the most important qualification whether they defined themselves as "independentists," "autonomists," or "centralists" on the political geography of the Basque Country.

In an earlier study in another region with a higher immigrant population, respondents thought one should "live and work in the Basque Country" in order to be considered "a Basque." Obviously, here the immigrant population wants to be considered part of the "us." Many of these citizens have lived in the Basque provinces for two or three generations, but if their last name is not Basque they still might be categorized by traditionalists as immigrants.

Attitudes about Basqueness are changing. It seems that a person can *become* Basque. Sabino Arana y Goiri is turning in his grave, and many diaspora Basques are just as incredulous. In several Uruguayan Basque organizations, an applicant for membership must have at least one Basque surname among the four grandparents to be admitted. "Non-Basques," defined as such because they do not have a Basque surname in their ascendancy, either cannot join these Basque centers or are accepted as nonvoting associates, or "friends of Basques."

Conclusion

I have summarized the ethnic separation of Basques throughout history in their homeland and have noted that though Basque ethnic awareness has existed since at least the times of Spanish colonization, Basque political nationalism became more intense with opposition to liberal reforms, industrialization, and

Spanish state-building in the 1800s. An "unfinished agenda" explanation for twentieth-century Basque nationalism seems appropriate. In this view, the assimilation into Spanish society of Galician, Catalan, Basque, and other ethnic groups and a successful Spanish nation-building agenda are incomplete (Douglass 1985). During the colonial period, imperial governments were so concerned with their colonies that autonomous regions within the metropole were ignored and issues that should have been resolved in the seventeenth and eighteenth centuries were postponed. As Spanish and British colonies one by one declared their independence, the separation by oceans gave a huge advantage to the colonists in any resulting struggle. But those lands closer and dearer to home could not be relinquished, as is the case with Britain vis-à-vis Northern Ireland and Scotland, and with Spain vis-à-vis Catalonia and the Basque Country.

Industrialization also served as a catalyst for uniting Basques against the changes to traditional culture and identity. Sabino Arana y Goiri ignited the contemporary nationalist crusade with pointed rhetoric exemplifying primordial identity. As industrialization and modernization diversified the Basque socioeconomic picture, so too did the nationalist movement diverge from the Aranist catechism. The review of the schisms in Basque nationalist ideology demonstrates that Basque nationalism has never been, nor is it now, a unified front with shared goals. The maturing of Basque nationalism and ethnic identity maintenance in the homeland and in the diaspora communities has brought me to my discussion of diaspora formation. The following chapters will describe the specific push-and-pull circumstances of Basque emigration to each host country, detail the birth of Basque ethnonational activity in diaspora communities, and analyze the results of written questionnaires and personal interviews.

While homeland nationalism has shifted its emphasis from race, language, and religion when defining and categorizing "Basqueness" to a more inclusive civic nationalism determined by living and working in Euskal Herria and by a person's desire to work for Basque culture, the diaspora has maintained traditional Aranist definitions of who and what is Basque. The Basques' perception of their history and identity idealizes their ancestors and the ancestral homeland, creating a strong ethnic group consciousness and solidarity among Basques. I now turn to the dispersal and creation of the diaspora; the expansion of migration for colonial ambitions or economic opportunity; and economic and political exile.

Chapter Three

The Formation of the Basque Diaspora

The political, economic, and social factors of migration are numerous, epoch-specific, and person-specific. New World economic and political opportunities, weighed against Old World uncertainties and upheaval, provided the general stimulus for emigration to the Americas. In the case of Basque emigration, the most salient push factors included Spanish colonization of the Americas and the demand for clerics, military personnel, and tradesmen in the colonies; the restricted economic opportunity in the homeland; the physical position of Euskal Herria between Spain and France and its use as a stage for Napoleonic military campaigns; the First Carlist War (1833–39) and the Second Carlist War (1872–76); and the Spanish Civil War (1936–39) and the subsequent Franco dictatorship. The Spanish liberalization of emigration in 1853 also encouraged thousands of persons annually to depart for Latin America, as did the Basque primogeniture inheritance system and overpopulated rural areas.

I will review how Basques pursued ethnically based trading networks to aid the expansion of their ambitions, and how this foundation of a trade diaspora was followed by economic, political, and sociocultural transnationalism. Until the beginning of the last century, trade, and military and religious conquests were the reasons for Basque emigration, an emigration that took place inside Basque trans-kingdom and trans-state networks, as well as within the framework of the Spanish empire. During the imperial period, Basque emigration to the Americas and the Philippines involved the transfer of skilled and influential individuals from an imperial country and its regions to its colonies—a colonial diaspora. This emigration was also often temporary, and young-male-dominated, and it was rare for an entire family to leave the Basque Country together.

The independentist movements in Latin American territories, compounded by the fact that Spain lost practically all of its colonies simultaneously and finally with the Disaster of the 1898 Spanish American War, drew a line that divides the history of Basque emigration into two phases. The second phase was part of a European wave of emigration to the former colonies in the New World, a transfer of people who were economically and/or politically oppressed.

Pulling them across the Atlantic were dreams of economic success, civil rights and political freedoms, and asylum. Some emigrants searched for opportunities while others fled difficulties, and the Basques were no exception. They were also no exception in that they sought out other Basques and used ethnic transnational networks in determining their destinations.

The Colonial Diaspora: Collaborators in Spanish Imperialism

Throughout the late Middle Ages, the Bay of Biscay's marine economy and trade required Basques to travel and contact other cultures and societies, and Basque place-names dot the landscapes in coastal regions of Europe, Scandinavia, and Newfoundland (Barkham 1989; Collins 1986, 235, 240–41; Caro Baroja 1971, 195–203).[1] The Flemish city of Bruges retains archives from the commercial consulate established there in the fifteenth century recording the presence of Bizkaian and Gipuzkoan merchants and demonstrating the trade networks between Basques in the Basque Country, the Low Countries, and England. Basque whalers, merchants, and shipbuilders, along with professional military personnel, were among the first emigrants. However, significant numbers of Basques did not begin to leave the Basque Country permanently until the 1500s, to participate in the colonial pursuits of the Crown of Castile and later Spain, and as part of the French colonization of North America and particularly of Newfoundland, where they worked in the fisheries and established a number of permanent settlements along the coast.

In the first phase of emigration at the beginning of the sixteenth century, Spain lacked sufficient population and economic resources to pursue colonialism on all fronts. Hence a militaristic policy of control rather than a colonial policy of settlement was applied to Spain's Mediterranean regions, and genuine colonizing efforts were reserved for the Americas. Both policies were heavily dependent upon two elements that predominated in the Basque region—sea power and iron products. Without military and commercial transportation, Spain could not possibly maintain its Old World holdings nor develop its fledgling New World colonies. Efforts to colonize would require reliable supplies of iron implements, and military campaigns would consume large amounts of weaponry. For the Basque economy, the opening of the New World was an immediate stimulant.

ETHNIC GROUP AWARENESS IN THE NEW WORLD CONTEXT

It would not be an exaggeration to state that no major Spanish expeditionary force and no ecclesiastical or secular administration in the New World did not include Basques. More important for this study is not the numbers of Basques involved in migration and settlement but the nature of Basque involvement.

I am concerned with demonstrating that Basques have often acted as a self-aware ethnic group, maintaining ties to each other and to their homeland. This has resulted in trade networks, collective action, mutual-assistance programs, schools for Basque children, associations and societies for the maintenance of Basque language, culture, and traditions, and a perception that Basques have a common stance toward outsiders and that Basques were set apart from other Iberian and New World–born persons of European descent.

One of the first instances of Basque ethnic solidarity in the New World involves the initial voyage of Columbus, which utilized the *Santa María*, Basque-owned and -manned and captained by Juan de la Cosa, as well as the *Niña*, which was Basque-manned (Caro Baroja 1971). When the *Santa María* was shipwrecked, Columbus left several men behind to found the first European New World colony at Fuerte Navidad, on the island of Hispaniola. When Columbus returned to find the colony destroyed by natives, the explanation was that the Europeans had split into two camps along ethnic lines, Basque and non-Basque. Divided ethnically and unwilling to work with the other colonists, the Bizkaians had caused a division that led to defeat by the indigenous population (Pérez de Arenaza and J. Lasagabaster 1991, 33; Galíndez 1984, 28–31).

Basques were involved in collective efforts at colonization, and in 1501 they attempted their own separate Basque colony on Santo Domingo. Although the colony was unsuccessful, it demonstrates ethnic collective action and solidarity by the Basques in the New World. Other Basque colonial encampments founded later in Mexico, Cuba, Peru, Bolivia, and Venezuela were also organized along ethnic lines—though in the historical record Basques were generally aggregated as all being "Vizcainos," or Bizkaians.

A different type of Basque began to arrive in the colonies once the native populations were conquered militarily—land developers, educated scribes seeking posts with the colonial administration, and many clerics sent by the Catholic Church to seek converts. The bishop of New Spain (now Mexico and the southwestern United States), named in 1527, was a Basque, Juan de Zumarraga, who surrounded himself with other Basques. The pull of proselytizing was strong for many Basque clerics, who requested and accepted appointments to the New World colonies. Basque explorers opened sea routes between New Spain and the Orient in Basque-constructed vessels, manned by Basques. Cristobal de Oñate and his brother Juan, also Basques, controlled the populations of Jalisco and founded the city of Guadalajara. Juan de Tolosa discovered silver at Zacatecas and initiated what was to become one of the most important mining operations in all of the New World. Francisco Ibarra explored more northerly regions between 1554 and 1564 and founded the province of New Vizcaya, named after his birthplace. While governor, Ibarra declared that the Fuero of Vizcaya would be the law of the new territory and that all colonists would be regarded as nobility and were to be exempted from royal taxation (West 1949, as cited in Douglass and Bilbao 1975, 78).

Colonial Basques also created their own mutual-aid societies and separate religious confraternities. This ethnic exclusiveness and economic independence from the Church created resentment on the part of Church authorities and caused problems for ethnic Basques. In Mexico, a priest who was turned away from an all-Basque chapel when asking for alms declared that there would be a trial by the Inquisition that would "exile all Vizcayans who were living in Mexico." He also prepared a list of resident Basques for the mayor to facilitate their deportation. Though this proposal was rejected, Basques decided to seek more protection for their activities (Obregón 1949, as cited in Douglass and Bilbao, 1975, 97). They proposed to build a major asylum in Mexico City to provide protection and shelter for young girls, widows, and descendants of Basque families. The College of Saint Ignatius (named after the Basque patron saint from Loyola, Gipuzkoa) would provide shelter and education in a living community with residents performing all the necessary tasks to keep it in order. The site was acquired in 1733, with the specific stipulations from Basques that it would remain free of Church control. This requirement led to many confrontations with Church officials in the following years, and the College, known as the College of the Vizcayans, did not open until 1767.

Although the Basques of Mexico were prone to collective action as an ethnic group, after a century of involvement in Spain's New World ventures some feared that their American successes were undermining their ethnic loyalties. In 1607, Balthasar de Echave published a work in Mexico City regarding loyalty to the Basque language as mother tongue, reminding Basques that their first and foremost loyalty should not be to the "Castilian Foreigner" or its language, Spanish, but to their "true and legitimate mother," that of Basque identity (Echave 1971, 84). Even in the 1600s, diaspora Basques tended to identify the Castilians as "the opposition" and demonstrated evidence of an idealization of their own ethnicity and a solidarity with co-ethnics.

Basque commercial and maritime interests were also prominent in Guatemala, as were ethnic tensions. In the seventeenth century, Juan Martínez de Landecho, a Basque, was deposed as president of the Audiencia de Guatemala because of fear that he would convert the Realm of Guatemala into a New Bizkaia with foral rights (Sáenz de Santa María 1969, as quoted in Douglass and Bilbao 1975, 80).

By the beginning of the seventeenth century, the Basque presence in Chile was extensive. Thayer y Ojeda concluded that immigration in Chile was characterized by "the father bringing over his son, the brother sending for the brother, the cousin inducing his cousin to come, the friend inducing the friend.... This Basque immigration, improperly called Vizcaino, was nothing more than a change of residence of various related families." The transnational networks of chain migration were well established in Chile. "By the nineteenth century half of all illustrious persons in Chilean history and society were of Basque descent" (Thayer y Ojeda 1904, as cited in Douglass and Bilbao, 1975, 81). However, anti-Basque sentiments were likewise prevalent in Chile. In Santiago de Chile, Bishop Francisco de Salcedo warned the king of Spain that the royal treasury was not receiving all it was due from the area. According to Salcedo, the reason was that all of the traders, or at least most of them, were Bizkaians; the harbor authority and the registrar who examined the cargos were both Bizkaian, as was the chief police authority. In all of the warehouses, Salcedo wrote, "the Bizkaians guarded their goods, which were great in quantity" (Thayer y Ojeda 1904, 13–14).

The end of the 1500s to the mid-1600s witnessed much ethnic conflict between Basques and non-Basques in present-day Bolivia and Peru. Beginning in 1582, Basque emigrants and emigrants from the Extremadura region of Spain fought each other in the mining districts of Potosí (Martín Rubio 1996). Dwellings were destroyed, and an ensuing forty years of violence was ethnically based. Madariaga cites evidence that jealous tensions and anti-Basque sentiment were in part due to Basque indiscretion in the display and use of their economic and political power. There was constant civil war, with one leader even advising his followers, "let all nations be united with the Creoles. This will quicken the destruction of these Vizcainos" (Madariaga 1950, 629).

In Peru, where the Confraternity of Aránzazu in Lima dates from 1612, Basques and non-Basques remained antagonistic, and between 1661 and 1665 there were bloody incidents in La Paz. In 1665 at the mining camp of Icazota, there was an aborted plot on the part of non-Basques to annihilate the Basque population. Again in 1666, eight hundred non-Basque men returned to Icazota and set fire to Basque businesses and houses, killing three hundred and fifty persons (Idoate 1957, as quoted in Douglass and Bilbao 1975, 83).

It is possible that envy of Basque economic and political success, as well as Basque clannishness and exclusiveness, were factors in the anti-Basque violence. Or perhaps the Basques remained close-knit and ethnically united out of self-protection from anti-Basque sentiments. Basques were prone to collective action in the New World, and they constituted a self-aware ethnic group in colonial societies—an ethnic group that was perceived as such by outsiders. Upon arriving in the colonies, they continued to define themselves as Basques and tried in many cases to recreate their Basque homeland's social, economic, and political structures, such as the *fueros* of Bizkaia. There were many examples of individualism and competition between Basques, too, but Basque activities were usually interpreted by non-Basques as being collective and bordering on an ethnic group conspiracy. The Basques initiated trading, religious, and employment networks based on ethnicity (Quiroz Paz-Soldán 1996), and certainly individual Basques used ethnicity to gain political favors or employment with each other, though not necessarily using their Basqueness to secure partiality from non-Basques.

Several generations of colonial expansion into the Americas were realized with Basque leadership, Basque capital, and Basque manpower (Azcona Pastór 1992; Vázques de Prada Vallejo and Usunariz Garayoa 1991; Gómez Prieto 1991; Douglass 1989). The social structure and economy of the colonies included numerous Basque landowners, business owners, administrators, soldiers, and clerics. The many Basque place-names record the efforts of these colonists and their tendency to cluster together. Basques were often viewed as potential subverters of Spain's interests, although in their roles as administrators, clerics, and mercantilists they also served the Crown's policies, which may have affected sentiments toward them. Ethnic rivalries were certainly prevalent, but in some cases anti-Basque activities could have been fundamentally opposition to the Crown yet aimed at the Basques because they were the controlling representatives of Crown interests. Yet in the cases presented here, usually the non-Basques favored the ruling king. The ample forces of maritime, military, and religious duties pushed Basques *out* of Euskal Herria to fulfill their responsibilities, oaths, and vows, while enticing economic forces with commercial promises of profits and economic success pulled them *to* the New World.

Basque, and especially Bizkaian, interests controlled more than Spanish shipping; they also "supplied capital, equipment and goods for trade as well as many of its personnel" (Lynch 1964, 154–55). Several previously established Basque commercial interests in Spain opened branch operations with kinsmen in the Indies, especially in Santo Domingo (Bilbao 1958, 192–209). Iparralde Basques also participated in the American ventures, and vessels from Donibane Lohitzun (St-Jean-de-Luz) were registered with authorities as Bizkaian. Lynch estimates that almost 80 percent of the New World traffic between 1520 and 1580 was Basque-controlled, and between 1580 and 1610 Basque interests represented at least 50 percent of the total. This accounts for nearly one hundred years of Basque domination in Spanish colonial efforts, pushing Basque maritime specialists toward the New World, where they established trade links back to their homeland.

Many Basques experienced the pull of family ties or other contacts from their home villages stemming from the time of this colonial stage, namely in Argentina, Uruguay, Paraguay, Venezuela, Colombia, Chile, Peru, Mexico, and Cuba. Spain's and France's colonial conquests provided new opportunities for overseas migration. Although France did not impose strict rules upon emigration, Spain did, requiring each emigrant to apply for a license and to depart through government-established channels. Violations were numerous, however, and the majority of emigrants left Spain illegally and so were not included in the administration's official count. Many Basques simply went to the north of Euskal Herria and departed from the French side, benefitting from Basque preferential treatment and aid. A seventeenth-century document states, "In 1640 three-fourths of the population of Vizcaya is composed of women due to the number of men who leave to never return" (Nadal 1966, 79, quoted in Bilbao Azkarreta 1992). Accurate numbers of emigrants by year or by destination are nonexistent because of the lack of exact record-keeping by departure-port authorities as well as the lack of detailed records by receiving authorities in the host territories, which lumped Basques, Galicians, Catalans, and other Spanish together. More recent records are no better. For example, Spanish official statistics give 1,042,775 emigrants leaving Spain between 1882 and 1930, but the receiving states show numerous millions of immigrants from Spain for the same years (Ruíz de Azua 1992, 266). Some of these emigrants departed from French ports, and others were only temporary residents abroad. The lack of consistency in data makes it unwise to infer from the records total percentages of Basque emigrants or numbers of people leaving the Basque Country itself.

Those Basques who departed without definite contacts in the New World to receive them knew from village lore that an established Basque group could be found in almost any of these New World trade regions. They knew about remittances to families in their areas and could see the construction of farmsteads, churches, and improvements in agricultural equipment that resulted from those remittances. It was only natural to expect that fellow ethnics would be useful in helping them adapt and acculturate to the new society. Particularly for Basques from the South of Euskal Herria, knowledge of the Spanish language and culture, plus experience with the customs and governmental workings of Spain, were beneficial in understanding and adapting to an already somewhat familiar Spanish societal structure in South America.

The Aftermath of War Pushes and Pioneerism Pulls Basque Migration

The Latin American colonies began declaring their individual independence from the Spanish empire in the early 1800s. As the period of Spanish hegemony and colonial domination was closing across the oceans, so was Spain's extravagance of ignoring its immediate neighbors and historical territories. Political upheaval across Europe and tremors of revolution could not be dismissed in Madrid or in the Basque Country. During and after the French Revolution, the northern Basque provinces were subjected to military occupation and their ancient foral laws were abolished. Basques were deprived of their lands and livestock, and some Basques were interned in camps by revolutionary officials. There was also a forced deportation of more than three thousand Basques who were accused of treason with Spain (Jacob 1994, 33–35). In 1793 in Baiona (Bayonne) alone, more than sixty death penalties were pronounced for "complicity in illegal immigration or correspondence with priests in exile" (Jacob 1985, 83). Napoleon's rise to power and push to conquer the Iberian Peninsula resulted in several wars being fought in the Basque Country, with Basques themselves being recruited and conscripted by both sides. Many escaped or deserted, as did forty-seven Basque soldiers from Itxassou alone (Jacob 1985, 86).

By the 1830s, Basque agents in Iparralde were recruiting emigrants to the safe haven of Uruguay. Official passenger lists for boats leaving from Baiona record that between 1832 and 1884, 64,227 persons emigrated from the department of Basses-Pyrénées, and by the late 1880s there were twenty-three travel agencies in Bordeaux alone working with Uruguayan agents specifically to service Basque emigration to Río de la Plata (Douglass and Bilbao 1975, 122–23). From the French side of the Basque Country, it is estimated that between 1832 and 1907 more than one hundred thousand persons emigrated to Argentina and that the provinces of Zuberoa and Behe Nafarroa lost between 20 and 25 percent of their total population. The *entire* population growth in Iparralde for the last half of the nineteenth century was canceled by emigration (Jacob 1994, 46).

The first of the Carlist Wars, described in chapter 2, commenced in 1833 with Catholic and regionalist Basques siding with the challenger to the Spanish throne. Financing the war meant heavy taxation in most areas of the Basque Country and conscription by the Carlist forces. The defeat of the Carlists in 1839 left Basques with political and economic war debt and retribution, and six years of war had disrupted the economy and agricultural output. An estimated eighty thousand war exiles fled to Argentina, Uruguay,[2] and Chile (Bilbao Azkarreta 1992, 231). A corn crop failure and the famine of 1846–47 aggravated already dire circumstances and gave impetus for many more Basques to abandon their economic, military, and political situations and seek relief in the Americas. The French Revolution of 1848 once again found the Basques fighting on the losing side against revolutionary goals, and memories of repercussions from the earlier rebellions again encouraged departures from the area. Between 1852 and 1855, there were 1,311 French Basque military evaders— almost one-half of the French total (Douglass and Bilbao 1975, 123). The Second Carlist War (1873–76) saw a repeat of the pattern of defeat and emigration to escape hardship. Maritime archives show that hundreds of men of military age avoided or deserted their obligatory three-year military service (Azcona Pastor 1996, 47), and others later fled the repercussions of the Liberals.

An exact accounting of Basque emigration in this time period does not exist because the pertinent recording agency, the Geographic and Statistical Institute in the Ministry of Agriculture of Spain, was not created until 1882. Though Argentine immigration data for the period between 1857 to 1930 record the arrival of 2,070,874 Spanish immigrants (Moya 1998, 1), some of these emigrants went back and forth, some returned permanently to Spain, and no records contain data that permits the calculation of the number of Basques among them. Pérez de Arenaza and Lasagabaster conservatively put the number of Basque-only emigrants in the same period at 200,000, but because of the illegality of emigration, repercussions and fines to families of emigrants, the lack of consistent record-keeping, and the lack of details in the records that were kept, other estimates of totals vary widely.

What is certain is that the preferred earlier destinations of Mexico, Venezuela, and Peru had changed by the mid-nineteenth century to Argentina and Uruguay. Therefore, for today's Basque population in Peru, the Basques in Peruvian history are connected to the Spanish conquerors and colonizers and are categorized by the general population as "Spanish," whereas Basques in the Río de la Plata region are distinguished as immigrant pioneers who fought for independence and built the new countries. "Basque" in Peru is a relatively unknown and misunderstood description of either a far-off history of the colonization of the Americas, in which the colonizers are seen as corrupt destroyers, or of a very few more-recent immigrants from the 1900s. However, "Basque" in Argentina and Uruguay carries a positive connotation based on more recent history and the creation of their respective societies, promoting for them a positive social status as creators.

Emigration during any of these time periods was by no means an unusual option or a last resort to remedy hardship. Like their forefathers, Basques in later centuries knew and heard of fellow Basques escaping poverty and political and economic oppression for employment and opportunity overseas. The key to migration may have been information. The choice of destinations and the time of departure depended on homeland circumstances, family and village ties, and employment opportunities. Because the economic and industrial development of Western Europe implied an increase in specialization, many small proprietors and tradesman were faced with a choice of finding alternative employment or emigration (Baines 1991, 14). Among Basques, chain-migration information networks facilitated the latter.

CIRCUMSTANCES AND INCENTIVES PULLING BASQUES TOWARD THE AMERICAS

The first expeditions to the Río de la Plata region were led by Basques representing the Spanish Crown. Basque Juan de Garay crossed the Andes from Peru and named the territory from the Paraná River to the ocean "New Bizkaia" (Pérez de Arenaza and Lasagabaster 1991, 47). He went on to found Buenos Aires in 1580. Thirty-four governors of the territory, and later province, of Buenos Aires were Basque, and of the province's founding council in 1810, 40 percent were Basque. Argentina's Declaration of Independence of 1816 was signed by twenty-nine deputies, ten of whom were Basque, and four of the five priests giving the blessing were Basques. For centuries, the "Ordinance of Bilbao" provided commercial regulatory codes for this region, until 1859 when Argentina created its own commercial codes. Sociologist and economist Juan José Guaresti has noted that Argentine law is based upon the Basque *fueros* (Anasagasti 1988, 16). Basque foral laws were an integral part of Basque identity in the New World because of their salience in the homeland, and their protection was the most significant factor in the Carlist Wars of the nineteenth century; Basque emigration thus included not only the transfer of persons but also of attitudes, values, and institutional principles.

Also pulling already frantic potential immigrants toward South America— now to Argentina and Uruguay specifically—were decades of success stories and the welcoming mentality first described by Basque essayist Juan Bautista Alberdi (1810–84), that "in America, to govern is to populate." European settlers were desired and specifically mentioned in Article 25 of the Argentine Constitution of 1853: "The Federal Government will foment European immigration and will be prohibited from restraining, limiting, and taxing the entrance to the Argentine territory, any foreigners who enter with the intent to till the soil, improve industries, and introduce and teach the sciences and arts" (Azcona Pastór 1992, 36). This was an open invitation to all, but especially enticing to suffering Basques who could likely procure information and possible assistance for a move. All categories of craftsmen, professionals, and laborers were needed for South America's expanding economies and societies. Spain's Royal Order of 16 September 1853 coincidentally relaxed emigration restrictions.

The 1879 military action by General Julio Argentino Roca (elected president of Argentina the next year) against the Araucanian natives opened vast areas of the pampas for control and increased the demand for European settlers. Updated immigration laws authorized advancing the costs of passage for certain newcomers, particularly Basques. The Argentine government utilized established Basque ethnic ties and sent recruiters to Euskal Herria to advertise economic opportunities and encourage the emigration of entire families. The government also subsidized transatlantic passages, offered land grants, and established facilities for free room and board, transportation, and employment for the new immigrants (Dupla 1992). These favorable factors convinced thousands of Europeans to leave their crowded homelands for South America. Pérez-Agote notes Argentina's worldwide popularity for migration by showing that between 1857 and 1915, there were 4,445,760 new immigrants (Pérez-Agote et al. 1997, 32).

Uruguayan governments, beginning in 1832, specifically requested Basque immigrants for the country's agriculture. The European Industrial Revolution created a high demand for wool, and the Uruguayan sheep industry was mainly controlled by Basques. There were agencies in Iparralde devoted exclusively to recruiting and transporting Basque emigrants to the Río de la Plata region. In 1852 alone, the Argentine consul in Baiona processed 2,800 emigrants—destination Buenos Aires. There is evidence that suggests that although some emigration was necessary as an escape valve to political and economic pressures of the region, emigration also seemed to create social problems such as lack of youth, laborers, and especially males for marriage. For a time, marriage ages rose, unmarried elderly women were common, and birthrates fell. In 1852, the bishop of Pamplona published a pamphlet entitled *Circular in Which the System of Hoodwinking Persons of Both Sexes in Order to Conduct Them to the American Continent Under the Seductive Promises of Establishing a Fortune and a Happy Future Is Demonstrated as Being Immoral* (Andriani Escofet 1852, quoted in Douglass 1979, 290). There is no clear evidence of his advice being heeded. The seemingly instant financial rewards encouraged recent arrivals to continue sending for relatives and fellow villagers, and encouraged those in the homeland to accept the challenge.

Upon arrival in Buenos Aires, Basque immigrants would most likely remain in the capital city or in a coastal town where the majority of the population of Argentina lived. Others moved on to the Uruguayan capital and its interior. Those from cities who were accustomed to administrative, factory, and commercial life stayed in the cities, while Basques from villages and rural homesteads were attracted to the agricultural rural life. By the 1840s, establishment of a sheep industry augmented cattle in the interior pampas regions, with Basque immigrants dominating both sheepherding and cattle raising.

Construction laborers, longshoremen, craftsmen, brickmakers, loggers, charcoal makers, and especially dairy producers and meat-salting plant operators all provided employment and social connections for Basque settlers, who dominated these industries in the latter half of the nineteenth century. Euskera was the working language spoken by both laborers and entrepreneurs (Siegrist de Gentile and Álvarez Gila 1998). Basques owned many of the stores and markets in Buenos Aires and Montevideo, and their economic success strengthened their influence in Río de la Plata financial circles. There were Basque ethnic neighborhoods such as the Barrio de la Constitución in Buenos Aires, where Basques enjoyed their own markets, shops, housing, schooling, and churches, and where Euskera was the language of communication (Olaizola interview, Buenos Aires, 1996). Certain Catholic churches were known as Basque churches, and there were sufficient Basque priests to hold masses, weddings, baptisms, and confirmations in Euskera (Álvarez Gila 1996). All of these factors point to a sustained ethnic consciousness and solidarity among Argentine Basques—three hundred years after the founding of Buenos Aires.

In the interior, a few Basques became land barons, and others gained tremendous fortunes in the cattle and sheep industries. Initially, many new Basque immigrants worked in teams as sheepherders and shearers, barbed-wire fence-stringers for livestock, and oxcart drivers, and thousands of others worked as ranch and farm hands. Successful ranchers needed additional hands and often sent passage to relatives from Euskal Herria, especially younger disinherited males from the rural regions. Basques opened hotels, restaurants, and bakeries. Artisans and craftsmen sent word to unemployed family and friends in the homeland that their specialties were needed, appreciated, and profitable in the Americas. Through hundreds of links, immigration from Euskal Herria produced a chain of transnationalism and bonds between the cone of South America and the Basque Country.

By the mid-1800s, a new destination attracting Basque emigrants was the United States, mostly in response to the discovery of gold in California, which also prompted secondary migration of Basques from South America to California. Before 1860, a few Basques who had no luck in their search for gold started raising sheep flocks to feed miners in the American West. Gold and silver strikes in Nevada and Idaho compounded the need for foodstuffs, and Basques raised cattle and sheep inexpensively and with high profit margins on the public lands. English was not necessary for agribusiness, and the presence of numerous non-English-speaking Basque immigrants encouraged Basques to seek each other's business and social company. Their physical isolation in the vast underdeveloped western territories made it easier to maintain language and customs because there was little contact with a uniform host-country culture.

The maintenance of Basque language and ethnicity was as prevalent in the 1800s New World as it was in the previous centuries. Early Basque emigrants pushed from their homelands by war, lack of economic opportunity, and political repression could not resist the magnetism of welcoming boisterous economies, political favoritism, and extended ethnic families. Urban life in Bilbao and Buenos Aires was comparable, and although the climate and terrain differed, rural daily life and agriculture in Argentina, Uruguay, and the American West at that time were analogous to that in Euskal Herria.

PRIMOGENITURE INHERITANCE IN RURAL EUSKAL HERRIA AND THE REVIVAL OF CARLISM

According to anthropologist Julio Caro Baroja, the single most important element in stimulating emigration out of Euskal Herria was the rules of inheritance followed in rural Basque society (Caro Baroja 1971; Bilbao Azkarreta 1992). Population density as well as high fertility and live-birth rates, along with the scarcity of available agricultural land and low agricultural output, resulted in limited expansion potential. The lack of industrial and urban growth until the late 1800s also limited possible options for employment and migration within Euskal Herria. Each farmstead could support only a single family in agriculture. People who had rental arrangements were less committed to the land and were more likely to emigrate because of their current instability. Those who owned their property and animals kept their holdings in the same family, and Basque common law discouraged the fragmentation or division of land through sales or inheritance. Consequently, most Basque farmsteads remained unchanged for many centuries, with each generation having a single heir.

The *fueros* guaranteed the practice of selecting one of the former owner's offspring as the new owner, and other siblings could be disinherited, although in practice they were usually provided with dowries. This meant that in every family there were most likely three or four siblings who were candidates for emigration. Even today, in certain villages the traditional rules of male primogeniture are followed. In other areas, a female heir is selected, while in parts of Nafarroa the heir or heiress is chosen according to individual merit without reference to gender or birth order (Lafourcade 1999, 167–74). Until recently, the remaining siblings had to depend upon the new owner for employment, accommodation, and care, but there usually was not enough work to finance the entire extended family. Unmarried siblings had the right to stay on the family farmstead as long as they stayed single; some married other heads of household, and others turned to religious professions or to military service. For thousands, a more viable alternative to alleviate hardship was emigration.

By this time, the typical emigrant was a single male between fifteen and twenty-five years old, sent for by relatives in the New World who needed agricultural laborers or going in search of relatives hoping they needed laborers. It was a prime age for escaping mandatory military service. At the end of the nineteenth century, few women emigrated with their husbands, and very rarely single women were sent to live and work with their kin in the Americas. More commonly, a husband traveled alone to find work and settle in the new community. After several years of saving money, he would either send for his wife and any children, or would return to the homeland with his savings. Emigrant bachelors utilized Basque social networks to find mates; Basque endogamy rates were high in Argentina (Moya 1998, 330), Uruguay (Azcona Pastór 1992), and the United States. One survey showed that in the United States, of 119 Basques who emigrated to Idaho between 1889 and 1939, 114 married other Basques (Edlefsen 1948, 65). Some Basque women married their fiancés in absentia in wedding ceremonies where a brother, uncle, or cousin stood in for the groom.

This way, the woman was already technically married and more acceptable for single travel when she left for America to join her husband.[3]

The Industrial Revolution of the nineteenth century disrupted traditional agricultural economic activities and displaced workers from both rural and urban areas. The cheaper manufacture of products left artisans searching for markets, which waited open-armed in the Americas. Industrialization may have provided new jobs for existing urban Basques, but it simultaneously displaced many workers as floods of migrants from the south of Spain made their way to the more industrialized Basque Country seeking employment. Basques had to compete with this cheaper labor in their home territory.

DIASPORA NATIONALISM, HOMELAND HARDSHIP, AND OPPORTUNITIES IN THE UNITED STATES

As previously documented in chapter 2, the Partido Nacionalista Vasco maintained branches disseminating information in nearly every important city and town in Bizkaia and Gipuzkoa, and in the capital cities of Araba and Nafarroa. Though nationalism itself was not a significant reason for emigration, people who did emigrate left the Basque Country with political ideas importantly different from their precursors, and they critically impacted the Basque immigrant communities that they joined.

Basque immigrants in each host society had organized themselves for economic, religious, social, and cultural reasons throughout the seventeenth, eighteenth, and nineteenth centuries. One of the first known emigrant political organizations was created by Buenos Aires Basques. Outraged by the abolition of the *fueros* after the Second Carlist War, they established the first Basque immigrant association in Argentina, the Laurac Bat (later changed to Laurak Bat—Four Are One—meaning the united four Basque provinces in Spain) in 1877. Its purpose was to unite Basques in the area, provide aid to new immigrants, and establish improved contacts with the Basque Country. The Laurac Bat organized political protests against the Spanish government's abolition of Basque ancestral rights in the homeland, keeping in mind the members' anticipated return to Euskal Herria with amassed fortunes (Velasco interview, Buenos Aires, 1997). The organization created a library, an orchestra and choir, a dancing troupe, and arranged numerous cultural and political events. It also provided assistance to needy Basques in Argentina and, because many Basques did not strike it rich in the Americas, Laurac Bat helped fund repatriation to the homeland. Mutual-aid societies were common in Basque diaspora communities in Argentina, Uruguay, Peru, and the United States. Established in 1908, the Sociedad de Socorros Mútuos in Boise, Idaho, paid medical expenses, funeral expenses, and repatriation for needy Basques and their families (Bastida interview 1999).

Concurrently, additional institutions for ethnic cultural maintenance continued to sprout in Argentina. In 1882, a Basque sporting club for handball, Plaza Euskara, was inaugurated. The Basque magazine *La Baskonia* began publication in 1893, educating its readers about current political news and cultural issues in the Basque Country as well as Basque immigrant activities and events, until the outbreak of the Spanish Civil War in 1936. The Basques of Bahía Blanca, Argentina, formed the Society of Mutual Aid for Basques in 1899. In 1901, the Asociación Cultural y de Beneficiéncia Euskal Echea (Cultural and Charitable Association, Home of the Basques) was created in La Vallol, near Buenos Aires, as an asylum for indigent elderly persons of Basque descent, combined with a boarding school for Basque orphans.

According to articles published in *La Baskonia* and Pierre Lhande, who conducted immigration research in this time period, there were approximately 250,000 Basque immigrants in Argentina by 1908 (Soraluze 1990, 32). Figures for Uruguay estimate a total Basque emigrant count by 1900 at 18,037 (Azcona Pastór et al. 1996, 66). These figures include only emigrants and not descendants of Basques; interestingly, for many of them this was their second or third move of residence outside of the Basque Country. It was not uncommon for Basques in Uruguay to have tried Buenos Aires, Caracas, or Rio de Janeiro first. The first Uruguayan Basque center was formed as the Laurak-bat in Montevideo in 1876. The shock and displacement of international migration were buffered by the numerous fellow Basques in these regions and by the available political, economic, and cultural involvement. Transnational ties were firmly in place among Basques in each host society and between Basques and their homeland.

Beginning with the first political exiles leaving France and Spain in the 1820s, the development of a relatively small political diaspora-Basque consciousness is also exemplified through various cultural expressions of songwriting and literary publications. From Argentina's *La Baskonia* and *Irrintzi* to California's two Basque-language newspapers, *Escualdun Gazeta* and *California'ko Eskual Herria*, by the early 1900s there were several Basque periodicals consistently published in the Americas that promoted the *fueros* and ethnonationalist ideas. Several shared readerships and distribution through international Basque networks. Though mostly disseminated to, and read by, an educated elite, the imagining of an interconnected Basque diaspora had taken form and would serve a significant role in aiding the forthcoming Basque government-in-exile.

Francoism, Political Exiles, and New Destinations

Displacement from rural society, changing urban society, unemployment, unrest, labor strikes, arrests and imprisonments related to a lack of civil rights, all preceded the cataclysm of the Spanish Civil War (1936–39). None of the previous battles with the central government over the *fueros* could prepare the southern Basque Country for the repercussions it would endure in the aftermath of fighting to preserve a republican form of government, nor had the North ever received such a profuse influx of exiles requiring immediate aid. After the Republican forces were defeated, Franco's victory guaranteed a central policy of Spanish nation-building and Basque nation-destroying. As described earlier, the horrendous indignities suffered—the dismantling of Basque institutions, the outlawing of manifestations of Basque culture, the dictatorial repression and lack of human and civil rights, the multitudes of death warrants—shoved Basques out of their homeland in pursuit of safe havens. Urban and rural dwellers, widowed mothers and children, orphaned teenagers, and Republican soldiers—thousands who had the connections and the means to escape the political and military crush—did so. Most evacuated initially to Iparralde, and there they chose their final destinations usually based upon family ties to regions in the New World or information they had obtained from family and village networks.

DIASPORA AID TO THE HOMELAND

In the diaspora communities, it was almost impossible for Basques to dam the pro-Spanish media flood of misinformation defining Basques as Communists and anti-Catholic.[4] The United States and Australian Catholic clergy praised Franco from the pulpit as the savior of religion in traditionally Catholic Spain, and Argentine, Uruguayan, and Peruvian Basque Catholics heard a similar sermon. In Belgium, however, Catholic relief organizations helped organize the fostering of thousands of children sent away from the Bilbao area just before the city fell to Falangist forces. Diaspora Basques were worried about the "red scare" and the blackballing of individuals suspected of being Communist sympathizers, yet knowing the truth they could not help but defend their families in the four provinces.

Little aid for the military cause came from Basque communities in the U.S. West, although they did provide humanitarian war relief. For example, in Boise, Idaho, the proceeds from an annual Sheepherders' Christmas Ball were used to purchase one thousand blankets for Basque women prisoners in Spain (Douglass and Bilbao 1975, 361). As the United States was drawn into World War II, Franco's identification with Hitler and Mussolini prompted U.S. government support for the exiled Basque government. After the war, the Basque government-in-exile maintained a delegation to the United Nations in New York City, and its presence influenced the local Basque center, Centro Vasco of New York, its "pro-Euzkadi Committee," and the publication of *Basques: Bulletin of the Basque Delegation in the U.S.A.* (Bilbao Azkarreta 1992, 237).

Interviews of New York–area Basques in 2003 still demonstrate a more politically aware membership than those of Basque communities in the western United States. For example, many New York Basque interviewees understood the details of partisan differences in the Basque parliamentary elections of 2001 and the significance of the PNV win.

The same cannot be said for the American West. In 1937, the Basque government delegate to the United States, Ramón de la Sota, visited Boise in order to inform the Basque community and attempt to raise money for the Basque war effort. Though many Basques attended events to hear news from the Basque Country, de la Sota was unable to create interest in financial support. In a 1938 letter to the Basque government-in-exile president, José Antonio de Aguirre, the Basque government delegate to the United States, Antonio de Irala, wrote of the Basques of Idaho, "there is a lack of national consciousness ... and their mentality in regards to patriotism is American" (my translation from San Sebastián 1991, 236). In 1940, Juan M. Bilbao was sent to Idaho and Nevada as emissary of the Basque delegation, but he found no significant interest in political mobilization, and his Boise tenure was short-lived.

Right-wing politics in Latin American states made speaking out against the Franco regime extremely dangerous. The Basque communities in Argentina, Uruguay, Chile, Venezuela, Cuba, and Mexico, however, did raise private funds to be sent to the Basque government-in-exile, and after the Spanish Civil War they enthusiastically received delegations from the Basque government-in-exile and thousands of political exiles. By the final collapse of the Spanish Republic in 1939, there were an estimated 150,000 exiled Basques, not counting several thousand children, orphans or youngsters sent away by their families for safety.[5] Those political exiles significantly influenced the diaspora communities' definitions and involvement in Basque identity maintenance by transporting the contemporary homeland nationalism of the day.

During the Spanish Civil War, Argentine-Basque women formed Argentine chapters of the PNV women's nationalist organization, Emakume Abertzale Batza (United Patriotic Women), sent financial and material aid to the Basque Country, and received thousands of Basque political refugees in Argentina. Though the world economic depression had strengthened xenophobic and anti-immigrant legislation in Argentina, one particular wave of approximately 1,400 Basques arrived in 1939 with the formation of the Comité Pro Inmigración (Committee for Basque Immigration), which obtained two decrees from Argentine President Ortíz facilitating the entry of Basque refugees into the country (Anasagasti 1988, 44). The Basque government-in-exile sent delegations to Uruguay, Argentina, Venezuela, Mexico, and the United States to help organize relief and promote the Basque cause. However, the political and economic climates changed rapidly. As the post–World War II Argentine economy declined, so did the number of people choosing Argentina as a destination. Basque immigration in the Río de la Plata region was reduced to a trickle; instead, there was substantial emigration to oil-rich Venezuela and to the English-speaking countries and booming economies of the United States and Australia. Belgium also served as host for political refugees and permanent immigration. Belgian socialist and Catholic relief organizations received over 5,130 Basque children evacuated during the war years (Artís-Gener 1976, 176); if the children were orphaned, many Belgian families adopted them permanently. Young adults who returned to Euskal Herria after their formative years and education in Belgium often felt like strangers in their own land; several returned to their Belgian families and have remained mainly in the Brussels and Antwerp areas for the last forty to fifty years.

Restrictive immigration policies of the 1920s and 1930s in South American countries and in the United States meant that many emigrants were unable to obtain entrance visas for their preferred destinations. Australia served as an acceptable second-best option. Australia's restrictive immigration laws translated to the "White Australia Policy" legislation of 1901 and encouraged desirable European labor for sugarcane cutting. In North Queensland, government-sponsored projects included free passage for European workers and cheap, easily available land contracts. Entry to Australia was uncomplicated if the emigrant had a personal sponsor there who would claim responsibility. One Basque woman in the Ingham area, Teresa Mendiolea, is documented to have sponsored hundreds of Basque men, advancing them travel costs, help with lodging, medical care, and employment (Mendiolea Uriguen Larrazabal interview, Townsville, Australia, 2000). As in the United States at this time, Basques in this Anglo host society were disadvantaged for socioeconomic mobility by the lack of communication and language skills, and the fact that the type of person migrating for manual cane-cutting labor was generally undereducated. These Basques relied on ethnic networks for employment, housing, medical care, and education (J. M. Goicoechea Ugarte interview, Townsville, Australia, 2000).

FRANCO'S POLITICAL REPRESSION AND THE BASQUE RESPONSE

Spanish Civil War refugees were received in Iparralde by Basque government-in-exile agencies, which were tolerated and ignored by the French government (Beltza 1977, 12). From the three northern provinces, waves of Basque refugees spread out to other European countries, especially the Soviet Union, Belgium, and England. Others tried to unite with relatives who had emigrated earlier to Latin America, and an estimated 35,000 refugees made their way to Mexico, Venezuela, and Argentina. The exiles were received by already established Basque communities and were provided with medical attention, housing, and employment. Although the overwhelming majority of Basque political exiles thought that Latin America would be a temporary refuge, more than fifty years later my interviews revealed numerous histories of exiles who could not return to the Basque Country for political or economic reasons.

Forced separation from family and homeland caused an intense hatred among exiles for all things Spanish and a repugnant abhorrence for memories of Franco. Two interviewees who as children were evacuated to London and who later married and moved to Melbourne, blame Franco for "robbing us of our loved ones, our homeland and personal possessions, our language and means of emotional communication and connection, and our unqualified spirit, soul, and identity" (Oribe interview, Melbourne, 1997; Belón Bilbao interview, Melbourne, 1997).

Many nationalist intellectuals, business elites, industrialists, merchants, writers, lawyers, and other professionals fled to Basque communities in the Americas, and as a consequence these communities prospered and became the sources of important financial support for the Basque government-in-exile. Diaspora communities in Mexico and Argentina published newspapers and information bulletins about diaspora resistance, which were then distributed in Euskal Herria. Clandestine radio broadcasts were transmitted first from Iparralde and then from outside Caracas, Venezuela, for thirteen years after the end of World War II. Local radio programs in Euskera from Boise and Buffalo, Wyoming, and in combinations of Spanish, French, and English in other Basque communities of the United States, ran for decades with homeland news and information from the Basque diaspora network. In Uruguay and Argentina, local programs did the same in Euskera and Spanish (Iguain interview, Montevideo, 1996; Vicente interview 1996).

Several Basque centers in Argentina and Uruguay tried to influence their host-country governments by protesting Franco's censorship of speech and press, often resulting in their own censorship. While official host-country media reports concerning Spain were typically pro-Franco, the diaspora communities also received information from their own and other exiles' families and friends relaying the reality of life at home. The frequent access to information through personal contacts affected Basque identity in each community. Interviews and questionnaires indicate that in Basque organizations that received political exiles from the Civil War, the contemporary ethnic identity of Basque descendants is more political, more nationalist, and more separatist than in communities that did not receive exiles. The effect of only a few political exiles in a community could outweigh the national and international media, host-society culture and attitudes, and time and distance away from the circumstances and events of the Franco regime. As mentioned previously, the primacy and consequence of diaspora transnational communication and of new immigration cannot be overstated for the Basques in these case studies, regardless of geography and host-country setting.

Escaping, for some, meant going "to the opposite end of the Earth" (Bengoa Berreciartua Arrate interview, Ayr, Australia, 1997). After World War II, Australia experienced an economic boom and a labor shortage, and it attempted to increase the country's population through more liberal immigration policies. In 1958, the Sugar Growers' Association of North Queensland sent a representative to Spain to recruit emigrants, and over the subsequent seven years, more than five thousand Spanish citizens entered Australia, approximately half of whom were Basque (Douglass 1978, 5). Cane-cutting was a seasonal occupation, and in the off-season many Basque laborers found additional work in Melbourne and Sydney in building construction; others traveled the migrant farm-labor circuit harvesting vegetables and fruit. With mechanization of the sugar harvest in the mid-1960s, most cane-cutters were put out of work and forced to look for other permanent employment in various government-funded infrastructure projects or in the private sector. Even for those who had learned English, current news and accurate information regarding homeland political developments were extremely difficult but not impossible to obtain. Basques in rural agricultural areas tended to be less involved with homeland politics, perhaps as a result of this lack of information. For example, in fifty-four interviews held in the Townsville, Ayr, and Ingham areas, not one person could recall firsthand, nor from hearing an older Basque recount, whether there had been any organized collective action from their area in response to the Spanish Civil War and the Franco regime. Basques who emigrated to North Queensland tended to be economic emigrants, whereas political refugees who fled to Australia were more likely to settle in Melbourne or Sydney, where they still exhibit stronger interest in the complex homeland politics. Basques from Melbourne and Sydney were, and are, more politically aware and involved, as evidenced in their collective mobilization and political actions in the 1970s and their knowledge and understanding of the various contemporary political factions in the homeland. Many in Sydney and Melbourne continue to hold double citizenship for Australia and Spain, in order to retain voting rights in the Basque Country.

The political and economic ideological fragmentation in the homeland nationalist movement during the 1970s confused Basques in Euskal Herria and most of those in the diaspora who were being asked to support the Basque government-in-exile, ETA, ETA, and ETA-*Berri*. "What is going on in our country?" and "Which group believes in what theories?" became the topics of exasperated discussion and the cause of many debates and problems in Basque communities around the world. Lacking information and, often worse, receiving conflicting descriptions and explanations of events, many Basques abroad stated that they began to lose interest because they could not keep straight all the arguments, factions, and movements inside what they judged should be a unified Basque nationalist movement for independence. Excluding Australia, the PNV had the advantage of a developed network and established communications with diaspora Basque centers, and the majority of Civil War exiles were familiar with PNV names, strategy, and goals. The ETA disagreements with the PNV, and subsequent splits within ETA, confounded an already extremely complex nationalist movement. The change in rhetoric of the New Left to class struggle and class identity rather than ethnic and cultural struggle and identity was not well received by Basques who had not lived in the provinces perhaps for decades. Of special note, during the 1970s most of the Basque centers in the diaspora modified their organizational statutes and practices and began describing themselves as apolitical centers, fearful of experiencing the same divisiveness descending upon their homeland. Politics slowly moved to the arena of home and private conversation, and the cultural activities of maintaining language, music, dance, gastronomy, literature, art, and sport moved to the forefront of diaspora institutional activity. The political layer of the Basque diaspora would be thin and short-lived on top of its trade and colonial substratum.

DIASPORA REACTIONS TO HOMELAND VIOLENCE

If Basques in the diaspora did not favor nationalist talk of workers' struggles, coalitions with Spanish labor unions, and abandoning demands for an independent Euskal Herria, they rejected outright the proposals of armed revolution and arbitrary violence advanced by Federico Krutwig. But because the Basque government-in-exile had been unsuccessful in manipulating any change or improvement for the southern provinces, its status and that of the PNV also waned, and diaspora Basques were more willing to listen to the original ETA goals. However, too many mutations, lack of information and communication, and general misunderstanding of the fragmentation in the nationalist movement caused many exiles to begin questioning whether there would ever be the same Basque Country to which they could return and, more upsetting for them, whether or not they would want to return.

Many in the diaspora Basque centers had been exiled now for at least forty years, enough time to have married and established families in their host countries. Some had taken adolescent children with them into exile, and those had now married with host-country residents and were producing grandchildren, making it even more distressing for immigrants to leave family for a return to an uncertain Euskal Herria. As would be expected, immediate daily pressures in the host society demanded attention, and Basques in communities abroad began to lose interest in, and understanding of, political events in the homeland. Still, ties among the Basques remained strong, with much associationism and numerous ethnic social networks that provided information—though specifics occasionally conflicted. What is significant is that the transnational ties of Basques in their separate host countries with individuals and organizations in the Basque homeland continued.

As is often the case, it took sensational political events with international media attention to demonstrate to the Basques and all others in the outside world that Franco's Spain was still not democratic and that civil and human rights in the Basque provinces were almost nonexistent. After the 1968 assassination of Spanish police commissioner Melitón Manzanas and the ensuing martial-law crackdown, Basques in Melbourne organized a dockworkers' strike in Canberra to protest at the seat of the Australian national government. Radio interviews included Basque community leaders giving their perception of the Franco dictatorship and the lack of civil rights in the Basque Country. In Sydney and in North Queensland, Basque communities sent hundreds of letters to the National Parliament demanding that the Australian ambassador to Madrid object to the treatment of the Basque suspects (Oribe interview, Melbourne, 1997; Garagarza Pérez interview, Melbourne, 1997). In Montevideo, Uruguay, there were street demonstrations, letter-writing campaigns to parliamentarians, and public denouncements of Franco by the Basque community and the hundred-year-old Basque center, Euskal Erria. Dozens of Basque centers in Argentina demanded that their government react to the Spanish government actions, and immediate fund-raising activity for the families of those imprisoned in Burgos resurrected latent nationalist sentiments. Surprisingly, in the typically apolitical U.S. Basque communities, private individuals, not centers, organized dinners, dances, and donation drives to send money for the Basque cause (M. C. Egurrola Totoricagüena interview, Boise, 1999; San Sebastián 1991). More than two hundred people met at the Boise Basque Center to compose a telegram to Franco requesting clemency for the Basques sentenced to death by the military tribunal (Bieter and Bieter 2000, 131). The governors of Idaho, Nevada, and Oregon sent official letters of protest to Madrid. Belgian student groups in Brussels demonstrated against their government's support or neutrality regarding Franco. However, conflicting perceptions from interviewees make it unclear whether or not these protests were led by Basques or Basque ethnic organizations. After the sixteen guilty sentences were announced, six being orders for execution, even the Vatican entered the arena, asking the Spanish government to exercise clemency.

Institutional leaders in Argentina, Uruguay, Australia, and the United States remember that Basque separatist activity and the justification of violence became new topics of conversation in their communities after the Burgos Trials (Velasco interview, Buenos Aires, 1997; Iguain interview, Buenos Aires, 1996; J. A. Ugalde Arranguena interview, Melbourne, 1997; Sarria interview, Boise,

1999). Dictatorial regimes in Argentina and Uruguay supplied daily reminders to Basques in those countries of how life in the homeland continued. Worldwide attention to the plight of the Basques as an oppressed people lent credence and justification for ETA actions. However, soon media coverage focused on ETA activities themselves, not the rationale or objectives behind them, leading host-country populations to equate Basques with violence and terrorism—a burden that diaspora Basques everywhere have had to carry.

Diaspora Basques repeatedly stated that they had grown weary of defending themselves against media reports that portray only ETA acts of violence against property and persons. They felt obligated to defend their homeland and continue to do so even though they may abhor the violence to innocent victims and to the society in general. They believe there was no equal media coverage of the state violence and repression suffered by Basques during the Franco regime or under the subsequent Socialist governments of Felipe González or the Partido Popular government of José María Aznar. In Argentina and Uruguay, where Basques have benefitted from a positive social status, some immigrants and their descendants chose to distance themselves from political affairs and continued to associate with the organized Basque community only for cultural events. In the United States and Peru, many Basque communities ceased celebrating Aberri Eguna as a day of Basque nationalism or else dropped the observation of this holiday altogether. As mentioned above, in diaspora organizations where transnational communications were maintained and where there were emigrants with first-person accounts of events in the homeland, solidarity for Basque separatism continued even if the means used to try to achieve it were doubted.

Regardless of the PNV conservative nationalism prevalent in the diaspora, anonymous responses in written questionnaires to the enquiry regarding opinions about the most desirable future of the Basque provinces, approximately half of the respondents chose a total separation from Spain and France declaring an independent state for the seven provinces. Basque nationalism as manifested in a desire for territorial independence remains strong even among the third-, fourth-, and fifth-generation descendants. Interviewees compared the Basque situation to the struggle of the Tupamaros in Uruguay, questions of "the Disappeared" in Argentina, the civil-rights movements of African Americans and especially Native Americans in the United States, the multiculturalism of Belgium, and the current politics of Aboriginal peoples in Australia. Each has affected Basque communities in those states, as Basque and host-state populations have been likely to equate Basque nationalist demands with those of minorities suffering discrimination and oppression in their own countries. During the Franco regime, the Basque communities in those host countries were perhaps more sympathetic to Basque nationalism.

Franco's death in November 1975 propelled many exiles to plan their return home with full expectation of the creation of a democracy and autonomy or independence for the Basque Country.[6] However, little changed in the first years of Franco's absence. Violence inspired defensive violence on both sides, and diaspora Basques had to react to these homeland activities and separate themselves from them in their own host societies.

Political Transitions Influence an End to Emigration

The transition to a democratic Spain, consisting of seventeen autonomous regions with differing degrees of autonomy, has taken place with numerous successes as well as with some difficulties. Much of the political oppression of Basque culture and politics publicly ceased, creating at least an expectation of democracy and political opportunity in Euskadi and separately in the Foral Community of Nafarroa. The entrance of Spain into the European Community and the conversion of the Basque industrial society to a postindustrial information-based society with a large service sector has created thousands of additional jobs. The open doors of European Union labor markets have facilitated Basques seeking employment and emigration to European countries rather than crossing the oceans to different continents where visas and work permits are required.

It is clear from interview information and questionnaire data that Basque emigration prompted by economic and political oppression has ended. Many scholars believe that without new immigration, diaspora communities will find it more difficult to maintain a distinct ethnic identity (Pérez-Agote 1999; Alday 1999; Douglass 1999; J. Echeverria 1999). This, however, assumes the traditional view of emigration as a one-way, one-time phenomenon; that emigration must be a physical move; that culture is stagnant; and that diaspora ethnicity necessarily must be synonymous with homeland ethnicity. This is not the case with the Basque diaspora, as return migration is now becoming more and more common as descendants of Basque emigrants return to Euskal Herria for study-abroad programs or to return to their roots. These long-term visits have resulted in numerous marriages between Old World and New World Basques. Travel is much safer and cheaper than ever before, making frequent visits practicable. New technology, such as the Internet (through which most Basque organizations in the diaspora are interconnected), facilitates networks between Basques in Euskal Herria and Basques in other communities in the world. The Basque diaspora is going through a critical phase in its existence. Its participation in the new frameworks of societal reality and global change are not those of colonial settlements, nor of communities needing mass migration to sustain them. The new media and the changing political realities of Europe and the homeland open new possibilities for future relations between and among Basques and for their ethnic identity maintenance. The necessity of chain migration and the energy infused into a community by new immigrants from Euskal Herria may be replaced by the "virtual migration" of Internet communications and the exchange of ideas and information. Diaspora Basques may no longer need new immigrants nor physical travel to the homeland. Basque ethnic identity, language, information, and culture might be maintained through electronic communications without ever leaving home—a "downloading" of identity.

Documented examples and descriptions concerning the formation of the Basque diaspora argue that Basque collective ethnic identity is not a recent reaction to modernization or to globalization. Basque ethnicity maintenance is visible in the historical record since the 1400s in the New World exploration and colonization processes, and it continues to this day with the creation of new institutions. This supports the argument that recent Basque ethnic identity salience is related to globalization, but not necessarily in a causal relationship or as a reaction to it. The "resurgence" is more specifically defined as a continuing phenomenon of Basque immigrants and their descendants consistently maintaining avenues for ethnic connection and identity manifestation in their host societies. Rather than nationalism and ethnic identity maintenance being a novel phenomenon, it may be that what is recent is academic attention to it.

It is also evident that the most significant push factors over time have included economic hardship and, in the twentieth century, political oppression. The magnetism of growing economies and democracies first in Argentina and Uruguay, then in the United States, Australia, and Belgium, pulled Basques to those host societies in search of opportunity and political freedom. Chapters 4, 5, and 6 will demonstrate that despite geographical and generational differences, the core elements of Basque ethnic identity are defined in a constant manner by self-defining Basques throughout the diaspora, and that their ethnic institutions have developed along similar patterns regardless of century and country. Mutual-aid funds for health care and aid to elderly Basques, funds for return trips to Euskal Herria, Basque cultural centers with choirs, dance groups, *mus* and *pelota* tournaments, cuisine development, schools and religious orders, and language-preservation programs are manifested in each host society regardless of the dates of initial Basque immigration.

Because the latest substantial waves of migration occurred when Basque homeland nationalism focused on the *ethnic* aspects of Basque identity proposed by Sabino Arana y Goiri (ancestry, language, religion), this tends to be the prevailing diaspora ideology. Trickling chain migration has slightly influenced this definition of "Basqueness" with a more modern civic definition that is only very recent in Euskal Herria. Diaspora definitions therefore remain exclusive and lag behind civic changes in the homeland.

It is the Civil War generation of emigrants and their offspring—people who left the homeland in the 1930s, 1940s, and early 1950s—who have most influenced contemporary Basque communities and their institutions in these six diaspora case studies. This group has guided the cultural and political paths taken by Basque centers throughout the diaspora and has added political links to previously colonial and trade transnationalism. Its influence over the later generation is evident in interview responses that dwell on Franco and political repression, desires for a united seven-province Basque state, and the focus on the Basque language and on nationalist definitions of *who* and *what* is Basque. Peru's official refusal to accept Basque political exiles impacted the size of Lima's Basque community but not its diaspora development. In a small Basque community, it only takes a few to impact the others.

Before the 1970s, expensive, unreliable, and slow communications meant that separate diaspora communities did not regularly contact each other between the different countries, or sometimes even within a country. Despite the efforts of the government-in-exile and diaspora political activists, the diaspora political activity tended not to be coordinated across countries, or across one host country. Political activity was most likely instigated by individuals and not by the Basque center institutions, and was town- or city-specific. As migration tended to be from a homeland micro-unit to a host country micro-unit, aid also tended to be from diaspora regions to their corresponding immigrants' region in the homeland.

Interviews demonstrated that the Burgos Trials served to ignite a more intense political consciousness diaspora-wide, but only temporarily. The political exiles of the Spanish Civil War have remained engaged in the politics of the four Spanish provinces, but recent generations and communities that did not receive a wave of political immigration are further removed from current events in the Basque Country. At the Laurak Bat in Buenos Aires, the Euskadi parliamentary election results of May 2001 were enthusiastically followed live via EITB Basque Television cable. However, at the Basque Museum and Cultural Center in Boise, pamphlets announcing Internet websites for real-time results lined the trash cans after that night's Mother's Day dinner.

(*top*) The typical dress at the end of the 1800s is shown by these two families who share their farmhouse. Photograph by Eulalia Abaitua; Euskal Museoa, Bilbao, Museo Vasco

(*bottom*) Workers unload coal at the Sendeja Street dock, Bilbao, ca. 1893. Photograph by Pedro Telesforo de Erraquin; Euskal Museoa, Bilbao, Museo Vasco

A dining hall for recent immigrants to Montevideo, Uruguay, ca. late 1800s.

Uruguayan Basques make their way to the interior of the country to reach their established employment, ca. late 1800s.

The Totorica Sheep Company in Grandview, Idaho 1935. One of the longest-operating–Basque family sheep businesses in history of the American west, 1895–1975. *Left to right:* Unknown, Segundo Totoricagüena, Urbano Totoricagüena, father José Totoricagüena, Teodoro Totoricagüena, Frank Baraysarra, not shown is brother Leandro Totoricagüena. Totoricagüena Family Collection.

Hundreds of Basques made the trip to Ingham, North Queensland, Australia, to make their living by hand-cutting sugar cane, 1932. Center for Basque Studies, University of Nevada, Reno

Argentine National Basque Week celebrations include a parade of Basque dancers and musicians through each year's host city, Mar del Plata, 1986.

The "Gure Txoko Basque Club Inc." Basques in Sydney, Australia, enjoy an annual Aberri Eguna picnic with a Catholic Mass and barbecue lunch, 1997.

(*top left*) Melbourne, Australia, Basque leaders of the "Basque Society–Gure Txoko," Miren Garagarza Pérez (*right*) and Jon Ander Bilbao, 1997.
(*top right*) Parents maintain and teach Basque traditions for future generations, Mar del Plata, 1986.
(*bottom*) The second home of the Laurak Bat Basque society, which was established in 1877 in Buenos Aires, Argentina.

The Laurak Bat Mixed Choir, Buenos Aires, Argentina, 1915.

The Emakume Abertzale Batza of Argentina celebrating the official arrival of the delegation of the Basque Government to Buenos Aires, 1939.

Oinkari Basque Dancers in Boise, Idaho, celebrate their annual festival of St. Ignatius in July 2001.

The Biotzetik Basque Choir performs at the annual dinner and songfest fund-raiser in Boise, Idaho, 2000.

Txantxangorriak musical group of Boise, Idaho, performs for the annual St. Ignatius Festival, 2001.

Boise'ko Ikastola teacher Nere Inda utilizes all Basque to instruct Boise students and visiting Basque Government officials, 2002.

Mus players at the Lima, Peru, Euskal Etxea, enjoy several games before their weekly dinner, 1996.

Basque-language classes at the Euskal Erria Basque center in Montevideo, Uruguay, 1986.

Father Jean Pierre Cachenaut, sent by the Bishop of Baiona to minister to Basques in the United States, celebrates masses in Euskara with the Basque communities of the American West, 1985.

Emakume Abertzale Batza of Rosario, Argentina, prepare Basque-style cuisine for the Argentine National Basque Week festival, 1996.

Basque dancers of Argentina demonstrate their skills in the dance of San Miguel during the annual Argentine National Basque Week, Rosario, Argentina, 1996.

Txistulariak from Argentina perform for the Argentine National Basque Week festival, 1996.

The gift shop of the Basque Museum and Cultural Center in Boise, Idaho, sells typical items symbolic of traditional Basque culture.

Pelotariak at the Gure Txoko fronton in Sydney, Australia. *Left to right:* Julianón, Oriñuela, Moro, Bilbao, Aguirrezabal.

Basques from Sydney, Australia, socialize together for various activities such as weekend "mushrooming."

Delegates to the 1999 Second World Congress of Basque Collectivities representing Basques from twenty-one countries, Vitoria-Gasteiz.

Delegates to the 1999 Second World Congress of Basque Collectivities discuss policies for the Four-Year Plan document for diaspora-homeland relations.

Basque youth from around the globe participate in the Gaztemundu 2001 program funded by the Eusko Jaurlaritza Basque Government.

Representatives of the city council of Gernika-Lumo meet with Idaho Secretary of State Pete Cenarrusa (center) in Boise, Idaho, as an exchange in their sister-city relations in 2000.

The Gaztemundu 2000 participants from Lima, Peru, meet with Lehendakari Ibarretxe.

The delegation of the Basque Autonomous Community to the European Union celebrated its opening in Brussels, Belgium, 1996.

Chapter Four

Ethnonationalism and Political Attitudes in the Diaspora

Basque communities in the diaspora have maintained collective memories that are intrinsic to their ethnic identity. Essential to that ensemble are the oppression and self-defense they perceive the Basque people to have experienced through the centuries, and the historical memory of the *fueros* and of self-government that is central to the reproduction of a nationalist project. Today, their established diaspora institutions are repeatedly described as nonpolitical, and although it is true that there have been few recent attempts at influencing their respective host societies' domestic politics, their members' past activities and interventions with host- and home-country politics were at times quite influential. In Argentina and Uruguay, a relative critical mass of Basques and the recognition of their contributions to each society have made it easier to gain political access and influence. In the United States and Australia, Basques are still a relatively unknown ethnic group and have only rarely collectively attempted to influence policy at the national level or in communities where they are geographically concentrated. Basques in Belgium and Peru are relatively insignificant in number and lack political clout. Since the 1980s, the impetus of the diaspora institutions has been cultural, and the political aspects of Basque diaspora nationalism usually have been consigned to individual choice, though this was not always the case.

Nationalism in the Basque diaspora exists separately from nationalism in the homeland. Neither a copy of nor opposition to homeland nationalism, diaspora nationalism is overwhelmingly *ethno*national, with a focus on the cultural and historical aspects of identity. Activists are eager to promote Basque ethnicity and the cultural strands of a shared history, language, and ancestry, and they encourage the transnational ties for such objectives, but demands for Basque statehood or territorial control have been, and are, rarely expressed publicly. The *ethno*national project is devoid of a specific state to control. There are minorities in each Basque community that harbor territorial and political goals of separatism and independent statehood for the seven provinces, but although homeland definitions of nationalism and "Basqueness" have progressed to more civic and inclusive nationalism, diaspora definitions have lagged behind. Exactly what does being Basque mean to these respondents?

Basque Diaspora Nationalism as Historically Both Political and Ethnic

In a 1995 survey conducted by the Basque Autonomous Government that included all seven provinces of Euskal Herria, 64 percent of the respondents defined themselves as "Basque," 24 percent said they were not, and the rest defined themselves as a mixture of Basque and French, or Basque and Spanish, or something else. Participants responding to a question asking, "What are the most important conditions necessary for a person to be considered a Basque?"[1] marked as "most important" "Born in the Basque Country" (59 percent); "Live and work in the Basque Country (51 percent); "Speak the Basque language" (27 percent); "Comprehend and defend Basque culture" (15 percent); "Have Basque surnames" (10 percent); and "Be a Basque nationalist (*abertzale*)" (7 percent).

Being "born in the Basque Country" and to "live and work in the Basque Country" received the highest selection rates. This shows a more civic definition of Basque identity, including more people in the Basque category, and the possibility of "becoming Basque." Euskera has lost its importance for a majority of the population, as have ancestry and the political aspect of promoting Basque goals. This demonstrates a change from the traditional Sabino Arana definition of "Basqueness" as being a Basque nationalist (*abertzale*), having Basque ancestry or surnames, and speaking Basque. Not included in this homeland survey was the respondent's attitude toward Catholicism and Basqueness, which was a significant criterion for early nationalists and remains salient in diaspora opinions.

Though homeland definitions of Basqueness and Basque nationalism have mutated, change in the diaspora has been almost imperceptible. When diaspora Basques have represented themselves politically rather than culturally, outcomes have varied widely. Argentina's 1940 Committee for Basque Immigration successfully lobbied the Argentine president, Dr. Roberto Ortíz Lizardi (of Basque ancestry), to declare a special circumstance with privileges for thousands of Basque political refugees after the Spanish Civil War. Uruguayan democratic leaders slighted Franco's Spain and openly celebrated the arrival of José Antonio de Aguirre y Lecube, president of the Basque government-in-exile, to the Euskal Erria Basque Center. Yet fifty years later in Montevideo, seven Basques were detained and judged for extradition to Spain as suspected ETA sympathizers and activists—the only such action in this century by the Uruguayan government against refugees pleading for political asylum. Uruguay's economic and political decline since the 1960s has necessitated its alignment with foreign powers, such as Spain, for aid, and the question of granting political asylum now holds dire financial consequences. Uruguayans' experience with political violence from a leftist rebel group, the Tupamaros, and the democratization of Spain most likely influenced this decision. Contrasting foreign policy decisions implemented by different leaders remind diaspora communities that their actions have the potential to cause conflict between themselves and their host-society government and between their host-society and homeland governments—hence the current concentration on cultural manifestations of identity and the argument that, despite generational, geographical, and gender differences in the diaspora, these Basque populations and institutions have developed in a similar manner, emphasizing cultural identity over political nationalism.

NONPOLITICAL AND NONPARTISAN? NOT EXACTLY

Personal interviews with past and present elected officials of the boards of directors of Basque centers, choral and dance-troupe instructors, religious leaders, artists, writers, academics, business and political leaders, recognized athletes—in general, Basques who have prestige and influence over other Basques—described identity maintenance and diaspora Basque-center agendas that were more cultural than political. Many interviewees stated that the centers are purposefully "apolitical" in order not to divide the members. "We are so few that we cannot afford to fight over politics" I heard often in each host country. Many of Basque centers' statutes state that the center and its subdivided sections (such as language classes, choir, musicians, athletes, and similar groups) are "apolitical" and will not promote or involve themselves in either the political process of the host country or of the homeland. Though many centers have allowed political candidates and parties to make presentations to their memberships, and in the U.S. have allowed candidates to attend center functions such as picnics and dances to distribute campaign paraphernalia, there have been no examples of center promotion or support for particular parties or candidates. Yet despite the rational strategy of the Basque institutional elite to maintain a strict cultural focus in their Basque community centers, there are still numerous examples of political nationalism.

One component of this began with the early-twentieth-century emigration of ardent nationalists. A group of twenty Basque nationalists moved to Argentina in 1900 and published their own diaspora journal, *Irrintzi* (Basque war cry), beginning in 1903, postulating the basic tenets of Basque nationalism and writings by Sabino Arana y Goiri. The following decades witnessed the development of several pronationalist associations. The first Argentine-Basque delegation to the national council of the Basque Nationalist Party, the Nationalist Communion of the Republic of Argentina, was sent to Euskal Herria in 1919. The Basque nationalist day, Aberri Eguna, was celebrated annually in Argentina and Uruguay at Easter, coinciding with the symbolism of the Resurrection. Curiously, it is argued that Basque nationalism was more widespread and welcomed by Basques in Argentina and Uruguay than among those in the homeland at the time (Ezkerro interview, Buenos Aires, 1996).

Political divisions among the members of the Laurak Bat resulted over the homeland politics of Arana and the nationalists. Pro- and antinationalist factions vied for control over the Laurak Bat, and in 1895 several Basques split to create the Centro Navarro (Navarrese Center) and others broke away to inaugurate the Centro Vasco Francés (French Basque Center). There are also some instances of Basque nationalism in Argentina before Arana (Álvarez Gila 1996, 176), and it is important to note that the contemporary Basque nationalism found in Basque centers today often still reflects the Arana ideology. The Aranist nationalist ideology, popular throughout the Buenos Aires, Rosario, and Montevideo urban areas, eventually spread to rural Basque communities. The Rosario Basque Center, founded in 1912, was named Zazpirak Bat (Seven Are One), referring to the true nationalist utopia of unification of the seven provinces.

Immigrants not interested in the ideologies of Sabino Arana or those of the Basque Nationalist Party fought for control of the established Basque centers, especially the Laurak Bat. However, the *abertzales* won elections more often than the *españolistas* (a derogatory term for persons of Basque descent who were not nationalists), and the centers continued their anti-Madrid politics. Linking themselves closely to Irish immigrants, Basques cheered Irish nationalism and, as in Euskal Herria, paralleled their demands with those of Ireland. The first public act of the Rosario Basque Nationalist Committee in 1911 was to demonstrate solidarity with the Irish community and its desired self-government in the delayed Home Rule Act. Basque nationalists continued to publish and disseminate political propaganda in Buenos Aires and Rosario and slowly spread this material to the interior. As recent immigrants joined the centers, they outnumbered the older *españolistas* and represented the growing Aranist ideology of nationalists in Euskal Herria. The ensuing ruptures in the established centers divided Basque culturalists, who envisioned a social gathering-place to foment sport, music, and friendship, from Basque political nationalists, who gained control with the votes of the ever-increasing emigrants escaping political repression. The Spanish Civil War and Franco's dictatorship provided the watershed of political exiles and a common enemy around whom the Basques unified their opposition, fervently pushing diaspora organizations to pronationalist stances.

At the turn of the century, there was an established diaspora nationalist press and information circulation network. In Argentina, the Basque periodicals *Revista Laurac Bat* (1878), *La Basconia* (1893), and *Irrintzi* (1904) were published in Buenos Aires, as were books with Basque nationalist themes, such as *Ami Vasco, Inocéncia de un Patriota, Aitor, Egi-Zale,* and *Patria.* In the United States, *Euzkotarra* originated from New Orleans (1907). By the time of the Spanish Civil War, there were *Eusko Deia, Galeuzka, Euskaltzaleak,* and *Tierra Vasca* in Argentina, *Euskal Ordua* in Montevideo, and other periodicals in Chile, Venezuela, and Mexico. These nationalist writings circulated throughout the Basque population in Uruguay, Argentina, Venezuela, Mexico, and the United States, and then clandestinely into Euskal Herria. Their Aranist and later anti-Franco direction "played an important psychological and emotional role in maintaining networks" and "kept hope for an end to the dictatorial repression" (Iguain interview, Buenos Aires, 1996). They also enlightened and updated readers regarding the Basque Country's political and socioeconomic reality.

In Uruguay, the distribution of *Ekin* and other informative bulletins sustained the political interest of those in Montevideo. Although the statutes of the Euskal Erria Basque Center state that the center was "apolitical," there were PNV activities as well as a party delegate specifically for Uruguay from the PNV-dominated Basque government-in-exile. Basques in Argentina, Uruguay, the United States, and Belgium all received the president of the Basque government-in-exile in some official and institutional capacity, and the Basque centers were often utilized as nuclei for mobilizing anti-Franco support and lobbying their respective host-country governments for foreign policies sympathetic to the Basque cause. The Basque president was not welcomed and did not enter Peru, and there were insufficient numbers of Basques in Australia to justify a visit or a Basque delegation.

Argentina opened its borders to thousands of Basque political refugees because of the influence of the Comité Pro Inmigración, which designated Buenos Aires and the Laurak Bat Center as the port of entry and host respectively (Anasagasti 1988). The Emakume Abertzale Batza women commanded an impressive effort to organize all the essential aspects of "preparing the new exiles with accommodation, employment information, Catholic masses in Basque, details of daily family life, and fundamental emotional and social support" through constant communication and contact with new arrivals at the Laurak Bat Center and the Zazpirak Bat Center in Rosario. Many interviewed exiles pointed to the efforts and dedication of the Basque women in Argentina as their "saving grace." Emigrants "felt accepted and welcomed" in the atmosphere of recognized nationalist political associations, and "a part of an international network of Basques helping Basques" (Irujo de Olaizola interview, Buenos Aires, 1997).

The Basque government-in-exile dispatched delegates around the world to the largest diaspora communities, sending a handful each to France, Belgium, England, the United States, Mexico, Cuba, Colombia, Venezuela, Chile, Uruguay,

Argentina, and the Philippines, among others. Though a few Basque government delegates were from the Republican Party, such as Ramón Aldasoro in Buenos Aires, the PNV enjoyed relatively unified political support in the diaspora, and although the delegates were expected to focus on administrative activities, for most people there was no separation between the PNV and the government-in-exile—to them, the Basque government *was* the PNV and vice versa. Hence the lingering diaspora approval of the Partido Nacionalista Vasco, although those endorsing it in interviews today could not describe its policies. Diaspora nationalists are loyal to the PNV because they believe it was the party that enabled their escape from Spain and the party that received and cared for them in the host societies. Party loyalty has stamped its third generation, with young adults who indicate their party preferences mentioning that their grandparents were PNV, and therefore so were their parents, and so are they. In each of the six case studies, the PNV remains the most popular party with diaspora Basques who distinguish between homeland parties.[2]

Political nationalism in U.S. Basque communities was prevalent during the Franco years when various center fund-raisers paid for household items to be sent to Euskal Herria's churches and families. Aid was not granted institution-to-institution but rather community-to-community through individual initiative. The decades of the 1940s through the 1960s were the years of the "long boom" in the United States but of stagnation and deprivation in much of Euskal Herria. Emigrant-generation interviewees stated that they "felt the responsibility to take care of those at home," and those involved with aid to ETA in its initial cultural-nationalism stages believe they were "defending their heritage."

An official Basque delegation of the government-in-exile was established in New York in 1938, and in 1941 the State Department granted a special visa to

TABLE 4.1 "Which political party in Euskadi most closely fits your political views?

Gender	PNV %	HB/EH %	I don't know enough about homeland politics to choose a party %	I stay out of Basque Country politics %
Female	11	5	61	18
Male	20	6	52	16

Total respondents = 832

President Aguirre y Lecube, who remained to lecture at Columbia University in New York. However, Basques' anti-Franco rhetoric and republican ties to socialists and communists during the Spanish Civil War aroused the interest of U.S. intelligence. Beginning in 1942, there were FBI investigations of Basque government-in-exile officials, Basque immigrants in the New York area, and those in the western states of California, Nevada, Oregon, Idaho, Wyoming, and Utah, as well as of the centers and political activities carried out in each community (Ordaz Romay 1996, 230). Obtaining U.S. government endorsement was imperative to the Basque cause and the priority objective for President Aguirre, so there could be no perceived connections to communism or revolutionaries. Eventually, Basques were hired as FBI agents who helped investigate the possibility of a plan by government-in-exile delegates José María Lasarte Arana, Telesforo Monzón Ortiz de Uruela, and Antonio de Irala e Irala to organize Basques in South America into counterespionage units to aid the United States with its World War II effort. In an FBI-intercepted letter from Aguirre to a Basque in Havana, the Basque president illustrated his fears about a possible agreement between Franco and the democracies and suggested that Basques everywhere must present an image of political unity with other republicans, even at the cost of sacrificing nationalist goals (J. Edgar Hoover, FBI Bureau File 10-14311-3, 1942, copy in Basque Studies Program Library, Getchell Library, University of Nevada, Reno).

Initial FBI investigations of Basque government delegates focused on possible services that the Organization of Basque Intelligence, with its ample networks in South America and Europe utilized for Basque exiles, could provide to aid U.S. intelligence-gathering. A communication from the U.S. legal attaché in Buenos Aires to Director J. Edgar Hoover depicts the level of entanglement between the FBI and the Organization of Basque Intelligence. It appears that the FBI was spying on its own spies in Basque Intelligence. The letter lists the categories of information that could be obtained regarding Argentine Basques' nationalist and/or communist activities, political ideologies, and religious affiliations (Ordaz Romay 1996, 235).

In the United States, there are few examples of homeland partisan involvement from the diaspora communities. In the 1970s in Boise, Idaho, a group that called itself Anaiak Danok (Brothers All) raised money for the Anai Artean in Iparralde to help the families of ETA political prisoners. However, the group disbanded by the end of the decade and never claimed any political party affiliation. Several American Basque families known to be knowledgeable about and involved in homeland politics stated that they had tried to influence U.S. foreign policy through their senators, namely Frank Church of Idaho and Paul Laxalt of Nevada, and through the governors of the states of California, Nevada, Idaho, and Oregon, where the majority of Basques live in the

West. It was a tremendous triumph for U.S. Basques when Senator Church, chairman of the Senate Foreign Relations Committee, visited Euskal Herria before Franco's death in 1975 in order to meet Basque representatives and see symbolic Gernika and the historic Basque Parliament; he did not visit Madrid or Spanish government officials. Idaho's secretary of state, Pete Cenarrusa, provided information regarding the Basque conflict to Washington and facilitated communication with Euskal Herria. The majority of U.S. Basques, uninterested in homeland politics, most likely were unaware of Senator Church's visit, and interviews conducted in Boise between 1995 and 2002 demonstrated that Basques under fifty knew almost nothing of Anaiak Danok unless their parents had been involved.

In October 1975, approximately two hundred Basques in Los Angeles protested the September Spanish trials and executions of two ETA militants, Angel Otaegi and Juan Paredes Manot. The Spanish flag had been hoisted over City Hall in celebration of Columbus Day and the Spanish and Spanish-American holiday Día de la Raza, both of which occur on October 12, and the Basques demanded that it be removed. In San Francisco, Basques marched on October 11 from Saint Mary's Cathedral to the Spanish Consulate, where a crowd of more than five hundred people "demonstrated their feelings of anger and hostility at the recent executions of Basque nationalists," and letters of support for the Basques from U.S. Congressman and California Senator Alan Cranson were read (Burgoa in *Voice of the Basques,* November 1975, 11).

In 1983, representatives from each of the Basque Autonomous Community's political parties traveled to the United States to visit Basques centers and to explain their positions on constitutional reform and autonomy issues. They were not well received in the sense that people were apathetic. In Boise, for example, approximately thirty people attended a reception at a Basque center that had more than seven hundred paying members. Most other centers had no reception whatsoever, and the tour was a complete failure. In the 1980s and 1990s, various homeland politicians made trips to the United States and were not officially received by any Basque centers. Informally, they were invited by individuals to dinners or social gatherings at private residences, but the directorships of the centers refused to become involved in partisan politics.

The lack of interest and involvement by U.S. Basques in the democratic transformations in the homeland during the 1970s and 1980s created an even wider gap in the political networks between the homeland and the U.S. diaspora. It also resulted in general ignorance among U.S. Basques of Euskal Herria's social, political, and economic reality. At the Second World Congress of Basque Collectivities held in Vitoria-Gasteiz in October 1999, the Peruvian, Australian, Argentine, Uruguayan, and Belgian delegates (as well as delegates from other countries) were all prepared to participate in discussions of the ETA cease-fire and the Lizarra Agreement,[3] but only two of six members of the U.S. delegation had even heard of it.

Another example of publicly manifest political interest occurred in March 2002, when Idaho Secretary of State Pete Cenarrusa and Idaho House of Representatives member David Bieter announced the introduction of a memorial asking the Idaho legislature to support a declaration regarding the Basque conflict. Five additional Boise Basques testified in favor of the memorial to:

(1) Express strong support for an immediate end to violence in the Basque homeland located in Spain and France and the establishment of peace through all lawful means available to the governments of Spain, France and the Basque Autonomous Region; and (2) Condemn all acts of terrorism and violence committed by any and all organizations and individuals within the Basque homeland and throughout the world, including those organizations, such as ETA, who are defined by the government of the United States as terrorist organizations pursuant to the applicable laws of the United States; (3) Reiterate its unqualified support of and participation with the government of the United States and those of all other nations in the war on terrorism. NOW, THEREFORE BE IT RESOLVED ... that the state of Idaho calls for an immediate cessation of all violence occurring in and near the Basque homeland, and that a peace process be immediately undertaken between the governments of Spain and France, the Basque Autonomous Government, and other groups committed to peace. The state of Idaho further supports the right of the Basques to self-determination. (Idaho Senate Joint Memorial No. 114, Idaho Legislature 2002)

This diaspora activity set off a firestorm of heated communications between the Spanish embassy in Washington and the State Department, the Office of the U.S. National Security Advisor, members of the Idaho legislature, and local press in Idaho and throughout Spain. Diaspora Basques in Australia, Argentina, Uruguay, Great Britain, Mexico, Cuba, and Venezuela, and hundreds more in the provinces of the Basque Country sent congratulatory e-mail messages to the participants, and to David Bieter and Pete Cenarrusa. On the last day of the Senate floor vote, *each* senator received between five and six hundred electronic messages, nearly shutting down the Idaho Capitol communications system. The measure passed unanimously in every committee and floor vote, and in May 2003 it was under consideration for discussion in the office of the U.S. senator for Idaho, Larry Craig.

Although the measure was politically significant for relations between the United States and Spain, as well as for Basque Country politics, the average Basque in Boise did not know or care about the memorial. "Some people are interested in Basque sports, others are interested in Euskera, and others are interested in Basque politics. Let each do their own thing," commented participant Julian Achabal. The majority of Basques in the United States remain interested in cultural manifestations of their identity and stay away from homeland political issues.

Preferred nonpolitical status is so intense that four of the thirty-three member centers of the North American Basque Organizations (NABO) have refused to participate in some Basque government programs because their leadership perceives these relationships as "getting involved in politics" (P. Etcharren interview, San Francisco, 2002; R. Echeverria interview, Elko, 1999). The Basque Autonomous Government has also requested from each U.S. Basque center official statistical registries of memberships detailing the members' names, place of birth, languages spoken, and citizenships, but by late 1999 there were still three centers refusing to participate or solicit this voluntary information of their members. The perception of embroilment with homeland political activity of any sort is negative for some center activists.

The current dilemma for centers in the NABO federation is to decide whether accepting Basque government grant funding and computers constitutes participating in politics. It does not legally jeopardize their nonprofit or charitable status. Basque centers in Susanville and Winnemucca have decided that Basque government "grants will one day have strings attached"; they have refused the computers and Internet services allocated for their centers, physically returning them to the International Relations Chairperson of NABO. These centers have voted not to accept Basque government grant funding because they understand this to be entering into political entanglements with the Basque government and the PNV, and they are opposed to such political activities. Other individuals have trepidations about receiving financial aid from Euskadi based on two separate issues. First, the Basque government requires that diaspora Basque centers be officially registered with its Secretary of Foreign Action in order to receive monies. This entails registering the members of the centers, as mentioned above. Almost two-thirds of the members have refused to supply this information, stressing the value of their personal privacy.

The Basque government has accepted this cultural difference and has allowed centers to register without a full accounting of their members. Although Franco has been dead for more than twenty years, the unhappy memories of these political exiles are not. Responses of U.S. interviewees indicated a lasting fear of politics in Spain. Only 14 percent "agreed" or "strongly agreed" that "admirers of General Franco and his politics are NO LONGER a threat to Basques." Reacting to the statement, "The Basque Autonomous Government should not trust the Spanish central government," only 16 percent disagreed. Conversations about the registration of diaspora Basque centers exhibit not a mistrust of the Basque government itself but rather fear of what could happen to such personal records in the hands of the Spanish government.

The second reason some U.S. Basques refuse Basque government economic aid is shame and embarrassment at the idea that the previously underdeveloped economy of Euskadi, where unemployment for youth hovered at 35 percent at the end of the 1990s, would be aiding Basque centers in the United States, where most members are comparatively wealthier than their homeland counterparts. For decades, immigrants sent remittances to families in the Basque Country in order to relieve their financial hardship. It is unfathomable to many that taxes collected in Euskadi, which they believe "should be invested in creating employment, educational opportunities, and improving health care and infrastructure," would instead be spent buying television sets so members of diaspora Basque centers can view videos sent by the Ministry of Culture (Steve Mendive interview, Boise, 1998). Knowing that "with a few fund-raisers each Basque community could purchase ten television sets if they chose to," the majority of the U.S. centers have not applied for financial grants from the Basque government since their inception in 1987 (J. Mainvil interview, Weiser, Idaho, 1998; R. Echeverria interview, Elko, 1998; Helen Berria interview, Nampa, Idaho, 1999).

Basque emigration to Australia was more economically than politically induced, although there are several Basques in Sydney, Melbourne, and North Queensland who describe themselves as political exiles fleeing Franco's repression. Because of the relatively small enclaves and the long distances between them, there has been little communication between the three Basque clusters. These Basques' political involvement and their knowledge of and contacts with other Basques in the diaspora are minimal. Although South American and U.S. Basques have interacted considerably despite long distances between them, except for contacts with homeland Basques those in Australia have been relatively isolated from each other and from Basque populations in other countries. Even so, there is still evidence of individual political involvement with the homeland and of a desire to influence Australia's foreign policies concerning the Basque Country.

Political involvement has included letter-writing campaigns to members of Parliament in order to influence Australian foreign policy toward the Franco government—expanded to demonstrations against the death sentences that Spanish judges handed down to convicted ETA sympathizers in the Burgos Trials of 1970. Basques from Sydney mobilized and organized buses to take marchers to Canberra to demand official Australian government reaction to what they described as "undemocratic and unjust judicial and general political practices in Spain." The same year, a general strike by Melbourne dockworkers (organized by Basques) demonstrated solidarity for Basque protests and general strikes in the homeland (Oribe interview, Melbourne, 1997). Pablo Oribe and his wife, Carmen "Mentxu" Belon—themselves exiled orphans of the Spanish Civil War—met with local politicians and several members of Parliament to educate them about the circumstances of Franco's repression in the four provinces. Oribe conducted radio interviews, lectured to community groups, and wrote media accounts of political persecution in the Basque Country.

During the 1960s and early 1970s, Oribe recounts that attempting to influence Australia's government about Spanish politics was "like talking to a rock." There was almost no interest in or sympathy for the victims of a remote homeland unknown to most Australians and unimportant in Australian foreign policy. Worldwide press coverage of ETA as radicals and communists was then mistakenly used by an uninformed public as a blanket description for all Basques, which hurt diaspora Basques' attempts to mobilize support for international pressure for change in Spain. Once again, individuals used their personal friendship and kinship networks to send material and financial aid to family and friends in the homeland. Because established Basque centers in Melbourne and Sydney organized various gatherings, Basques in these areas were more likely to share information and discuss possible collective actions. Those in the North Queensland areas of Ingham, Townsville, and Ayr were fewer in number, more isolated, and acted individually, if at all. Close to one-third of the interviewees remember their parents or themselves contributing funds for relief of families in the homeland, and they believe these funds to have been general nonpartisan humanitarian aid sent mostly to relatives.

A more recent example of individual interest in political nationalism involved a controversial Herri Batasuna Party campaign video advocating the use of all possible means (including violence) to achieve a united Basque state. Released in 1996 for upcoming elections, the tape resulted in the subsequent trials and imprisonment in Spain of the entire national directorate of the Herri Batasuna Party for up to seven years.[4] A copy of the video obtained through personal connections made its way among homes in Sydney and was reproduced to expand its audience in Australia. Conversations at the Gure Txoko Basque Center in Sydney indicated outrage that the "supposed democracy" of Spain could imprison the entire directorship of a legal political party for advertising its political ideology. "Nothing has changed since Franco died. State terrorism will create reactionary defensive terrorism," stated one member.

Closer to the homeland, Basques in Belgium have benefitted from the abundance of current news and information and the advantage of proximity resulting in cheaper, easier travel and access to Euskal Herria. The majority of the Basque population in Belgium are first- and second-generation political exiles of the Civil War and Franco years, and several are representatives of the thousands of orphan children cared for by Belgian families during the Civil War. They tend to endorse either the traditional nationalist Partido Nacionalista Vasco or the radical nationalist Herri Batasuna, though the HB is losing popular support because of the perception that its "targets are no longer symbolic of the Spanish government but rather are Basques themselves." In Belgium, as in the other case studies, political activity is carried out by individual actors. As I shall discuss below, the existence of the Herri Batasuna "embassy" and the Basque Autonomous Government's Delegation to the European Union make it easy for the Brussels Txalaparta Center to propose more cultural manifestations of identity. Comparative attitudes and opinions exemplify this Basque population's heightened knowledge and understanding of homeland politics because of the relative ease of communication: "We watch TV news from France and Spain almost every day."

CURRENT HOMELAND PARTISAN REPRESENTATION IN THE DIASPORA

As I demonstrated above, the ethnic-identity manifestations of those diaspora populations cannot be described as either apolitical or nonpolitical. In 1998, there were 31,600 persons in the diaspora who held Basque citizenship rights and were qualified to vote in the Basque Autonomous Community; of those, 26,396 registered to vote: 3,699 in Argentine; 2,010 in the U.S.; 1,022 in Uruguay; 977 in Belgium; and 429 in Peru (figures for Australia are not available).[5] By 2001, the number of registered diaspora voters had increased to 32,858. In addition, there are 12,690 Nafarroans in the diaspora, as well as Basques from Iparralde (official numbers not available). Because these diaspora Basques are qualified to vote in all elections, it would seem natural to assume that the homeland political parties might solicit their support, but they do not.

Although the number of qualified diaspora voters per country was available for 1998, the number of actual voters per country was not. In the 1998 parliamentary election, there were 26,396 eligible diaspora voters, and 6,888 of them actually voted—a 26.1-percent participation rate. In Euskadi itself, voter turnout for the same election was 73 percent, and again the PNV was the most popular party, creating a coalition government after "winning" with 28 percent of the electorate's support. In the 2001 parliamentary elections, Jaime Mayor Oreja was presented as the presidential candidate of the conservative Partido Popular. Media coverage of candidates and party platforms reached especially disturbing levels of biased reporting favoring the right, and on May 13, as voters watched polling results on television and via the Internet, many expected the first loss of the Basque nationalist PNV. Interest in several Basque diaspora communities in Argentina, Uruguay, and Australia resulted in an increase to 32,858 voters abroad registering; 10,552 of them actually voted, a 32-percent diaspora voter turnout. The PNV/EA coalition won the 2001 elections with 39.5 percent of the popular vote, the highest percentage it had ever achieved.

In Argentina, the Acción Vasca (Basque Action) and Emakume Abertzale Batza (United Nationalist Women), both of which are PNV subsectors initiated in the 1930s, function openly as subgroups within several of the Basque centers. Though not currently strongly connected to party politics, the Acción Vasca and Emakume Abertzale Batza have served dual political and cultural purposes throughout their histories. Of the six countries, Argentina is the solitary example where PNV groups function, but in the past two decades they have become less involved in homeland PNV party politics and have attracted fewer new members. The Emakume of Rosario, Argentina, actually has almost nothing any longer to do with the PNV but retains the original name of the organization. It began as the women's branch of the Rosario Zazpirak Bat Basque organization, which accepts only men as members. The practice of gender-specific organizations continues today in Rosario, and the two groups sponsor several joint cultural activities each year, but none that are political party events (Arregui interview, Buenos Aires, 1997).

The leftist nationalist party Herri Batasuna mails informational pamphlets from the homeland to a few Argentine Basque centers, but it has no formal ongoing institutional communication with either FEVA (Federation of Basque Entities in Argentina) or with any Basque center in Argentina (M. Egibar e-mail communication 1998). The Sydney Gure Txoko also receives Herri Batasuna publications, which are made available to interested members, as does the Boise Euzkaldunak Inc. Basque center in the United States. There is unofficial personal censorship of Herri Batasuna's publications in several centers on this party's mailing list. Often an employee (usually the bartender) or a person responsible for opening mail discards HB publications, thereby censoring and influencing that entire Basque community's access to information (Arozarena interview, Buenos Aires, 1997). Directors of Herri Batasuna affirmed in personal interviews that they know this occurs and that they are fighting and losing a propaganda battle with the PNV, which controls the Basque government. Karmelo Landa, a national director of Herri Batasuna, said that the party planned to solicit the diaspora population for political support (Landa interview, Euskadi, 1996), but as of late 2002 nothing had been launched to the centers. Instead of pamphlets being thrown away in the bar, there are occasional e-mail messages, which are deleted.

Belgium is the only case that has had formal representation of another political party besides the PNV, and also has permanent official political representation of the Basque government. Partisan representation is exemplified at the Herri Batasuna's Herri Enbaxada (Embassy of the Homeland) in Brussels. This "embassy" was established as the official headquarters and residence of the Herri Batasuna's European Union parliamentarians elected as representatives from Euskadi. The office and five-bedroom residence serves for HB administrators and is often utilized by party members, union leaders, activists, and others traveling to Brussels for European Union matters. The office managers are political exiles charged with participating in and collaborating with ETA activities in the Basque Country. They have been granted political asylum in Belgium and are residing legally in Brussels. These HB Enbaxada employees inform the appropriate EU agencies of alleged human and civil rights abuses by the Spanish government, gain media attention for the Basque nationalist cause, and publish information regarding Basque political prisoners and the current political situation in Euskal Herria. In the early 1990s, they arranged lectures regarding the situation in the Basque Country, as well as cultural exhibitions of Basque art and music, which were attended by twenty to thirty Basques and non-Basques per event. Interested participants have included Flemish nationalists (who have actually established a Basque bar and meeting site) who identify with the Basque ideal of self-determination. Some Belgian interviewees responded that they had attended events at the Enbaxada but had since decided to disassociate themselves because of connections between HB and ETA. They felt that their "attendance at any Enbaxada events could be misconstrued as support for the HB and therefore ETA." They wanted to share their "Basqueness with other Basques and associate with other Basques, but in a nonpolitical way," and they did not believe they could accomplish this with Herri Enbaxada personnel or at HB activities.

Three kilometers from the Herri Enbaxada is the Euskadiren Ordezkaritza Bruselan, the Basque Autonomous Community's official delegation to the European Union, which functions as the stateless region's informal embassy. Its civil servants are mostly PNV members, though this is not a condition for employment or internship. Other Basque "Eurocrats" employed in Brussels do not necessarily define themselves as Basques and are there representing their own business interests, according to Alex Aguirrezabal, Director General of the Delegation. In a 1997 survey, 90 percent of the Basque civil servants in EU employment in Belgium stated that they planned to return to Euskadi, and 60 percent said that if they could find a job in Euskadi they would return immediately (Aguirrezabal interview, Brussels, 1997). This gives an indication of their short-term mentality, maintained networks with the homeland, and lack of desire to build any permanent diaspora relationships or investment in a cultural institution or other Basque organization. "They are always thinking of when they will be back in Euskadi" (Mendibelzua interview, Brussels, 1997).

Of the Belgian respondents participating in this research project, a large percentage were familiar with the Herri Batasuna's Enbaxada, but many did not know that the Basque government's Ordezkaritza existed. Their interview on the Ordezkaritza premises was the first time they had visited and become aware of the Basque government's representation in Belgium and in European Union politics and economics. Neither the government's Ordezkaritza nor the HB Enbaxada has reached out to the Belgian Basque diaspora population, nor do they believe they have any reason to do so, with the exception of the HB's mobilization of people in Brussels to protest Spanish government policies to the EU. The Euskadiren Ordezkaritza operates more in an economic and business capacity for the Basque government by researching EU mandates, rules, and restrictions for business and international trade and by promoting Basque companies. Therefore, although there is an official delegation of the Basque Country in Belgium and an embassy of the Herri Batasuna, neither seems to have affected the diaspora population in any significant way, politically or culturally.

A third factor of influence on the Belgian Basque population is the Txalaparta Basque Center. This organization is similar to Basque centers in other countries, with cultural dance and music groups, a choir, sporting events, dinners, and an in-progress clubhouse project. With the aid of Basque government grants, the Txalaparta has purchased a three-story building in a prime area of Brussels real estate, with a restaurant and bar, a salon for dance rehearsals, and a small indoor *frontón* for *pala* and *pelota* that can be converted for large celebrations and other activities. Partisan politics in Txalaparta became the catalyst for membership splits, broken friendships, members abandoning the organization, and ultimately the disintegration of the association itself. Since Txalaparta was loosely organized in the mid-1970s, members have often disagreed regarding the extent of political involvement that the organization should exhibit. While some members were sheltering Basque political refugees and/or were political refugees themselves, initiating political events, discussions, and political action, others desired a social association and were more interested in a Basque bar and restaurant. The diverse political opinions of Euskal Herria reached the Txalaparta and, as in the homeland, divided members and crippled the association at the end of the 1980s. The resurgence of Txalaparta beginning in 1995 seemed to be a result of renewed interest from the Belgian Basque population, buttressed by promised grants and financial aid from the Basque government to carry out cultural activities. However, many interviewees did not know that the Txalaparta had ever existed, or else that it was resuming activities and inviting additional memberships. Interviewees stated that Belgium is so close to the "real thing" that they do not have to reproduce Euskal Herria in Belgium. They travel to the Pyrenees easily and inexpensively, maintaining a transnational identity, a luxury not available to Basques in the other five countries.

Summarizing Belgium's political and partisan activities in comparison to those in the other diaspora communities, Belgium retains three distinct Basque networks operating simultaneously and separately from each other, each in its own sphere of influence. The Delegation of Euskadi focuses on business and trade, the Herri Batasuna Embassy concentrates on nationalist politics, and the Txalaparta promotes culture. Unlike other diaspora Basque organizations, these generally do not mix or overlap in membership and participation, and they do not feel the same need to act collectively for protection and brotherhood or to maintain their identity. They are able to manifest their cultural and political interests by traveling to Euskadi. As of 2002, the Txalaparta had disbanded.

In the United States, Peru, Australia, and Uruguay, there are no formal organizations representing homeland political parties. Some individuals are privately active and establish dual citizenship for voting purposes, but there is no systematic official representation of party politics. During the dictatorships suffered in Peru, political socialization has taught people to stay out of politics and to keep any criticism quiet. One Lima Euskal Etxeak member, Francisco Igartua, had his news magazine *Oiga* (Listen) censored and closed by the Fujimori government for exhibiting too potent critiques of Peruvian power politics (Igartua interview, Lima, 1996). Interviewees stated that in previous decades, international press accounts replayed in the Peruvian media associated Basques with leftist radicals and violence. After the Soviet Union aided the Republicans in the Spanish Civil War, Basques around the world were branded as communists, and anti-Franco rhetoric was received negatively in Peru as well as in the other five countries, although in Belgium to a lesser degree. Basques in Peru stated that they knew of no Basque political movements or party representation, nor could any interviewee from the Basque center remember any political coloring to activities of the Euskal Etxeak of Lima. They celebrate Sabino Arana's Aberri Eguna as the nationalists' holiday of the rebirth of Basque nation, but for most it is perceived as more of a cultural and social gathering, not connected to the PNV or to any particular political ideology. Questionnaire responses regarding the "importance of celebrating Aberri Eguna as a day of Basque nationalism" showed agreement throughout the diaspora, with the holiday's importance rated 100 percent by Basques in Peru, 91 percent in Belgium, 91 percent in Argentina, 73 percent in Australia, 69 percent in Uruguay, and 68 percent in the United States.

Diaspora Basques have not consolidated as a Basque lobby to influence domestic politics, but as a group they have shown an interest in homeland politics. Unlike what is often expected of immigrants (that they unite for instrumental economic purposes or for protection and use their ethnicity to obtain special treatment from their governments), Basques in these countries have not followed this pattern. In response to a question asking respondents whether "claiming an ethnic identity can help me get a special government benefit," not a single respondent from Peru or Uruguay marked *yes*, and the highest affirmative response was a low 4 percent in Belgium. Common political interests of diaspora Basques have continued to center around the circumstances of the homeland, not those of personal economic gain.[6]

The Euskal Erria Basque center members in Montevideo differ from their brethren in that they continue as an institution to receive all ideologies and politicians from the Basque Country regardless of party, and needy centers from the Uruguayan interior have all applied for Basque government financial aid, dismissing any political conflict of interest. The PNV, HB, Eusko Alkartasuna (Basque Solidarity), and Euskadiko Ezkerra (Basque Left), as well as Basque Country labor-union leaders, have been invited to present their projects to the board of directors at the Euskal Erria. A separate center in Montevideo, the Euskaro, formerly the Euskaro Español, is often scorned by members of Euskal Erria as not being nationalist because it had the word Spanish in its original name and until recently displayed a Spanish flag next to the Basque *ikurriña*. Its members are less concerned with the politics of the homeland and focus more on culture and sport, unless an extreme circumstance erupts, as it did in the 1992–94 crisis of extradition proceedings for seven suspected ETA members living in Uruguay.

In this incident, members of the Basque centers of Montevideo and thousands more from the general Uruguayan community participated in demonstrations in support of hunger-striking Basque political exiles and suspected ETA sympathizers who had been jailed in Montevideo while waiting deportation to Spain. A few Uruguayan Basques were also erroneously jailed and subsequently released. Demonstrations by thousands of Uruguayans took place daily, eventually in front of the hospital where the hunger strikers had been moved; at one critical point, shots fired by the Uruguayan military police killed a citizen (Iguain interview, Montevideo, 1996; Sarazola interview, Montevideo, 1996; M. Zuazola interview, Montevideo, 1996). This was simultaneously a consolidating and a divisive event. Non-center Basques protested and showed solidarity in opposition to extradition and in favor of self-determination of peoples, as banners proclaimed. Non-Basque leftists spray-painted "Gora Euskadi" (Long Live the Basque Country) next to "Gora Che Guevarra" (Long Live Che Guevarra) already painted on houses and buildings. Demonstrators experienced at shouting union slogans and pro-Tupamaro and antigovernment chants also joined in the mobilization. Homeland representatives from HB, lawyers from human-rights groups, and delegates from Basque peace organizations flew to Montevideo to plea for refugee and exile status for the detained, but their pleas were refused. The president of the Autonomous Basque Government, José Antonio Ardanza, telephoned President Gurutz Iguain of the Euskal Erria

Center, asking that the center publicly denounce ETA and political violence in the homeland (Iguain interview). The recently reelected President Iguain of the Euskal Erria Center refused this request to involve his institution in an official political statement. Basque government President Ardanza then stated in an interview in the Uruguayan daily *El País* that "a position close to ETA had taken control of the Euskal Erria Center" (*El País*, 30 October 1994).

This "erroneous accusation" (Iguain interview) created a defensive reaction and intense negative feelings from some center members toward the Basque government. The Basque government had rarely meddled in any center's activities and had never "requested" a center to make a public political statement. Despite a major uproar in Montevideo and in Latin American foreign-policy circles, and of course in Spain, Basques in the interior of Uruguay did not participate in any demonstration of support for the political exiles, nor were they encouraged to do so. There was no attempt to synthesize interior Basques to make a united formal statement—not that they would have done so, according to their presidents (Celia Bessonart interview, Trinidad, Uruguay, 1996; A. Irigoyen interview, Durazno, Uruguay, 1996; Zaldua interview, Salto, Uruguay, 1996). Uruguay granted extradition, and five of the seven detainees were transported to Spain and sentenced. The breakdown of amicable relations between the Basque Autonomous Government and the Euskal Erria Center continued for several years.

In November 1996, Karmelo Landa Mendive again traveled to Uruguay to coincide with a visit by Spain's King Juan Carlos and Queen Sofia, using the opportunity to meet with Uruguayan parliamentarians to discuss the possibility of Montevideo hosting initial peace talks between a consortium of Basques and the Spanish government. He was not granted any appointments or joint media time with the king, and he made his negotiations offer through the Uruguayan press. There was no response, and there has been no progress because Karmelo Landa and his fellow HB directors were in prison from November 1997 until July 1999 because of the political video incident. Today, HB-EH[7] has supporters in Montevideo, but because of the chaos caused by the detentions and extraditions, and by the homeland judgments for imprisonment of the party leadership, plans for utilizing the diaspora in political causes have been postponed.

This demonstrates the nature of individual choice in political manifestations of ethnic identity. Institutionally, some of the Basque centers have kept democratic principles of admitting and receiving various ideologies, promoting or favoring none. They have given their members the opportunity to inform themselves and individuals a private choice of whether or not to act. Of course, cultural strategies are in general preferred to political activities as less threatening to host societies, for there is no challenge to the sovereignty or power of the host country's political actors, or to its territory or military. Diaspora cultural activities are also more acceptable to homeland politicians, because they will not be upstaged for authority and legitimacy, nor will there be much criticism of public policy in Euskadi. Host governments also would favor the cultural strategy, goals, and collective action of diaspora communities that police and control themselves and any radical political tendencies. Still, in many countries, for economic, political, racist, or xenophobic reasons, ethnic minorities are regarded suspiciously enough for the host government to involve itself with members' activities, as was the case in the United States with the FBI investigations of Basques. In Uruguay, three interviewees suspected that their telephone lines were regularly tapped by police looking for information about ETA and/or political exiles living in Uruguay, and one also believed his telephone was tapped when he visited Euskadi.[8] In Belgium, one family revealed that police had forced themselves into their home searching for information about political exiles in Belgium. Families sheltering refugees claimed that the Belgian police had watched their homes and personal movements for months.

Involving oneself in political nationalism carries much greater risk than the cultural manifestations of everyday ethnicity, and most diaspora Basques do not solicit that risk. In sum, Basques outside the homeland, whether recent emigrants or fifth-generation, have infrequently involved themselves with the political aspects of homeland issues and host-country involvement. I now turn to what diaspora Basques individually know about homeland politics and to what degree and in what ways they are involved in the contemporary politics of Euskal Herria.

Comparing Respondents' Personal Attitudes Toward Politics

POLITICAL PARTICIPATION

Despite generational, geographic, and gender differences in the diaspora population, the core elements of diaspora Basque identity are similar, and I argue that they are overwhelmingly cultural and nonpolitical. Specific comparisons are in order to build this argument. If politics were a salient factor of diaspora Basque identity, it follows that a significant number of questionnaire participants would be interested in or know something about homeland political parties. This is not the present situation with either gender, between the generations, or in any host country.

When comparing the six cases, in every country the PNV was the most popular party, and in all but Peru—where the Partido Popular (PP, Popular Party) and the Partido Comunista de España (PCE, Communist Party of Spain) tied for the second-highest response rate—the Herri Batasuna was the second-most popular party. More telling than the choice of party was the respondents' willingness to select "I don't know enough about Basque Country political parties to answer this question." Except for Belgium, where most respondents are recent emigrants and where news concerning the Basque Country is published in the media and Basques travel frequently to the homeland, in each of the other countries this "I don't know" response received the highest percentage: in the United States, 75 percent; in Uruguay, 61 percent; in Australia, 46 percent; in Argentina, 43 percent; and in Peru, 39 percent. The lack of Spanish and Basque language skills among many Basques in the United States plays a part in their not obtaining information or understanding contemporary homeland politics. The mostly economically motivated migration to the United States is also a factor in these Basques lack of political interest, as compared to Argentina where thousands of political exiles sought refuge. In all host countries combined, there was a 9-percent difference between males and females and whether or not they knew enough to choose a political party. The additional 9 percent of males who claimed sufficient knowledge chose the PNV.

Comparison between generations demonstrated the same pattern, with respondents selecting the PNV as the most popular party and HB second, across five generations from emigrants themselves to fourth-generation Basques born in the host country. In the emigrant generation there was much higher support for the PNV, with 37 percent acknowledging support, compared to the other generations' 7 to 17 percent. Only 28 percent of emigrants claimed they did not know enough about homeland politics to select a party, compared to between 55 and 72 percent in the other categories. Age groupings, regardless of generation, repeated the pattern, with the PNV as the most popular party and HB in second place, but again the response with the highest selection rate was "I don't know enough about the Basque Country political parties to answer this question."

The argument that, regardless of geography, generation, and gender, diaspora Basques prefer cultural to political manifestations of ethnicity is strengthened with the following data, while the assumption that males take care of politics while females guard cultural aspects of ethnicity is erroneous. Responses agreeing with the statement favoring cultural over political involvement prevail in each independent variable. When comparing age cohorts, a similar pattern emerges, with a preference for cultural manifestation of Basque identity expressed by between 78 percent (ages 31–45) to 88 percent (ages 76–90). Between countries, the consistent pattern is weakest in Belgium, although almost two-thirds of respondents still agreed or strongly agreed.

Skeptics could claim that Basques are nonpolitical in general and do not demonstrate political interest in their host societies either. However, questionnaire responses demonstrate that diaspora Basques are associated with their host-country politics. Although in Peru 79 percent do not participate in politics, personal interviews explained that this is the result of a lack of civil society, low political efficacy, and struggling democratic ideals of individual participation. Many recent migrants to Belgium explained that they tend not to involve themselves with their host country's political issues because they do not have Belgian citizenship. Overall, respondents tended to connect politics to civic rather than ethnic identity. No conflict between being Basque (ethnic) and being Uruguayan or Argentine or American, etc. (civic) appeared.

There are differences between Basques in each country and their support for liberal versus conservative parties. An overview of diaspora Basques' self-categorization in host-country political parties follows in table 4.3. The highest political-party identification rates are in the United States, with 85 percent of Basques reporting an association with a political party, and the lowest are in Peru, with 21 percent reporting a party association. Interviews in Peru

TABLE 4.2 "I prefer to participate in Basque cultural events and not Basque political events."

	Strongly Agree or Agree %	No Opinion %	Strongly Disagree or Disagree %
Gender			
Female	82	8	10
Male	79	13	8
Host Country			
Peru	92	8	0
United States	83	10	7
Uruguay	81	12	7
Argentina	81	10	9
Australia	75	13	13
Belgium	58	8	33
Generation			
Immigrant	77	12	11
First	80	11	9
Second	84	8	9
Third	84	9	7
Fourth	76	17	7

Total respondents = 832

uncovered a general lack of trust in Peruvian politics and were likely influenced by the recent nondemocratic Fujimori regime.

Political participation in host-country activities that affect other Basques would also indicate an interest and/or willingness to be involved with a political aspect of Basque identity. However, with the exception of Belgian Basques, who, as discussed above, take advantage of the European Union's institutions to promote information about Euskal Herria's political and economic situation,

TABLE 4.3 "Which political party do you usually associate yourself with in (host country)?"

Host Country	Political Party Preference by Basques %	Other Parties %	I do not participate in (host-country) politics %
Argentina	2 Partido Justicialista 36 Unión Cívica Radical 10 FRESPASO	7	44
Australia	47 Labour 13 Liberal 10 Country	5	25
Belgium	8 Parti Comunist 12 Parti Ecologist 5 Christelijke Volkspartij 9 Parti Social Chrestien	7	59
Peru	7 Cambio 90/Nueva Mayoría 14 Unión por el Perú 0 Alianza Popular Revolucionaria Americana	0	79
United States	42 Democratic 43 Republican 1 Reform	11	4
Uruguay	15 Partido Colorado 47 Partido Nacional (Blancos) 15 Encuentro Progresista	2	21

Total respondents = 832

responses from the other five countries are similar, with participants overwhelmingly marking that they have not participated in any activities that affect Basques.

Diaspora Basques do not seem to think participation in political activities is a factor of their Basque ethnic identity. Though reasons for preserving ethnic identity vary widely, in several other diasporas, such as the Irish, Armenian, and Jewish, promoting a political awareness in the host country of one's homeland situation is often popular. Not among the Basque populations. Only Belgian Basques showed an interest in this expression of their ethnicity, with 50 percent selecting "I want to promote an awareness of the political situation in the Basque Country to (host country population)." Elsewhere, positive responses to this same item ranged from Argentina's 16 percent to the United States' 7 percent. No significant gender differences materialized, with only 10 percent of females and 15 percent of males wishing to promote political awareness, and support ranged from 10 percent to 17 percent between the five generation categories.

Because Basques abroad are eligible to vote in homeland elections, their political attitudes and opinions may become more important to homeland parties planning on campaigning abroad and mobilizing qualified participants. Though no party currently campaigns in the diaspora for election votes, they may in the future.

DIASPORA HOPES FOR THE HOMELAND'S FUTURE

What are the diaspora populations' hopes for the homeland? Remembering that currently three provinces (Lapurdi, Behe Nafarroa, Zuberoa) are a part of France, and that Euskadi (Araba, Bizkaia, Gipuzkoa) and Nafarroa are two separate politically autonomous regions in Spain, respondents were asked their opinion of the "most desirable situation for the future of the seven provinces." Again, an average of 49 percent across the six host countries answered, "I do not know enough about the situation to answer this question." Males tended to be more in favor of separatism and more likely to claim knowledge about home-country politics. While 57 percent of females and 40 percent of males answered that they did "not know enough," 32 percent of females and 46 percent of males chose "declaring independence from Spain and France and forming one separate country for all seven provinces" as their most desirable preference for the future of Euskal Herria. Of those respondents who had chosen the Herri Batasuna as their homeland party of choice, 96 percent favored total independence and statehood for all seven provinces, as opposed to 64 percent of the PNV supporters.

Maintaining the present political situation was favored only by 2 percent of females and 4 percent of the males, 3 percent of self-identified PNV supporters,

TABLE 4.4 "While living in (host country) have you ever participated in any political movements (rallies, letter-writing, protests, fund-raisers, etc.) specifically because it would affect Basques?"

Reply	Argentina %	Australia %	Belgium %	Peru %	United States %	Uruguay %
No, because there have not been any political movements that would affect Basques.	40	52	30	67	41	17
No, because I do not get involved in politics.	54	45	26	33	51	75
Total Percentage	94	97	56	100	92	92

Total respondents = 832

and not a single HB supporter. When comparing the different generations' preferences, there are no highly significant differences in the data. All generations' responses fell between only 1 percent (second-generation, born in the host country) and 7 percent (emigrants born in Euskal Herria) favoring the current political divisions, while 32 percent (first-generation, born in the host country) to 46 percent (third-generation, born in the host country) favored total political independence. However, there were marked differences between the age groups and between host countries.

Basques in each of the host settings have had to educate their friends and neighbors about each of these options, as well as about separatism, ETA, and

TABLE 4.5 "There are many differing opinions of a possible future for the Basque provinces. In your opinion, which of these is the most desirable situation for the future of the seven provinces?"

	Iparralde stays with France; Euskadi and Nafarroa remain two separate parts of Spain %	Iparralde stays with France; the four unite and remain as one part of Spain %	All seven declare independence together and form one separate state %	I do not know enough to answer this question %
Age Category				
18–30 yrs. old	4	7	61	28
31–45 yrs. old	3	8	38	51
45–60 yrs. old	3	11	36	51
61–75 yrs. old	5	12	29	55
76–90 yrs. old	2	10	18	70
Host Country				
Argentina	1	5	62	31
Australia	3	14	30	52
Belgium	9	9	73	9
Peru	8	25	17	50
United States	5	13	18	64
Uruguay	1	4	43	52

832 respondents

ETA's activities toward independence for the Basque Country. Although initially ETA objectives and activities were cultural, acts of violence soon became the dominant subjects of media reports about the Basque Country presented around the world since the 1970s (I. Zabaleta interview, Reno, 1998). In the early years, there was a collective silence or public silence regarding protest against Franco, but by the 1960s ETA provided a voice and spoke for the Basque community at home and abroad. Though most respondents would not comment publicly that they favored ETA tactics, many agreed with what they perceived ETA was, and is, fighting for, "independence and defense of Basques' human and civil rights." Later in the 1980s and 1990s, diaspora communities began to doubt ETA's tactics but not its goals. Interviewees expressed a certain weariness with explaining or defending ETA's political violence, whether active or reactive to Spanish state violence. Yet in half of the countries studied, less than a majority disagreed that "these tactics were effective in achieving additional autonomy."

More than twice as many Basques in Peru as in Australia disagreed that political violence had been successful in achieving increased political autonomy, and very few in Peru had no opinion on this topic, whereas one-third of Australian Basques marked this option. Peru's experience with the rebel Sendero Luminoso movement and Uruguay's with the Tupamaros may have affected these answers, though this possibility was not included in interviews or in the questionnaire as an independent variable. Gender was not an indicator for difference, as 42 percent of females and 44 percent of males disagreed with the effectiveness of political violence as a factor in increasing autonomy, and 19 percent of females and 29 percent of males agreed. As expected, of those diaspora Basques who identified themselves with the PNV, 30 percent agreed (58 percent disagreed) with the effectiveness of political violence, while 76 percent of Herri Batasuna supporters agreed (only 7 percent disagreed) that violent tactics were useful in obtaining increased political power.

The cease-fire declared by ETA in September 1998 should have been an important topic of discussion in Basque centers and in personal circles if the diaspora Basque population is a political diaspora. Centers were contacted by e-mail or fax three months later to inquire if their organization had included this information in newsletters or if the cease-fire had been mentioned or discussed formally at center events. Approximately half of the Basque centers responded to the enquiry, and of those, half replied that there had not been any institutional discussion, and the other half did not know anything about the cease-fire. Though this could reflect the ignorance of the center's Internet communicator, it is not likely, because the computer communicators tend to be among the most informed and active people at the centers.

TABLE 4.6 "Whether or not I agree with its use, I think political violence has been effective for achieving more autonomy in the Basque Country."

Reply	Peru %	Uruguay %	Belgium %	Argentina %	United States %	Australia %
Disagree or Strongly disagree	69	58	54	41	41	31
No Opinion	8	33	13	31	36	37
Agree or Strongly Agree	23	9	33	28	22	33

Total respondents = 832

"Basqueness" as Defined in the Diaspora

Are these diaspora Basques following traditional Sabino Arana nationalist definitions of Basqueness: race, language, and religion? Or are they synchronized with homeland changes to a more civic nationalism and inclusive ethnic identity of those who live and work in Euskadi and want to be Basque? Not immune to secularization, Basques, once fervent Catholics at home and in the diaspora, are turning more to ethnicity for their identity and sense of belonging (Pérez-Agote interview, Euskadi, 1998). Pérez-Agote argues that with the decline of religion, meaning—in this circumstance, ethnicity—becomes socially constructed. However, for Basques, the Catholic religion has been a salient factor that solidifies the boundaries of ethnic identity. The Aranist conservative construction of Basque identity emphasized Catholicism and Basqueness as inseparable. The focus on ancestry and language is also problematic for the diaspora because of intermarriage with host-country natives and diminished Basque-language skills.

ARANIST AND TRADITIONAL BASQUENESS

An aspect of Basque identity significant to traditional nationalists was the maintenance of the Catholic religion, and this remains important to diaspora Basques. Males and females agreed that "continuing Catholic beliefs and traditions in our families" is of "great" or "very great" importance. However, 71 percent of females and 69 percent of the males agreed that Catholicism was only of "some degree of importance" to them. For each gender, 17 percent did not think that religion was of any consequence to Basque culture and identity, nor should it be to the Basque people living in the diaspora or the homeland. Aggregate responses ranged from Belgium's 57 percent who do not believe that Catholicism is important to continue and maintain, to only 8 percent in the United States. Belgian Basques, as the most recent emigrants, exhibit an attitude closer to that of the homeland population. In the United States, where Basques often felt discriminated against because of their religion, Catholicism is still fundamental to their ethnic definition, whereas in countries where Catholicism is a state religion, such as Peru, Argentina, and Uruguay, it is not considered an essential factor of identity. There is a steady decline by age category of a belief in religion's importance to Basqueness. Overall, 46 percent of the eighteen-to-thirty-year-olds do not believe religion to have any importance at all, and this pattern tends to point to Catholicism's decline in future ethnic definitions as well. In personal interviews, some respondents said they are religious, but they do not connect religiosity to ethnicity: "I am not more Basque because I am Catholic." Several female emigrants in different host countries, but all from Bizkaia originally, said they were actually anti-Catholic because of the Church's abandonment of the Basques and siding with Franco during the Civil War.

Endogamy between diaspora Basques in this sample was lowest in Uruguay (13 percent) and highest in Belgium (35 percent). Basque emigrants in Belgium had usually married another Basque emigrant from Euskal Herria or had married while living in Euskal Herria and then emigrated together, so this was not a case of a later-generation Basque marrying another later-generation Basque as in Uruguay. When asked if "Basques should try to marry other Basques," only between 4 percent of respondents in Belgium and 20 percent in the United States agreed or strongly agreed. The high percentages of people with "no opinion" indicate that future attitudes could result in different conclusions. Overall, 28 percent of respondents had no opinion, and in the United States, where answers were the most conservative, 38 percent answered "no opinion." In each of the U.S. communities, interview statements of Basques 18 to 25 years old included comments such as, "I do hope I'll marry a Basque guy. Life would be so much simpler because then I don't have to explain all this stuff to him" (second-generation female), and "Yeah, I'd like to marry a Basque because I think we'd have the same ideas about raising our children and about how important our families are" (third-generation male). In several interviews in the six countries, participants would have agreed with this third-generation Peruvian: "I don't want to sound racist or like I have a superiority complex, but I think it is special to be Basque and we are different from other people. I don't want to lose that and I want to marry another Basque because he'll understand that and would want to come to all the Basque activities." Although United States interviews included references to children who were "only half Basque" or "only a quarter Basque" or "more Basque than—," some respondents did not distinguish or classify hierarchically according to ancestry or lineage. This abandonment of Aranist definitions is least prevalent in the United States and most frequent in Belgium, which has been influenced by recent chain migration and specifically by younger emigrants employed in the Euskadi Delegation in Brussels.

Diaspora Basques tend to be more exclusive, even though this is self-defeating to their communities. It might seem rational to be more accepting in the diaspora, to include others who want to share in the maintenance of Basque culture even if they were not born Basque and are not Basque by ancestry. As Basques intermarry with host-country populations, it would seem they would want to include spouses in their group categories. However, the data show the opposite results.

These affirmative numbers fortify the argument that diaspora definitions of Basqueness tend toward the Aranist traditional conservative nationalism including race or ancestry. As stated previously, in the homeland only 10 percent of my questionnaire respondents listed as a condition of Basqueness "to have Basque surnames," which translates to ancestry. Belgian Basques, with the most frequent communications with the homeland and the most recent migration with a more civic definition of Basqueness and Basque identity, were the smallest segment agreeing with the ancestral criterion. The other countries have critical masses of earlier emigrants with an Aranist definition of Basqueness perpetuated in their Basque community activities and attitudes, and they have fewer and less-frequent contacts with the homeland. Most Basque centers also require at least one grandparent with a Basque surname for membership; therefore, the sample reflects this institutional bias as well.

Diaspora opinions regarding permanent residents of Euskal Herria and their acceptance as Basques whether or not they were born there ranged from only 29 percent of United States Basques to 51 percent of Uruguayan Basques agreeing or strongly agreeing with acceptance. This was a serious issue of conflict for traditional nationalists, as mentioned earlier, and it remains so, because internal migration from Spain to the Basque Country is high. In a 1995 survey conducted by the Basque Autonomous Government's Department of Culture regarding resident respondents' "ethnocultural origins," investigators found that those persons born in one of the seven provinces of Euskal Herria to parents also native to Euskal Herria were 47 percent in Euskadi, 70 percent in Nafarroa, and 62 percent in Iparralde (Aizpurua 1995, 50). In the Basque Country, one of the reasons nationalism has transformed to a more inclusive ideology is because of this high percentage of residents who were not born Basque but have "become Basque." People have moved to the provinces and raised their families, learned Euskera in many cases, support Basque culture and political and economic autonomy, and some even support independence.

TABLE 4.7 "A person must have Basque ancestors to be a Basque."

Host Country	Agree or Strongly Agree %	No Opinion %	Disagree or Strongly Disagree %
United States	91	2	6
Peru	83	0	17
Australia	73	4	23
Uruguay	69	6	26
Argentina	62	8	29
Belgium	50	4	46

Total respondents = 832

Inconsistent responses from the diaspora arise when people were asked about the importance of "accepting as Basques those who feel and identify themselves as Basques" (which to respondents must have denoted more emotional involvement than the previous question of merely living permanently in Euskal Herria). Seventy-six percent of respondents in the United States to 95 percent of those in Belgium agreed that this was of "some," "great," or "very great importance." Younger diaspora Basques, 94 percent of the 18-30-year-olds, thought acceptance consequential. While respondents agreed that "to be Basque one must have Basque ancestors," they also agree that it is important to "accept as Basques those who feel and identify themselves as

TABLE 4.8 "To be considered a Basque, a person should speak the Basque language."

	Strongly Agree or Agree %	No Opinion %	Strongly Disagree or Disagree %	Respondents who speak Basque fluently or with some difficulty %
Host Country				
Belgium	13	4	83	42
Peru	8	8	83	23
Uruguay	12	6	83	2
United States	15	9	76	46
Argentina	24	8	68	16
Australia	36	13	52	56
Gender				
Female	18	9	73	31
Male	21	8	71	32
Age Category				
18–30 yrs. old	19	8	73	25
31–45 yrs. old	20	6	74	26
46–60 yrs. old	20	7	72	27
61–75 yrs. old	18	12	70	38
75–90 yrs. old	16	14	69	61

Total respondents = 832

Basques." As younger Basques assume positions of leadership, policy-making, and influence, we might expect a continued change in diaspora mentality, moving closer to inclusive homeland definitions of Basqueness and further from the exclusive primordialist Arana categories.

Euskera still has not secured itself as a crucial factor in Basque ethnicity. In the homeland itself, various areas have long since been hispanicized, and during the Franco dictatorship Basque was outlawed as a means of communication. Consequently, many emigrants of the political-exile era did not speak the language. Though Basques are extremely proud of their unique language and its complexity, most do not consider it a defining factor in categorizing a person as Basque. Sociolinguistic research in all seven provinces has demonstrated that while Basque speakers almost unanimously define themselves as Basque and believe that the most important criterion of Basqueness is actually speaking Basque, bilingual and Spanish-monolingual participants selected "To have been born in Euskal Herria" as the most salient factor. Nevertheless, all three language-ability groups chose as the second-most important criterion of Basque identity "To live and work in Euskal Herria" (Aizpurua 1995, 95).

Only 8 percent of Australian respondents know no Basque language at all, compared to Uruguay's 66 percent, and this has affected their responses. Obviously, respondents who do not speak Basque themselves would not want this to be a determining factor because it would eliminate them from their own ethnic identity. The extreme similarities between male and female respondents fortify the argument of a lack of gender difference and negate the assumptions in this case that females are more interested in, more likely to use, and more likely to favor ethnic language than males. Although there are no marked differences between age groups in opinions regarding language and identity, there are variances in their abilities with Basque language. Only half as many youth as elderly can converse in Basque, which bodes ill for its maintenance. Some Argentine, Uruguayan, and United States Basque centers offer language courses, but only small minorities show interest. Even in the 1995 homeland survey, 35 percent of Euskal Herria's residents stated that they had "no interest in the Basque language," referring to learning or using it.

THE DEVELOPMENT OF DIASPORIC CONSCIOUSNESS AND SPECIFIC DIASPORIC BASQUE IDENTITY

I suggest that there is a specific Basque diaspora identity. Many of the participants in my research retain or have acquired dual citizenship, and the globalization of communications networks enables their ties with the homeland to be preserved, strengthened, and even reinvented. Collective (sometimes idealized) memory, maintained ties to the homeland, solidarity with other Basques, and the creation of an enriching life in their host countries (Cohen, *Global*

Diasporas, 1997) points to a genesis of something original: not a hybrid identity mixing old-country with new host-country traditions, which all immigrants share in different ways, but an actual diaspora identity. Because diaspora Basques maintain ties with the homeland, their sense of identity is different from what would result among people who have no interest in preserving connections with the homeland and wish to assimilate fully into the host-country culture.

The term *diaspora* still implies to many the forced dispersion found in Deuteronomy 28:25, and the Old Testament warning that a "scattering to other lands" was the punishment for a people who had forsaken the righteous paths and abandoned the old ways (Cohen 1996, 507). The word has become associated with Jewish traditions, although its origins are Greek. The Greek expression originally meant "to sow widely," and it was used to describe military expansion, colonization, and migration, usually with a positive connotation. Although the opposing notion of a "victim diaspora" may better describe the Jewish, Armenian, African, Irish, and Palestinian dispersions (Cohen, *Global Diasporas*, 1997, 31–54), early Basque diasporas connect to the Greek definition of active colonization; the Franco-era exiles better reflect a negative victim diaspora.

When reviewing Cohen's list of "common features" of diasporas, it is evident that the Basque emigrations can be categorized as diaspora. However, all diasporas do not necessarily manifest all features. For example, the Basque diaspora would identify least with the seventh feature because there are no adversarial or "troubled" relationships between Basques and host-society populations in any of the six countries studied. I have described the dispersal of Basques to many lands for trade, colonization, and economic and political reasons, and have summarized their perceived collective history, real and imagined. These populations exhibit an idealization of the homeland and show a collective commitment to its maintenance and restoration with their remittances and attempts to influence host-country policies toward the Basque Country.

The diasporic idea of "return" to the homeland need not be a physical return but can be a constant turning to the homeland by way of information, communications, home-life traditions, food, music, language, etc., and to each other as fellow countrymen. The orientation toward the homeland may be manifest in many ways. The youngest respondents (32 percent) were most likely to indicate that they may return to Euskal Herria some day to live permanently. In comparisons between the countries, Basques in the United States had the highest rating, 72 percent, for "I have my own life in (host country) and plan to return to Euskal Herria only to visit." However, only 25 percent of Basques in Belgium responded that they would stay in Belgium. For most, physical location is not strongly related with ethnicity. One does not stop being Basque because one lives in Peru, and practicing the traditions of host societies does not equate to terminating traditions of the homeland. Both can be exercised simultaneously. There has been a strong ethnic-group consciousness based on distinction and sustained for centuries outside of the homeland, corroborated by historical fact and confirmed by the fifth generation participating in the Basque organizations. The transnational networks and ties to the homeland and the creation of host-country Basque associations and cultural centers demonstrate this consciousness and interest in ethnic identity maintenance.

The eighth of Cohen's criteria suggests that diasporas can be constituted in the imagination when feeling solidarity with fellow ethnics outside the homeland and in a similar situation. The creation of communications among diaspora Basques was initiated with Basque government funding for computer and Internet hook-up for Basque organizations. However, diaspora Basques have been aware of other Basque populations and have had limited contacts through trade and personal relationships for centuries. In the age of globalization and cyberspace, a diaspora can be held together or recreated in the mind through cultural maintenance and a shared imagination such as is present in the Basque centers. Identification with a diaspora serves to bridge the gap between local and global identities (Hall 1991). The Basques' strong identification with the past, and not their inability or lack of desire to assimilate in the present, permits their diasporic consciousness. Reacting to the statement "Basque immigrants should try to assimilate and practice the traditions of their new country," 32 percent of Uruguayan Basques had no opinion, but another 59 percent agreed or strongly agreed, and the other five countries' participants also "agreed" or "strongly agreed" by between 72 percent and 79 percent.

The age of globalization points to a shift to de-territorialized social identities. The world is being organized vertically by nation-states and regions, but also horizontally by an overlapping, permeable, multiple system of interactions. This new system creates communities of interest and not of place, based on shared opinions, ethnicities, religions, and other factors. Rather than globalization creating a single homogeneous global culture, perhaps multiple cultures are resulting from mixes of a variety of cultures blending differently in each setting (Hall 1990). Whereas modernity demanded state and nation-state building, loyalty from citizens, conformity, and obedience to a uniform state-culture identity, postmodernity, or the age of globalization, allows for multiple affiliations and associations, including diasporic allegiances. There is no longer the need to choose one or another identity—a person can be both Australian and Basque simultaneously. Survey research results demonstrate this self-identification with both categories. With a low of 3 percent in the United States and 28 percent in Uruguay defining themselves as only host-country (i.e., Uruguayan without a hyphenation), almost three-quarters of the

Basques surveyed described themselves as a combination either Basque–host country, or host country–Basque.

This question of dual loyalty surfaces often when dealing with political topics. However, interviews with Basques in these six countries revealed a strong civic loyalty to their host country and plans to remain living in it. They did not necessarily perceive any conflict between their host country's values and Basque values, but majorities "prefer Basque values" (by 92 percent in Peru) to their host-country population's values. Except for the Peruvian Basques, others interviewed did not perceive significant differences between themselves and the citizens of their adopted host countries. They have emigrated to countries whose populations are largely European and Catholic, or else allow freedom of religion. Their loyalties to their host country versus the Basque Country have never been tested, since the Basque Country is not a separate state. Therefore this population can claim true dual loyalties because these people do not foresee the possibility that the two would ever conflict. Others stated that they "do not like the concept of dual loyalties because it implies that one is exercised at the expense of the other," which they did not believe to be the case.

Basques also reported their loyalties to their host countries as a "civic responsibility," but their loyalty to Basque ethnicity was not described as a civic loyalty by way of residence in a territory or allegiance to a form of government. Rather, their loyalty to "Basqueness" was felt and not rationalized—"a responsibility to ancestors," to "a special and unique history." It is rational that homeland Basques would shift toward civic nationalism, accepting as Basques those who live in Euskal Herria, but Basques living in the diaspora need some way to separate themselves, to keep an insider status, and that is why ancestry remains so salient to them. Otherwise, anyone could be a Basque, and the uniqueness of the ethnicity would diminish.

Basques maximize the option of negotiating their identities depending on the situation. This situational or circumstantial identity does not mean that they are "Basque" sometimes and "Australian" at other times. Rather, depending on the environment and people with whom they are associating, diaspora Basques often emphasize one identity *more* than another; ethnic identity more than civic identity. "What ethnicity are you?" or "What is your background?" becomes more salient than "In which country do you live?" or "Which state's passport do you have?" and vice versa. This identity switching is often mistaken for and misunderstood as instrumental behavior for personal gain; however, often it is a response clarifying one's identity to an "other" person. In Australia, describing oneself as "Australian" is not as useful as defining oneself to another Australian (of, say, Greek ancestry) as a Basque. If a Basque from Uruguay is communicating with a person from Brazil, he would more than likely identify himself as Uruguayan. These are more equivalent comparisons; Brazilian to Uruguayan, and Basque Australian to Greek Australian. Societal contexts and processes influence the self-definition and self-consciousness of diasporan identities in issues of self-representation.

Diaspora Basques have been aware of and known about each other for hundreds of years, and during the twentieth century, in addition to trade and religious missions, they have collaborated in joint political, immigration, and cultural projects. International *mus* card game championships and exchanges of musicians, dance groups, students, and athletes have occurred regularly between diaspora communities and between diaspora communities and the Basque Country. Just as important are the interactions of diaspora Basques with other diaspora Basques when both are visiting their families in the homeland. Frequent returns to Euskal Herria have served to heighten diasporic consciousness because of these encounters with other Basques similar to themselves. Although a Basque from the United States is unlikely to travel with a sole purpose of meeting Basques in Argentina, Uruguay, Peru, or Australia, he will meet Basques from these countries during visits to Euskal Herria. Just as one's parents emigrated to the United States, homeland neighbors might have relatives who emigrated to Australia, and during a visit to Euskal Herria there are ample social opportunities to meet and compare experiences. In the same way that contact between diaspora Basques in different host societies has contributed to a diasporic consciousness, so too have their exchanges while in their common homeland. "Just in our *portal* of apartments in Ondarroa, my family emigrated to Australia, the neighbor across the hall has an uncle in Chile and a daughter in Uruguay, the lady downstairs has one brother in New York and one in Cuba. I think Basques could take over the world if we ever got organized" (first-generation, Australia).

Conclusion

In other diasporas such as the Armenian, Croatian, and Jewish, the politicization of attitudes regarding the homeland has pitted members against themselves and fueled serious divisions inside the ethnic community (Winland 1995, 11). This has not been the case with Basques. With the exceptions of the Centro Vasco Francés and the Centro Navarro in Buenos Aires, the Euskaro Español and Euskal Erria in Montevideo, and the Txalaparta in Brussels, political disagreements have not tended to evolve into institutional divisions.

Elderly interviewees remembered the decades of the Franco dictatorship as years of political cohesion in diaspora Basque centers. This unified behavior was an appropriate stance against the common enemies, the central Spanish government and oppression in the homeland. The divisions in the homeland that erupted with the creation of democracy and autonomy in Spain reinforced the nonpartisan and nonpolitical aspects of the diaspora Basque centers. Again, unlike what occurred with the Armenian, Jewish, or Croatian diaspora populations, democratization, independence, or autonomy in the homeland did not seriously affect the diaspora Basque populations' general disinterest in political aspects of their ethnic identity.

Heterogeneous or hyphenated diaspora Basques do not see themselves as inferior to "pure" homeland Basques, and diaspora populations "need not apologize for their alleged lack of authenticity or for the hybridity of diasporan identity, as if it represented mere decline from some purer homeland form" of identity (Tölölyan 1996, 7). Diaspora Basques have achieved multiple belonging on their own terms, utilizing their own definitions. This development of a diaspora consciousness is evident in increased understanding and communications between diaspora Basques without homeland intervention or facilitation.

Although these diaspora communities had not collaborated intensively, their actions and reactions regarding twentieth-century events corresponded with collective efforts on behalf of homeland Basques. There were parallel attempts to influence host-country governments regarding the Franco regime and ensuing political oppression in Euskal Herria. Individual and collective efforts have followed a pattern in which Basque center or institutional leadership is absent, neither hindering nor promoting, but preferring cultural leadership instead. This vacuum of political stewardship has resulted in a widespread lack of interest, understanding, and knowledge on the part of individuals and has influenced the definition of Basqueness while advocating the status quo, which was the PNV. Although there may be a self-selecting nonpolitical bias reflected in comments by respondents associated with Basque centers, nonmembers have not established any political-action groups in any of these host countries either, nor have the HB or the PNV had relations with Basque groups from outside the centers in these six countries (Karmelo Landa interview, Euskadi, 1996; M. Egibar e-mail communication 1997; I. Aguirre interview, Brooklyn, 1999). My research data indicates that homeland definitions of Basqueness have progressed to a more civic nationalism, whereas diaspora definitions tend to preserve the traditional conservative Sabino Arana definition. Continuing chain migration into Belgium's Basque community and its more numerous transnational networks have kept it closer to contemporary homeland ideologies, but the other diaspora communities seem to be promulgating an early-twentieth-century Basque nationalism.

There were no significant differences between males' and females' responses on any questions regarding definitions of "Basqueness," demonstrating that gender does not seem to affect the definition or attitudes toward factors of

Basque identity. Politically, males were more likely to claim knowledge of homeland politics and more likely to favor separatism. Though living in dissimilar societies with varying attitudes regarding gender roles, diaspora males and females do not vary significantly in their attitudes by host country, generation, or age.

Attitudes toward autonomy and stateless political power are especially pertinent here because diasporas can be precisely that—a form of stateless power. However, because of diaspora Basques' general preference for ethnonationalism over political nationalism and their proclivity for selecting cultural rather than political factors for their identity, the Basque diaspora will not likely shift course to engage in transnational political networks.

Chapter Five

Basque Ethnicity Affirmation and Maintenance

Basque diaspora populations have historically demonstrated their preferences for cultural rather than political activities relating to ethnic identity maintenance in their individual actions, Basque center activities, and now in their direct personal responses to my interviews and questionnaire. Specifically *which* traditions are maintained, and *how*, in these six countries will be examined in this chapter. The question of *why* this Basque identity persists is equally intriguing, and statements from interviews will be incorporated with questionnaire results from individuals.

The formation of diaspora communities seems to be common in many human migrations. Personal and institutional networks transmit information between home communities and diaspora communities and back again. The degree to which these networks are maintained by members of an ethnic community is critical to the establishment of patterns of migration and to a strong sense of ethnic identity and the creation of a community outside the ethnic homeland. Murphy and Leeper distinguish the ethnic institutions that are of particular importance in establishing these networks:

1. Formal and informal family and community institutions;
2. Religious institutions;
3. Economic associations, which are often closely linked with ethnic political organizations;
4. Cultural organizations, which promote both internal cohesion of ethnic identity (informal institutions) and interaction with host societies (formal organizations). (Murphy and Leeper 1996)

I will indicate the role played by these ethnic networks and institutions in the Basque diaspora specifically and focus on how the core elements of Basque diaspora identity are defined in a constant manner and how Basque ethnic institutions fomenting cultural activities have developed according to similar patterns. I have suggested that a resurgence in this cultural ethnic identity salience is related to globalization, though not a partner in a causal relationship nor a defensive reaction to it. I will now explore the veracity of these statements, utilizing past research and diaspora questionnaire and interview results.

When considering the question of identity, Ernest Gellner's "potato principle" (1983) refers to the strong territorial identity and feeling of "rootedness" that he assumes to be prevalent among peasants where social mobility is limited and people are tied to places and kinship networks. This contrasts with more fluid identities in more modern societies. It may be that these Basque emigrés, coming mainly from agricultural environments, chose to recreate the "rootedness" of their homeland in their new host societies, but they did so regardless of whether their host society was industrialized at the time they emigrated. Again, this was not a reaction to industrialization or modernization per se, but rather to the migration itself. T. H. Eriksen believes social identity becomes most important when it becomes threatened, which is often related to some kind of change, such as migration (Eriksen 1993, 68). An assured continuity with the past, which can be a weighty source of self-respect and self-authenticity in an alien society, is fundamental to a sense of belonging. I will describe and analyze Basque diaspora ethnicity maintenance by exploring these assumptions and questioning the impact of globalization.

Social, Educational, and Cultural Functions of Basque Institutions

The development of migrant networks and institutions is studied in theories of chain migration, networks, and in defining cultural capital (Boyd 1989; Fawcett 1989; Coleman 1993). Ethnic networks comprise relationships that link former, current, and future migrants. Van Hear (1998) dissects networks and their importance to chain migration and disseminating information about means of travel and entry, finding accommodation and employment, and adaptation to new environments. Even though the disruption in a migrant's life may be overwhelming, the "organic development of personal, family, kin, friendship, community and ethnic ties mean the networks are the strongest when they embrace links with the established populations of the countries of destination" (Van Hear 1998, 60).

The networks enhance migrants' capacities to adapt to new circumstances. In these case studies, the web of Basque centers provided the fundamental link toward adaptation. Diaspora associations, especially those that have a physical office or cultural Basque center, help fortify inter-Basque networking for friendship, employment, information, and news of the homeland. Newcomers, whether visiting or studying, still tend to go directly to the community's Basque center for instant companionship and information.

The Basque collectivities have progressed over time in very similar manners. Since the 1612 founding of the Confraternity of Our Lady of Aranzazu of the Basque Nation in Lima and the founding of the Confraternity of the

Basque Nation in Arequipa, Peru, in 1630, through the 1800s in Argentina and Uruguay, and later in the other countries I studied, *socorros mútuos* (mutual-aid societies for alleviating the costs of medical care, funerals, and repatriation) have been present in every country case study. They have provided local Basques with familial-type networks, financial aid for health care, communications with family in the homeland, and repatriation costs.

Basques in the Buenos Aires area created the Euskal Echea (Basque Home) in 1901, an institution for Basque senior-citizens' retirement, and simultaneously a boarding-school facility for Basque children. It still functions successfully as initially planned—a care center and home for the elderly surrounded by the energy of children. Throughout Argentina and the United States, Basque-owned boardinghouses and their employees served as surrogate homes and families where Basques could stay short-term while traveling to town for doctor visits or live during the off-season of agriculture or livestock raising. In Argentina, the United States, and on a smaller scale in Uruguay and Australia, these Basque "hotels" served as information centers for news from Euskal Herria and for networking for employment (J. Echeverría 1999; Douglass 1996; Mendiolea Uriguen Larrazabal interview, Townsville, Australia, 1997). In Argentina, stores and markets also served as meeting places for Basques (Iriani 2000). The significance of the facilities emanates from chain migration, which fomented continued interaction with contemporary information and attitudes directly from the homeland for inter-Basque-community relations (homeland to diaspora) as well as intra-Basque-community relations (Basque to Basque inside one ethnic community in the host society).

Once employment stabilized and single Basque immigrants were joined by families, permanent housing diminished the need for boardinghouses, and as Basque employment in agriculture decreased so did the numbers of customers. The transformation resulted from the end of chain migration and there no longer being a need for a "home away from home." Basques had made their own homes, whether in the rural pampas, the sugarcane fields, the Sierra Nevada, or the cosmopolitan cities of Montevideo, Sydney, and New York. Established immigrants no longer needed temporary room and board or an informal employment agency; they needed a place to socialize, to communicate with others in their own language, and to practice their own traditions and culture. The institutions of the boardinghouse and the Basque hotel were replaced by the Basque center.

CULTURAL ADAPTATION

Basque immigrants creating and recreating these centers have chosen to emphasize similar elements of Basque identity. Basque diaspora culture has been constructed, reconstructed, blended, rediscovered, and reinterpreted—combining the past, present, and expectations for the future in the immigrants' self-definition of Basqueness. Just as homeland Basque culture has developed and changed, so have the diaspora cultures, and much in the same way.

The Basque diaspora's institutions have transformed and developed, as have the demands from their members. Initially, immigrants needed employment and social services, to learn the host country's language, and to understand the host country's social, political, and economic institutions; in contrast, the later generations need the reverse—to maintain cultural attachment to their heritage and homeland. Individuals participate in ethnic choral and dance ensembles, language and cooking classes, athletic activities, dinners and dances, and various festivals. The original functions of the Basque networks and organizations, as with ethnic organizations in other host societies, were intended to reduce the strain of the newcomer status and facilitate cultural adaptation. The Basque centers provided immigrants with economic and social services, along with instant acceptance, friendship, and belonging. Older interviewees praised the organizations' volunteers, who aided their families' acculturation, and several confessed that they might not have successfully endured without the haven of a center to escape to, or the anticipation of a monthly Basque dinner or ethnic gathering. The efforts of women volunteers to aid newcomers in day-to-day integration were lauded by numerous interviewees in each country.

Ethnic identities are created through time and subsequent generations, and through space as immigrants carry culture from one place to another. The progression of these Basque collectivities include the development of a diasporic community while simultaneously reacting to the effects of continued immigration. The new immigrants' incorporation into the established diaspora community could pose various problems. Sometimes, new immigrants disappointed older immigrants by not sharing their values, because of course the homeland's culture had evolved during the time since the older generation left. New immigrants might also be disappointed to find a diasporic community focused on the past and on historical myths and nostalgia that were not a part of their generation's homeland reality. Basque diaspora communities that experienced frequent contact with the homeland or continuous chain migration were less likely to experience cultural conflict or cultural authenticity conflict, or disparate cultural identities between established and recent immigrants.

Interviews with more recent immigrants revealed that upon arrival in the new host society they were likely to categorize the established Basques negatively as "out of touch with homeland reality," "Basque nationalists from the prewar period, even though it was the 1970s," or as "living in the past."

Earlier immigrants were likely to describe more recent immigrants as "troublemakers," "probably ETA sympathizers who don't know their own history," or "more Marxist than Basque." The Basque centers' apolitical stances helped alleviate divisions between generations of Basques and promoted integration by focusing on cultural aspects of Basque identity that were not time- or generation-specific.

The end of continuous Basque immigration has changed the necessary function of today's organizations to that of cultural identity defenders and preservers. Participation in these centers is voluntary and now serves psychological, emotional, and social fulfillment rather than economic need. Daily member-to-member interaction has been replaced by monthly dinners and social gatherings, *mus* card game tournaments, annual festival celebrations, and institutional newsletters. The same organizations that provided host-country language classes and found accommodation and employment for recent Basque immigrants are now disseminating genealogical information for Basques to research their heritage, teaching Basque rather than the host-country language, collecting travel brochures about Euskal Herria, and helping members organize tours to their homeland. Basque immigrants initially needed the services that these organizations provided; later generations, however, are optional consumers.

Basque diaspora organizations' roles have changed significantly, as exemplified by a historical Basque Museum and Cultural Center in the United States, and by various organizations in Argentina devoted to researching and preserving the history of Basques *in Argentina,* not in the homeland. Whereas Jewish, Polish, Irish, Armenian, and Italian diasporic ethnic communities have mobilized politically for antidiscrimination and political representation in many host countries (Erdmans 1995; Bakalian 1993; Waters 1990; Alba 1990), Basque organizations have stressed cultural more often than political activities and have mobilized occasionally for homeland politics but not for host-society representation.

As the needs met by Basque diaspora institutions involve fewer daily survival functions for Basque immigrants and their descendants, it may become more difficult for these cultural organizations to interest and enroll new members. They are now focusing almost entirely on the preservation of Basque culture and no longer serve to aid integration into host-country culture. Recent migrants are more likely to be temporary and to have entered their respective host countries with employment contracts and already established contacts. Because they have no need to join ethnic organizations in order to remind themselves of or to "prove" their Basqueness, they "have no need for the institutions as they have evolved today." There are multiple examples from each case-study country where very recent Basque immigrants living in one of the six host societies do not participate in local Basque association functions (dinners, dances, festivals, choirs, art shows, and so on) because they simply are not interested (Urquizu interview, Buenos Aires, 1997; Pagoaga Gallastegui interview, Brussels, 1997; Mendibelzua interview, Brussels, 1997; Urriz Larragan interview, Brussels, 1997). "I know I am Basque and I don't need to go to the Basque center dinners and sing old songs to prove I am Basque to anyone" (German Garbizu interview, Lima, 1996). The organizations need the new immigrants, however, for authenticity, legitimacy, language regeneration, and updating personal networks with the homeland.

The economy of the Basque Country has progressed, and there are now many more opportunities for employment in Euskal Herria and in the European Union. Continual democratic change in Spain has all but ended the compulsion for political exile. There are no longer significant numbers of new emigrants to any of these six countries, with the exception of Belgium and the administrative functionaries living in Brussels who are employed by the Basque Government Delegation or by institutions of the European Union.[1] They do not consider themselves immigrants, but they do influence the existing permanent Basque population in Belgium with chain-migration factors. Because the diaspora population is maturing, there are no longer formal institutional networks or programs to provide for immigrants, and sporadic needs are usually accommodated informally by personal networking with activists from the Basque communities.

Basque ethnics have the best of both worlds because Basque institutions do not usually make any demands on their members. Manifestation of ethnic identity is completely voluntary for later-generation Basques who speak their host-country language perfectly and form a part of Christian-European host societies where white Catholics fit in and participate in the dominant state religion (as, for example, in Argentina, Uruguay, and Peru). The host society does not tend to categorize and separate them as Basques, although they may identify and separate themselves as Basques. It is a "community without cost" (Waters 1990, 149). The social and political costs and consequences of being Basque are quite different than those of nonwhite and/or non-Christian ethnic groups in all six countries. Though there were respondents whose Basque ethnicity favored them for employment, in the greater part of these Basques' daily lives their ethnicity does not matter (housing, schooling, social integration, etc.). They tend to take for granted that, when it does matter, it is largely a matter of personal choice for positive status or for enjoyment. It may be that for each Basque person, ethnic identity maintenance is voluntary, costless, and a matter of personal preference. However, it is made ever so much easier because they live in societies dominated by Christians of European descent. The selective aspects of voluntary ethnicity are so easy and enjoyable for many Basque individuals because they do not experience the racism connected to their ethnicity that Asians, Middle Easterners, or Africans do in these same countries.

However, ethnicity is historically variable, and it did have costs for Basques in different locations and time periods. Catholics were not particularly welcomed in the United States, and several interviewees in Idaho and Nevada stated that they were discriminated against at school, being called "black Basco," and when seeking employment, because of their Catholic religion. Nevertheless, Catholicism was not so different a religion to necessitate the establishment of religious institutions for ethnic purposes, as is the case for the Jewish, Armenian, or Chinese diasporas. In areas with substantial Basque populations, the Vatican sent Basque priests to the diaspora, and there were regular Catholic masses in the Basque language. There are still Basque priests in San Francisco, Sydney, and Buenos Aires assigned to the diaspora populations. Other Basque priests have coincidentally been sent to areas that have large Basque populations (which are not difficult to find in South America) but have not been sent specifically as Basque priests for a Basque population. Many of those priests coincidentally assigned between the 1970s and 1990s did not speak Basque anyway.

In analyzing the comparative adaptation of immigrants to Australia and their emotional and psychological health, Scott and Scott determined that most immigrants tend to regard their new circumstances as an improvement over those they left behind, except in the areas of employment and friendship, and that those who settle in rural areas tend to be more satisfied with their jobs and are better assimilated. Men are more likely than women to profess emotional well-being and high self-esteem (Scott and Scott 1989, 168–69). My interviews of Basques supported this research, with males more likely to talk about their varied employment, meeting new friends at work, and learning the host-society language and customs, while many women discussed the loneliness and difficulties experienced while working at home without significant adult companionship, friendships, and communication skills. Those who emigrated from rural areas in Euskal Herria to urban regions in their new settings also experienced this additional rupture in their understanding of their surroundings.

ETHNOMUSICOLOGY: COMPOSING A DIASPORA IDENTITY

For diaspora populations, the study of the combination of ethnicity, identity, and music, known as ethnomusicology, is central to linking homeland and "here-land" with a network of sounds connecting the memories of childhood with the present. Ethnic music is a symbolic mode of affiliation for present-day diaspora Basques. Preservation of music, and in particular choral music, is an element of ethnicity maintenance in each of the case studies. Though the choirs of Australia are less formally organized, and that in Belgium is temporarily disbanded during the construction of a new Basque center, very similar types of music have served as the cornerstones of their repertoires. Many have nationalist lyrics, and the repertoires of Basque choirs are often filled with patriotic love songs to the homeland. Music is highly portable and "is an extraordinary multi-layered channel of communication, nesting language itself, that primary agent of identity, within a series of strata of cultural meaning . . . before the microchip, music has been wired into the mobile body, forming earliest memories and later evoking deep-set emotions" (Slobin 1994, 244). Ethnomusicologists argue that perhaps only the aroma of familiar foods has the same power to evoke memory, and "music makes specific connections with family members, politics, and significant moments for which melodies are the milestone" (ibid.).

Basque organizations affirm these links through music with formal and informal performances by established Basque choirs and various genre musicians, by teaching folksongs to children, and with background music at social and cultural events. The seemingly mundane piped-in music in Basque center bars and restaurants, as well as the music performed at religious masses and celebrations and during festivals for singing and dancing all contribute to the shared memories, experiences, and connectedness of the diaspora Basques. Musical performances in each of the six countries were very similar, with homages to the Tree of Gernika, national anthems, nationalistic hymns of fallen warriors, and mothers' lullabies. The love songs are not to people but to Euskal Herria, and there are both traditional and contemporary examples.

Young people who travel to the homeland return with the latest CDs of Basque folk rock by such performers as Oskorri, Ruper Ordorika, Xabier Lete, Txomin Artola, Amaia Zubiria, and Benito Lertxundi, who all sing in Basque. Although many diaspora customers do not understand the language, they recognize the melodies. Many homeland performers, such as Ene Bada, Alboka, and Tapia eta Leturia, have become popular enough to travel to Basque festivals in Uruguay, Argentina, Venezuela, Mexico, and the United States for successful tours to Basque collectivities. Consequently, when first-time travelers to Euskal Herria participate in the fiestas and social scene, they recognize the music and can sing along with the homeland populations, and when visiting other diaspora communities' Basque-festival celebrations, they also are "insiders." Music is often the main means of identification for diasporic groups, as well as local and regional subcultures (Gastezi interview 1998). Regardless of age, respondents agreed overwhelmingly (between 89 and 96 percent) that "singing traditional songs in Basque" is of "some," "great," or "very great importance" to them. Geographical location did not seriously affect attitudes, with between 84 percent in Australia and 96 percent in both Uruguay and the

United States agreeing to music's importance. It is not uncommon for individuals to be able to sing a song in Basque and not understand a single word.

Almost every Basque collectivity has initiated a folk-dance group. Numbering anywhere from a few adolescents to troupes of sixty young adults, these groups have served the purpose of ethnic socialization for youth and entertainment at ethnic functions. The larger groups also perform for non-Basque gatherings and educate the host-country public about Basque culture. *Txistularis* (players of a unique three-holed Basque flute) and accordionists accompany the dancers and often give their own separate performances. Conversations with spectators at musical performances and festivals revealed that because the *txistu* is a Basque instrument, it is preferred over accordions, guitars, and pianos—not because audiences enjoyed the sound more—it can be quite shrill—but because they equated Basque functions with Basque music played on Basque instruments.

The dancing groups and choirs have served as powerful factors in ethnic socialization because dancers and musicians share their ethnic identity experiences as a group. Peer encouragement to remain active in association programs is tied to personal friendships and loyalties, strengthening the desire to continue membership and interest. Performers learn the meanings of the dances and the lyrics and coincidentally learn the history and anthropology of Euskal Herria. Older interviewees in communities with established dance groups or choirs regularly mentioned that they had made most of their Basque friends as youngsters in a choir or dance group. These musical associations then tie members to the music and its symbolism and language, to each other, and to their youth.

PRESERVATION OF TRADITIONS AND CULTURE

In every case of this research, if there was a physical Basque center, there was a kitchen. The association of ethnic identity with ethnic food, as mentioned above, is strong. Basque centers typically offer monthly membership dinners and several special-occasion feasts with Basque-style selections ranging from typical peasant home-cooking to contemporary Basque nouvelle cuisine. As in the homeland, often it is the men who rule these *txokos*, or private kitchens, though home-cooking tends to remain the domain of the women. Although 91 percent of the total respondents believed that it is of "some," "great," or "very great" importance to "teach and use Basque cuisine and food preparation in our homes," the reality was that a combined average of 63 percent actually do prepare Basque-style meals in their homes at least "a few times a month." When combining "every day," "about once a week," and "a few times a month," there were no significant differences in gender responses, although in personal interviews a few males confessed that they did not really know which of the dishes their wives prepared were Basque-style or something else. There were differences in country responses, which tend to reflect past and recent migration and specific details of Basque organization activities. In Peru, a substantial number of men meet every Thursday to create a Basque-style meal for each other, demonstrating and maintaining cuisine as a significant factor in their lives and in the activities of the Lima Euskal Etxea. Recent migration to Belgium shows emigrant and first-generation Basques preserving food traditions. Overall, 96 percent of interviewees in Belgium reported eating Basque-style food at home "at least a few times every month," compared to 93 percent in Peru, 75 percent in Australia, 73 percent in the U.S., 56 percent in Argentina, and 33 percent in Uruguay.

Earlier migration being to Argentina and Uruguay translates to fourth-and fifth-generation Basques continuing cooking traditions. If the next category of "a few times a year" is included, Argentina would add another 36 percent and Uruguay another 43 percent. Cross-tabulations of generation and cooking frequencies show a steady decline in Basque-style food preparation with later generations. From those born in Euskal Herria to the fourth generation or more born in their host countries, combining the percentages for eating Basque-style food at home "at least a few times a month," the percentages follow a pattern: born in Euskal Herria, 89 percent; first-generation, born in host country, 73 percent; second-generation, born in host country, 51 percent; third-generation, born in host country, 31 percent; and fourth- or later-generation, born in host country, 30 percent.

Many of the Basque centers in Uruguay, Argentina, and the United States have restaurants attached that are open to the general public. Cooking classes are organized sporadically, but few people participate regularly. The Basque government has sponsored diaspora tours by homeland award-winning chefs, and centers and private restaurants in Mexico, Venezuela, and Chile have hired Basque chefs to infuse the tradition of ethnic cooking (Garritz interview 1999). Mexico enjoys a separate Basque center devoted entirely to Basque cuisine, the Sukalde Asociación Civil. Several centers have annual celebrations of Basque gastronomy, and in Necochea, Argentina, there is a week-long festival of Basque food.

Card-playing, whether for the International *Mus* Tournament Championship of Basque diaspora collectivities in twenty-one countries or sitting at a Basque center bar playing for fun, produces another avenue for ethnic identity reinforcement and shared experiences. Twenty years ago, Sunday nights would find the majority of Basque centers in all six countries filled with *mus* and *briska* players (Totorikaguena de Velasco interview, Buenos Aires, 1997; Juan Pedro Arin interview, Montevideo, 1996, Oribe interview, Melbourne, 1997; Igartua interview, Lima, 1999; Salazar interview, Sidney, 1999), but today the typical generation gap exists. The grandparent and teenage generations are present, playing cards, football, or *pelota* (Basque handball), or practicing their dancing. The missing generation is that in the parenting years, between the ages of twenty-five and fifty.

The Basque diaspora world congresses in 1995 and 1999 stressed as a matter of utmost importance—as did every interviewee in a position of center leadership in all six countries—their fear of a collapse of the Basque centers if the current generation does not "come back" to its roots.[2] The Basque associations do not collect generational data from their members, so there is no consistent available information about which generations these members represent. My research was conducted on stratified samples to ensure the representation of each generation. However, respondents were asked on the questionnaire whether family members before them, and currently, participated in Basque institutions in the host country, or whether they were the first in their extended family to participate. Results show there are many first-timers. Overall, in responses from the fourth generation or more born in the host country, 52 percent were "the first one involved from my family," which demonstrates a turn to ethnicity by those not previously participating in diaspora ethnic institutions.

Broken down by generation, 52 percent of respondents born in Euskal Herria indicated that they were the first in their families to participate in a Basque organization in their host countries. Among the first generation born in the host country, 16 percent were the first in their families to participate; among the second generation, 25 percent; among the third generation, 39 percent; and among the fourth generation, 52 percent. Broken down by host country, in order of the major migration periods, 63 percent of respondents in Belgium identified themselves as the first in their family to participate in a diaspora Basque organization; 35 percent of those in Australia; 39 percent of those in Peru (although Peru experienced the earliest migration during Spanish colonization, people currently involved in the Basque center represent migration during the 1920s); 18 percent of those in the U.S.; 33 percent of those in Argentina; and 49 percent of those in Uruguay. These figures support the figures given for interest by generation: it appears that throughout the diaspora, ethnic interest ebbs in the first generations after immigration then rises in subsequent generations.

Since 1985, there has been unprecedented institutional growth in the Basque diaspora; there are thirty-nine additional Argentine Basque diaspora organizations, some new and some re-established, ten in the United States, and six in Uruguay. Belgium is re-creating its one center in Brussels, and in the North Queensland area of Australia activists are making plans for initiating a Basque cultural association. With new societies being formed and previously established organizations attracting people who have not participated before, perhaps the centers are healthier than they think. Twenty-six percent of the respondents had "never married and had no children," but 34 percent had "children [who] participated as youth and continue to participate," or "children [who] did not participate as youth, but currently do." Compare this to 23 percent of those having "children [who] participated as youth, but no longer do" or "children [who] did not participate as youth, nor do they currently." Both trends—the later generations joining the organizations as first-timers and more children continuing on with their parents than are leaving or not participating—point to maintenance, and possibly growth, in the numbers of Basques identifying with their ethnicity through community centers and associations. Anthropologists have argued that ethnicity becomes more important late in life (Stoller 1996; Climo 1990; Simic 1985) and also when consolidating a new identity, as teenagers do, or when people become parents, move, or retire. These numbers look to a promising future for the ethnic institutions.

The Basque collectivities also promulgate the continuation of Basque sports and athletic events. The same activities are practiced regardless of country: competitions in wood-chopping, weight-carrying and weight-lifting, team tug-of-wars, *jai alai*, *pelota* (handball), and *pala* (similar to racquetball). Though the weight-carrying, lifting, and wood-chopping are for exhibitions during festivals, there are regular games of *pelota* and *pala*, and if the *frontón* (court) is large enough, *jai alai* is also played. International exchanges and tournaments of *pelota* and *pala* players for festivals are common and enthusiastically received by Basque audiences. Teaching and "practicing the Basque sports such as *pelota, jai alai*, wood-chopping, weight-carrying, and lifting" were singled out for "some," "great," or "very great" importance to the respondents, from a low of 70 percent in Belgium to a high of 93 percent each in Peru, the United States, and Uruguay, where there are numerous public and privately owned *frontóns* in addition to those at the Basque centers. However, the numerous *frontóns* are often devoid of players. In each country, there is a national players' association whose leaderships are extremely worried that interest in these Basque sports might die out. There is much encouragement from the organizations and the crowds, but the physical hardship of handball played by Basque rules (no hand protection whatsoever) deters younger players from learning. The nerve damage, permanent swelling, and hand surgeries suffered by experienced players easily convince youngsters to try other athletic entertainment.

At the American Congress of Basque Centers in Buenos Aires in 1997, the groundwork was laid by diaspora organization delegates to create a network of Basque libraries for interlibrary loans and information exchange. Many of the facilities in Argentina, Uruguay, Chile, Venezuela, Mexico, and the United States served as repositories for Basque government-in-exile documents, and there are thousands of publications in the diaspora that are not available in

Euskal Herria itself (Ugalde interview 1999; Larumbe and Astigarraga 1997). Masses of clandestine materials were smuggled out of the Basque Country during the Civil War and the Franco dictatorship, and exiles in diaspora communities published their own works from the safety of their host societies. Utilization of the library exchanges will greatly depend on researchers' language abilities in Spanish and Basque.

Though the library materials have been available for decades, interviews with librarians in each country revealed that few members utilize these vast resources. One librarian stated, and others agreed, that "it takes much time and effort to read all this old and very formal Spanish. Unless the person is doing research or is an historian or anthropologist they are not coming in here to wrack their brains. In Lima we are starting to receive children's books from the Basque Government, but unless a parent is teaching his children Basque, no one is interested in that either" (Guarrotxena Larragán interview, Lima, 1996). There is, however, general interest in the history books. Over 88 percent of all respondents believed that learning about their history and about other Basques in the diaspora to be of "great" or "very great" importance, but going to the center, browsing through the sources, and actually checking out and reading a book takes time and energy. In any society, whether immigrant or native, some people are motivated enough to do it, but a majority are not.

Basque diaspora associations provide newsletters that facilitate information distribution in host countries and often have short articles in the Basque language, which the majority of the readership cannot understand. These newsletters are more social in nature and record the marriages, births, and deaths of members, remind readers of upcoming ethnic events and fund-raisers, and may include special vignettes of Basque culture, history, or anthropology to educate their audiences. Many Basque associations exchange newsletters between and within countries, expanding the ethnic imagination of their readers. Today, ten to fifteen organizations also post their newsletters on the Internet for the diaspora audience.

There is a wide variety of additional ethnic activities carried out through the Basque organizations, ranging from art exhibitions to lectures and conferences on literature, to medical research of Basque physiology. Those interested in a given topic are encouraged to establish meetings or seminars and to invite and educate others regarding their interest. The most important aspect of the associations may be the informal socialization that takes place among the Basques themselves. Whether sitting at the bar cheering a football team, enjoying a wedding celebration, or attending a Basque cinema event, the exchange of information and shared experiences tie these people to each other through their Basque connections, reinforcing the associations' and the individuals' identities.

Language Maintenance

Linguists argue that language makes order possible in the world. It functions as the organ of thought, conscience, and reflection, granting the spirit and the mind autonomy over experience. It also provides a basis of support for one's identity (Grinberg and Grinberg 1989). The Basque organizations have served as the motor for language maintenance and preservation. During the twentieth century, because of continued migration, Basque was often spoken at center events and celebrations, though second- and third-generation members usually joined speaking only the host-country language. With the end of chain migration, the necessity of learning Euskera to communicate with monolingual immigrants diminished, and the Basque speakers already present lost the opportunity to communicate in their native language with native speakers.

Currently, there are various combinations of bi- and trilingualism (utilizing two or three languages interchangeably) and diglossia (utilizing one language for specific situations and a different language for other specific situations). In diaspora Basque families, it is not uncommon to find parents who speak to each other in Basque but to their children in French or Spanish, or children who speak to their parents in Basque, Spanish, or French but to their siblings in the host-country language. In the United States and Australia, there are later generations who speak English and Basque, some who speak English and French, some who speak English and Spanish, and some who speak only English. Similar combinations exist in Spanish-speaking Argentina, Uruguay, and Peru, and among the French-speaking Belgians.

Changes in social identity are accompanied by changes in language attitudes, favoring host-country language over the homeland language (Gudykunst 1988), and the necessity of communication skills for education and employment make the host-country language fundamental. However, according to ethnic studies in migration and language development, many immigrants feel alienated, as though they are "in disguise" when they speak the new language, and that they have lost the language in which they feel "authentic" (Grinberg and Grinberg 1989, 112). Children seem to assimilate new languages more easily than adults, and in these case studies of Basques, the child immigrant often became the interpreter for Basque parents, which reversed the roles of authority and respect.

Later-generation interviewees often articulated that they wished their parents had forced them to learn and speak Basque. They lamented that they had ridiculed their parents for not speaking in the host-country language perfectly, or for their "embarrassing" accents. In the South American countries, participants were especially remorseful that they had not learned Basque, because since their parents already spoke Spanish, they only had to learn one other language. Though there are trilingual families, interviewees in Australia and the United States explained that they, or their parents, had to decide which language to use at home—Basque, Spanish, or French—and usually Spanish or French was selected. Immigrants believed they needed to give their children an economic advantage with a second language, and most immigrated during the Franco years when Basque was outlawed, had very low status as a language of peasants, and was diminishing in utility.

> Why should I teach my daughter Basque when people in the Basque Country don't even speak it? Everyone there speaks Spanish, and she can also travel anywhere in South America or get a job for a Latino company in Brussels. (Zabala interview, Antwerp, 1999)

> My parents spoke to us in Basque not out of any political or identity statement but because they spoke to their own parents in Basque and because they spoke to each other in Basque. I think in their village, Nabarniz, they didn't really speak Spanish, so maybe they [the parents] didn't really know it very well when they came to Australia. (Achurra Etxebarria interview, Ayr, Australia, 1997)

> Oh God, we were so embarrassed to go anywhere with Ama. We thought she was really dumb. Actually I guess we thought other people would think she was dumb. *We* were so ignorant. She'd talk to us in Basque in front of our friends. We didn't understand that she was so much smarter than us for all she had learned and overcome. My mom knows English, Spanish, Basque, and some French. Now who's dumb? (Lasuen Arrieta interview, Emmett, Idaho, 1999)

Euskera as a factor of individual Basque ethnic identity has lost much of its importance among these diaspora populations. In Euskal Herria itself, various areas were totally hispanicized by the mid-1800s, and later, during the Franco era, Basque was outlawed as a means of communication. Consequently, many emigrants of the political-exile era did not themselves speak Basque. Though Basques are extremely proud of their unique language and its complexity, most do not consider it an important factor in their own personal ethnicity. As seen in chapter 4, speaking Basque as a prerequisite for "being Basque" has also lost support in the diaspora populations.[3]

Though traditional Sabino Arana Basque nationalism stressed the importance of the Basque language, and the last influential wave of migration was of people with this ideology, Basques in these diaspora countries no longer consider this of such importance. Because so many of them do not speak Euskara, they would not want to eliminate themselves from their own category. There are no significant differences between the responses of males and females. Language loss is evident from the data in table 5.1, which shows how few Basques are actually able to speak and utilize Euskera, and how many are illiterate in their ancestral language. Respondents were asked to describe their linguistic abilities and frequency of usage. Overall, only 5 percent use Basque regularly, and another 5 percent "use Basque every day, switching back and forth between languages and using Basque equally with other languages." Australian and United States Basques had the highest frequencies in both categories.

It is important to compare the first and second columns indicating knowledge and use of Basque. Many respondents know a few words but do not actually use them. For example, in Peru, 46 percent of respondents know more than just a few words and selected either "a basic conversation," "fluent with some difficulty," or "fluent" to describe their language knowledge. But only 15 percent are using their Basque for more than just a special greeting or

TABLE 5.1 Language Knowledge, Usage, and Literacy by Host Country and by Age Category

	"I know only a few words" or "none" %	"I only use Basque for special phrases" or "None" %	"I can write a few words in Basque" or "None" %
Host Country			
Uruguay	94	98	95
Argentina	69	84	68
Peru	54	85	54
United States	41	67	58
Belgium	38	71	46
Australia	37	53	56
Age Category			
18–30	65	77	65
31–45	60	77	70
46–60	60	76	70
61–75	50	73	59
76–90	32	63	54

Total respondents = 832

special phrase. The higher numbers in column 2 reflect a lack of language *usage*, which is different than language *knowledge*. Sociolinguists who study language planning, language shift, and language vitality and death have demonstrated that if a population does not utilize the language it knows (however little that might be), the decline in usage is followed by people not even learning it (Fishman 1989, 1997; Fishman et al. 1985). This reflects the situation of the Basque diaspora population.

There are Basque-language programs at the Basque centers in Argentina, Uruguay, Australia, and the United States; university language courses in Argentina and the United States, and *ikastolas* (Basque-language schools for preschool through approximately year eight) in Argentina and the United States. Although the students and parents put forth a tremendous effort, sociolinguistic studies demonstrate that without a social or economic reason for learning and using a language, it is not likely to be maintained. Diaspora Basques can use Euskera with each other (if they both know it), but they can also utilize their host-country language. When traveling or communicating with relatives in Euskal Herria, those from Peru, Argentina, and Uruguay can easily use Spanish, and those from Belgium might use French. It is the Australian and United States Basques who must learn a second language to communicate with other Basques in the homeland or in the diaspora, and they tend to take school courses in French and Spanish. Interviewees in Australia and the U.S. often mentioned the economic benefits of learning Spanish or French for future employment, whereas those in Argentina, Uruguay, and Belgium were learning English. Ironically, French-speaking Basques from Belgium and Spanish-speaking Basques from Uruguay have utilized English rather than Basque to communicate with each other over the Internet.

Homeland Connections

The preservation of contact with the homeland is a defining feature of any diaspora. Globalization may make contact more efficient and convenient, but each of these many generations of Basques has maintained relationships with their respective homeland generations utilizing the means of communication of their time—word of mouth, written letters, telephone conversations, faxes, videos, then e-mail, video conferencing, real-time chat rooms, and frequent physical visits home.

Links to the ancestral homeland based on family ties diminish with each generation removed from the immigrants' experience, and the diasporic associations have assumed the responsibility for reconnecting members to their ethnicity. Some respondents were never disconnected and have always felt themselves attached to Euskal Herria. Tölölyan (1996) distinguishes between ethnic community and diasporic community in the latter's commitment to maintaining ties with the homeland and with other kin groups outside the homeland. Basques certainly exhibit a diaspora mentality and imagine themselves as connected to the homeland and to each other through the following networks.

ECONOMIC AND PERSONAL TIES TO EUSKAL HERRIA

In addition to stock-market investments and banking accounts, diaspora Basques also maintain other material and financial links to Euskal Herria by means of property and/or business ownership. These include a wide range of interests and are not only family inheritances remaining from decades ago; 46 percent of those with financial ties were individuals under forty-five who visit the Basque Country regularly. Among Basques in Belgium, 57 percent reported financial and/or material ties to Euskal Herria; in Peru, 31 percent had such ties; in Australia, 25 percent; in the U.S., 17 percent; in Argentina, 12 percent; and in Uruguay, 7 percent.

The majority of these Basques keep themselves informed about homeland current events and issues through personal contacts at least once a year (every participant in Belgium and Peru reported that they communicate with friends and family in Euskal Herria at least once a year; in Argentina, only 8 percent did *not*; in Australia, 10 percent did not; in the U.S., 12 percent did not; and in Uruguay, 15 percent did not) and by regularly reading newspapers or journals from, or with information about, the Basque Country. Though Australia's respondents demonstrated a low level of frequent reading, it is important to note that Australian cable television transmits one hour of Spanish broadcast news daily, which includes stories from the Basque provinces. Interviews revealed that rather than trying to find printed information about the Basque Country, Australian respondents could just turn on the television for daily news and watch or tape-record the program. However, on a monthly basis, significant numbers everywhere reported some reading of newspapers from or about Euskal Herria: in Peru, 79 percent; in Belgium, 75 percent; in the U.S., 65 percent; in Argentina, 61 percent; in Uruguay, 39 percent; and in Australia, 34 percent.

Consistent rather than sporadic communications, together with personal connections with family, friends, and institutions, foster the diasporic mentality among these collectivities. While there is no longer continued migration of people, the chain linking the populations has become a virtual one in the imagination. Television broadcasts, information exchange, informal circulation of personal journals and newspapers, sharing music CDs and videos from the Basque provinces, and stories from personal travels all recreate and maintain ties to the homeland.

INSTITUTIONAL CONNECTIONS AMONG BASQUES

The availability of homeland media information has greatly increased through the Basque government publications made available to the diaspora organizations, such as *Euskal Etxeak,* which is published quarterly with articles concerning homeland and diaspora news and events. The Office of the Presidency of the Basque Government sends a steady stream of videocassettes to Basque centers, which were also provided with televisions and VCR equipment. The videos engage a diverse range of topics, from Basque cuisine to sporting championships to history and anthropology. Hook-ups to the Internet provided through Basque government grants have also aided those who understand computer technology. As of late 2002, there was Basque television transmission from Euskadi via satellite to cable television in Argentina, Uruguay, Venezuela, Mexico, and the eastern United States, enabling Basques in the diaspora to experience the same media communications as Basques in the homeland.

In addition to media communications, there is abundant movement of people as well. Asked if they had planned a trip to Euskal Herria before 2000 (within two or three years of the sample), more than one-third of the total answered "yes." Eliminating the oldest age group, 76–90, for whom it usually is the most difficult to travel, I found that 41 percent had plans for study or tourism in at least one of the seven provinces. There were differences between the countries in the percentages of respondents who had never lived in or visited Euskal Herria. In Belgium, the recent migration and proximity to Euskal Herria resulted in every single participant having lived in or having visited the Basque Country at some time in his or her life; but in Uruguay, 63 percent had never lived in or visited their homeland. In neighboring Argentina, with similar historical migration, 34 percent had never traveled to Euskal Herria, and in the United States, Australia, and Peru, the percentages were 17 percent, 10 percent, and 7 percent, respectively. Income did not seem to be a factor in this decision, because there was only a high of 3 percent difference between those who traveled and those who did not in each of the six cross-tabulated economic categories. Strong familial and territorial links encourage interaction and facilitate movement between the communities. Although the geographic proximity of Belgium adds to the ease of travel, everywhere it is the diasporans who are much more likely to return to visit relatives and not the reverse, emphasizing the importance of a temporary "return" to the homeland as well.

Travel and interstate exchanges between *mus* players, athletes, dancers, choirs, and elected Basque center officials in the diaspora and homeland are increasing in frequency. Various annual encounters strengthen personal and institutional networks and, most important, the diasporic mentality. Basques are allowed to experience another Basque community's festivals and to see how similar they are to those of their own community. They return to those home communities with photographs and stories of the Basque exchange and of similarities and differences between themselves—and the diasporic imagination is thus invigorated and fortified (Bastida 1998; Negueloua 1998; Goyenetche 1998). There have also been planning congresses of delegates representing Basque collectivities from all over the world, held sporadically in the 1980s and more regularly thereafter with conferences in 1989 (Argentina), 1995 (Euskal Herria), 1997 (Argentina), and 1999 and 2003 (Euskal Herria). Discussions and projects of the conferences have concentrated on such organizational issues as increasing youth membership, maintaining current programs for cultural preservation, and improving relations with the Autonomous Basque Government.

Basques have multiple and constant interconnections across state borders, and their identities are shaped according to more than one culture. Is transnationalism a transgenerational process? Many migrants have transnationalized their existence by physically moving between host and home countries, or by establishing social networks that transcend state borders. Basques who can afford it are likely to spend July and August in the homeland with relatives or friends, or by leasing an apartment there. They describe themselves as "kind of natives—kind of vacationers. I'll tell you, everyone at the market knows us and all of our neighbors know us, we feel at home there too" (Iguain and Oyarbide 1997). Many Basques have created a transnational identity for themselves that is superimposed upon civic, religious, gender, racial, and ethnic identities.

Banal Nationalism and Daily Ethnic Socialization

The idea that home decoration and jewelry choices are reinforcers of ethnonationalism has been heretofore overlooked as female triviality and therefore not worthy of academic research. However, I have found that both of these forms of expression recreate ethnic identity through the use of intimate objects and psychologically reinforce ethnicity and ethnic socialization for the individual and the family. In addition, they also demonstrate "Basqueness" to home visitors and the public. The resurgence in the use of Basque given names for children is also prevalent and marks an ethnic boundary for that person for the rest of his or her life. The Basque given name is another constant reminder, especially in Anglo societies, every time it is spelled, explained, and its pronunciation corrected, that one is Basque.

HOME DECORATION

House decoration tends to be the domain of the female head of household, and in many of these cases non-Basque women married to a Basque also tended to use ethnic symbolic objects in home decoration. A home provides the setting for modern intimacy and moral community. Values and expectations are transmitted and intensified by the objects selected for display, and many diaspora Basques utilize their homes and home decoration to create and express their identity. Photographs of family and ancestors, family farmhouses, and villages in Euskal Herria punctuate the importance of descent and connection to the Basque Country. Mementos from homeland tourist gift shops are placed in areas of importance and displayed with care.

Carved wooden busts of *amumas* (grandmothers) and *aitxitxes* (grandfathers), Tree of Gernika artistic representations, coats of arms of the seven provinces, pictures of *txistularis,* and *ikurriñas* everywhere greet visitors to thousands of homes of Basques living in the diaspora. This day-to-day reminding and remembering of one's ancestors and ethnic identity creates an example of what social psychologist Michael Billig calls "banal nationalism" (Billig 1995). Everyday habits, language, food, and the display of cultural artifacts imprint these Basques' minds and remind them that they are Basque. Interviews in each of the six countries were conducted in Basque homes, and the majority utilized ethnic cultural decoration. Though I was specifically looking for it and noticed it quite easily, the Basques welcoming me into their homes affectionately pointed out their objects, not necessarily to "prove" their Basqueness to me but to emphasize the importance their ethnicity had for them.

Basque women utilize their flag's red, green, and white for a myriad of purposes, from combinations of red, green, and white for dressing a table, to painting the house exterior and trim, to the colors of flowers planted in the garden. Several women mentioned (without being prompted) that they will not plant red and yellow flowers together because those are the colors of the Spanish flag. Whether in clothing, jewelry, or house decoration, because they use quantities of green and red, many stated that they seldom buy anything yellow just to ensure they never mistakenly put the two together. Everything from choices of wedding or funeral flowers,[4] furniture fabric to stoneware glaze seemed to be at least subconsciously affected by whether it might promote a Basque awareness, or neutrality. What is conscious is the deliberate separation of red and yellow, which when together seem to trigger a negative response, especially from emigrant and first-generation men and women.

PERSONAL ADORNMENT

Personal ornaments and jewelry have often been utilized as expressions of group identity with intense symbolic significance. In India, for example, there are rigid laws of caste that restrict the wearing of gold to people of certain groups only (Untracht 1997). In the Basque population, gold religious medals for baptisms or First Holy Communions are customary, and although some of the younger interviewees stated that they do not wear their medals regularly to host-country social functions, they almost always wear them to Basque functions. *Lauburu*[5] emblems, rings, earrings, and necklaces are also popular with males and females, as are T-shirts, baseball caps, belt buckles, and car bumper stickers with Basque themes. A few males in Australia and the United States have tattooed *lauburus* or "Euskadi" on their arms, and *ikurriñas* are sometimes found tattooed on women's ankles.

Besides public displays of Basqueness, there are also symbols closer to the heart, such as that of Juan Miguel Salaberry, an elderly gentleman from Rosario, Uruguay. For decades, Juan Miguel has worn his grandfather's *txapela* (beret) every day, and in his wallet he has carried a small tattered paper *ikurriña*. He says that together they keep him safe—the memories of his ancestors combined with the spiritual and emotional strength of Basque ethnicity (J. M. Salaberry interview, Rosario, Uruguay, 1996). After migrating to Melbourne, Nekane Kandino legally changed her given name from a Spanish "Rosarito" (Basque given names were not permitted in the four Spanish provinces during the Franco years) to the Basque "Nekane." This was an act of self-actualization for her because, as she described herself, "Being Basque is primordial. There are thousands of years of Basqueness in me. I am not Nekane who also happens to be Basque. I am Basque and that shapes how I manifest myself as Nekane" (Kandino interview, Melbourne, 1997). These insignificant daily demonstrations of Basqueness may be "banal," "symbolic," or "leisure-time ethnicity" to some academics, but for Juan Miguel and Nekane, and thousands more like them in the diaspora, maintaining Basque identity is not only a rational matter but also one of great instinct, emotion, and spirit.

Ethnic identity is increasingly voluntary in the diaspora communities to which Basques have migrated. Because Basques are not distinguishable by skin color, garments, diet, or general behavior in these European-settler countries, maintaining "Basqueness" is a choice; even in Peru, which is not a European-settler country, Basques distinguish themselves from others of European descent. Basques are marking their own group-identity boundaries rather than being marked by other outside groups, and the importance of names is an example of this phenomenon. Just as Nekane needed a Basque name to fulfill her identity, young parents of all generations are increasingly giving Basque first names to their children. There are numerous Mirens, Amaias, Nekanes, Idoias, and Maites, as well as Aitors, Kepas, Josus, Mikels, and Iñakis. In Australia and the United States, special attention must be given to how English-speaking people will pronounce (or mispronounce) a name and to the psychological impact that a unique name has on a child. As adults, interviewees stated that they are proud of their given and surnames, although as children a few hated them because of endless childhood teasing and the constant misspelling and correction of pronunciation. In the Anglo-Australian and United States societies, where it is customary for a woman to drop her own surname and assume that of her husband, Basque women in the last twenty years have increasingly not followed this practice and kept their maiden surnames when marrying a non-Basque. This is another constant demonstration and reminder of ethnic identity.

Haizpak: Sister to Sister

Geographically disconnected from each other and from their homeland, Basque women in the diaspora have endeavored to perpetuate ethnic identities for themselves and their families. Curiously, their struggles, and the ensuing results, are similar throughout the disparate settings to which they have emigrated. Women are both maintainers and modifiers of social processes, and the role of women as reproducers of ethnic ideologies is often related to women being perceived as the "cultural carriers" of that ethnic group.

Is there a Basque sisterhood, a *haizpak* (sister of a female)? Or are women always a brother's sister, *arrebak*, and defined in relation to a male? Few languages other than Basque distinguish between these different relationships. Are there established homeland women's roles that are perpetuated by diaspora women (and men)? In the 1970s and 1980s, Basque anthropologists argued the concept of a Basque matriarchy. Yet while the study of real women was brushed aside, Basque mythology about feminine identities was pervasive. However, Basque feminist anthropologists found that in Euskal Herria the elaboration of the myth of a Basque matriarchy constituted a "gendered tool" that had been used in the development of the ideology related to radical nationalism, and Basque matriarchy provided a powerful ethnic marker. Even though the arguments regarding real female power were dismantled by these analyses, the ideology affected the key issues of Basque identity and therefore continued (Del Valle et al. 1985, 44–54, quoted in Del Valle 1993).

MIGRATION EXPERIENCES

Women have essentially been omitted from early studies of migration. When considered, females are generally perceived as amendments to the men who migrate, nonthinking, nonemotional appendages with no choices, comparable to the valuable things packed in traveling trunks. They have been treated more as migrants' wives, daughters, and mothers than as migrants themselves, relegating their roles in international migration as secondary, although in some instances, such as the United States, female migrants outnumber male migrants (Brettle and Simon 1986, 4). Because women are intimately involved with men, changes in women's status affects the men and vice versa, and it is erroneous to perceive women as nonworking dependents. Many Basque men did migrate solo, planning to send home saved earnings until they could return to the homeland; when a husband and wife migrated together, the move would most likely be permanent.

In family migration, married couples tend to move to where the husband has the greatest opportunity for employment, leading to great difficulty disentangling men's and women's individual motivations and aspirations for migration (Chant 1992). Once in the host country, men tend to work outside the home, learning the host-country language, customs, and expectations, and how to "move" in the new society. The Basque woman's experience has not often been so positive, especially in the English-speaking United States and Australia. Many women told of tremendous loneliness, isolation, and depression, and of a lack of both self-esteem and a sense of self-worth because of their inability to express themselves. They had been "robbed of their youth, of their own dreams, and careers." Hence the salience of the Basque organizations as an outlet for these women to communicate through their ethnicity. Ethnic identity provides empowerment and recognition, as it has for these *haizpak*. It gives one a history, a collective feeling, support from the "family" of other ethnics, and self-worth.

Women interviewees who migrated to Argentina and Uruguay entered host societies where Basques were highly regarded with a positive social status. Those in the United States were usually categorized as Spanish or French, and in Australia Basques were and still are commonly mistaken for Italians or Greeks. The shock of migration for many Basques derived not only from a change of country-to-country culture, but from a change of rural to urban culture. Basques migrating to New York, Lima, Montevideo, Buenos Aires, or Rosario entered urban settings with hundreds of thousands, or millions, of residents—quite a shift from the agricultural and fishing cultures of the small villages and farmsteads from which they had come. Whether in Melbourne or Mar del Plata, San Francisco or Sydney, the demands of city life compounded by geographical and cultural change could be overwhelming. The transition from traditional to modern life was, and is, not a simple or linear one.

Costs of migration are personal and emotional, with a shift in the quality of family relationships away from ties built by daily interactions in the homeland to brief interactions in letters, telephone conversations, and now e-mails. There is much stress that accompanies surviving in a transnational double world, forcing migrants to adapt rapidly and frequently to considerable changes in habits and expectations (Basch, Glick Schiller, and Szanton Blanc 1994, 242). The lack of belonging and/or acceptance in both their homeland and host country is especially frustrating. In the host country, they are described as "the Basque woman"; in Euskal Herria, they are, for example, "the Australian woman." "En el limbo," neither here nor there, was a phrase repeated often in each country, usually by emigrants themselves, but also by the first generation born in the host country. These women did not feel singularly connected either to their homeland or to the host country, to a territory or to a culture, but they do feel solidly connected to each other because of shared experiences.

Physical disconnectedness from Euskal Herria is replaced by an emotional and intellectual interconnectedness with other Basque women. Emigrants understand each other's horrors of political exile, loss of family and friends, and fears of coping in their new host countries. The first and second generation born in the host countries understand each others' upbringing and how they are different from host-country non-Basque friends. From constantly spelling and explaining their surnames, describing food preparation, and interpreting ETA activities, women of all ages in each of the six settings declared that they believe they "have more in common with each other in different countries than we do with other women equivalent to ourselves in this country." Their imagined connection is through their Basque ethnicity and its experiences. The *Euskal Etxeak* journal was often cited as an example in conversations when women compared themselves to other Basques in different countries. "They celebrate San Ignacio and have dancers and choirs the same way we do. I even found a story about a girlfriend from my hometown, and she is just like me except she ended up in the United States and I escaped to Belgium. I imagine she has worked at many dances frying as many *chorizos* and *tortillas* as I have" (Urriz Larragan interview, Brussels, 1997).

Do women more than men preserve Basque traditions, and what is the woman's role in the reproduction and development of ethnicity in her family? As I mentioned above, women are often perceived as the "cultural carriers" of any ethnic group. Women are thought to be the main socializers of children and the teachers who transfer cultural traditions to the next generation. In the case of the emigrant generation, women are often less assimilated linguistically and socially within the wider society because they work at home. In addition to these general assumptions, the concept of the Basque matriarchy is promulgated in the diaspora, where it might be expected that women would play the most significant role in ethnicity maintenance. However, my research data from the Basque diaspora communities show no significant difference between males and females in their attitudes toward mothers or fathers being more influential in preserving and maintaining Basque ethnic traditions. Asked to react to the statement, "Mothers have been more influential than fathers for teaching Basque culture to their children," a majority disagreed or had no opinion. More than one-third—36 percent of males and 40 percent of females—agreed with this statement. Multisocietal socialization of young people by host-country peers, school, physical surroundings, media, and other influences combines with Basque ethnic socialization at home, in the Basque centers, and at cultural events with other Basque families, and by both their mothers and their fathers.

There is a difference among the women themselves regarding the salience of religion with Basque identity. Catholicism was a significant factor of Basque identity in the first half of the twentieth century, and it continues to be so in the diaspora populations, with 71 percent of females and 69 percent males agreeing that "continuing Catholic beliefs and traditions in our Basque families" is of "great" or "very great" importance. However, when comparing the female responses separately, the older the women the higher the percentage who believed Catholicism was of "great" or "very great" importance. Of 402 women who responded to this question, only 36 percent of the youngest— those from 18 to 30 years of age—felt that Catholicism is important. Of the next group, those 31 to 45, 54 percent responded positively. Among those 46 to 60, 62 percent; among those 61 to 75, 71 percent. Of the oldest group, those 76 to 90, 76 percent believed Catholicism of "great" or "very great" importance to their Basque identity.

In the United States, where many interviewees mentioned experiencing discrimination against Catholics, 80 percent of the females responded that Catholicism is of "some," "great," or "very great" importance to maintaining Basque beliefs and traditions. Basque females in Belgium were the least likely to agree with the religion factor being important to Basque identity, with only 33 percent agreeing. Fifty-four percent of Uruguayans, 66 percent of Argentines, and 67 percent of Australians also agreed.

There are numerous personal decisions and motivations involved in international migration. For many, their homeland conditions *as females* have much to do with the decision to migrate, especially for single women. Both women and men are escaping political, economic, and social oppression and searching for a better life. Women also migrate to escape forms of oppression unique to them as women. Several female interviewees stated that, together with economic hardship in Euskal Herria, their influence had helped convince their husbands, brothers, or fathers to migrate. Because many Basque women experienced economic and social status gain in their new host countries, they were not as motivated as their male counterparts to return to the homeland. For economic and familial reasons, 66 percent of females responded that they have their own lives in their host countries and plan to return to Euskal Herria only to visit. The pull of family in the Basque Country has been replaced by the pull of the families they have created—children and grandchildren—in the host country. Moreover, these women report that they are accustomed to the host-country life-style.

Besides institutional women's organizations, such as Emakume Abertzale

Batza in Argentina or the Aiztan Artean in the United States, there is an informal sisterhood between the females, regardless of age and generation, in the host country. Female interviewees spoke of a connection to other Basque females who understood one another's suffering in an ethnic context—the separation from family and village, traditions and customs, language and society. Thus the importance of the Basque centers and institutions for first-generation immigrant women as an environment to connect with others and to manifest their identity through ethnicity. Later-generation females, especially teenaged girls, reinforced this pattern through their lasting friendships with other Basques. Teen interviewees who participate in dance groups, choirs, and sporting sets reaffirmed what their parents hope for—they believe their "Basque center friends will be friends for life."

Basque women have tended to be the transnational communicators between homeland and host-country families. They have served as the principal correspondents, sustaining family and friendship relations. Kinship networks and a broad range of social and economic links have been cultivated by the women. They have befriended new immigrants and relieved each other's anxieties. They have introduced each other to the social realities of everyday life in the host country and have informally counseled and consulted each other. Increasingly in the last two decades, women have also been elected to leadership positions in the Basque centers of five countries, but not in Peru, where males continue to dominate.[6] Women represent centers in the Basque federations in Argentina, Uruguay, and the United States, and they no longer consider their own contributions inconsequential or trivial. So, if enquiring of a female Basque immigrant to any of these six countries what she does in the Basque community and the answer is "nothing really," she most likely has served fellow Basques as counselor, teacher, real-estate agent, employment officer, household manager, tourist guide, taxi driver, interpreter, and communicator. She has cooked and sold several hundred *tortillas* and *chorizos,* set and moved several thousand chairs for dinners and dances, and year after year taught the *txikis* (little ones) Basque songs.

My findings show that although men and women understand and experience the act of migration and the process of acculturation differently, gender does not tend to affect cultural ethnic identity maintenance or the definition of "Basqueness" among diaspora Basques.

The Age of Globalization Is Also the Age of Ethnic Identity Resurgence

Manuel Castells describes today's world as one with conflicting trends of globalization, the information technology revolution, and the restructuring of capitalism all creating a transformed network society, a culture constructed by an interconnected and diversified media system, versus an increase in powerful expressions of collective identity that challenge modernization and globalization in favor of a local, communal, separate identity and cultural distinctiveness (Castells 1997, 1–2). On the one hand, then, we have globalization and an outward-expanding model of identity and subsequent homogenization; simultaneously, we have ethnonationalism that converges on the historical, the traditional, a known ethnic identity and ensuing heterogeneity and cultural difference. Multitudes around the world are choosing to revert from the unknown future to the known and understood traditional past.

BASQUE DIASPORIC IDENTITY

Basque diaspora identity salience is related to globalization but not necessarily as a partner in a causal relationship, nor as a defensive reaction to it. The tools of global communications are being manipulated and utilized by the homeland and diaspora populations to educate and intercommunicate, and these networks are perceived as positive media for ethnic identity re-creation, maintenance, and enhancement. The homogenization potential is received in the diaspora organizations as a possible means of unifying the Basques in various diaspora communities, not as a threat of cultural imperialism by the United States or as the standardization of all world culture and identity.

Identity in this setting is a person's way of giving understanding and meaning to life experiences and events. The various identities that one person has do not necessarily conflict with each other; rather, they may tend to be complementary. There is a symbiotic *diaspora identity* that incorporates and synthesizes the two, Basque and host-country identities. Glick Schiller et al. (1995) consider this the emergence of what they have named "transnationalism".—the formation of social, political, and economic relationships among immigrants that cross several societies. It is a new sort of migrating population, whose activities and patterns of life encompass both their host and home societies (Glick Schiller et al. 1995, 1). The emergence of interstate societies and diasporas are examples of these deterritorialized cultures. When respondents were asked to describe themselves as "Basque" or "host country" (Peruvian, Uruguayan, American, etc.), or as a combination of the two, or "other," 73 percent identified themselves as either Basque–host country or host country–Basque.

These Basques' identities are configured in relation to their host country *and* to their home country. As is the case with other ethnic groups, there is a continuum of interest in ethnicity, ranging from assimilationism to integration to ethnic fundamentalism. Often, the diasporic person has "double and multiple consciousness," an identity that crosses boundaries and resists totalization (Tölölyan 1996, 28). The world can no longer, if ever, be understood as international, in the sense of being made up of independent, separate nations with solid boundaries. Instead, it has become a transnational, interdependent system where national borders are increasingly permeable (Sorensen 1995, 107). People may live in several different locations and/or take part in networks that transcend boundaries, and this influences their daily lives and outlook. In the age of transnationalism, identities are contextualized and become transnational, binational, pan-national social relations (ibid., 108).

For many diasporic populations, including the Basques, experiences and means of orientation are divorced from the physical locations in which they live and work. They are able to simulate environments of homeland at the centers and with each other. The globalization process has opened up the world for increased contact, and the Basque cultural centers are benefitting. Some academics argue that the difficulties of accepting these changes are reasons why "localism" or a return to some sort of "home," be it real or imaginary, become important themes (Featherstone 1995, 103). The global and local are bound together and not necessarily mutually exclusive. The regularity and frequency of contacts with a group of significant others are what sustain a common culture, and the creation of powerful emotionally sustaining rituals, ceremonies, and collective memories tie these Basques together in their respective communities and also to each other as they imagine each other practicing and remembering the same rituals and ceremonies.

Basque ethnics are able to strengthen symbolic modes of affiliation and belonging through their diasporic consciousness, and they utilize their ethnic identity to undermine existing symbolic hierarchies and create their own ethnic space for their own purposes, which tend to be more psychological and emotional than rational. However, this is not a new phenomenon for them. What has progressed are the mechanisms used to maintain the Basque identity.

WWW.IDENTITY.ORG

The Autonomous Basque Government of Euskadi has provided funding for each officially registered diaspora Basque organization to obtain a computer with Internet access for its members. These communication possibilities have increased the frequency of intercommunication between Basques in different communities and countries, including communication between Basques in the homeland and Basques in the diaspora, and between diasporic Basques themselves. While diasporic Basques reported knowing about Basques in other parts of the world, communications had been restricted to personal contacts between relatives and close friends, or occasionally with Basques traveling to another country who took the time to visit the local Basque center and meet other Basques there. As mentioned previously, visits to the homeland could also result in diasporic Basque contact. For example, several Australian Basques reported meeting with, and learning about, Basques from the United States while each was vacationing at home in Bizkaia (Garagarza interview, Melbourne, 1997; Kandino interview, Melbourne, 1997). It is now common for diaspora Basque institutions to create their own websites and receive e-mail communications from other Basques around the world making inquiries about family genealogy, Basque center activities, and Basque-language learning materials. These institutions are no longer serving only Basques in their physical locale because now they incorporate a global audience.

"Virtual ethnic communities" utilize telecommunications technology to replace mass media with targeted or "addressable" media and specialized and more homogeneous audiences (Elkins 1997). These technologies allow ethnic communities to support their diaspora populations and attempt to retain their language and culture. The key is the availability of easy, frequent, and inexpensive interactions without physical proximity. Elkins does not argue, nor would I, that virtual communities will replace existing ethnic communities. However, technologies do allow existing dispersed ethnic groups to find new means of support, persistence, and interest. The telecommunications technologies enable and facilitate communication and information exchanges among Basques themselves and among Basques through their institutions, creating additional shared experiences for those persons utilizing this method of individual development.

Technology enables and facilitates but does not determine situations. The availability of Internet exchanges and the hundreds of Basque-topic websites do not translate to equally distributed usage in the diaspora. At the Basque center in Peru, there were only a few younger members who understood how to use e-mail and Internet searches, and none frequent the center often. Nevertheless, there is a willingness to utilize modern technologies in each of the centers, and there is the beginning of a cadre of likely recruits for the expanding virtual Basque community.

DIASPORA BASQUE ETHNICITY = POSITIVE SOCIAL IDENTITY

Tajfel's social-identity theory argues that the process of social categorization enables the individual to define his or her position in society as a member of the groups to which he or she belongs. Social identity is defined as that part of a person's self-concept that derives one's knowledge of membership in a social group together with the value and emotional significance attached to that membership, and people strive for a positive social identity (Tajfel 1978, 1984; Tajfel and Turner 1979). Socioeconomic status is usually a reliable indicator of social categorization. Though Basques think of themselves positively, they do not tend to do so at the expense of other ethnic groups. Their perceived positive social status does not translate to a "higher socio*economic* status." My questionnaire responses indicated that in the U.S., 31 percent of those queried agreed that Basques enjoy a higher socioeconomic status than other immigrants (31 percent disagreed). In Peru, 31 percent agreed and 50 percent disagreed; in Belgium, 29 percent agreed and 33 percent disagreed; in Argentina, 15 percent agreed and 49 percent disagreed; in Australia, 6 percent agreed and 59 percent disagreed.

Perhaps being Basque is individually relevant in the countries I studied. If the chosen ethnic identity is determined by an individual's perception of its meaning to different audiences, its salience in different social contexts, and its utility in different settings, joining and participating in Basque ethnic activities or joining a Basque center would have an individual and social impact. Diaspora Basques might also utilize this positive status of their ethnicity for personal gain. They strive for a positive social identity and tend to believe they are perceived positively in each of their host societies in comparison to other ethnic groups, even if their socioeconomic status may not be higher. In every country, a majority of Basques admitted that their own maintenance of Basque identity was tied to the Basques' positive work-ethic reputation. Indeed, in the U.S. 90 percent of those interviewed admitted that they preserved their Basque identity because they were proud of the Basques' reputation as honest, hardworking people. In Peru, 85 percent of my respondents made this admission; in Australia, 81 percent; in Uruguay, 72 percent; in Argentina, 71 percent. In Belgium, 59 percent of those queried indicated that they valued this aspect of the Basques' reputation—a somewhat high number when taking into consideration that the Basques have had much less time to establish any reputation at all among the Belgians.

The positive association between "Basque" and "honest and industrious" is equivalent to social praise, and Basques reported the pride they experienced when telling new acquaintances that they are Basque. Some individuals in Argentina, Uruguay, and the United States even admitted that they *expect* the person's reaction to be actual words of praise. In Sydney and Melbourne, Australia, they count on needing to give an explanation of what Basque ethnicity is and a short geography and history lesson, though most people in the North Queensland area are more familiar with Basques. Basques in Belgium reported that they usually have to disassociate themselves from ETA and political conversations. The majorities in each case still agreed that Basques have a positive social status in their host society and—although future research should test this by asking non-Basques what they think of Basques—the positive perception definitely exists with among Basques themselves.

Basque ethnic festivals and collective activities serve to fulfill a psychological need to belong, and at the same time they offer the individual aspiration of uniqueness. Basques can manifest their unique Basqueness to the outside host society and simultaneously be part of a group of fellow ethnics. Given a list of fourteen statements made by other diaspora Basques explaining why they maintain their ethnicity, 58 percent of the males and 62 percent of the female participants agreed that one of the main reasons they preserve their Basque identity is specifically because it makes them feel they "have a special connection to each other," and 53 percent of both groups agreed that their Basque identity makes them "feel special and unique."

Respondents were also asked if they had ever been treated favorably or unfavorably "specifically because you are Basque." Instrumentalists contend that ethnicity is circumstantial and often utilized for gaining resources or services. In the case of Basques, the evidence does not consistently support this argument. Table 10 presents the percentages of respondents who believe their ethnicity has definitely affected the outcomes of certain situations either "favorably" or "unfavorably." If the respondents thought their Basqueness had no effect on the outcome of the situation, they were instructed to leave this section blank.

The results for employment are difficult to interpret, because in interviews some men explained that although they believe Basques tend to have a positive reputation in comparison to many other immigrants in their societies, if their Basque ethnicity had aided them with gaining employment it was because another Basque had hired them, not because a non-Basque had hired them. The only way of ascertaining this point would be to interview all of the employers and ask if an applicant's Basque ethnicity favored his candidacy or not. The same question applies to the other circumstances as well. In interviews in the United States, several respondents did not want to admit that they had received special treatment because they "did not want to get anyone in trouble." One former miner stated that when once he was waiting in an application line, the foreman walked down the line asking if there were any Basques, and those who answered "yes" were taken to the front and hired immediately. Though this incident was fifty years past, he had never admitted to what he thought was unfair treatment because of positive discrimination. What is important in positive social-identity theory is the Basques' perception of themselves and whether or not they believe their ethnicity is a help or hindrance for instrumental gain. The data reveal that a majority perceive it as neither.

Though instrumentalists argue that ethnicity must have a practical function in order to be viable and depict ethnicity as an instrument for competition for scarce resources, T. H. Eriksen focuses on ethnic identity as those distinctions that are socially relevant to the individual who maintains them (Eriksen 1993, 61). Though not an instrument of competition, Basques' social status can be

TABLE 5.2 Percentages of respondents who perceived "Favorable" or "Unfavorable" treatment because of Basque ethnicity.

Treatment	Uruguay Fav %	Uruguay Un %	Peru Fav %	Peru Un %	Australia Fav %	Australia Un %	United States Fav %	United States Un %	Argentina Fav %	Argentina Un %	Belgium Fav %	Belgium Un %
Joining a club	15	8	50	7	18	2	23	1	19	5	4	0
Admission to school or university	10	9	21	7	13	4	7	1	21	5	8	4
Selection for award or scholarship	4	8	0	14	12	2	9	2	7	4	0	0
Buying or renting accommodation	7	8	14	14	10	2	9	1	9	4	0	4
Receiving a government benefit	2	10	0	14	11	2	5	2	5	5	5	0
Getting a job	7	11	28	0	22	2	26	1	19	4	25	0

Total of 832 responses from written anonymous questionnaires. Respondents were asked to leave blank if they had not been affected "favorably" or "unfavorably" by their Basque ethnicity.

extremely relevant psychologically and emotionally though not used for material gain. Several authors have argued that utility is the most important factor in accounting for the ethnic identity maintenance. This instrumentalist argument regards identity as contingent on political mobilization. However, perceptions of utility itself are cultural creations, and the boundary between what is useful and what is meaningful becomes blurred (Eriksen 1993, 74). Basques in the diaspora may understand their ethnicity as being meaningful, but there is not enough convincing evidence to argue that they view it as useful for anything material.

Conclusions

Basque emigrants have surmounted numerous life-altering experiences of changing languages, cultures, and societies, and they found strength in each other through Basque center activities. Ethnic identity is not restricted only to those people who live inside a certain physical boundary. We see from thousands of Basques in the diaspora that maintaining a connection to one's ethnicity is a personal choice. It is demonstrated in such personal ways as wearing *lauburu* earrings to planting red-flowered gardens.

Basque diaspora institutions utilize modern technology and the Internet, and individual respondents explained that "actually modernity makes preserving ethnicity easier" because of additional media for communication and information. Travel is easier and cheaper, and the interconnectedness of diaspora organizations intensifies the "us" feeling to a global sense of "we Basques." Globalization trends and telecommunications technology have increased the availability of information and communications between Basques, and there is no evidence that these trends have scared them into any reactionary activities. In the United States, Alba (1990) found that ethnic identity salience rises with educational level. It is quite chic now to be ethnic. This pattern is replicated in diaspora populations participating in Basque activities, with 65 percent of questionnaire participants having university training and 13 percent postgraduate studies.

The technologies of globalization have greatly affected the ability of these diaspora groups to maintain ties with the homeland and with each other. It is important to remember the interconnectedness of these communities. It is not a two-way connection between one Basque center and the homeland, but one between and among all the participants.

Mary Douglas (1983) categorizes some people as ethnic anomalies—people who are "neither-nor" or "both-and," depending on the situation and/or the wider context. Diaspora Basques tend to feel this way, as though they are both Uruguayan and Basque, not one or the other. They congregate with others at the Basque centers who are in the same position and can share similar circumstances. Though public protests regarding homeland and/or host-society politics are often perceived as threatening to host-country populations, Basques have tended to prefer cultural manifestations of their ethnicity, preventing any questioning of hierarchies of loyalty.

The progression of the role of Basque centers, from helping Basque immigrants integrate into the host society to functioning as an ethnic organization and a regenerative source of ethnicity by creating and recreating ties to the homeland, to serving as an extreme tourist agency and vacation guide, has less to do with globalization, geography, or gender than with the change in migration patterns and the change in the category of people traveling, and the purpose of their visits. There has been a historical decline in the need for economic functions and services provided by ethnic social structures such as the Basque centers—but it does not coincide with a declining importance of Basque ethnic identities.

What is significant about this type of ethnicity is its lack of political salience. These second-, third-, and fourth-generation immigrants have no need to consider their ethnicity in an economic light and hence do not tend to politicize this aspect of their identities. Their economic well-being and education have not been compromised by their ethnicity as their parents were. There is no need to bolster their ethnic identity daily and actively. The later generations tend to experience their ethnicity by voluntary individual choice but continue to preserve a collective identity.

Chapter Six

Basque Government–
Diaspora Relations

The Spanish Constitution of 1978 attempts to offer a solution to demands for self-government from the state's various regions while retaining centralist elements. Thus Article 2 begins with the "indissoluble unity of the Spanish nation" but later recognizes the "right to autonomy of the nationalities and regions of which it is composed," establishing two levels of "national/regional identity." Araba, Bizkaia, and Gipuzkoa approved the Statutes of Autonomy of the Basque Country, also known as the Statutes of Gernika, in October 1979, and elected their regional parliament in March 1980, with creation of the Basque government following shortly thereafter. Nafarroa achieved separate autonomy in direct governmental negotiations with Madrid with the 1982 act affirming the region's historic rights. In this chapter, I shall analyze diaspora relations with the government of Euskadi, and I shall use the term "Basque government" to refer to the government of the three autonomous provinces of Euskadi.

In recognition of the financial, political, and cultural contributions that supported the Basque government-in-exile for forty years, the Basque Autonomous Government of Euskadi has collaborated with the diaspora communities via a policy of subsidies and grants, giving aid for their internal operating costs and their educational and cultural activities. Basque organizations abroad have been presented with computer communications equipment, audio-visual materials with information about the homeland, such as sports, history, anthropology, tourism, and cooking, and with audio tapes and printed materials for studying Euskera. The Basque government is interested in utilizing the diaspora Basque centers for the promotion, development, and diffusion of information about the contemporary reality of the Basque Country. In the current environment of continuous globalization and internationalization, Basque communities can serve as a "stimulator for social, cultural, economic, and political relations" (Exposition of Motives, *Ley 8/1994*).

Basque diaspora-homeland transnational networks, previously personal and occasionally institutional, experiencing swings from latency to frenzied activity, began a period of stabilization with the establishment of the homeland autonomous government. In the early years of the new Basque government, policymakers included returnees from political exile. In 1982, the Minister of Culture invited delegates from various diaspora communities to participate in a congress regarding the future of the diaspora, but no objectives or proposals were confirmed by the congress. The Service for Relations with the Basque Centers was established in the Ministry of Culture in 1984, and its first assessor, Jokin Intxausti, traveled through Europe, the Americas, and the Philippines investigating the current circumstances of the Basque diaspora organizations. His untimely death in 1986 was followed by the appointment of Josu Legarreta, who further developed the goals of his office and expanded communications between the homeland government and the diaspora centers. Diaspora visits by Basque government officials, including that of the Lehendakari (president of Euskadi) in 1988, were received with profound emotion equal to what had greeted the visits of José Antonio de Aguirre a generation earlier. Previous diaspora-homeland links consisted of chains of transnational personal networks between individuals in diaspora communities and relatives in their Euskadi hometowns and acquaintances in other areas, and a very few institutionalized relationships, such as the University Studies Abroad Consortium (USAC) of the University of Nevada, Reno, and the Boise State University–Oñate study programs. Now the Basque government was giving recognition and significance to Basques abroad that magnified their pride in the achievements of homeland autonomy.

The Government of the Foral Community of Nafarroa opened communications with a few Basque centers in the 1990s, mostly as a response to diaspora queries. Nafarroa has not established a specific office to deal with relations with diaspora Basque communities, but its government tries to accommodate requests for information, especially about tourism, through the Basque centers. The three provinces in Iparralde have no formal local government–diaspora relations. However, nongovernmental organizations, cultural associations, and privately funded activities foster networks. There is relatively recent emigration from Zuberoa, Behe Nafarroa, and Lapurdi to the United States and to Belgium. Therefore, regardless of the lack of institutional relations, personal networks between these areas are recent and strong. Basque dance troupes, choirs, athletes, and musicians from Iparralde have toured the diaspora communities through personal invitations from Basque center leaders and through personal and center funding. The government of Euskadi often incorporates various institutions and artists from Nafarroa and Iparralde into its diaspora projects, and it continues to promote the nationalists' concept that the seven provinces, although divided politically, are united through ethnicity, history, language, and culture. The foral government of Nafarroa did not, and has not yet, reached out to Basques abroad in an equivalent manner, though in 2001

President Sanz visited Navarrese centers in Argentina with success. Relations between Nafarroa and diaspora communities thus remain as personal contacts and networks rather than as institutionalized relationships.

By 1994, the Basque government decided to make a qualitative change in relations between the institutions of the homeland and those of the Basque communities abroad. The institutional development of Euskadi and its increasing self-government and the judicial and political framework of the Law on Relations with Basque Communities (*Ley 8/1994*), provided a substantial foundation for a new start.

Law of Relations with the Basque Communities in the Exterior—*Ley 8/1994*

REVERSING TRENDS

The Law of Relations with Basque Communities Outside the Autonomous Community of the Basque Country, *Ley 8/1994*, was passed by the Basque parliament in May 1994. It signaled a new stage in the history of relations between the Autonomous Basque Government and Basque institutions in the diaspora, and was described as being a means of repaying "our historic debt to Basques overseas and to the countries that welcomed them" (Sainz de la Maza 1994, 14). This law was presented to the diaspora communities as a "commitment that begins with recognition and gratitude toward the Basque Communities for their efforts and labors in the interest of the Basque cause" (President José Antonio Ardanza Garro, Introduction to Parliamentary debate on *Ley 8/94*, cited in *Law of Relations with Basque Communities and Centers Outside the Autonomous Community of the Basque Country*, 1994, 8). President Ardanza described the law as a starting point that would mark a new direction in relations between the Basque Country and diaspora Basques and their centers around the world (ibid., 9).

The law provides for a Registry of Basque Centers, for which each center is required to collect the names, birthplaces, ancestral homeland town names, languages spoken, and citizenships held by its members. Originally, the 1994 law stipulated that this information was to be made a matter of public record, but following complaints from several countries, especially the United States, regarding privacy and security, the registry is now a private databank of the Basque government, ordered by Decree 106/1996. This registry of Basque centers is officially recognized by the Basque Autonomous Government, and the law also establishes the requirements for members of those centers to register and be recognized for possible benefits. It endows registered members of Basque institutions who are also registered with the Basque government with material benefits as well as psychological empowerment. The material benefits

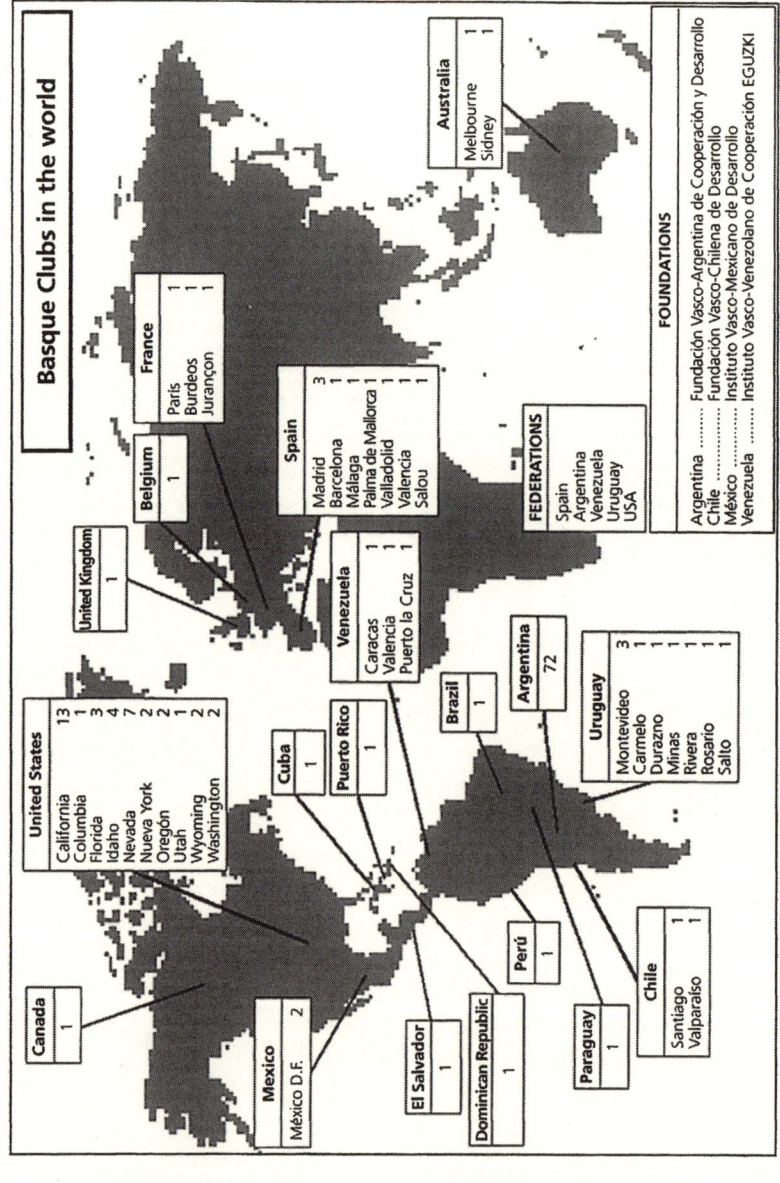

Map 6.1. Officially registered Basque centers around the world, 2003. Benan Oregi, Eusko Jaurlaritza, and Jill Berner, Center for Basque Studies

include, among other things, the ability to attend a university in the Basque Country and acceptance of degrees on equal footing with homeland residents, to receive health benefits and social assistance, to qualify for public housing in Euskadi (only in the three autonomous provinces) equally with other legal residents without needing to meet residency requirements as other immigrants must, and to apply for grants for diaspora community projects. The law sets the requirements of eligibility for personal benefits and distinguishes between benefits for members of Basque centers (Title III, Articles 9, 10, 11) and those for the institutions themselves. It also distinguishes between benefits for Basques who remain overseas and for those who return permanently to the Basque Country.

Ley 8/1994 created an Advisory Council for Relations with Basque Communities, which meets annually (Article 6.1 of Decree 234/1995) for discussion and analysis of diaspora programs and communications between diaspora communities and appropriate institutions in the homeland. It consists of three persons selected by the Basque government who have lived in and/or have researched the diaspora communities. Although the law was passed in Euskadi, this Advisory Council also communicates with Basque institutions in the Foral Community of Nafarroa, and with the three French Basque provinces in Iparralde. *Ley 8/1994* institutionalized social, cultural, political, and economic relations that were previously mainly personal networks. Diaspora political organizations, academic institutions, private Basque associations, or for-profit Basque institutions such as restaurants or hotels are not qualified for subsidies.

The law also prescribes a Congress of Basque Collectivities to be held every four years as a forum for social, cultural, and economic relations among the diaspora communities themselves and between the diaspora communities and the homeland government. Basques in each country are allowed to elect three delegates to represent them, and additional special invitations are extended from the Lehendakari of the Basque government to academics and special guests. The First Congress of Basque Communities, held in Vitoria-Gasteiz in November 1995, facilitated the establishment of intercommunications among the diaspora communities. By personalizing the congress with ample opportunity for social functions and time for delegates to meet and discuss questions informally with each other, the congress established personal relations that are evolving into institutional ties. For example, the president of the North American Basque Organization and the president of the Argentine Federation of Basque Entities have regularly visited each other's National Basque Festivals. Exchanges of Basque dance groups were organized between the United States and Argentina in 1996 and 2001, and exchanges of *pelota* players between the United States and Venezuela were also initiated. The Jaialdi International

Basque Festival in Boise attracted representatives from Basque communities in Canada, Mexico, Peru, Uruguay, and Australia, as well as several hundred guests from the Basque Country.

Article 1 of the law stipulates a desire to preserve and reinforce links and to support and intensify relations between the Basque government and homeland institutions with Basque communities and centers in the diaspora. It also specifically mentions promoting activities to disseminate, stimulate, and develop Basque culture and Euskadi's economy (Article 1, Section 3). This has led some diaspora and homeland opposition-party members to question the Basque government's instrumental motives in using the diaspora for economic gain to the homeland economy, then subsequently exploiting this economic gain to further political party—specifically, PNV—election objectives. Government officials deny this allegation and insist that any relations that are good for the Basque Country are good for everyone equally, not only certain citizens from the PNV (Aguirre Arizmendi interview, Vitoria-Gasteiz, 1999; Legarreta interview, Vitoria-Gasteiz, 1999; San Sebastián interview, Vitoria-Gasteiz, 1999; Esnal interview, Vitoria-Gasteiz, 1999).

The law creates a legal framework and infrastructure for the grants and subsidies already provided to the diaspora since 1987 and establishes the permanence of budgetary categories. It foments networks between Basques in the diaspora with those in the Basque government and with various academic, cultural, economic, and religious institutions in the homeland.

BENEFITS TO BASQUE ORGANIZATIONS AND CENTERS

For Basque centers and organizations to take advantage of the Basque government's benefits, they must be "recognized" by proving they comply with the requirements of *Ley 8/1994*. They must have a valid constitution in accordance with the judicial system of the state in which they reside; must include as fundamental objectives the maintenance of Basque culture and social and economic ties with the Basque Country, its people, history, language, and culture; must be organized around democratic internal structures and functions; and must request formal recognition and follow the procedures to obtain it. Centers must also respect the objectives set down in *Ley 8/1994*. Failure to follow any of these requirements could lead to withdrawal of recognition.

The Basque government also has recognized federations of Basque centers in Argentina (Federación de Entidades Vasco Argentinos—FEVA); in the United States (North American Basque Organizations—NABO[1]; and in Uruguay (Federación de Instituciones Vascas de Uruguay—FIVU. Private interviews with homeland government officials and institutional officials reveal an official desire for the centers to remain formally federated, thereby facilitating communication between all parties involved. To communicate with U.S., Uruguayan, or

Argentine Basques, the homeland party need only contact the federation and is sufficiently sure that all participating centers in that country will receive the same information. But in Australia and other countries with more than one Basque organization, the homeland institution or organization must contact each center or organization individually. Often, requests for information from the diaspora to the homeland are not coordinated and are thus repeated or redundant. The federations also keep the Basque government out of the "internal" affairs of the host countries' Basques and prevent antagonism between the diaspora and the homeland, though often creating schisms among the diaspora Basques themselves in a single country. Interviews with leaders of smaller organizations in Uruguay, the United States, and Argentina revealed that several of them perceive the larger and more established centers to be the recipients of a disproportionate amount of funds. In the United States, discussions at several NABO meetings have included the issue of Boise, Elko, and San Francisco regularly receiving grants "because they have better connections than we [Los Banos] do." In Uruguay, Basques in Salto have stronger communications with Basques in Argentina than with others in their own country, and those in Minas, Rosario, and Carmelo believe they should get more funding because their organizations are new and attempting to establish themselves. Argentine Basques from Buenos Aires' Laurak Bat, and from Rosario and Mar del Plata mentioned concerns about the Basque government's funding "new small organizations that will fold after they find out how much work it is to keep paying the bills. It is a waste of their [the Basque Government's] money."

However, because FEVA, FIVU, and NABO are federations, they share power with the individual organizations and do not have the authority to stop individual organizations from going directly to the Basque government or other homeland institutions for aid or information. For example, NABO had asked its centers to channel all applications for grants and subsidies through the federation so that they could be jointly submitted to the Basque government. NABO has no authority to prioritize or favor any applications for aid. However, the Boise Euzkaldunak Incorporated Basque Center went directly to the Basque government for subsidies for the 1995 and 2000 Jaialdi cultural celebration, and the San Francisco Basque Cultural Center also communicates directly with the Euskadi Pelota Federation to request players for exhibitions and competitions of handball. Individual centers regularly invite Basque Country music groups and ask for Basque government aid to cover costs—and their requests have been granted. When questioned about this, the Director of Relations with the Diaspora Communities stated that it was not the business of the Basque government to meddle in internal affairs among the diaspora organizations or to disrupt any federation directives of which it is not a member, so the problem remained one for NABO to settle between its delegates. Obviously, it would be easier for the Basque government to deal with a single federation than to work individually with the dozens of centers in Argentina or in the United States.

The statutory benefits specifically given to diaspora Basque centers include:
1. Access to information of a public nature, with a social, cultural, or economic content, prepared by the public administration of the Autonomous Community of the Basque Country (any Basque center that requests it will also receive the *Official Bulletin of the Basque Country* free of charge);
2. The right to participate in different forms of expression of Basque homeland social, cultural, and economic life that contribute to the external diaspora projection of such;
3. Treatment identical to that of associations situated in the territory of the Basque Autonomous Community in regard to access to its cultural heritage, artifacts, and special collections;
4. The right to ask the Basque Autonomous Community to participate in activities organized by a diaspora center to promote Basque culture;
5. Basque center participation in programs, missions, and delegations organized by Basque homeland institutions in the centers' territorial area;
6. The right to request and receive advice on social, economic, or labor matters in the Basque Country;
7. The right to a supply of published and audio-visual material designed to facilitate the transmission of knowledge of Basque history, culture, language, and social reality, for display and distribution among members of Basque communities;
8. Collaboration in activities to spread the word of the situation of Basque communities through means of communication centered in the Autonomous Community, such as Basque Radio and Television, and the *Euskal Etxeak* journal;
9. The right to be heard via the Advisory Council and to attend the Congress of Basque Collectivities;
10. The organization of courses to learn the Basque language (Article 8, Section 1 of *Ley 8/1994*).

Diaspora Basque centers also qualify to receive financial and other types of assistance that the homeland public administration might establish within the framework of this law. The law specifically mentions support to temporarily cover the operating costs of centers and maintaining and improving the infrastructure of the actual buildings, for the promotion of activities and programs related to the homeland, and as economic assistance for especially needy members (Article 8, Section 3).

INDIVIDUAL RIGHTS AND BENEFITS

Basques are now in a post-exilic stage and may go home if they desire and can afford it. There are no longer political barriers to return, though there are financial barriers for many families. The "members of Basque communities" to whom the benefits and rights apply are defined as those resident abroad and their dependents. Included are those who fall under Article 7, Section 2 of the Statute of Autonomy, individuals "who specifically request it shall enjoy the same political rights as those living in the Basque Country, if their last legal residence in Spain was in Euskadi, and provided they retain their Spanish citizenship." However, according to Josu Legarreta, Director of Relations with the Diaspora Communities, it is possible to receive benefits even if a person has dropped his or her Spanish citizenship by exhibiting birth records showing the place of birth in the Basque Country (Josu Legarreta interview, Vitoria-Gasteiz, 2002). Individuals evacuated during the Spanish Civil War and those exiled after the war are specifically listed for aid.

The principle of territoriality has been raised when determining to whom these rights belong. Should they belong to Basques born in any of the seven provinces of Euskal Herria or just those born in the three provinces that incorporate the contemporary political boundaries of Euskadi? Presently the government of Euskadi is funding these benefits, and it has determined that anyone born in one of the seven provinces who returns to one of the three provinces in the jurisdiction of Euskadi shall qualify for these services, although in actuality problems arise if the applicant was not born in Euskadi. There has been a case where a person born in Nafarroa was not given a special exemption that would have been granted had he been born in one of the three territories of the Basque Autonomous Community.

Specific rights for members of diaspora organizations are also enumerated, including access to Basque cultural-heritage events and libraries, archives, museums, and other cultural property and institutions for the dissemination of culture, under the same conditions as citizens in the Basque Autonomous Community. Language curricula are provided to Basque centers so that members may study Euskera free of charge, and procedures have been established to grant certificates of Basque-language proficiency awarded by the Basque government to those who qualify. Educational, cultural, and economic exchanges are promoted by the Basque government, such as with the Gaztemundu (World of Youth) program for uniting diaspora youth in the homeland. The University of the Basque Country, with three campuses in Vitoria-Gasteiz, Donostia-San Sebastián, and Leioa, recognizes qualifications and transcripts awarded by other universities that are similar to the qualifications established by the University of the Basque Country. A Basque with a university degree from Macquarie University in Australia could apply to the University of the

Basque Country for graduate work and would automatically be accepted equally to residents of Euskadi, or a Basque from the Universidad de la República in Montevideo studying international law could begin courses in Montevideo and transfer for the final year to the University of the Basque Country in Donostia-San Sebastián and not have to duplicate any course work, or take entrance exams as do other foreign students. This could be extremely beneficial for South American Basque students who are looking to future careers in Europe. With Spanish as a native tongue, they would not experience the language difficulties of second-language study, as would Belgian, United States, and Australian Basques. Additionally, earning a degree or diploma from a university in Spain may carry more prestige for European employment than would a South American university equivalent. After education, any diaspora Basques who are interested in creating a business in the homeland can receive "technical and legal advice in regard to the creation of the business" (Article 10, Section 1.G).

The benefits described are to be carried out through the Basque centers, which presents a problem in several of the diaspora organizations. Some needy members would like to apply for economic assistance but are too proud to let others know and certainly do not want other center members or the directors to know or control any assistance they might receive (Olaizola interview, Buenos Aires, 1999; Velasco interview, Buenos Aires, 1997; Tomás Egibar interview, Brussels, 1999). All of the centers are operated by volunteers who tend not to be appropriations specialists or account executives. Many do not want the responsibility of being fiscal officers or of determining whether a subsidy is being used for the project for which it was intended. The Basque government has not told the centers *how* to do this job, just that they are the institutions to "carry out the benefits," leaving the implementation open to interpretation and confusion.

For those diaspora Basques returning permanently to the homeland, automatic residency is granted, eliminating the mandatory waiting period for other immigrants. Benefits include access to health and social services and to public housing, and those who qualify financially "may have access to means of support able to be used to facilitate their return voyage to the Basque Country with the view of establishing their residence there" (Article 11, Section 3).

Several Basques in Argentina have argued that they "have a right" to Basque government benefits whether or not they are registered members of centers, and that anyone born in the Basque Country should have full access to all benefits even if they cannot go to the homeland to receive them. For example, if there are old-age pensions for returning diaspora Basques who move to the homeland, the same pensions should be available to those who, for whatever reason, stay in their host country. Some diaspora Basques are demanding "rights" and benefits from the homeland while they stay in the diaspora.

This is an interesting turn of events. During the Civil War and the subsequent Franco regime, diaspora Basques sent material and financial aid to homeland Basques and supported the government-in-exile from their host countries. However, to some Basques who stayed in the homeland, those who left were traitors, abandoning the country when they were most needed, escaping political oppression and "making it big" in the Americas. Now, diaspora Basques (a majority of whom did not make it big or they would have had sufficient money to return), especially a few in economically depressed countries in Latin America, are expressing their opinion that they are "owed" these benefits by their brothers who remained in Euskadi. A representative analogy would be a *baserri* (family farm) that cannot support all of the siblings. Several siblings leave the family farm to seek opportunities in the cities (perhaps for adventure and change, and/or because they feel they have no economic options and have been pushed off the farm). None is at fault, for their choices are a result of economic circumstances, personalities, birth order, gender, etc. Part of the wages earned from the city job is sent back home to the family. The city sibling marries and makes a home in the city and becomes a city person, though always loving and remembering with nostalgia the family's farm life. The economy shifts, and now the city employment has moved elsewhere and the farm has become prosperous. Now the city sibling needs the help of those on the farm. Should the city dweller have to move back to the farm to receive assistance, or should the family support the city dweller as the city dweller earlier supported the farmers? The Basque government answers that one must live on the farm to be supported by the family; the Argentine diaspora Basques argue that family is family and should be supported no matter where they live.

Though this philosophy is related to the diaspora Basques' transnationalist philosophy and their connection to "Basqueness" not necessarily being territorial, the implementation and administration of social and health benefits to Basques in various countries around the globe would surely result in a financial and administrative nightmare. The centers do not want to become banks or points of exchange between the Basque government and beneficiaries abroad, nor are they going to provide the necessary services directly. In the Basque Parliament of Euskadi, there has been brief and very general mention of the idea of providing senior-citizen pensions for Basques abroad who were born in the Basque Country, but no specific legislation has been introduced or policy appropriations granted.

Policy Formulation for the Diaspora

In Euskadi in 1990, the General Secretariat of Foreign Action was created under the Office of the Presidency, and the Program for Relations with the Basque

Centers was moved in order to consolidate and unify foreign relations for the Basque government into one area and to emphasize the importance of international affairs. Utilizing local contacts facilitated by the diaspora, the Basque government created transnational political and economic ties with several foreign state and sub-state actors. By the end of 1991, there was evident a clear policy of utilizing the Basque centers to facilitate meetings between Basque government and business leaders and individuals in the highest levels of government and business in the host countries.

The aging of the emigrant collectivities relates to the Basque government's conscious attempt to utilize institutional relations in order to create a postmodern Basque diaspora. It has an interest in promoting the reality of today's Basque Country to its own diaspora so that the diaspora communities can spread the word about tourism, culture, economic development, and political autonomy. Occasionally, rhetoric from Basque government officials traveling to diaspora communities is almost pedantic in that it seeks to educate diaspora Basques about "Basqueness." The government is trying to promote a nontraditional and non-Aranist attitude that "one can be Basque in this way, or one can be Basque in that way" (Garmendia 1997), rather than following the stale definitions of older generations. It is attempting to create institutionalized bonds that will update the exclusive ancestral definition toward the homeland's inclusive civic definition of "Basqueness."

THE ADVISORY COUNCIL FOR RELATIONS WITH THE BASQUE COMMUNITIES

The Advisory Council for Relations with the Basque Communities was created by *Ley 8/1994*, and appointments were made in June 1995. This is the official consultative body of the public administration of the Basque Autonomous Community for diaspora affairs. Its function is to propose to homeland institutions the promulgation or modification of provisions relating to Basque communities. The Advisory Council reacts to and attempts to implement the Four-Year Plan for Institutional Action, which coincides with the World Congress of Basque Collectivities stating diaspora goals for the next four-year period. This Advisory Council consists of the president of the Basque government and his appointees, the Secretary of Foreign Action and the Director of Relations with the Diaspora Communities, and representatives from each of the cabinet posts of Culture, Tourism, Labor, Social Security, Education, Housing, Finance, and Industry and Commerce. There is one representative from each of the *Diputaciones* of the three provinces, one from the Federation of Basque Municipalities, two representatives of the Basque parliament, one from the University of the Basque Country, one from the Basque Language Academy, and three assessors "designated by the Congress of Basque Collectivities" (Article 12, Section 3).

Because *Ley 8/1994* specifically describes the assessors as "three representatives from Basque centers designated by the Congress of Basque Collectivities," delegates to the First World Congress in 1995 assumed that they would be selecting these three representatives. However, the Basque government had already appointed three persons living in Euskadi who had resided in or studied the diaspora. A select committee of the Congress with one representative per country had heated discussions regarding this topic, because several delegates believed they should represent themselves and wanted the authority to elect their own representation. Disputed was whether or not these "assessors" would comprehend the diaspora situations if they were not living in or were not from the diaspora. The question of "trustee" versus "delegate" representation was debated, with Argentina taking the lead, advocating three *elected* assessors *from the diaspora*. Basque government officials from the Office of Diaspora Relations intervened in the debate to attempt to soothe misunderstandings by emphasizing that the assessors would have minimal input in twice-yearly meetings of the Advisory Council, which was only intended to facilitate carrying out the Four-Year Plan with homeland institutions, not to propose projects or to establish anything not already in it. They can only react to what the centers request, not initiate their own requests. Some delegates had understood that the assessors would have power over the distribution of grants and subsidies and wanted the prerogative to determine for themselves who would represent the best interests of Basques in their country.

Until this discussion, there was no evident conflict between the diaspora and the homeland, nor among the diaspora groups themselves at the Congress. However, the prospect of money often divides, as does the question of fair

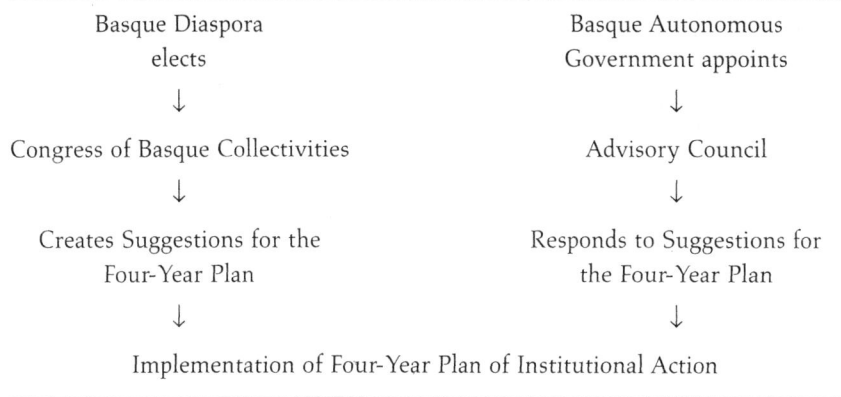

FIG. 6.1. Diaspora Policy Creation and Implementation

representation. The diaspora-versus-homeland question raised several points. Seven of the nineteen diaspora countries' delegates did not want the assessors to be appointed by the Basque president or to come from the homeland. They did not believe that a person could adequately represent a group of people of whom he or she is not a part. Others worried that because one of the appointees had lived in Chile for many years he would be partial to Chile. They questioned whether, if they were elected by all the delegates, the assessors would feel obligated to represent all equally, and whether assessors who did not live in the diaspora would be able to judge which proposals for support, grants, and aid were the most needed or most appropriate?

The other twelve delegates either did not care who represented them, as long as there was trustee representation, or understood that the three assessors do not have a vital role to play on the Advisory Council or in the granting of funds. Typically, the smaller countries (those with fewer Basques) assumed that assessors from the United States or Argentina or Venezuela, with their numerous centers and their federations, would be elected because of their numbers. However, because every country is allotted three delegates regardless of the size of its Basque diaspora population, the voting would not be proportional to population, and perhaps lobbying and voting blocs would develop to elect an assessor. The blocs could result in geographical, linguistic, or specific interests.

The need for ethnic missionaries in Australia and the United States demonstrates the economic viability of these Basque populations but also their lack of personnel or expertise for teaching language and dance or for athletic training. The South American centers have many "Basque experts," but the economic

TABLE 6.1 Possible Voting Blocks for Advisory Council Assessor Representation

Block Category	Assessor 1	Assessor 2	Assessor 3
Geographical	South America	North America/Australia/UK	Europe
Linguistic	Spanish-speaking	English-speaking	French-speaking
Interest	Maintaining infrastructure and membership; needs of financial aid for centers and members	Strengthening networks with homeland; needs of human aid and cultural exchange	Frequent access to homeland institutions, facilities, and benefits

crises in Argentina, Uruguay, and Peru have affected the organizations' ability to maintain themselves and that of their members to pay their dues and participate in social activities. Basque centers in Belgium and France represent every economic group, but their proximity makes it easier and cheaper for all to travel to the Basque provinces. Their frequent visits allow them ready access to libraries, educational facilities, special collections, museums, and galleries, and allow them the same rights to transportation, health care, and social benefits that residents enjoy.

The three assessors actually appointed in 1995, the delegates agreed, were knowledgeable, fair, and would be effective representatives; the point of contention was the manner of selection and not the representatives themselves. The Basque government had intended that the Congress would rubber-stamp its appointments, but the delegates had understood they would be actually electing the assessors. Subsequent interviews with Basque government officials preparing for the Second World Congress of Basque Collectivities in October 1999 confirmed that the assessors' roles and the selection process would remain unchanged unless the newly elected president of the Basque government, Juan José Ibarrexte Markuartu, should desire a change (Iñaki Aguirre interview 1999; Aintzane Aguirre interview, Vitoria-Gasteiz, 1999; Josu Legarreta interview, Vitoria-Gasteiz, 1999). At the 1999 Congress, delegates again raised this issue, which resulted in two of the three previous assessors returning and one being replaced by election of the delegates.

LEGAL FRAMEWORK OF BASQUE GOVERNMENT FOREIGN POLICY

The 1979 Statute of Autonomy of the Basque Autonomous Community enumerates the powers granted specifically to the Basque Autonomous Community of Euskadi and those reserved for the central state government of Spain. Regarding diaspora populations, Article 6, Section 5 states: "Given that 'Euskera' is the heritage of other Basque territories and communities, the Autonomous Community of the Basque Country may request that the Spanish Government, in addition to whatever ties and correspondence are maintained with academic and cultural institutions, to conclude and, where necessary, to submit to the Spanish State Parliament for authorization, those treaties or agreements that will make it possible to establish cultural relations with the States where such territories lie and communities reside, with a view to safeguarding and promoting Euskera." This article has been interpreted to include Basques in Nafarroa, France, and the Basque communities abroad and has strengthened ties for teaching and promoting the Basque language. Article 7, Section 1, stipulates that "for the purpose of this Statute, the political status of 'Basque' shall be accorded to all those who are officially resident, according to the General Laws of the State, in any of the municipalities belonging to the territory of the

Autonomous Community." Section 2 continues, "Persons residing abroad, and their descendants, who officially request it, shall enjoy the same political rights as those living in the Basque Country, if their last residence in Spain was Euskadi, and provided they retain their Spanish citizenship."

Two main principles govern citizenship and naturalization in most political administrations: *ius soli* (birthplace) or *ius sanguinis* (blood ties). For example, in France under *ius soli*, French-born children of foreigners automatically become citizens, and likewise in the United States. However, in Germany it is virtually impossible to obtain German citizenship unless blood ties can be proven. Article 116 of the German constitution says that all ethnic Germans who lived within the boundaries of 1937 are considered to be German, and it also includes individuals who have never lived therein if they are ethnic Germans. The proof can be by descent. The law of ancestry is *ius sanguinis*, and nationality is transmitted to children through blood: even second- and third-generation immigrants born in Germany are denied citizenship, yet under *ius sanguinis*, anyone of German ancestral origin living in Argentina can be considered German, even if the link is centuries old and the person speaks no German (R. King 1993, 2).

The Basque government has tried to combine the two principles: anyone born in the Basque Country who emigrated enjoys the same rights as permanent residents, and anyone born to people who left, no matter the generation, has the same rights. The sole requirement is that they must become members of a recognized and officially registered Basque organization in the diaspora or else return to the Basque Country and become permanent residents. As mentioned above, however, the specific conditions for receiving benefits have created issues of contention for a small minority in the diaspora.

In consideration of international treaties, a 1991 ruling by Spain's Constitutional Court allowed the *Generalitat* of Catalonia to promote by international treaty its cultural values outside Spain, so long as it did not compromise national sovereignty or generate state responsibilities vis-à-vis third parties (C. Garcia 1995, 126). Officials of all seventeen autonomous communities carry out external activities; ten have opened commercial offices in Brussels similar to that of the Basque Delegation to the European Union, and in 1995 there were at least seventy-four different treaties in twenty-five countries, mostly with sub-state actors (ibid., 127). The Basque government, then, has the legal authority and the political and economic ability to forge ahead with its diaspora successes. Utilizing local contacts facilitated by influential Basques abroad, they have created transnational political and economic ties with several governmental, nonprofit, and commercial entities.

By the end of 1991, there was evident a clear policy of using the Basque centers to facilitate meetings between Basque government officials and those in the highest levels of host-country governments. President Ardanza was received with the same protocol as a head of state while in Chile, Mexico, Cuba, Argentina, and Uruguay, and he met with Vice President Al Gore and various congressional leaders in the United States, as a result of the influence of host-country Basques (Andoni Ortúzar interview, Vitoria-Gasteiz, 1997). These foreign-policy meetings have enhanced the status of the Basque government abroad and have caused profound concern for some politicians in Madrid. However, Basque government officials need only point to the mentioned precedent setting the court ruling and to appropriate articles in the Spanish constitution (Article 42) and in the Statutes of Autonomy (Article 6, Section 5; Article 7, Section 2; and all of Article 22) that empower the Autonomous Community to conclude agreements and treaties with other governments "for the management and provisions falling under their exclusive jurisdiction" (Article 22, Statutes of Autonomy of the Basque Country).

Article 42 of the Spanish constitution addresses the right of return for refugees—over which the Basque Autonomous Government also exercises powers—by allowing for the use of government funds to financially aid needy returnees and by providing resident services. The Basque government must submit treaties and international agreements with the host countries of Basque communities to the Spanish parliament for authorization. Since the passage of the Basque parliament's *Ley 8/1994* detailing the specifics of returnees, only a handful of people have requested aid based on their needy circumstances (Aintzane Aguirre interview, Vitoria-Gasteiz, 2002). Many diaspora Basques returned in the 1980s before *Ley 8/1994* was passed and, though they could request aid now, they have not done so. Several of the returnees whom I interviewed did not know that the benefits exist and in agreement with others said they would not apply anyway (B. Goitiandia interview, Kuna, Idaho, 1999; Foruria interview 1999; Arrubarrena Arozamena interview, U.S., 1999; Oleaga interview 1999).

Parliamentary debate on *Ley 8/1994* and its effects on Euskadi's foreign policy consisted mostly of positive emotional accounts regarding the influence of the diaspora in maintaining the government-in-exile, the reception and care given to thousands of political refugees, the work accomplished by the centers and their members in presenting a positive image of the Basque Country, and the important work of maintaining Basque culture, language, and identity. Jon Ażua Mendia (PNV) gave a more instrumentalist angle when he spoke of the "two-way relations which are also going to benefit the Basque Country. In a world that is ever more international, our country needs to open out and look overseas, and Basque communities can play, and are in fact playing, an interesting role in stimulating international awareness of the Basque Country, as a professional 'lobby,' in brief, a basic permanent reference in those markets we want to tackle" (Azua Mendia, quoted in *Law of Relations ...*, 1994). The debate from Eusko Alkartasuna's voice, Intxaurraga Mendibil, raised the point of the several thousand Basques who had escaped to Russia and then were not allowed to leave, and the EA did not want to discriminate between Basques living overseas and those living in the homeland and argued that both groups of needy Basques deserved equal treatment. Others had personal stories of relatives who had lived in exile and of their efforts to maintain ethnic identity and language. There was no mention of creating rifts with Madrid over foreign policy, nor of competing with other autonomous communities for international resources.

Ley 8/1994 institutionalizes the relations and networks of Basque transnationalism and formulates mechanisms that facilitate cooperation and communication between diaspora communities and homeland institutions and among the diaspora communities themselves. The Advisory Council mobilizes the highest spheres of Basque governmental, educational, and cultural institutions in the effort to enhance foreign-policy ties with the diaspora. The successful and positive relations have opened the floodgates for horizontal exchanges among diaspora Basques themselves and have fortified vertical ties between the Basques abroad and their homeland. Exchanges have occurred among dance groups, musicians, chefs, center and federation officials, and athletes. Newsletters are exchanged among diaspora communities, and Internet users check each others' webpages. Policies, communications, and relationships have been extremely "efficient," "fair," "successful," and "positive," according to the homeland and diaspora leaders involved.

Congresses of Basque Collectivities

The First World Congress of Basque Collectivities convened in 1995 to discuss the draft Four-Year Plan of Institutional Action proposed by the Basque government, as well as additional topics, such as allowing non-Basque participation at diaspora Basque centers; Basque-language maintenance; attracting new center members, especially youth; and keeping current center members active. The success of the meeting of delegates was largely the result of an extremely well-planned conference with goals and expectations for participants to create a communications infrastructure. The conclusion of the Congress included the pronouncement that the Basque diaspora communities were ready to promote a substantial change in relations between themselves and the institutions of the homeland and that both the diaspora delegates and the homeland institutions were enthusiastic about future collaborative projects. The Law of Relations with the Basque Communities and the Centers proved to be a helpful legal and political tool that enabled the Basque government and the diaspora communities to reinforce their joint activities and establish future plans.

FOUR-YEAR PLAN OF INSTITUTIONAL ACTION

The delegates to the 1995 First World Congress of Basque Diaspora Collectivities debated and approved the following Four-Year Plan of Institutional Action. It began with the general objectives: (1) to keep the structure and infrastructure of the Basque centers; (2) to promote and maintain the Basque identity, culture, and language; (3) to establish effective channels of communication and information with the Basque Country; and (4) to associate the younger generations with the life and activity of the Basque centers, and through the centers to Euskal Herria.

All centers regardless of size or history would be considered as equal when applying for material support, and special attention would be given to developing telecommunications and computing systems. The Basque government approached credit and banking institutions in Euskadi regarding preferential financing for Basque centers renovating or improving their physical infrastructure, and it was approved in 1998. Once a year, the Book Service of the Ministry of Culture would distribute publications of the Basque government to diaspora Basque centers and would also help fund the cost of publishing by the centers themselves.

An International Day of the Basque Language was chosen to be celebrated in the homeland and in the diaspora (December 3), and language-study materials were sent to the centers. Further discussion with individual centers planned the funding for sending diaspora students to the Basque Country for intensive language training and for sending homeland teachers to diaspora communities to teach Euskera. An International Association of Basque Sports was created to promote Basque handball and *jai alai*, as well as rural sports competitions unique to Euskal Herria. Basque centers with *frontón* courts might be sent coaches and trainers if possible, but this would need further consideration from the Basque government administrators responsible for arranging such exchanges.

The Basque government also made a commitment to intensify the stream of information from Euskadi to the diaspora communities by way of encouraging and using Internet and particularly e-mail telecommunications. Basque Radio and Television (Euskal Irrati Telebista—EITB) began broadcasting one television channel and two radio stations via satellite and cable to Europe and the Americas. Improved communications would also affect the commercial and economic missions of Basque government institutes and foundations, and homeland institutions would provide information, posters, and pamphlets, and other materials about Basque Country tourism to help the centers promote group tours.

The social assistance described in Article 3, Sections 1 and 2, of *Ley 8* would be augmented by payment of travel costs for needy Basques planning a permanent return to Euskadi. Public housing would be available on an equal basis with current residents, and all diaspora members registered with their organizations would be guaranteed medical and hospital assistance while traveling in Euskadi.

As of 1999, 95 percent of the plan had been implemented according to the Director of Diaspora Relations and the positive affirmations of the seventy-five delegates to the 1999 Second World Congress on Basque Communities. Delegates were not able to complete a plan for social-security benefits for returnees because the Spanish central government exercises authority over these budgets, not the Basque Autonomous Community's regional government.

The Second World Congress also resulted in various successes and in the construction of additional networks of communication and exchange. Six Basque government ministers gave added significance to the Congress with their participation, as did the presence of the president of the University of the Basque Country and representatives of provincial and municipal governments. The Second Four-Year Plan proposed that priority be given to educating youth about contemporary Euskal Herria, job placement for diaspora persons in homeland businesses, welfare programs for the needy, university exchanges, economic and tourist programs, and maintenance of Basque culture.

Seventy-seven separate points covered the details of everything from on-line courses from the University of the Basque Country for diaspora students to the Basque centers' collecting the histories of their institutions and the emigrants' experiences to produce a series of publications. Basque centers would consider establishing an International Association of Friends of the Basques in their respective countries, which would be comprised of notable personalities and would help obtain greater international recognition of Basque culture. Members of Basque centers who are medical doctors now have the right to practice in public hospitals belonging to the Basque Health Service (Osakidetza), and all registered members of a center abroad are guaranteed health care in Euskadi whether they are temporary visitors or permanent residents. The issue of benefits for the needy was again discussed, and both homeland and diaspora representatives agreed to continue looking for ways to "create, together with the Institutions of those countries where exiles settled as a result of the Spanish Civil War and especially those in South American nations, an assistance fund to attend to any needs which those exiles may have and thus guarantee them a minimum level of income in accordance with the economic situation of the country where they have settled" (Second Four-Year Plan Article B, Section 6). For individual needy members in desperate emergency situations, the General Secretariat of Foreign Action would research the possibility of providing assistance through subsidies or grants.

Not mentioned in the first action plan but included in the second were the responsibilities of reciprocal aid that the homeland might expect from diaspora communities. Whereas the diaspora needs tangible materials in the form of books, tapes, videos, and ethnic missionaries, the homeland needs a voice. According to Iñaki Aguirre, Secretary of Foreign Action, the Basque government wants the centers' thousands of members to act as goodwill ambassadors for the Basque Country. It "wants the personal testimonies of diaspora Basques to spread the good news about Euskal Herria and its reality today" (Iñaki Aguirre interview 2000).

For future plans, the General Secretary of Foreign Action for the Basque Government would also like to facilitate and participate in the creation of an Internet network of worldwide Basque interests, including the medical, business, industrial, educational, and political interests of the Basque Country and respective host-society governments. The idea is to establish a databank and an exchange of information and of opportunities for Basques by Basques, and to create win-win relations. Though these are the ideas of individuals and do not reflect any formal policy positions of the government or of a political party, the ideas nonetheless are likely to be acted upon because of the type of people who favor them—politicians and upper-level civil servants in the homeland and industrialists and leaders in the diaspora.

In general, the Basque government has been more reactive than proactive with the diaspora communities, responding to center and individual requests as received. Each host country's Basque organizations have different predicaments at different times, rendering it inefficient and ineffective to create one uniform policy for all the diaspora. Thus the importance of the open-ended Four-Year Plan and the grant possibilities for customizing relations.

CONGRESS OF AMERICAN BASQUE CENTERS: BUENOS AIRES 1997, NECOCHEA 2000

As a result of the positive rapport begun at the World Congress in Vitoria-Gasteiz and Argentina's desire to continue the discussion and activities planned, FEVA organized midway congresses of Basque collectivities in Buenos Aires in 1997, and in Necochea in 2000. FEVA invited all the Basque centers in the Americas to discuss the Four-Year Plans of Institutional Action passed in 1995 and 1999. These American Congresses of Basque Centers evaluated their own performance on the goals set in Vitoria-Gasteiz and discussed themes that were tabled there because of lack of time. Seminars included the following themes: the selection of the three assessors for the Basque Government Diaspora Advisory Committee; the fact that there are many Basques in the diaspora who are not members of centers and therefore do not qualify for any grant aid but who are needy and deserving; creation of a worldwide databank of blood donors (already existing in Uruguay, Argentina, and Chile) of the rare RH-negative blood abundant in the Basque population; increased frequency and quality of communications among diaspora centers; the expansion of this American Congress to include all the Basque centers of the world; and the creation of an international nongovernmental organization that would function at the level of the United Nations, European Union, and similar political and economic alliances.[2] The Argentine delegation's proposal included raising again the issue of Basques who are not members of registered centers and who therefore do not qualify for aid, which they argued is unjust. They also proposed an identity card for diaspora Basques to utilize while in Euskadi that would identify them as beneficiaries of residents' rights.

The discussions have been analytical and evaluative and have raised many questions regarding the responsibilities of the Basque government and homeland institutions versus those of the diaspora centers and individuals. For many delegates, these opportunities to interact have provided the first instance in which they have seriously contemplated the scope and relevance of their activities, or realized the salience of their personal and institutional transnationalism. They have embraced it fervently.

The Impact of Telecommunications

Ernest Gellner and Benedict Anderson regard print culture as a crucial factor in the construction of nations because it interconnects people over space and time (Gellner 1983; Anderson 1991). The possibility of a nation depends on the book and the newspaper and on a literate public able to read these publications and imagine themselves as a community. Basque government publications and the Internet provide a print culture to a global audience of Basques in the construction of a diaspora and in enhancing the imagination of a Basque diaspora community.

Basque communities abroad have recognized their role in countering media reports since the beginning of the Spanish Civil War with their efforts to inform their host-country audiences about the falseness of Francoist propaganda while emphasizing their own Catholicism and anticommunist ideology. The government-in-exile utilized the diaspora for decades to spread the word of homeland circumstances, and the current elected Basque government hopes the diaspora will continue to fulfill this role. Iñaki Zabaleta has researched negative media images of the Basque Country and their effect on public opinion. He found that between 1991 and 1998, 96 percent of news in the *New York Times* concerning the Basque Country was negative and related to terrorism. Only the inauguration of the Guggenheim Museum in Bilbao broke this streak (Zabaleta 1999). Though media research demonstrates the negative image of the Basque Country spread in international communications, the ETA cease-fire of 1998–99 did not receive the same attention. The Basque government would like word of mouth to counter the international media, which is a difficult task. To thwart this one-sided image of Euskal Herria, the Autonomous Government intends to utilize the Internet, Basque Radio and Television, and the *Euskal Etxeak* journal to keep Basques and non-Basques informed of the Basque Country's reality. Each is also fundamental to continuing transnational links and to the maintenance of ethnic identity.

DOWNLOADING IDENTITY

Internet links established in 1995 among the majority of the Basque diaspora's centers have produced an explosion of personal communications among younger Basques who understand how to utilize electronic mail. Information, invitations, Basque-language lessons, and Basque website addresses are shared. Since 1995, when the Basque government financed the "wiring" of the diaspora centers, one can witness profound developments in intercommunications. Lists, chatrooms, and over a thousand websites (Adoni Alonso interview 2002) give Basque "surfers" a myriad of choices in information and entertainment on Basque themes. Inquiries that otherwise might be disregarded because they were too difficult to answer are now made and answered simply with several clicks of the mouse. Basques from the United States interested in investing in real estate in Argentina have utilized Basque-center e-mail and connections to get information. Basques from Belgium desiring to practice their English have made institutional and personal contacts through the centers in the United States, Canada, and Australia. Researchers and journalists are provided with opportunities to make connections and to arrange fieldwork while benefiting from the institutional networks. Whereas previously established communication among centers tended to be instrumental *for the institution,* Internet communication has the capability to encourage personal and personally instrumental interactions.

Internet access will likely provide the most significant catalyst for exponential increases in intra-diasporic communications. The Internet allows the construction and manipulation of a virtual identity that breaks free from traditional paradigms of territoriality, ancestry, and language and enables a construct of identity based on the actor's own definition. The exploitation of telecommunications introduces expanded dimensions for the creation and re-creation of ethnicity and carries the potential to unite virtually what is impossible to unite physically. Diaspora populations are accustomed to psychological and emotional ties without the benefits of physical contact. However, the Internet does not give a public or social identity and is therefore not perceived as a threat to the Basque centers or to cultural organizations. Because technology is available only to those with some degree of knowledge and financial ability, it is currently utilized at the Basque centers by a few skilled members and at home by those who can afford a computer and Internet access. Television is much more accessible and effective for information transfer and entertainment.

Basque public television and radio (EITB) has made inroads in the South American market and is transmitting to Basque communities through cable television in Mexico, Peru, Chile, Argentina, Uruguay, Venezuela, and the eastern United States. It is hoped that consistent homeland transmission from EITB will show a different perspective on current events in the Basque Country and will educate and update those who watch. It has been a very popular idea among Basques in these diaspora countries to be able to receive twenty-four-hour current news broadcasts, films, game shows, sporting events, and cultural entertainment in Basque and in Spanish. EITB also broadcasts documentaries and reports regarding the diaspora population to the homeland audience. This promotes more realistic and less symbolic or nostalgic mutual knowledge. The influence of the media and the globalization of telecommunications are being utilized to achieve positive results for Basque ethnic identity as Basques are becoming more and more interconnected with each other around the globe. The imagined community is expanding into a virtual reality.

EUSKAL ETXEAK: AN INTRA-DIASPORA JOURNAL

In May 1989, the first issue of the Basque government's journal *Euskal Etxeak* was published for the diaspora with the aim of "presenting the contemporary Basque reality" to those not living in the homeland (Ardanza 1989, 2). Basques were invited to submit articles, thus establishing the first systematic network of communications for the diaspora populations. The journal has provided a common forum in which diaspora collectivities enhance their awareness and knowledge of one another's activities and is the primary source of information regarding Basque government initiatives with respect to the diaspora.

Euskal Etxeak is published for the diaspora communities three or four times a year by the Basque government, with news and information regarding Euskal Herria and Basques all over the world. Financed by the Basque government, it is mailed to the Basque centers and to most members' home addresses. This extremely popular periodical is published in Spanish and English editions with a few short articles or titles in Basque, and includes current reports from the homeland about sports, politics, economics, history, and language, as well as editorials and reports of activities from diaspora members. Numerous interview respondents pointed to it as an example of prestige and legitimacy, mentioning, "We even have our own magazine, you know?" To these people, being part of an organized and mobilized diaspora community is socially and psychologically significantly different from being just one more descendant of another immigrant in their host society. Conversations with Basques in each host country included the influence of the journal and the ability to compare themselves with other Basques around the world. This publication has been the most effective to date in creating a united diaspora mentality that demonstrates to all Basques who encounter it the similarities among diaspora populations. Readers compare the celebrations, programs, histories, and problems of Basques in other areas of the world and have concluded that there are more similarities than differences.

One phenomenon resulting from this initial unification sees diaspora Basques trying to find lost relatives in other diaspora communities. A first step for many Basques on their return to ethnicity may have been looking for homeland family, investigating histories of immigrant ancestors, and making an emotional visit to the ancestral home in Euskal Herria. Now those Basques and others who are part of a continual line of ethnic maintenance are branching out and looking for relatives who emigrated to other parts of the world. Internet websites advertise their ability to research family genealogy, but detailed records on Basques are often scarce and occasionally unreliable. Historical research, such as looking for great-aunts and great-uncles and other distant kin entails looking through poorly kept emigration and immigration records and more specific Basque-center membership lists. Finding information about a Basque who was not a Basque-center member is extremely difficult. On the contrary, discovering a live relative who participates in any Basque institution anywhere is relatively simple if the searcher knows the complete name and place of birth. Subscribers to *Euskal Etxeak* have discovered pictures and names of relatives when reading about other countries, and individual e-mail requests to Basque centers for information is customary (Patty Miller interview, Boise, 2002; Jean Curutchet interview, San Francisco, 1997; Miren Arozarena interview, Buenos Aires, 2002; Kate Camino interview, Reno, 2002).

Abundant homeland information will undoubtedly affect diaspora opinions and questions regarding public policy. The Basque government may find that the diaspora, rather than blindly following homeland policy and "obeying" and being "loyal" to established governmental policy, may raise criticisms. By empowering and encouraging diaspora populations to involve themselves with each other and with the homeland, the Basque government has opened a Pandora's box. The growing self-assertiveness of the Basques abroad and the fact that they have survived without the Basque government's aid until now means that the transmission of criticism from the diaspora toward the homeland may have serious repercussions. If the homeland's leadership perceives that its diaspora should maintain constant contact, express loyalty, and provide the homeland with services in the host country (for example, by utilizing the centers as free "embassies"), there could be considerable tension. Perhaps the Bakersfield and Los Banos groups are justified in their "strings attached" concerns about the free computers offered by the Basque government. Clearly stated objectives and expectations in communications between the Basque government and the diaspora communities would perhaps eliminate any future strained relations.

Euskadi's Commitment to the Diaspora

BASQUE GOVERNMENT FINANCIAL SUPPORT FOR THE DIASPORA

The various Basque diasporic communities maintain vertical relations with the homeland and horizontal relations with each other in the different host societies. Each of the sample diaspora populations presented here, with the exception of North Queensland, has institutional relations with the Eusko Jaurlaritza, the Autonomous Basque Government of Euskadi. *Ley 8/1994* recognizes the Basque centers as cultural delegations of Euskadi—representations of embassies for a stateless people. Josu Legarreta, Director of Diaspora Relations with the Basque Communities during the 1980s and again beginning in 1999, asked that the centers "continue as until now, as ambassadors of the Basque Country, being a collective acknowledgment of what our country is and has been among the nations of the world" (Legarreta, quoted in *Euskal Etxea*, 1989, 10). As table 6.2 indicates, the Basque government has supported its rhetoric with pesetas to help subsidize these cultural embassies.

TABLE 6.2 Basque Autonomous Government Appropriations to Diaspora Communities

Host Country	1998 $	1999 $	2000 $	2001 $	2002 $
Argentina	445,476	478,451	614,770	516,605	355,625
United States	81,219	95,547	94,520	173,590	153,186
Uruguay	97,757	70,738	69,056	60,756	47,047
Belgium	43,242	18,465	—	—	—
Australia	16,921	11,587	9,616	8,414	11,000
Peru	12,221	10,330	9,015	7,992	5,000

Figures in United States dollars calculated from Spanish pesetas for each year's average exchange rate.

Grants were funded even before *Ley 8/1994* passed, with initial appropriations for the entire combined diaspora communities in nineteen countries applying for aid in 1987 totaling 5 million pesetas ($40,650 U.S.). This figure increased to 213,870,301 pesetas ($1,108,131 U.S.) in 2001. The grants support functions such as Basque-center building maintenance, cultural celebrations and promotion, language courses, expenses for choirs and dance groups, athletes, conferences, academic research on Basque themes, and a fifteen-book series that compiles the histories of the fifteen most important diaspora communities.

In addition to grants, in 1998 the Basque government negotiated with the Banco Bilbao Vizcaya to allow special low-interest rates for loans to diaspora centers, with the Basque government acting as guarantor. The 4.75-percent interest rate is extremely advantageous for centers in countries with floating interest rates and where borrowers normally pay more than triple that rate. Sixteen centers in Argentina, Uruguay, and Mexico have taken loans to carry out investment in infrastructure and to improve their facilities. Each of the centers so far has received the total loan amount for which they applied, and the total loans equal approximately $1.6 million U.S. (*Euskal Etxeak* 41 [1999]: 10).

The effects of the subsidies on the Basque organizations are debatable. The creation of fifty-seven new organizations since 1985 in just these six case-study communities coincides with the granting of subsidies by the Basque government, but it also coincides with the autonomy of the Basque provinces, which boosted Basque morale in the diaspora. This change in political status can have profound effects on a homeland's diaspora—as witnessed in Polish Catholic communities that revived their trans-state activities motivated by the emergence of Solidarity and the democratization of Poland (Sheffer 1986, 4) and in Croatian communities that revived and created ethnic organizations after the break-up of Yugoslavia and intensified their activities as Croatian ethnics (Winland 1995). In Argentina, the resurgence of Basque ethnicity also coincided with the embarrassment of the Malvinas/Falkland Islands War with Great Britain and the shame of Argentine identity (Zavaleta interview, Buenos Aires, 1997). One could argue that the increase in Basque awareness follows a trend of general ethnic-identity resurgence around the globe.

Basque government grants are intended only for special one-time projects and are not intended for, nor are they sufficient to provide for, the construction or permanent maintenance of buildings. However, Arnold Strickon argues, with reference to his analysis of Norwegian immigrants and national independence, that "once a target population does respond to the overture of the home country, the ideological and material inputs into the emigrant population can themselves become a motivation, resource, and reinforcement of ethnic identification and activity" (Strickon 1984, quoted in Winland 1995, 6). The Basque government representatives for diaspora relations do not believe there is a positive causal relationship between grants funded and the increased numbers of Basque organizations (Andoni Ortuzar interview, Vitoria-Gasteiz, 1999; Benan Oregi interview, Vitoria-Gasteiz, 1999; Iñaki Aguirre Arizmendi interview, Vitoria-Gasteiz, 2000; Josu Legarreta interview, Vitoria-Gasteiz, 2001), and neither do the overwhelming majority of interviewed leaders from the forty-three Basque communities that participated in this research.

To obtain these grant funds, representatives of the Office of Relations with the Diaspora Communities make requests for appropriations to the Basque Autonomous Government Parliament. A governmental decree establishes that the president shall name, by resolution, an Evaluation Commission made up of the Secretary General of Foreign Action as president; the Director of Relations with Basque Collectivities, and two others, also selected by the president of the Basque government. Favored grants are those that will affect the most people and will have "staying power." The gathering of historical materials and oral histories pertaining to the exile of Basque citizens after 1936 has been singled out as a priority. Proposals for festival production costs might include requests for everything from bringing homeland dancing groups and athletes to Australia to paying for special gifts for dignitaries in Argentina. Those requests might receive only partial funding.

One section of the grant petition requests the solicitor to offer ideas about how the proposal could be funded in the future—intending to encourage the centers and individuals to move on to self-support. In 1999 only five of the ninety-nine applicants answered this question. There is a creeping concern among a few policymakers in the homeland administration that diaspora communities in the countries hard hit with economic decline will continue to make grant requests without considering the *necessity* versus the *desire* for a certain project. Festivals can be successful and effective at promoting and enhancing Basque culture and identity, and they can be efficiently administered without superfluous accessories. However, Basque government officials working in diaspora relations are adamant about not interfering in the internal decision-making of diaspora organizations. In 1995, there were sixty-eight applications for financial aid, and by 2002 this number was ninety-seven. During the same years, the budget for the Diaspora Relations office decreased. In 2001, its budget was $1,274,076 U.S., and in 2002 it was $1,084,815 U.S., although it worked with other departments to ascertain additional funding for certain diaspora programs.

In 2002, ninety-four of the ninety-seven separate proposals for grant consideration received partial aid. Rather than fully fund a few projects, the Evaluation Commission examines each proposal for its breadth and depth and, of course, its cost. Each grant application has to be approved by the officially registered Basque organization of which the solicitor is a member. The Basque government does not meddle in these internal affairs, and each center can make its own rules regarding how its members make proposals. The centers can relay on to their federations every single grant application from its members, or send them all directly to the Basque government, or screen the applications and deem some unworthy or unworkable. Of course, it is to the centers' benefit to submit all applications and compel the General Secretary of Foreign Action to act as hatchet man. This action avoids personal conflict and internal problems in the centers and lays the blame for rejection on an unknown homeland appointed official and his civil servants.

The Office of Relations with the Basque Communities (1998 budget: $1.5 million U.S.) shares foreign-policy responsibilities with other directorates under the General Secretary of Foreign Action. The organizational structure of the Basque government's Foreign Action includes another entity known as the Presidential Commission for Foreign Relations, which answers directly to the Lehendakari (president). This commission participates in European affairs where the various recognized Regions have direct representation in decision-making and policy-making. There are also two programs of aid that allow collaboration and financing of projects in Iparralde.

FUNDACIONES, INSTITUTOS, AND CONFUSION

The Basque government has established political and economic policies to promote international business networks utilizing the positive reputation and status of the Basque populations in their respective host communities. Benefitting from the positive social status of Basques, top Basque business leaders,

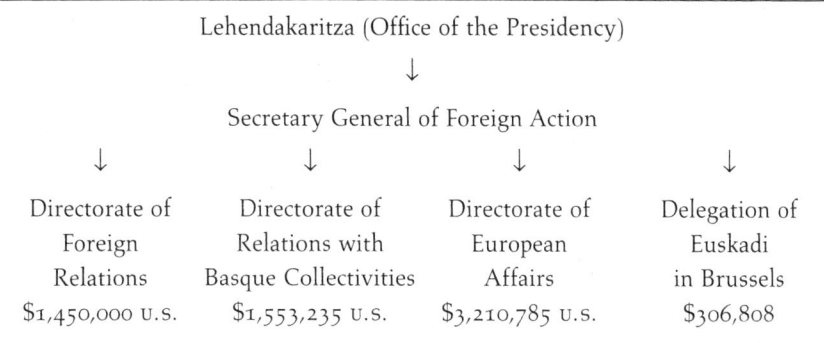

FIG. 6.2. Foreign-Policy Responsibilities of the Basque Autonomous Government and the 2002 Budget

engineers, and lawyers from the host society have joined with expert economists and specialists from Euskal Herria to create business and economic *institutos* and *fundaciones* charged with producing and designing international trade between homeland and diaspora.

In 1992, the Basque government created the Basque Foundations and Basque Institutes of Chile, Mexico, Argentina, Venezuela, and later that of the United States. An economic-network concept established in the diaspora, the idea was to create industrial and business relationships between the homeland and various host-country enterprises where Basques had high social status and economic clout. The homeland businesses would use the diaspora Basques' contacts and personal networks to make inroads into the South American Mercosur trading bloc with investment, production, and distribution for the reconversion of industrial societies. In the United States, the American Basque Foundation had a lobby office in Washington, D.C., that helped get Basque government public-debt bonds introduced in United States markets and served as the official Registered Agent and legal representative of the Basque government for the issuance of these bonds in the U.S. It also aided political relations with Vice President Al Gore and several congressional leaders and committee chairpersons. Though the American Basque Foundation has since dissolved, the others continue to expand, even to the point where in 2002 the Mexican Institute was elevated to a Delegation of Euskadi in Mexico. The change in judicial and political status is expected to expand to the other institutes and foundations in the remaining countries. These institutes and foundations mediated the investment of thirty-five Basque firms in Latin America during 1997 and 1998 alone (Josu Legarreta interview, Vitoria-Gasteiz, 1999). It is highly unlikely that Belgian Basques can influence European Union policy or add to the Basque government's weight in EU regional committees' political or economic decisions (Andoni Ortuzar interview, Vitoria-Gasteiz, 1997), so there are no plans to establish an institute or foundation in Belgium, and the established Delegation of Euskadi in Brussels already performs these economic functions. In Australia, the Basque diaspora population does not meet the critical mass necessary for political or economic influence, and the General Secretary of Foreign Action stated that, though Australia would be a natural opening to Asian markets, there are no plans yet for expanding to Australia. In 2002, the Basque Society for the Promotion and Reconversion of Industry (SPRI) opened an office in Shanghai.

The creation of these foundations and institutes caused many misunderstandings between their employees (mostly professional economists and marketing and business specialists), the centers and their memberships, and the Basque government. The centers had been told in speech after speech by the Basque president and in numerous communiqués from diaspora relations officials that *they* were the "embassies of the Basque Country," that all communications and relations between the homeland and the diaspora would be achieved through Basque center–Basque Autonomous Government channels. Now there were "institutes" and "foundations" created separately by diaspora Basques that were receiving business and government representatives from homeland and host country.

One former president of a Basque center in Argentina described his embarrassment and disappointment when at a business lunch an associate asked why he, as president of the local Basque center, had not attended a reception for a delegation from the Basque Country interested in building a machine plant in their city. He knew nothing about it because the institute had not notified him or anyone else at the local Basque center. The interviewees at the institute replied, "Why would we? Why should we? These are business meetings, not Basque dance or art exhibitions. We have work to do, and just because there is a Basque cultural organization here does not mean we are going to ask permission or clear our business presentations with someone who does not know anything about the topic" (Urquizu interview, Buenos Aires, 1997).

When asked about money to be made from these arrangements or about personal rivalries or jealousies between the two groups, members of the centers overwhelmingly replied that they only wanted from the institutes the information and recognition that they had been told they were granted. They only wanted to be informed, not consulted for permission; only be made aware of additional ties and links being established in order to be knowledgeable and up to date about homeland-diaspora relations of all kinds. A few of the foundation and institute personnel believed that the center leaders were worried about losing or having to share their status as spokespersons for their respective Basque communities but not necessarily interested in personal material gain, which is practically impossible to obtain through the foundations or institutes.

The centers are not professional structures and do not have continuous leadership by the same individuals. Volunteers make up the boards of directors, and these people cannot possibly do the work of the foundations and institutes. The Basque government needs expert professionals to foment business and industrial communications, and they will remain separate from the centers (Irazusta interview, Buenos Aires, 1997). The diaspora relations director asked to have the FEVA and NABO federation presidents on the boards of their institute and foundation respectively, and in Chile, Mexico, and Venezuela those involved with the institutes are the same people who are usually on the boards of directors anyway. Homeland policymakers and civil servants admit that personality conflicts inside diaspora organizations and among them are indeed issues of discussion and slight concern. However, they uphold a "no-entanglement" policy.

This continuous aspect of homeland-diaspora relations involves the entwining of economic and financial resources, as did colonial-era enterprises, migration chains, and activities during the Civil War and the following Franco years. Grants appropriated by the Basque government for the established diaspora Basque centers, the private ownership of land or businesses in Euskadi by diaspora Basques, and resources connected to joint ventures all strengthen the contemporary transnational bonds between the homeland and the diaspora, although these bonds are qualitatively changed now with the element of a recognized government as an actor for the first time. The evolving relationship may prove to be problematic. Gabriel Sheffer, examining the behavior of homeland governments toward their established diaspora, notes that governments want to promote their own interests and if there arises a conflict between homeland and diaspora needs, homeland economic and political interests come first (Sheffer 1996, 44).

Future relations between the Basque government and diaspora Basque centers will most assuredly continue to be dominated by cultural concerns and will focus on expansion and preservation of ethnic identity. Although the PNV has not directly introduced partisan politics into the relationship, when campaigning at home the party benefits from the international status it has created by using the position of the Basques in the host societies and from the institutes and foundations. Infant networks of Basque centers, federations, Basque institutes, and individuals will soon further impact the "imagining" of a global Basque diaspora. The daily manifestations of ethnic identity preservation, therefore, are more likely to evolve into a diasporic-Basque identity rather than a host-country Basque identity.

GAZTEMUNDU: PREPARING DIASPORA YOUTH FOR FUTURE LEADERSHIP

A special program encouraging youth to visit the contemporary Basque homeland, not the idealized and romanticized myth perpetuated by generations of diaspora Basques, was initiated in 1990. The other goal of Gaztemundu (World of Youth) is to educate and prepare the future leaders of Basque organizations. The program is not a two-week tourist trip through the provinces. Diaspora Basques who are members of an officially registered center and between the ages of twenty and thirty are invited to apply to be one of sixty chosen to participate in the program each autumn. The Basque centers must carry out their own preselection process and forward no more than three nominations per organization. Countries that have only one Basque center are allowed to send up to ten delegates. Applicants are required to create an individual project regarding one of three themes: (1) promotion of Basque cultural activities in their center and in their host country; (2) economic and industrial relations between their host country and Euskadi; or (3) attracting and keeping youth active in the diaspora organizations. The participants present their research papers conference-style and then discuss their solutions and proposals for improvement in their topic group. Each selected person pays up to $500 U.S., and the Basque government subsidizes the remaining costs.

This program is perceived as an effective investment in the future of diaspora-homeland relations. The Basque government is molding the self-selected future leaders of the institutions and preparing them to work inside the current framework of relations. The Gaztemundu initiative has been successful in achieving its stated goals as well as in meeting the peripheral objectives of strengthening ties among diaspora communities through these youth conferences. Gaztemundu participants interviewed from one month to six years after attending their conference stated that they remain in constant contact with at least one person from a different country and regularly exchange ideas for each other's centers. The Gaztemundu programs for Basque youth are similar to Irish programs for diaspora youth to experience the *Gaeltacht* Gaelic-speaking western counties and to the Israeli summer kibbutz-work programs, where contact with the homeland is expected to spark interest in ethnicity preservation. These young people represent the generation most likely to understand and utilize telecommunications, and the homeland government and institutions have an interest in capturing their attention and allegiance with the goal of maintaining and promoting positive relations. The Gaztemundu program is creating institutionalized bonds between hyphenated Basques and the Basque Country to secure the allegiance of the former for the latter's economic and political agendas, in both the Old and the New World (Douglass 1999).

Diaspora Political Commitment to Euskadi

VOTING

It is not uncommon for homeland politicians to campaign to their diaspora populations. Israeli parties organize inexpensive airline charters to allow diaspora Jews to travel and vote in homeland elections. Haitian and Filipino leaders actively solicit their United States diaspora populations for political support (Basch et al. 1994). In the Spanish Autonomous Community of Galicia, the diaspora vote actually makes an electoral difference, as it did recently by giving the necessary percentage to elect Fraga Ibarne president. Fraga Ibarne had traveled through Galician diaspora communities campaigning, and the approximately 500,000 votes from outside the Galician homeland made the difference in the outcome (I. Aguirre Arizmendi interview, Vitoria-Gasteiz, 1999).

No Euskadi or Nafarroan political parties campaign for the parliament or for the presidencies outside their respective autonomous communities because the diaspora vote does not make an electoral difference. The total number of qualified diaspora voters for the 2001 parliamentary election in Euskadi was 32,858—of whom only 10,552 actually voted—and 160 of those votes were nullified for various reasons. This represents only .7 percent of the total 1,414,269 votes cast in that election. The main focus of the diaspora Basque-center activities remains cultural, and in questionnaires the majority of respondents stated that they are not interested in politics and also admitted that they do not know enough about homeland politics to distinguish between the various homeland political parties.

Table 6.3 demonstrates the political-party preferences of those diaspora populations who do vote. After going to the trouble to become eligible to vote, a very low percentage actually do so.[3]

Although *Euskal Etxeak* explained to its readers the registration and voting procedures, Basques in Sydney erroneously thought they had to go to the Spanish Embassy (they could go to any consular office), and in Peru, Uruguay, and the United States some received their ballots by post after the election day. It is clear that many diaspora Basques are interested in homeland elections, but many, many more are not aware that they qualify to vote and have the right to do so. As shown in chapter 4, the majority do not know enough about politics to distinguish between the political parties and/or do not involve themselves in homeland partisan politics.

Though the World Congresses and the American Congresses all included the need for the diaspora to actively promote a positive view of the Basque Country to counter negative images of political violence, there is a notable lack of information in diaspora communities regarding homeland elections or even regarding the significant ETA cease-fire. When leaders of the communities that participated in the questionnaires and interviews in 1996 and 1997 were contacted again in 1998 and 1999 regarding the imprisonment of the National Directorate of Herri Batasuna in the fall of 1997 for the production of a campaign video and about the ETA cease-fire that began in September 1998, they reported that their communities were generally ignorant of both events. Individuals with access to Basque media via the Internet "may be interested," but none of the communities I contacted had held any kind of informative meetings for their members or tried to contact their local press. None had discussed either of the topics formally at members' dinners or other gatherings. Center bartenders also reported very little discussion of either event. This is consistent with questionnaire data that almost two-thirds of the diaspora populations researched do not know about or purposefully stay out of Basque Country politics. Though elite leaders had agreed to the idea, these diaspora

TABLE 6.3 Diaspora Voting in the 1990, 1994, 1998, 2001 Elections

	1990 Diaspora		1994 Diaspora		1998 Diaspora		2001 Diaspora	
Registered Voters	7,005		14,373		26,396		32,858	
Actual Voters	2,152	(30.7%)	3,119	(21.7%)	6,888	(26.1%)	10,522	(32%)

Diaspora Votes

	1990		1994		1998		2001	
PNV	647	(30.1%)	978	(31.4%)	2,011	(32.%)	PNV/EA 4165	(39.5%)
PSOE	523	(24.3%)	858	(27.5%)	1,500	(24.3%)	PSE-EE/PSOE 2161	(20.5%)
PP	205	(9.5%)	431	(13.8%)	1,343	(21.7%)	PP 2898	(27.5%)
HB/EH	204	(9.5%)	312	(10%)	522	(8.5%)	EH 625	(5.9%)
IU	0		31	(1%)	256	(4.2%)	EB-IU 384	(3.6%)
EA	105	(4.9%)	251	(8.1%)	378	(6.1%)		
Others	468	(21.8%)	258	(8.3%)	166	(2.7%)	159	(1.5%)
Nullified votes	0		0		712		Nullified/Blank 160	(1.5%)
Total	2,152	(100%)	3,119	(100%)	6,176	(100%)	10,522	(100%)

Election data compiled from Basque Government Department of Interior published results and *Euskal Etxeak* 40 (1998). PNV = Partido Nacionalista Vasco; PSOE = Partido Socialista Obrero Español; PP = Partido Popular; HB/EH = Herri Batasuna/Euskal Herritarrok; IU = Izquierda Unida; EA = Eusko Alkartasuna.

communities were not fulfilling their part of the Four-Year Plans, which called for an active lobby to promote a positive image of Euskal Herria.

Conclusions

The leaderless diaspora is no more. There is a marked difference between the passive policy of the 1980s and the active one of the 1990s and the new millennium. The Basque government has only begun to harness the potential of the diaspora communities. It has been nudged to recognize a diaspora waiting since the days of the government-in-exile, but it has not yet made the mistake of attempting to control its diaspora populations, nor has it alienated them by telling them they are not a part of the homeland or no longer understand it.

The Basque communities are proving to be effective and significant nonstate actors, proceeding on behalf of their homeland government, institutions, and businesses. Though the role can be evaluated for its importance, the "unofficial ambassador" status has been influential in the cases analyzed here. However, I have also shown that diaspora communities do not operate as monolithic blocs of ethnic or political consciousness and that there are personal conflicts and individual agendas that interfere with the effective administration of grants and economic and political ties between and among the diaspora and homeland populations. For example, the question of benefits for needy Basques residing in the diaspora remains unresolved.

Basques in these communities abroad are constructing and consuming identity in a very different fashion than they have in the past, thanks to the impetus of the Basque government to "connect" them and to its organizational and legislative efforts. Each new advance in transportation, telecommunications, and the Internet utilized by the groups reduces the physical and conceptual distance between San Sebastián, San Francisco, and Santa Fé. The 1994 Law of Relations with the Basque Communities in the Exterior propagated the multiplication and intensification of homeland-to-diaspora and diaspora-to-diaspora relations and interactions, which in general have been described as extremely successful and positive. The Basque diaspora, previously sedentary and without unified direction, still has no collaborative political or cultural project. Instead, there are generalizations from the first and second Four-Year Plans that address typically noncontroversial issues and programs in which communities may or may not participate. This voluntary aspect may be the key to maintaining productive, beneficial, and favorable relations.

There are currently more than 160 Basque organizations in twenty different countries, and the government of Euskadi recognizes 137 of those. The unprecedented proliferation in the number of Basque centers points to an expanding web of communications between Basques. The Basque government's decision to prepare a qualitative change in relations, along with the judicial and political framework of *Ley 8/1994*, the World Congresses, the Gaztemundu program, the *Euskal Etxeak* journal, the grants and subsidies, and the avenue of globalized telecommunications have all synthesized to overcome the geographic disconnection and establish a psychological connection.

Chapter Seven

Amaia: An Interconnected Disconnectedness

The history of Basque transnationalism challenges the sociospatial assumptions of community, for these active ethnics have linked themselves simultaneously to networks of relationships and meaning from both host and home country since the time of marine trade and Spanish colonialism, through the Basque government-in-exile period, to contemporary Basque centers. "Communities are to be distinguished, not by their falsity/genuineness, but by the style in which they are imagined" (Anderson 1991, 6). These dispersed Basque diaspora communities are similarly imagined as ethnic diaspora communities (utilizing Cohen's categorization), promoting cultural preservation and sustained ethnic identity over centuries in some cases; as groups maintaining homeland trade, labor, immigration, and cultural ties; as exhibiting solidarity with co-ethnics; and as a community with a shared collective history and myths of its idealized homeland.[1]

I have traced the history of Basque migration and shown that Basque ethnic group awareness existed in their European and later New World trading networks and in the imperial diaspora inside the Spanish colonial framework. Economic conditions, the aftermath of wars, primogeniture inheritance systems, and chain migration from Basque villages to the New World facilitated a Basque labor diaspora. From the 1930s through the 1970s, a political diaspora of exiles escaping oppression, prison, and death sentences under the Franco dictatorship provided the last wave of Basque emigration. It is this most recent cohort of Basques who have affected the diaspora communities and their contemporary ethnic identity manifestations. As a means of concluding the results of this project, I aim to summarize the comparisons of Basque diaspora communities in Argentina, Australia, Belgium, Peru, the United States, and Uruguay; to compare the Basque diaspora to other ethnic diasporas; and to propose its place in present and future Basque studies.

"Belonging Here and There": Expressions from the Basque Diaspora

I have demonstrated support for the argument that despite geographical and generational differences, the core elements of Basque ethnic identity are defined in a constant manner, focusing on ancestry, music, dance, sport, cuisine, and religion, and decreasingly on language, in each of the six case studies. The various ethnic institutions and Basque centers developed in much the same way—as ethnic societies for mutual financial aid and as host-country adaptation facilitators with a focus on preserving a Basque cultural identity, and not as political organizations promoting a political or partisan ideology. The centers have also followed a transition pattern similar to institutions that are now facilitating host-country Basques' "return" to ethnicity in general and often to the home country specifically. The research responses demonstrated that though the majority of people queried had no intention of a permanent physical return, many maintain a psychological and emotional commitment to the Basque Country—one of the elements of diasporic identity.

A diasporic identity, however, is not merely an extension of the homeland. Boundaries of multiple loyalties shift and can differ from one diaspora location to another. The subjective nature of Basque diaspora identity—the sense of belonging that it entails and the connection to positive social status as argued by Tajfel—is important because it provides a sense of unity that transplants the sense of belonging from a specific physical homeland to a transnational consciousness. The subjective identity may also entail a responsibility to survive as a conscious collective (Bakalian 1992, 2–3), a concept that only a few interviewees expressed explicitly in interviews but that was supported by questionnaire results.

Separate research has concluded that women are more likely than men to implement ethnic food consumption, holiday celebrations, and childhood socialization patterns (Stoller 1996, 146), but responses to my interview and questionnaire questions did not find this a statistical reality with the Basque population. Though there were differences between males and females in their reported knowledge of homeland politics and in their migration experiences, gender was not a significant factor in defining "Basqueness," and the majority of both genders disagreed that mothers had been more influential than fathers in preserving Basque ethnicity maintenance. This adds another dimension to the Basque feminist anthropologists' contentions that a Basque matriarchy does not exist in reality. Though the myth of a Basque matriarchy continues among Basque populations in Euskal Herria and abroad, questionnaire responses fortified Teresa Del Valle's conclusion (Del Valle et al. 1985) that mothers are not necessarily more influential than fathers in perpetuating Basque traditions and identity.

I have illustrated that these diaspora definitions of "Basqueness" tend to cling to the traditional exclusive Sabino Arana identifiers—ancestry, religion, and language—although the homeland's understanding (following Catalonia) has been modified to a more inclusive category of those who live and work in

Euskal Herria and those who want to be Basque and work for the maintenance of Basque culture. There were high percentages of respondents who did not know or had no opinion on these questions, which opens the possibility of a shift occurring in the diaspora population's mentality. However, regardless of geography, gender, and generation, there are prevailing core elements of cultural ethnonationalist tendencies and ethnic institutions that have developed according to similar patterns. Though the majority of the Basques who are members of ethnic organizations in the diaspora consider themselves *abertzales*, or patriots, they understand this more as an ethnic commitment to fight for the preservation of Basque culture, language, and autonomy, though not necessarily for territorial sovereignty and statehood.

The most recent Basque immigrant population, that in Belgium, demonstrated opinions closer to those of the homeland, and interviewees there stated that their relatively easy access to Euskal Herria facilitated their personal and informational networks. Because geography is less and less a barrier to interaction, distance-shrinking technology theories propose that as communication and transnational networks intensify in substance and frequency, these Basques, especially those in the "I do not know" and "No opinion" categories, are likely to be influenced by images and information received from the homeland that will influence their attitudes toward inclusivity of Basqueness.

Categorizing the Basque Communities as a Diaspora

Academic definitions and common features of "diaspora" distinguish these Basque communities as indeed diaspora. Their dispersal to many lands over time was traumatic and forced, as it was for Carlist War veterans and Franco-era political exiles, or by choice, as exemplified by the Basque mariners, and military, cleric, and commercial migrants inside the Spanish imperial diaspora. Basques have departed their homeland in pursuit of commerce and because of established trading networks that provided information and improved possibilities of success. They created bilateral trade on their own with foreign political entities and also as part of the Spanish domination of the Americas. The Basque Autonomous Government is renewing and re-creating commercial networks long left dormant by utilizing Basque diaspora communities to further homeland business through *institutos* and *fundaciones*.

The shared understanding of a particular nationalist Basque history creates a perception of victimization and continuous attempted domination by Castilian Spain. For Basques, their "golden age" includes defense from invaders, including the Romans and Moors; autonomy from Castile; superiority of seamanship; the democratic and collective society ruled by the *fueros*; and a rural life-style where Basque culture and language are maintained. These collective memories were a part of each Basque community, regardless of the time of migration, the size of the community, or the host country. This is not surprising, because it is the same nationalist history that was promulgated in the homeland. Regardless of its "veracity" or "genuineness" to different historians, what is important is that these memories are accepted and believed as the truth by the diaspora Basques themselves. This common understanding foments ethnicity maintenance and diaspora consciousness. These particular Basques feel they have a responsibility to their ancestors and to the "maintenance, restoration, safety and prosperity" (Cohen and Layton-Henry, eds., 1997, 26) of Euskal Herria, even if they rarely act politically upon these feelings.

However, the idealization of the Basque Country and the diaspora's historical perceptions of the Basques as victims of incessant domination may change as the diaspora witnesses homeland democracy and administration at work. In other ethnic communities, the creation of the Israeli state and an independent Croatia, and the establishment of democracy in Poland and the Ukraine, removed these diaspora populations' ideas of themselves as a superior ethnic group, above political corruption and inefficiency. There will be problems in the autonomous communities of the four provinces in Spain, as there are in any administration, and Basques will be confronted with this cognitive dissonance.

Many migrants left the Basque Country believing they would return after making their fortunes, but these were individualized plans and there was no collective "return movement" for Basques to their homeland until the Civil War wave of exiles. Previous emigrants had chosen to leave, albeit pushed by economic hardship and war reparations, and had moved as individuals or as families. The Civil War exiles were thousands who moved at once, traumatically and involuntarily. Their return depended upon the elimination of Franco and also became a myth as the decades wore on. There is no evidence of a contemporary collective permanent-return movement. The majority of exiles who returned did so between Franco's death in 1975 and the early 1990s. Nevertheless, though it may not come to a physical fruition, many continue to speak of the day when they will go back to Euskal Herria, though for the majority it is not feasible to return for family or economic reasons. For most, there is no desire for a permanent return because they live successful and enriched lives in their host countries. The "return" need not be permanent, and my research demonstrated that a high number of diaspora Basques have visited and/or regularly visit their homeland, while others have virtual visits daily on the Internet, reinforcing a transnational diasporic identity.

Many Basques have exhibited their salient ethnic group consciousness by manifesting mutual preference in trade, labor, and chain-migration networks since the 1500s. This time-proven cohesiveness separates diasporas from recent immigrant communities. Though the Basque communities in Belgium and Australia are relatively recent compared to those in South America, Basque participants in Peru, Uruguay, and Argentina continue to maintain their ethnic identity after more than six generations. They do not perpetuate the idea of a "common fate" for all Basques, and when this concept was discussed in interviews many associated the idea with the Jewish diaspora and a negative punishment and banishment that they said had nothing to do with their own situations. They were more individualistic and likely to say that they could do whatever they chose to do, separately from other Basques. Neither had they collectively experienced problems *as Basques* in their host societies. For other diaspora communities, this defense of their ethnic group increases ethnic solidarity and identifying with ethnicity. For the Basque communities, reported problems came from their being Catholics in the western United States and from their being mistaken as Italians in Australia. However, participants in the ethnic organizations reported no collective discrimination in any of their six countries.

The shared history and experiences as immigrants contribute to these Basques' sense of empathy and solidarity with other Basques abroad, especially for women, and more intensely for women who migrated to English-speaking host countries. This fellowship is transcending the single Basque community-to-homeland bilateral relationship and is recently incorporating diaspora-to-diaspora relations as well as multilocal networks and relationships among the homeland and several communities abroad. Basques participating in the Euskal Etxea of Lima in Peru reported feeling a similar connection to Basques in Belgium, in Argentina, or in the homeland. The scale of their ethnic identity changes from local—during community celebrations, festivals, or dinners at their center—to global when they click on the EITB website to read news about other Basques around the world on the Canal Vasco. Ethnic identity transforms from intimate identity with family, home decoration, foods, and family ethnic traditions to public manifestations of Basqueness at World Congresses. Because my research does not include Basques who are not members of or do not participate in some way in ethnic organizations, this generalization cannot be applied to their ethnic consciousness or lack thereof.

Having utilized Cohen's nine common features of diasporas, the one that did not apply to the Basques was the "troubled relationship with the host societies" (Cohen and Layton-Henry, eds., 1997, 26). Rather than speak in terms of "dual" identity, which tends to simplify ethnic and civil identities as the same and is often seen as the cause of trouble in host societies, I have emphasized that the two are different designations. Interviewees were unlikely to confuse their patriotism for their host country with their Basque ethnic consciousness and a desire to maintain their ethnic ties. Most were proud to live in their host countries and could not imagine moving elsewhere, including to

Euskal Herria. However, neither could they imagine not being Basque. Being Basque does not equate to physical location or country of residence. The remaining eight features did pertain to these communities abroad in varying degrees, though some were more salient than others at various times and stages in the layering development of Basque diaspora formation.

Globalization: Shrinking World—Expanding Diaspora

The effects of globalization have aided the Basque diaspora with the development of safe, easy, and inexpensive communications and travel. This era "creates communities not of place, but of interest," making it more likely that people loosen their affiliation and allegiances to nation-states (Cohen 1996, 517). Stanley Brunn (1996, 259–72) stresses the impact of modern technological progress as a major factor in the proliferation of diasporas. Though the resurgence in ethnic identity and newly established centers and globalization are correlated, there is no strong evidence to argue that globalization *causes* the creation or growth of diasporas themselves or of diaspora consciousness.

A swelling in interest in Basque identity maintenance is not a defensive reaction to globalization but includes an unplanned embrace of the tools and results of globalization. Basque diasporans manifest the transnational networks and identity on a global scale that globalization facilitates. A renewed interest in ethnic identity in some Basque communities resulted in their reestablishing diaspora organizations, while other communities created new associations, but there is no reason to suggest a direct causal effect. Many of these new organizations in Uruguay and Argentina were founded before the Internet became available, and in towns that would not be considered transnational cosmopolitan globalized communities. The functioning of these associations continued in much the same fashion as those of the 1930s through 1980s, until the Basque government began to implement its consolidation of diaspora communications. The scope and speed of information flows have minimally influenced their cultural patterns, but at the same time, there have been political and ideological transformations with the spread of liberal democracy, economic liberalism, and the growth of private enterprise (Van Hear 1998, 252), and an acceptance and almost expectation of multiculturalism in democratic societies. However, these elements do not predate the resurgence.

Globalization facilitates transnationalism in the Basque diaspora by aiding the creation and maintenance of communications among Basque collectivities abroad and with the homeland. The technology age implies that physical location is no longer required for the practice of community. Globalization of telecommunications eases the "interlacing of social events and social relations 'at distance' with local contextualities" (Giddens 1991, 21). However, Basques will not likely be practicing or celebrating their culture exclusively via electronic screens; the local scale of places where they live, the centers, and the people with whom they socialize are integral parts of their ethnic identity.

The United Nations Research Institute for Social Development summarizes globalization as a configuration of economic, technological, geopolitical, cultural, and ideological changes, along with an accelerated integration and interdependence of the world economy and the mobility of capital, and the liberalization of world trade in goods and services. These developments have been made possible by rapid technological advances, particularly in electronics, communications (especially telecommunications), and transportation, which also aids temporary returns to the homeland. These communications also give added value to global media and the Internet (Van Hear 1998, 251). The Basque government's program funding computers and Internet hook-up for each diaspora Basque center found some organizations unprepared and unacquainted with the technology, but since 1996 the centers have "caught the wave" and are now intercommunicating via the Internet. Media transmissions by Euskal Telebista are also likely to impact those communities receiving it with constant and consistent positive images of the Basque Country. The more positive the images, the more likely currently uninvolved Basques may "return to their roots" and connect with the positive social identity and communal belonging of the Basque centers.

There are also counter-tendencies to globalization, such as the increase in nationalist movements, religious fundamentalism, and racism. No interviews revealed any attitudes regarding the promotion of "Basqueness" or of the Basque centers at the expense of other ethnic groups in their host societies, though this is hardly a "politically correct" topic of conversation with an academic researcher and would not likely be volunteered in an interview. Though one can experience a religious conversion at any time in life, the data indicated that there is a declining connection between religious identification and Basqueness. The younger the interviewees, the less likely they were to agree that Catholicism was important to their ethnic identity.

Along with globalization, transnationalism broadly refers to multiple ties and interactions linking people or institutions across the borders of states (Vertovec 1999, 447). New technologies foment transnational ties with increasing speed. Despite the great distances and the extended time periods of immigration, transnational ties between the Basque communities have been strengthened with the globalization of communications. The frequency of communication and contact among the diaspora communities and between the diaspora and the homeland will likely continue to increase. Cautious of predicting, Manuel Castells (1996) argues that though new technologies are at the heart of today's transnational networks, the technologies themselves do not create, but instead reinforce, new social patterns. We have seen how Basques are utilizing these new telecommunications networks to increase the frequency and intensity of their relations with each other and with the Basque Autonomous Government.

Transnationalism is also defined by Glick Schiller et al. as "the formation of social, political and economic relationships among migrants that span several societies" and people whose "networks, activities and patterns of life encompass both their host and home societies (Glick Schiller et al. 1994, 1). This definition seems to fit these self-defining Basques who participate in their organizations. Many exhibited an unconscious multidimensional identity, not merely a hybrid two-dimensional one. They embodied Basque identity, host-country identity, and a diaspora identity. They are transnational actors as they go back and forth between two societies, and the societies that they traverse are also becoming more transnational from the effects of globalization. They tend to move between local and global-scale identities with ease. Perhaps the diaspora populations are better prepared for the future trends of globalization and transnational consciousness and do not need to react to them because they are already living them. "Transnational bonds no longer have to be cemented by migration or by exclusive territorial claims. In the age of cyberspace, a diaspora can, to some degree, be held together or re-created through the mind, through cultural artifacts and through a shared imagination" (Cohen 1996, 516).

The Basque Autonomous Government and the Foral Government of Nafarroa may also be better prepared for the future as the conceptualization of political units and administration evolve. Their understanding of non-state actors' roles in global politics is based on experience, not hypothetical. Their relationships with diaspora constituents may prove to be equally important to those with homeland residents. As seen in chapter 6, in these case studies the social, economic, and cultural networks and ties remain nonpartisan and, in comparison to other diasporas, relatively nonpolitical.

Diaspora identity bridges the gap between local and global-scale identities. Globalization has enhanced the abilities of diasporas to continue growing in numbers and to intensify their ethnic identity. By creating faster, cheaper, and easier communications and travel, globalization also promotes a deterritorialization of identity. While a homogenized global culture is emerging, simultaneously the proliferation and resurgence of local identities, mixed with the overarching global culture, produces different combinations. "Globalization and diasporization are separate phenomena with no necessary causal connections" (Cohen, *Global Diasporas,* 1997, 175), but Basque ethnic identity maintenance and diaspora strength are increased by the effects of globalization. The previously negative connotation of not fitting here or there is now likely to be perceived as belonging here *and* there.

Choosing the Basque Option

Ethnicity can be utilized as an optional identity, and diaspora Basque ethnicity varies widely in depth and in salience for each person. It is more accurate to describe it as a continuum from low-intensity to ethnic fundamentalism, "from an optional identity to a total identity" (Pieterse 1996, 371). Scholars see ethnicity as circumstantial and situational, as voluntary (Lyman and Douglass 1973), and/or as constructed (Nagel 1994). There is now less emphasis on ancestry and more on subjective orientations of identity. I have shown that Basque–host-country identity is not hierarchical but multilocal, with sentimental ties to villages, regions, nations, and states. They are not one or the other; they are both and several, simultaneously.

Basque ethnicity is increasingly a personal choice of whether to be ethnic at all. Optional ethnicity comes from the paradox of a quest for community and a desire for individuality, and from the circumstances of creating a costless community (M. Waters 1990, 147). However, if one's own ethnicity is a volunteeristic personal matter, it is difficult to understand that race or ethnicity for others is influenced by societal and political components. Basque ethnicity is historically variable. In the past in the United States, it had social costs associated with it—particularly the element of Catholicism—yet it also enjoyed positive status in many South American regions. Basques are free to "exercise an ethnic option" because they are European and Christian in European- and Christian-dominated host countries. If invoking an ethnic background is increasingly a voluntary, individual decision, and if it is done for personal enjoyment related to that ethnicity, then ethnicity itself takes on individual and positive connotations. Optional ethnicity persists because it fills the need for belonging to a community and also of individualism without individual costs (M. Waters 1990, 164).

For the first generation, ethnicity is a "concrete, unreflective, lived experience, while for subsequent generations it becomes more abstract, idealized, reflective and ultimately optional" (Kivisto 1989, 67). Basques vary in their level of intensity of publicly demonstrating their "Basqueness." Some people do not perceive ethnicity as something for public consumption, and understand it as a more emotional, sentimental feeling about ancestors, homeland, language, culture, and private personal identity.

The transmission of Basque identity has largely been accomplished through the Basque center activities where individuals can manifest their ethnic identity in a social setting. Alba (1990) notes the decline in ethnic social structures but the continuation of ethnic identities. Some Basque organizations have declined or disappeared, such as the *socorros mútuos* and the boardinghouses, and some of the centers have declined in membership and their ability to attract younger Basques, but there are many new centers recently established, and there are new members joining old centers.

Different identities produce different demands on the centers. Emigrants need one thing, fourth-generation members need something else, and the centers are attempting to cater to all their customers and fill all their ethnic needs. Each wave of migration has introduced a version of Basque culture shaped by the political and economic evolutions of the homeland. Compared to the Polish diaspora communities where divisions between new and established immigrants have caused ruptures in the ethnic associations (Erdmans 1995, 18) the Basque organizations seem to have provided politically sterile environments that have incorporated all generations and ideologies. Further research could pursue Basques who have left the organizations and inquire about their reasons to ascertain if these were political or instrumental motives, or merely reflecting a lack of interest. There are many Basques in various stages of leaving the ethnic communities, but my questionnaire results also showed others who are in various stages of entering the organizations for the first time.

The Basque diaspora once relied on kinship and personal networks, but now identity maintenance and ethnic solidarity are manifested through modern bureaucratic organizations—the Basque centers, the Basque Autonomous Government, the institutions and foundations, and so forth. Cultural associations have been fundamental to the Basque diaspora, and though their objectives and roles are in the process of changing, there is no evidence that suggests their demise in the near future. There has been a shift in the services they provide—services that orient "customers" or members firmly planted in the host country to the homeland, and no longer helping those from the homeland orient themselves to the host country. Volunteers and leaders at the centers now require different skills. Whereas earlier they needed to speak the home-country and host-country languages to help the emigrant in the host community, now they need both languages to aid later-generation Basques plan trips, research, study, and other activities in the homeland. Previously, a knowledge of the host country was necessary; now a knowledge of Euskal Herria is essential.

Interviews and questionnaire responses gave no indication of the straight-line assimilationist assumptions of the disappearance of Basque ethnic identity in the diaspora communities. Without political or economic reasons for maintaining ethnic solidarity, the importance of ethnic identity and allegiance supposedly declines. However, these diaspora communities maintain their identities, and some communities are forming new organizations. There was no evidence that Basque identity survives as a response to instrumental goals of collective political interests in any of the six countries. None of the respondents utilized ideas that could be interpreted in terms of rational-choice theory of personal profit, risk, or utility maximizing, and the revitalization surge predates the Basque government grants program. The dimensions of ethnic identity that did emerge from interviews were closest to Tajfel's positive social-identity theory (Tajfel 1981, 1982; Tajfel and Turner 1979), chain-migration and migration-flow theory (Baines 1991), and those theories of diaspora and transnationalism detailed herein (Cohen 1997; Shain 1994; Sheffer 1984, 1996; Basch et al. 1994).

Social-identity theory aided in explaining why interviewees constantly refer to the high status of Basques, particularly in Argentina and Uruguay, and in communities of critical-mass populations in the United States. Their pride in being Basque is connected to their perceptions of social identity and the status attributed to that Basque ethnic identity. There is a social function to being Basque in these ethnic communities abroad. Basques themselves perceive there to be a positive social status even though they do not believe that Basques to have an actual higher socioeconomic status than other immigrant groups. Yet there was no strong evidence of Basque identity being used instrumentally in the pursuit of social interests, except for the approximate quarter of my respondents who believed they had gained employment because of their Basque ethnicity. Basqueness provides a sense of communal belonging and a simultaneous individual sense of self-selected uniqueness.

If It Ain't Broke, Don't Fix It: Maintaining a Nonpoliticized Diaspora

The political significance of diasporas often depends on their origins and development, and on their relations with their host and home countries, as well as their own ideological dimensions. Basque diaspora populations have not acted in any way to create hostilities inside their host societies, and there is no evidence that they are perceived as a threat in any of the six countries or that their civic loyalty has ever been seriously questioned. None of these communities has been perceived as a threat to the homeland government either, because they have not involved themselves in the domestic politics of Euskal Herria. None of them has as yet made any formal or institutional criticisms of homeland political groups, ideologies, or policymaking. Traditionally, these Basque communities have not been political; until recent developments in communication technology, information transfer was slow and it was difficult to participate in the political life of the homeland at such distances and with such delays, and more recently the Franco dictatorship discouraged all vestiges of Basque political life. Today, easily accessible information, the Internet, and Basque TV could change that disinterest or lack of political efficacy. There is still no independent inter-diaspora press, only the Basque government–produced

Euskal Etxeak, which publishes government-regulated information. However, as information access increases through Euskal Telebista and Internet availability, diaspora Basques may find that the more they know about the homeland, the more there is to critique. However, I believe this is unlikely, given the general disinterest in homeland politics exhibited by the diaspora populations in my research.

The Basque government's relations with each diaspora institution are similar. Therefore, expected gradual shifts from traditional Sabino Arana definitions of Basqueness to a more civic and inclusive definition are likely to reach the Basque centers almost simultaneously and to affect these institutions in a like manner. Though this increased frequency and intensification of contact may initially highlight differences, misunderstandings, and conflict (Forbes 1997), the Basque diaspora is not a politicized community, so conflict is likely to be kept at a minimum and not cause the political divisions it has with the Armenian (Pattie interview 1998), Jewish (Liebman 1991; Hertzberg 1996; Jakobovits 1991), Polish (Erdmans 1995), and Filipino (Okamura 1998) diaspora groups. Increased contact could result in conflict, or in greater commitment. The general idea of the "triadic relationship" (Sheffer 1986; Safran 1991; A. D. Smith, *Zionism and Diaspora Nationalism*, 1995, 16) between the diaspora community, the homeland, and the host country is being exhibited in these communities incrementally as the Basque Autonomous Government and the economic *institutos* and *fundaciones* intensify their activities.

In other ethnic communities, expanded activities and links between homeland and diaspora populations are creating "deterritorialized" nations, as shown in studies of political parties establishing offices abroad, homeland groups lobbying diaspora communities, and diaspora communities lobbying host-country governments in regard to homeland politics (Basch et al. 1994; Panossian 1998; Subtelny 1991). However, the Basque diaspora populations in this study have been shown to be nonpoliticized communities whose individuals exhibit little interest in and knowledge of homeland political issues, parties, and future goals. The majority of my respondents were willing to admit that they did not know enough about homeland politics to respond to the political items in the questionnaire. Basques do not tend to have the diaspora-homeland divisions seen in some other diasporas because the Basque diaspora populations have stayed out of the homeland political arena and have promoted a cultural *ethno*nationalistic identity.

Diaspora Basques are just now involving themselves with policies that affect the diaspora through *Ley 8/1994*, and especially the law's provisions for the World Congresses to create a Four-Year Institutional Plan for Action. None of the diaspora communities I studied had institutions or individuals who claimed interest in affecting domestic politics in the homeland, though this does not preclude its future possibility, and thousands of diaspora Basques vote in homeland elections. The Filipino and Caribbean diaspora populations in the United States find that voting in homeland elections and dual citizenship are made difficult by their home governments (Basch et al. 1994, 277), but the Basque Autonomous Government has facilitated diaspora registration and voting procedures and has encouraged them. It does so in spite of the fact—or perhaps *because* of the fact—that the totality of the diaspora vote has not been influential, in comparison to the Galician diaspora that tips regional elections in Galicia.

A specific role for the diaspora in the internal affairs of Euskal Herria is absent for now. There are no foreign-based Basque political parties and no foreign campaigning for diaspora electoral support. This contrasts with Armenian diaspora communities, which have established diaspora parties such as the Armenian Revolutionary Federation and the Armenian Democratic Liberals, which lobby for preferential host-country foreign policy toward Armenia and campaign for the diaspora's, and even the homeland's, vote in homeland elections. There are Armenian diaspora-based parties that actually win homeland elections. Though representatives of Basque homeland political parties have visited diaspora communities in an official capacity, the visits have been more educational and social in nature. Neither have the Basque homeland parties utilized the diaspora as an election campaign issue in Euskadi or Nafarroa.

Diasporas may be a foreign-policy or economic asset that home governments are eager to exploit (Esman 1986, 345). The Basque Autonomous Government is successfully using the diaspora in pursuit of its own external economic goals with the establishment of the institutes and foundations. Though the homeland government is capitalizing on the Basque status and reputation for an economic advantage, there is no evidence to demonstrate a political or partisan motive for mobilizing the Basques abroad. Whereas the Basque government-in-exile encouraged diaspora communities to utilize their host-country status and to act politically in its support, there is only unofficial talk of this for the contemporary Basque Autonomous Government's political future.

A recent phenomenon in the Basque diaspora finds that the roles of "donor" and "recipient" have been reversed. The homeland population has historically been the recipient of migrants' aid, with emigrants sending remittances home. Now the homeland, via its institutions and established autonomous government, is sending financial and human-resources aid to the diaspora. This contrasts with the Filipino, Croatian, Ukrainian, Haitian, or Puerto Rican diasporas (Okamura 1998; Winland 1995; Subtelny 1991; Basch et al. 1994). Similar to other diasporas,[2] the Basque homeland government has recently established a specific administrative unit to deal with "Basques in the exterior." The Office of Relations with the Basque Collectivities is the starting and finishing point for individuals and diaspora organizations wishing to establish or fortify already existing transnational networks with homeland institutions.

I have shown that the Basque communities in these six case studies have not attempted to influence host-country domestic politics toward themselves and have not formed ethnic-interest lobbies to influence internal policy. Nor is there any evidence that they have attempted to utilize transnational links to influence Basque Country domestic policymaking. However, they *are* becoming more interested in homeland policymaking regarding the diaspora, as demonstrated in the debates and discussions that took place at the 1995 and 1999 World Congresses of Basque Collectivities, as well as the 1997 and 2000 American Congresses of Basque Centers.

It is argued that transnational communities "involve various rather puzzling new forms of linkage between diasporic nationalisms, delocalized political communications and revitalized political commitments at both ends of the diasporic process" (Appadurai 1996, 220). However, as demonstrated here, there is no evidence to suggest that the Basque diaspora communities are politicized, nor that they will soon utilize collective transnational networks to mobilize. There is no conclusive evidence to describe the Basque diaspora as a pluralistic one, either. For example, Jakobovitz (1991, 45–51) describes British Jews and American Jews as markedly different. Though I chose the most disparate host countries by oldest and most recent dates of emigration, farthest and closest in physical proximity to Euskal Herria, European versus New World settler societies, host countries with same versus different languages, democracies and dictatorial political systems, communities with a critical mass of hundreds of thousands versus a few hundred, and those based on chain migration as opposed to Peru and Uruguay without, there still was a lack of decisive differences manifested between these diaspora Basques' reasons for, and manners of, preserving their ethnicity. Nor can I declare a universal diaspora Basqueness. Belgian Basques' closest proximity enabling easy personal communications and their most recent immigration tended to follow current homeland values and opinions a little more closely on issues of religion and on who should be included as a Basque. Responses from Basques in Peru in regard to political questions differed most—likely as a result of their experience with political violence and nondemocratic regimes.

Future Study: The Trajectory of Basque Diaspora Studies

My attempt to answer a few questions regarding Basque diaspora identity has actually mushroomed into research on an enigmatic dynamic. Apart from supporting the arguments I made, I have discovered a plethora of untouched academic themes. The "area" in area studies must be extended to nonphysical territories of interest and diaspora. Basque studies have exceptional potential for expansion in the areas of homeland government–diaspora relations, the effects of diaspora networks on homeland populations and institutions, the effects of the Law of Relations with the Basque Communities, and the progress of the recently established Basque organizations. Comparisons of the Basque to Catalan, Galician, and other Spanish regions' diasporas and of Spain's reactions to these regional governmental functions would benefit diaspora studies as well as Spanish studies.

The trajectory of the Basque diaspora will likely include continued intensification of relations with the Basque government—relations that are significant for research. If the PNV loses control of the Basque government in a future election, it will be interesting to see how a different party perceives the importance of the diaspora to homeland politics, and whether or not appropriations for diaspora grants and investments continue. Of course, this is also assuming that the Basque economy continues to flourish and provide enough money to consider maintaining a budget for diaspora projects.

Basques have perceived the Castilian Spanish as their opposing "other" for centuries, but now that there is an autonomous Basque government it is difficult to blame all economic, social, and political problems on Madrid. The idealization of a democratic homeland and the desirability of Basques ruling Basques may be disappointing when the reality of the complexities of political administration and bureaucracy deprive diaspora Basques of their utopian myth of Euskal Herria. As with other newly independent or newly democratic homelands, the Basque diaspora may see that several of the problems that were attributed to their "other" still exist.

Different diaspora generations have experienced the same historical events, such the Spanish Civil War, the Burgos Trials, ETA media coverage, the death of Franco, and political autonomy, at different stages in their lives. My interviews and questionnaires reflect people's ideas at one point in their lives, and further longitudinal research could track changes over time.

While ethnic identity maintenance is easy to identify through personal and collective activity, organizations, and institutional linkages, assimilation is not. It is difficult to judge whether or not Basques who do not participate in Basque ethnic organizations or their activities have the same ethnic feelings or thoughts. Just because these Basques do not manifest their ethnicity publicly or socially does not mean it does not exist; they simply pose a more challenging situation for researchers. *Assimilated* is also quite a subjective term (Olzak and Nagel 1986; Alba 1990; M. Waters 1990; Glazer and Moynihan 1975; Spicer 1971) and tends to describe overt behavior but not psychology or sentiment.

Regarding diaspora studies in general, Khachig Tölölyan points to the fact that the terms *immigrant, expatriate, refugees, guest workers, exile communities, overseas communities,* and *ethnic communities,* and the vocabulary of "transnationalism" are being incorporated in an inclusive "diaspora" definition (Tölölyan 1996, 4–5), but that diaspora should be a "collectivity," not merely "a scattering of individuals" (Tölölyan 1996, 8). Safran prefers to limit the definition of *diaspora* to those who meet the following criteria: dispersal from an original center to two or more peripheral regions; retention of a collective memory of the homeland; partial alienation from the host society; a myth of return to the homeland; commitment to the preservation of the homeland; a collective consciousness and solidarity from a relationship with the homeland (Safran 1991, 81). Cohen argues that no one diaspora will manifest all features of his list common to diasporas, but he adds to and modifies Safran's list with the "possibility of a distinctive yet creative and enriching life in host countries with a tolerance for pluralism," and he eliminates the necessary catastrophic or traumatic dispersal from a homeland. The simplest categorization is that of Milton Esman: "a minority ethnic group of migrant origin which maintains sentimental or material links with its land of origin" (Esman 1986, 333).

In comparing transnational communities, Van Hear utilizes three minimum criteria for a diaspora: (1) a population dispersed to two or more other territories; (2) an enduring presence abroad, although exile is not necessarily permanent and populations may move between homeland and new host; and (3) some kind of exchange—social, economic, political or cultural—between and among the separated populations comprising the diaspora (Van Hear 1998, 6). Researchers must be careful about categorizing a group as a diaspora merely because there are diasporic elements to their behavior. Distance has ceased to be a barrier to interaction and communication, and many groups and individuals make decisions about movement on the basis of networks, communication, and information. The political significance of diasporas will continue to grow because of the globalization of economies and international relations (Claval 1996, 444). Diasporas influence their homelands and host countries, and contribute increasingly to worldwide transnational networks that have yet to be studied.

I have attempted to explain why the Basque diaspora populations maintain their ethnic identity by utilizing theories of positive social identity, opposition, primordial identity, as well as instrumentalist, chain-migration, and diaspora approaches. The maintenance of ethnicity and the creation of networks are mutually reinforcing. Diasporas create networks because they maintain their ethnicity, and they maintain their ethnicity because they are involved in these networks. A combination of these theories clears the Basque diaspora picture, though none of these explanations by itself answers these questions. Facilitated by factors of globalization and the growing realization in host countries that ethnic pluralism is a given, diaspora populations no longer confront the necessity of assimilating and changing or of exchanging their ethnic identities.

Other research on the Basque diaspora has described historical accounts of Basques, but none has included, as did this, Basque government–diaspora relations, institutional networks, or material and financial links between homeland and diaspora. This work has created original data for Basque diaspora populations in six different countries and has compared, for the first time, the Basque diaspora to other ethnic diasporas. It is the first attempt to document contemporary Basque diaspora populations and to analyze their ethnic identity maintenance and transnational networks. It is also the first time diaspora Basques have been asked to describe themselves and to explain their ethnic identity maintenance, establishing a foundation for future research.

The honeymoon period is just now ending, and the euphoria in Euskadi and in the diaspora over having an autonomous Basque government, enjoying economic prosperity with gifts of grants and subsidies for the centers and their members, and a "no questions asked" attitude of acceptance by the diaspora for government policy may not last forever. Control of the Basque government by nationalist coalitions may not last either, and the nonpartisan, nonpolitical, and heretofore almost nonpoliticized and nonmobilized diaspora may flirt with a change of status.

A change in the Basque government's ruling parties could alter the relations with the diaspora in perhaps less favorable ways, with lower appropriations for diaspora Basque centers and less support for economic development. Regardless of which parties lead, future Basque governments could utilize the effects of globalization and transnationalism to the advantage of all, with diaspora business and economic development, cultural enhancement, language revitalization, and spiritual and psychological augmentation and intensification to ethnic identity. Or, to the detriment of all Basques, it could underestimate the power of ethnic identity and patronize the diaspora with condescension, or ignore the new model of deterritorialized loyalties—and waiting opportunities.

Notes

CHAPTER ONE. ETHNICITY, ETHNIC IDENTITY PERSISTENCE, AND DIASPORA

1. The United States' relatively weak party system and influential interest-group activity make it easier for groups small in number to gain access to domestic political and economic resources, yet there has been no such activity by the Basque communities.

CHAPTER TWO. BASQUE COUNTRY HISTORY, THE DEVELOPMENT OF BASQUE NATIONALISM, AND CONTEMPORARY HOMELAND IDENTITY

1. For works on psycholinguistics and sociolinguistics and the effects of language in ethnic identity, see Bamgbose 1991; Landau 1986; Fishman 1989, 1997; Fishman et al. 1985.
2. One husband and wife whom I interviewed were quite certain that the kings and queens of Castile had to kneel in front of the Tree of Gernika and the representatives of the Basque towns to swear *their* support for the *fueros* and Basque autonomy. After much discussion, they decided they had seen it in a famous painting, so it must be true. They likely were referring to Francisco de Mendieta's *Oath to the Fueros of Ferdinand the Catholic*, which depicts such a scene and is very famous and widely reproduced in the Basque Country.
3. Basques tend to respect and empathize with the Catalans as a result of their simultaneous struggles and shared anti-Franco history.
4. This study was greatly facilitated by what I term "my biological credentials" and by the fact that I was accepted as an "insider" with all Basque last names. Both of my parents being from Gernika added symbolic legitimacy to me as a Basque, and as a researcher. My ability to participate in all of their Basque activities (knowing the dances, singing the Basque songs, playing *pelota* with children, even cooking a Basque meal for the Peruvian Basque Center) made me "as Basque" as the people I interviewed.
5. Dorothy Legarreta's *Gernika Generation* provides a detailed country-by-country account of the evacuated children and their chaperones. Many of my interviewees in Brussels had originally gone to Belgium as one of these children and had returned to their Belgian families as orphans or returned as adults for education or employment and then stayed permanently. One couple had met in the evacuee camps in England, married, and emigrated to Australia.
6. The Fifth Assembly was the fifth general meeting of ETA members during 1966–67. After this, there were annual assemblies that made up the Executive Committee and

controlled ETA training and activities. However, among later factions, ETA-V also came to mean those who followed the plans and ideas of the Fifth Assembly.

7. Numerous interviewees recounted stories of telephone hotlines spreading the news, impromptu champagne parties and emotional celebrations. Several who were children at the time remembered being allowed to eat all the sweets they could stomach, and others celebrated with *turrón*, a special sweet—then scarce in the diaspora—typically reserved only for Christmas.

CHAPTER THREE. THE FORMATION OF THE BASQUE DIASPORA

1. Samuel Champlain's Newfoundland charts of 1612 show Port-aux-Basques. Other Basque place-names in Newfoundland noted on contemporary charts and documents include Baya Ederra, Aingura Charra, Etchaire Portu, and Portucho Çaharra. See Selma Huxley Barkham.

2. Basques who chose to emigrate to Uruguay were unfortunately obligated to fight in the Uruguayan Grand War upon their arrival. They fled one conflict only to find themselves in another, forced to fight in the Uruguayan Basque Battalion.

3. Much later, in the 1950s, the Catholic Church in Euskal Herria sponsored emigration programs for single Basque women to Australia, where scores of single Basque men had emigrated to cut sugarcane.

4. In 1940, the *Boise Statesman* (Idaho) printed an article by the president of the Independent Order of Spanish-Basque Speaking People of Idaho, Inc., who issued a public declaration denying that Basques were communists, after allegations to the contrary (Bieter and Bieter 2000, 93–95). In Melbourne, Paul Oribe and Carmen Belón Bilbao recalled church sermons praising Franco's fight to save Catholicism.

5. The Basque government-in-exile estimate in 1939 was 150,000 Basque exiles in Iparralde alone (Dupla 1992, 130), plus several thousand children spread throughout Europe (Legarreta 1984).There are no official Basque government statistics for Basques who entered other host countries as political refugees.

6. There are no official statistics of the numbers of returnees because the details of a person's reasons for requesting residency and his prior residency are not recorded, and many exiles did not officially register with government officials fearing possible future retribution (J. Egurrola Albizu interview, Gernika, 1999).

CHAPTER FOUR. ETHNONATIONALISM AND POLITICAL ATTITUDES
IN THE DIASPORA

1. Respondents allowed to mark more than one "condition necessary to be Basque." Data from Aizpurua 1995, 206–7.

2. Table 6.3 demonstrates diaspora voting results from the 1990, 1994, 1998, and 2001 elections.

3. The 12 September 1998 Lizarra-Garazi Agreement was signed by the Partido Nacionalista Vasco, Herri Batasuna, Izquierda Unida, Abertzaleen Batasuna, Euskal

Notes

Alkartasuna, Batzarre, Zutik, Partido Carlista, Iniciativa Ciudadana Vasca political parties, as well as by trade unions and social organizations, with the main purpose of facilitating a peace process and democratic settlement in the Basque Country.

4. The national directorate was given early release in July 1999 by the Spanish Supreme Tribunal as a result of its ruling that the seven-year sentences constituted an excessive penalty (*El Diario Vasco,* 22 July 1999, 1).

5. Numbers provided by the Secretariat for Foreign Action, Basque Autonomous Government, 1999.

6. To be investigated in chapter 6 are the more than 26,000 diaspora Basques who have registered with their diaspora Basque institutions and are eligible for benefits from the homeland government.

7. Herri Batasuna changed its name to Euskal Herritarrok in the spring of 1999. For events occurring before that date, I use the name *Herri Batasuna*; for anything after that date, I use HB-EH.

8. Uruguayan police followed me and identified themselves after I interviewed legal political exiles and HB's Karmelo Landa.

CHAPTER FIVE. BASQUE ETHNICITY AFFIRMATION AND MAINTENANCE

1. These countries' immigration records still tend to be dominated by state citizenship and do not separate Basques in the "French" or "Spanish" categories. The United States and Australia have an optional ethnic classification used in census-taking, but these numbers do not specify new immigration.

2. The international diasporic congresses and relations with the Basque government regarding this topic are detailed in chapter 6.

3. See page 113 for homeland attitudes toward speaking Basque, and table 4.8 for diaspora attitudes toward speaking Basque.

4. Commonly, diaspora Basques' funeral wreaths are red, green, and white. Interviewees also stated that funeral masses would likely have Basque music and songs, and many people are buried with a Basque flag.

5. A *lauburu* is a four-headed symbol common in Basque archaeological finds. It is found on tombstones and is believed to be a symbol for the sun. However, to Basques it also represents the four seasons, or a Basque Catholic cross. For some, it represents the four Basque provinces in Spain.

6. The Lima Euskal Etxeak activities are mainly dominated by a group of approximately thirty men who meet weekly for a Basque dinner at the center, much like the homeland *txoko*-style male gastronomy club. The women dominate the choir, dance, and music activities.

CHAPTER SIX. BASQUE GOVERNMENT–DIASPORA RELATIONS

1. NABO chose its name in 1974, after having originally met as the "Western Basque Convention." According to leaders Miren Rementeria Artiach, Julio Bilbao, and Albert

Erquiaga, discussions allowed the possibility for groups from Mexico and perhaps Canada to join. Though NABO maintains relations with centers in both countries, none have actually joined.

2. The people of these Basque centers are all part-time volunteers, not international business moguls or high-status politicians. However, they know how to mobilize their memberships and how to contact and network with other influential Basques. They assume the Basque ethnic connection to be enough to open the door and be heard, and they have often been correct (Eiguren 2002; Garritz 1997; Felipe Muguerza interview, Argentina, 1998).

3. In Euskadi, there is an abstention rate in elections that hovers between 30 and 35 percent.

CHAPTER SEVEN. *AMAIA:* AN INTERCONNECTED DISCONNECTEDNESS

1. Basque literary conclusions and theatrical final acts are designated with the name and title *Amaia*. It is the beginning and the end, the answer to a mystery, puzzle, or question.

2. In 1997, the president of Armenia signed a decree creating the State Council for Relations with the Diaspora (Panossian interview 1999).

Glossary

Aberri Eguna: Day of the Fatherland (coincides with Easter Sunday). Traditional Basque patriotic holiday.

abertzale: Patriot. Refers to someone who supports the cause of Basque autonomy or independence.

Aiztan Artean: "Sisters All." Basque women's organization in Boise, Idaho.

Araba: Alava, one of the four Basque provinces in Spain.

arreba: A female sibling of a male.

barrio: Neighborhood.

baserri: Farmhouse. Refers to the traditional Basque rural landholding.

Batua: The standardized and unified Basque language currently taught in Euskadi and elsewhere.

Behe Nafarroa: One of the three Basque provinces in France.

berri: New.

Bilbo: Bilbao, capital city of Bizkaia.

biltzarrak: Elected popular assemblies that traditionally governed the Basque Country.

Bizkaia: Vizcaya, one of the four Basque provinces in Spain.

Castilla: Castile.

chorizo: Typical sausage used in Basque cooking.

Donostia: San Sebastián, capital city of Gipuzkoa.

Donibane Lohitzun: St. Jean-de-Luz.

Emakume Abertzale Batza: United Patriotic Women. The women's branch of the PNV.

ertzaintza: Basque police.

españolista: A person who loves things Spanish; a derogatory term for Basques who are not considered nationalists or patriots.

Etarra: A member of ETA.

Euskadi: Basque Country. Refers to the current autonomous political entity comprising Araba, Bizkaia, and Gipuzkoa.

Euskadiko Ezkerra (EE): Basque Left. Contemporary political party.

Euskadi 'ta Askatasuna (ETA): Basque Homeland and Liberty. Contemporary Basque independentist organization.

Euskaldun: A person who speaks the Basque language. *Euskaldunak* (plural) refers to Basque-speaking people.

Euskal Etxeak: Literally, Basque houses or homes; name given to numerous Basque centers outside the Basque Country.

Euskal Etxeak: Journal published by the Basque government for diaspora Basques.

Euskal Herria: The Basque Country as a historical entity, including all seven provinces in Spain and France.

Euskal Herritarrok: Literally, "those from Euskal Herria." Contemporary leftist Basque nationalist political party; formerly known as Herri Batasuna.

Euskera: The Basque language.

Eusko Alkartasuna (EA): Basque Solidarity. Contemporary Basque political party that split from the PNV.

Eusko Jaurlaritza: Contemporary government of the Basque Autonomous Community.

Euzkadi: Sabino Arana's original term for the Basque Country, including all seven provinces. Currently refers to the Basque Autonomous Community.

fueros: Local charters and laws that formed the traditional basis for government in the Basque Country.

fors: French equivalent of *fueros*.

frontón: Two- or three-walled court used to play handball (*pelota*) and paddle ball (*pala*).

Fundación: Foundation. The foundations established in the contemporary diaspora by the Basque government encourage economic endeavors between the Basque Country and diaspora host countries.

Gasteiz: Vitoria-Gasteiz, capital city of the Basque Autonomous Community.

Gernika: Guernica.

Gipuzkoa: Guipúzcoa.

Guardia Civil: Spanish Civil Guard utilized as military police.

haizpa: A female sibling of a female.

haizpak: Sisters.

Hegoalde: South. Refers to the southern Basque Country, the four provinces in Spain (Avala, Bizkaia, Gipuzkoa, Nafarroa).

Herri Batasuna: People's Unity. Basque leftist nationalist party, political arm of ETA. The name was changed to Euskal Herritarrok (those from Euskal Herria).

ikastola: School that utilizes the Basque language for instruction.

ikurriña: Basque flag.

Instituto: Institute. Refers to institutes established in the diaspora by the Basque government to encourage economic endeavors between the Basque Country and the host country.

Iparralde: North. Refers to the northern Basque Country, the three provinces in France (Behe Nafarroa, Lapurdi, Zuberoa).

Lapurdi: One of the Basque provinces in France; in French, Labourd.

lauburu: A Basque symbol with four heads, similar to a Greek cross.

Laurak Bat: Literally, "the four are one," referring to the four Basque provinces. Also the name of numerous diaspora Basque centers and publications.

Lehendakari: President of the Basque government.

mus: Traditional Basque card game.

Nafarroa: One of the four Basque provinces in Spain; in Spanish, Navarra; in French and English, Navarre.

pala: Traditional Basque ball game, similar to paddle ball.

Partido Nacionalista Vasco: Basque Nationalist Party. Longstanding Basque political party, commonly known as PNV.

pelota: Traditional Basque handball game.

Pyrénées-Atlantiques: French administrative department that includes the three Basque provinces of Zuberoa, Lapurdi, and Behe Nafarroa.

Reconquista: The historic reconquest of Muslim Spain by the emerging Spanish Catholic kingdoms, occurred between 718 and 1611.

Sociedad de Socorros Mútuos: Society of Mutual Aid. Refers to Basque diaspora organizations dedicated to mutual support.

tortilla: Traditional Basque egg omelette, typically served as an appetizer.

txistu: Traditional Basque three-hole flute.

txistulari: A person who plays the *txistu*.

Vizcaya: The Spanish spelling for Bizkaia, one of the four Basque provinces in Spain.

Vizcaínos: Spanish term for people from Vizcaya.

Zazpirak Bat: Literally, "the seven are one," referring to the seven Basque provinces. Also the name of numerous diaspora Basque centers and organizations.

Zuberoa: One of the Basque provinces in France, known in French as Soule.

Sources

BOOKS AND ARTICLES

Abrams, Dominic, and Michael A. Hogg. 1988. "Comments on the Motivational Status of Self-Esteem in Social Identity and Intergroup Discrimination." *European Journal of Social Psychology* 18: 317–34.
———, eds. 1990. *Social Identity Theory: Constructive and Critical Advances.* New York: Harvester Wheatsheaf.
Adelman, Jeremy. 1995. "European Migration to Argentina, 1880–1930." In *The Cambridge Survey of World Migration,* edited by Robin Cohen. Cambridge: Cambridge University Press.
Aizpurua, Xabier. 1995. *Euskararen Jarraipena: La Continuidad del Euskera.* Vitoria-Gasteiz: Servico Central de Publicaciones del Gobierno Vasco.
Alba, Richard D. 1985. *Italian Americans: Into the Twilight of Ethnicity.* Englewood Cliffs, N.J.: Prentice Hall.
———. 1990. *Ethnic Identity: The Transformation of White America.* New Haven: Yale University Press.
Alday, Alberto. 1999. "Vasco-Navarros en el Nuevo Mundo: Una Identidad Dual." In *The Basque Diaspora/La Diaspora Vasca,* edited by William A. Douglass et al. Reno: University of Nevada, Reno, Basque Studies Program and University of Nevada Press.
Alter, Peter. 1994. *Nationalism.* 2d ed. London: Edward Arnold.
Altman, Ida. 1995. "Spanish Migration to the Americas." In *The Cambridge Survey of World Migration,* edited by Robin Cohen. Cambridge: Cambridge University Press.
Álvarez Gila, Oscar. 1995. "La Formación de la Colectividad Inmigrante Vasca en los Países del Río de la Plata (Siglo XIX)." *Estudios Migratorios Latinoamericanos* 10: 215–48.
———. 1996. "Vascos y Vascongados: Luchas Ideológicas entre Carlistas y Nacionalistas en los Centros Vascos del Río de la Plata (1900–1930)." In *Emigración y Redes Sociales de los Vascos en América,* edited by Ronald Escobedo Mansilla, Ana de Zabala Beascoechea, and Oscar Alvarez Gila. Vitoria-Gasteiz: Universidad del País Vasco.
Amezaga Clark, Miren. 1991. *Nere Aia: El Exilio Vasco en América.* San Sebastián-Donostia: Editorial Txertoa.
Anasagasti, Iñaki, ed. 1988. *Homenaje al Comité Pro-Inmigración Vasca en Argentina (1940).* San Sebastián-Donostia: Editorial Txertoa.
Anderson, Benedict. 1991. *Imagined Communities: Reflections on the Origin and Spread of Nationalism.* London: Verso.
Anthias, Floya. 1992. "Cultural Identity and the Politics of Ethnicity." In *Ethnicity, Class, Gender and Migration: Greek-Cypriots in Britain.* Aldershot, Engl.: Avebury.

Anthias, Floya, and Nira Yuval-Davis. *Racialized Boundaries: Race, Nation, Gender, Colour, and Class and the Anti-Racist Struggle.* London: Routledge. 1993.

Appadurai, Arjun. 1996. *Modernity at Large: Cultural Dimensions of Globalization.* Minneapolis: University of Minnesota Press.

Aramburu Zudaire, José Miguel, and Jesús María Usunáriz Garayoa. 1991. "La Emigración de Navarros y Guipuzcoanos hacia el Nuevo Mundo durante la Edad Moderna: Fuentes y Estado de la Cuestión." In *La Emigración Española a Ultramar, 1492–1914,* edited by Antonio Eiras Roel. Madrid: Ediciones Tabapress.

Arana y Goiri, Sabino de. 1965. *Obras Completas de Arana y Goiri-tar Sabin.* Buenos Aires: Editorial Sabindiar Batza.

Aranaz Zuza, Ignacio, et al. 1992. *Navarros en América: Cinco Crónicas.* Pamplona: Gobierno de Navarra.

Archdeacon, Thomas. 1985. "Problems and Possibilities in the Study of American Immigration and Ethnic History." *International Migration Review* 19 Spring): 112–34.

Artís-Gener, Avelí. 1976. *La Diáspora Republicana.* Barcelona: Editorial Euros.

Astigarraga de, Andoni. 1986. *Abertzales en la Argentina.* Bilbao: Ediciones Alderdi Argitaldaria.

Azcona Pastór, José Manuel. 1992. *Los Paraisos Posibles: Historia de la Inmigración Vasca a Argentina y Uruguay en el Siglo XIX.* Bilbao: Universidad de Duesto.

Azcona Pastór, José Manuel, Fernando Muru Ronda, and Inés García-Albi de Biedma. 1996. *Historia de la Emigración Vasca al Uruguay en el Siglo XX.* Montevideo: Ministerio de Educación y Cultura, Archivo General de la Nación.

Bachvarov, Marin, and Andrei Pantev. 1996. "The Forgotten Bulgarians." In *The Network of Diasporas,* edited by Georges Prévélakis. Nicosia: Cyprus Research Center KYKEM.

Baines, Dudley. 1991. *Emigration from Europe 1815–1930.* London: Macmillian Education Limited.

Bakalian, Anny P. 1993. *Armenian Americans: From Being to Feeling Armenian.* New Brunswick, N.J.: Transaction Publishers.

Balfour, Sebastian. 1995. "The Loss of Empire, Regenerationism, and the Forging of a Myth of National Identity." In *Spanish Cultural Studies: An Introduction, The Struggle for Modernity,* edited by Helen Graham and Jo Labanyi. Oxford: Oxford University Press.

———. 1997. *The End of the Spanish Empire 1898–1923.* Oxford: Clarendon Press.

Bamgbose, Ayo. 1991. *Language and the Nation: The Language Question in Sub-Saharan Africa.* Edinburgh: Edinburgh University Press.

Barahona, Renato. 1989. *Vizcaya on the Eve of Carlism: Politics and Society, 1800–1833.* Reno: University of Nevada Press.

Bard, Rachel. 1982. *Navarra: The Durable Kingdom.* Reno: University of Nevada Press.

Barkham, Selma Huxley. 1989. *The Basque Coast of Newfoundland.* Plum Point, Newf.: Great Northern Peninsula Development Corporation.

Barth, Frederik, ed. 1969. *Ethnic Groups and Boundaries: The Social Organization of Culture Difference.* London: George Allen and Unwin.

Basch, Linda, Nina Glick Schiller, and Cristina Szanton Blanc. 1994. *Nations Unbound: Transnational Projects, Postcolonial Predicaments, and Deterritorialized Nation-States.* Amsterdam: Gordon and Breach Science Publishers.

Basu, Sajal. 1992. *Regional Movements: Politics of Language, Ethnic-Identity.* New Delhi: Indian Institute of Advanced Study.

Beltza [pseud.]. 1977. *El Nacionalismo Vasco en el Exilio 1937–1960.* San Sebastián-Donostia: Editorial Txertoa.

Ben-Ami, Shlomo. 1991. "Basque Nationalism Between Archaism and Modernity." *Journal of Contemporary History* 26: 493–521.

Bengoetxea, Joxerramon. 1991. "Nationalism and Self-Determination: The Basque Case." In *Issues of Self-Determination,* edited by William Twining. Aberdeen: Aberdeen University Press.

Ben-Rafael, Eliezer. 1994. *Language, Identity, and Social Division: The Case of Israel.* Oxford: Clarendon Press.

Berberoglu, Berch, ed. 1995. *The National Question: Nationalism, Ethnic Conflict, and Self-Determination in the 20th Century.* Philadelphia: Temple University Press.

Berry, John. 1986. "Multiculturalism and Psychology in Plural Societies." In *Ethnic Minorities and Immigrants in a Cross-Cultural Perspective,* edited by Lars Ekstrand. Berwyn, Penn.: Swets North America.

———. 1992. "Acculturation and Adaptation in a New Society." *International Migration* 30: 69–85.

Berry, John W., and R. C. Annis, eds. 1988. *Ethnic Psychology: Research and Practice with Immigrants, Refugees, Native Peoples, Ethnic Groups, and Sojourners.* Lisse, Netherlands: Swets and Zeitlinger.

Bieter, John, and Mark Bieter. 2000. *An Enduring Legacy: The Story of Basques in Idaho.* Reno: University of Nevada Press.

Bilbao Azkarreta, Jon, ed. 1992. *América y los Vascos.* Bilbao: Deia, and Vitoria-Gasteiz: Eusko Jaurlaritza.

———. 1958. *Vascos en Cuba, 1492–1511.* Buenos Aires: Editorial Vasca Ekin.

Billig, Michael. 1995. *Banal Nationalism.* Thousand Oaks, Calif.: Sage.

Blanco Fernández de Valderrama, Cristina. 1994. "Inmigación e Identidad Colectiva: Reflexión sobre la Identidad en el País Vasco." *Papers: Revista de Sociología* 43: 41–61.

Blount, Ben G. 1974. *Language Culture and Society: A Book of Readings.* Cambridge: Winthrop Publishers.

Boski, Pawel. 1988. "Retention and Acquisition of National Self-Identity in Polish Immigrants to Canada: Criterial and Correlated Attributes." In *Ethnic Psychology: Research and Practice with Immigrants, Refugees, Native Peoples, Ethnic Groups, and Sojourners,* edited by John W. Berry and R. C. Annis. Lisse, Netherlands: Swets and Zeitlinger.

Bottomley, Gillian. 1991. "Culture, Ethnicity, and the Politics/Poetics of Representation." *Diaspora* 1: 303–20.

———. 1992. *From Another Place: Migration and the Politics of Culture.* Cambridge: Cambridge University Press.

———. 1995. "Southern European Migration to Australia: Diasporic Networks and Cultural Transformations." In *The Cambridge Survey of World Migration*, edited by Robin Cohen. Cambridge: Cambridge University Press.

Boyd, Monica. 1989. "Family and Personal Networks in International Migration: Recent Developments and New Agendas." *International Migration Review* 23: 638–70.

Branaa, Jean-Eric. 1989. *Les Basques de l'Amérique/Basques from America*. Bayonne: Jean-Eric Branaa.

Brass, Paul R. 1991. *Ethnicity and Nationalism: Theory and Comparison*. New Delhi: Sage Publications.

Breton, Albert, et al., eds. 1995. *Nationalism and Rationality*. Cambridge: Cambridge University Press.

Brettell, Caroline B., and Rita Simon. 1986. "Immigrant Women: An Introduction." In *International Migration: The Female Experience*, edited by Caroline Brettell and Rita Simon. Totowa, N.J.: Rowman and Allanheld.

Brunn, Stanley D. 1996. "The Internationalization of Diasporas in a Shrinking World." In *The Network of Diasporas*, edited by Georges Prévélakis. Nicosia: Cyprus Research Center KYKEM.

Campani, Giovanna. 1995. "Women Migrants: From Marginal Subjects to Social Actor." In *The Cambridge Survey of World Migration*, edited by Robin Cohen. Cambridge: Cambridge University Press.

Caro Baroja, Julio. 1971. *Los Vascos*. 4th ed. Madrid: Ediciones ISTMO.

———. 1998. *Ser o No Ser Vasco*. Translated with an introduction by Antonio Carreira. Madrid: Editorial Espasa Calpe.

Carr, Raymond. 1982. *Spain 1808–1975*. Oxford: Clarendon Press.

Castells, Manuel. 1996. *The Rise of the Network Society*. Vol. 1 of *The Information Age: Economy, Society, Culture*. Oxford: Blackwell.

———. 1997. *The Power of Identity*. Vol. 2 of *The Information Age: Economy, Society and Culture*. Oxford: Blackwell.

Castles, Stephen, and Mark J. Miller. 1993. *The Age of Migration: International Population Movements in the Modern World*. London: Macmillan.

Castles, Stephen, et al. 1996. "Australia: Multi-Ethnic Community Without Nationalism?" In *Ethnicity*, edited by John Hutchinson and Anthony D. Smith. Oxford: Oxford University Press.

Cavalli-Sforza, Luigi Luca, and Francesco Cavalli-Sforza. 1995. *The Great Human Diasporas: The History of Diversity and Evolution*. Translated by Sarah Thorne. Reading, Penn.: Addison-Wesley.

Cava Mesa, Begona. 1996. "El Asocianismo Vasco en Argentina: Política Cultural." In *Emigración y Redes Sociales de los Vascos en América*, edited by Ronald Escobedo Mansilla, Ana de Zabala Beascoechea, and Oscar Alvarez Gila. Vitoria-Gasteiz: Universidad del País Vasco.

Caviglia, Maria Jorgelina, and Daniel Villar. 1994. *Inmigración Vasca en Argentina: Vete a América*. Vitoria-Gasteiz: Departamento de Cultura Gobierno Vasco.

Chant, Sylvia, ed. 1992. *Gender and Migration in Developing Countries*. London: Bellhaven Press.

Chapin, Wesley D. 1996. "The Turkish Diaspora in Germany." *Diaspora Journal* 5 (Fall): 275–301.

Clark, Robert P. 1979. *The Basques: The Franco Years and Beyond*. Reno: University of Nevada Press.

———. 1984. *The Basque Insurgents: ETA, 1952–1980*. Madison: University of Wisconsin Press.

———. 1992. "Territorial Devolution as a Strategy to Resolve Ethnic Conflict: Basque Self-Governance in Spain's Autonomous Community System." In *Ethnic and Racial Minorities in Advanced Industrial Democracies*, edited by Anthony M. Messina. Contributions in Ethnic Studies, No. 29. Westport, Conn.: Greenwood Press.

Clark, Robert P., and Michael H. Haltzel, eds. 1987. *Spain in the 1980s: The Democratic Transition and a New International Role*. Cambridge: Ballinger.

Claval, Paul. 1996. "Diasporas and Politics: An Overview." In *The Network of Diasporas*, edited by Georges Prévélakis. Nicosia: Cyprus Research Center KYKEM.

Clifford, James. 1997. "Diasporas." In *The Ethnicity Reader: Nationalism, Multiculturalism and Migration*, edited by Montserrat Guibernau and John Rex. Cambridge: Polity Press.

Climo, Jacob. 1990. "Transmitting Ethnicity Through Oral Narratives." *Ethnic Groups* 8: 163–80.

Cohen, Anthony P. 1993. "Culture as Identity: An Anthropologist's View." *New Literary History* 24: 195–209.

Cohen, Robin. 1994. *Frontiers of Identity: The British and the Rest*. London: Longman.

———. 1996. "Diaspora and the Nation-State: From Victims to Challengers." *International Affairs* 72: 507–20.

———. 1997. *Global Diasporas: An Introduction*. London: University College London Press.

———. 1997. "Diasporas, the Nation-State, and Globalization." In *Global History and Migrations*, edited by Wang Gungwu. Boulder, Colo.: Westview Press.

———, ed. 1995. *The Cambridge Survey of World Migration*. Cambridge: Cambridge University Press.

Cohen, Robin, and Zig Layton-Henry, eds. 1997. *The Politics of Migration*. Cheltenham, Engl.: Edward Elgar Publishing.

Collins, Roger. 1983. *Early Medieval Spain: Unity in Diversity, 400–1000*. New York: St. Martin's Press.

———. 1986. *The Basques*. Oxford: Basil Blackwell.

Collinson, Sarah. 1994. *Europe and International Migration*. London: Royal Institute of International Affairs.

Comet I Codina, Robert. 1990. "Minority Languages in Spain." In *Minority Languages*, Vol. 2 of Monographic Series 71, *Western and Eastern European Papers. Fourth International Conference on Minority Languages*, edited by Durk Gorter et al. Clevedon, Engl.: Multilingual Matters.

Congleton, Roger D. 1995. "Ethnic Clubs, Ethnic Conflict, and Ethnic Nationalism." In *Nationalism and Rationality*, edited by Albert Breton et al. Cambridge: Cambridge University Press.

Connor, Walker. 1972. "Nation-Building or Nation-Destroying?" *World Politics* 24: 319–55.

———. 1978. "A Nation Is a Nation, Is a State, Is an Ethnic Group, Is a ..." *Ethnic and Racial Studies* 1 (October): 377–400.

———. 1984. "The Impact of Homelands upon Diasporas." In *Modern Diasporas in International Politics*, edited by Gabriel Sheffer. London: Croom Helm.

———. 1993. "Diasporas and the Formation of Foreign Policy: The U.S. in Comparative Perspective." In *Diasporas in World Politics: The Greeks in Comparative Perspective*, edited by Dimitri C. Constas and Athanassios G. Platias. London: Macmillan.

———. 1994. *Ethnonationalism: The Quest for Understanding*. Princeton: Princeton University Press.

Constantinou, Stavros T. 1996. "Greek American Networks." In *The Network of Diasporas*, edited by George Prévélakis. Nicosia: Cyprus Research Center KYKEM.

Conversi, Daniele. 1990. "Language or Race?: The Choice of Core Values in the Development of Catalan and Basque Nationalism." *Ethnic and Racial Studies* 13 (January): 50–70.

———. 1993. "Domino Effect or Internal Developments? The Influences of International Events and Political Ideologies on Catalan and Basque Nationalism." *West European Politics* 16 (July): 245–70.

———. 1995. "Reassessing Current Theories of Nationalism: Nationalism as Boundary Maintenance and Creation." *Nationalism and Ethnic Politics* 1: 73–85.

———. 1997. *The Basques, the Catalans and Spain: Alternative Routes to Nationalist Mobilisation*. London: Hurst.

Corcuera Atienza, Javier. 1991. *Política y Derecho: La Construcción de la Autonomía Vasca*. Madrid: Centro de Estudios Constitucionales.

———. 1979. *Orígenes, Ideología y Organización del Nacionalismo Vasco (1876–1904)*. Madrid: Siglo XXI de España Editores.

Dahan, Michael, and Gabriel Sheffer. 2001. "Ethnic Groups and Distance Shrinking Technologies." *Nationalism and Ethnic Politics* 7 (Spring): 85–107.

da Silva, Milton M. 1975. "Modernization and Ethnic Conflict: The Case of the Basques." *Comparative Politics* 7 (January): 227–51.

Decroos, Jean F. 1983. *The Long Journey Home: Social Integration and Ethnicity Maintenance Among Urban Basques in the San Francisco Bay Region*. Reno: University of Nevada, Reno, Basque Studies Program.

Del Valle, Teresa. 1985. "Basque Ethnic Identity in a Time of Rapid Change." In *Iberian Identity: Essays on the Nature of Identity in Portugal and Spain*, edited by Richard Herr and John H. R. Polt. Berkeley: University of California Institute of International Studies.

———, ed. 1993. *Gendered Anthropology*. London: Routledge.

———. 1997. "El Genero en la Construcción de la Identidad Nacionalista." *Ankulegi: Revista de Antropología Social* 1 (November): 9–22.

De Vos, George, and Lola Romanucci-Ross, eds. 1975. *Ethnic Identity: Cultural Continuities and Change*. Palo Alto, Calif.: Mayfield Publishing Company.

Díez Medrano, Juan. 1994. "The Effects of Ethnic Segregation and Ethnic Competition on Political Mobilization in the Basque Country, 1988." *American Sociological Review* 59 (December): 873–89.

———. 1994. "Patterns of Development and Nationalism: Basque and Catalan Nationalism Before the Spanish Civil War." *Theory and Society* 23: 541–69.

———. 1995. *Divided Nations: Class, Politics, and Nationalism in the Basque Country and Catalonia.* Ithaca: Cornell University Press.

Dillman, Don A. 1978. *Mail and Telephone Surveys: The Total Design Method.* New York: John Wiley and Sons.

Doomernik, Jeroen, and Hans Van Amersfoort. 1996. "Turkish Immigrants in the Netherlands." In *The Network of Diasporas,* edited by Georges Prévélakis. Nicosia: Cyprus Research Center KYKEM.

Douglas, Mary. 1983. "How Identity Problems Disappear." In *Identity: Personal and Socio-Cultural, A Symposium,* edited by Anita Jacobson-Widding. Atlantic Highlands, N.J.: Humanities Press.

Douglass, William A. 1978. "Basques in Australia." In *University of Nevada, Reno, Basque Studies Program Newsletter* 18 (March): 4–6.

———. 1979. "Basque Immigrants: Contrasting Patterns of Adaptation in Argentina and the American West." In *Currents in Anthropology: Essays in Honor of Sol Tax,* edited by Robert Hinshaw. New York: Mouton.

———. 1980. "Inventing an Ethnic Identity: The First Basque Festival." *Halcyon 1980: A Journal of the Humanities*: 115–30.

———. 1983. "Counting Basques: The 1980 U.S. Census." *University of Nevada, Reno, Basque Studies Program Newsletter* 28 (November): 3–7.

———. 1984. "Sheep Ranchers and Sugar Growers: Property Transmission in the Basque Immigrant Family of the American West and Australia." In *Households: Comparative and Historical Studies of the Domestic Group,* edited by Robert McC. Notting, Richard R. Wilk, and Eric J. Arnould. Berkeley: University of California Press. Pp. 107–29.

———, ed. 1985. *Basque Politics: A Case Study in Ethnic Nationalism.* Reno: University of Nevada, Reno, Basque Studies Program.

———. 1987. "The Basques of Nevada." *Nevada Public Affairs Review* 2: 56–60.

———. 1988. "A Critique of Recent Trends in the Analysis of Ethnonationalism." *Ethnic and Racial Studies* 11 (April): 192–206.

———. 1989. "Factors in the Formation of the New-World Basque Emigrant Diaspora." *Essays in Basque Social Anthropology and History,* edited by William A. Douglass. Basque Studies Program Occasional Papers Series, No. 4. Reno: University of Nevada, Reno, Basque Studies Program.

———. 1993. *Through the Looking Glass, or Becoming the Datum.* Donostia: Eusko Ikaskuntza.

———. 1993. "A World Eclipsed: Economic Changes Cause an Identity Crisis for Basque Americans." *The World and I: A Chronicle of Our Changing Era* (December): 256–65.

———. 1996. *Azúcar Amargo: Vida y fortuna de los ortadores de caña italianos y vascos en la Australia tropical.* Bilbao: Servicio Editorial Universidad del País Vasco.

———. 1999. "Creating the New Basque Diaspora." In *Basque Politics and Nationalism on the Eve of the Millennium,* edited by William A. Douglass et al. Basque Studies Program Occasional Papers Series, No. 6. Reno: University of Nevada, Reno, Basque Studies Program.

Douglass, William A., and Jon Bilbao. 1975. *Amerikanuak: Basques in the New World.* Reno: University of Nevada Press.

Douglass, William A., and Joseba Zulaika. 1990. "On the Interpretation of Terrorist Violence: ETA and the Basque Political Process." *Comparative Study of Society and History: An International Quarterly* 32 (Fall): 238–57.

Dow, James R., ed. 1991. *Language and Ethnicity: Focusschrift in Honor of Joshua A. Fishman on the Occasion of His 65th Birthday.* Vol. 2. Amsterdam: John Benjamins Publishing Company.

Dupla, Antonio. 1992. *Presencia Vasca en América 1492–1992: Una Mirada Crítica.* Donostia: Tercera Prensa-Hirugarren Prentsa.

Durando, Dario. 1993. "The Rediscovery of Ethnic Identity." *Telos: A Quarterly Journal of Critical Thought* 97 (Fall): 21–31.

Echave, Baltasar de. 1971. *Discursos de la Antigüedad de la Lengua Cantabra Bascongada.* Bilbao: Edición Separada de la Gran Enciclopedia Vasca.

Echeverría, Jeronima. 1999. *Home Away from Home: A History of the Basque Boardinghouses.* Reno: University of Nevada Press.

Edwards, John. 1985. *Language, Society and Identity.* Oxford: Basil Blackwell.

Eiras Roel, Antonio, ed. 1991. *La Emigración Española a Ultramar, 1492–1914.* Madrid: Ediciones Tabapress.

Ekstrand, Lars, ed. 1986. *Ethnic Minorities and Immigrants in a Cross-Cultural Perspective.* Berwyn, Penn.: Swets North America.

Elazar, Daniel J. 1984. "The Jewish People as the Classic Diaspora: A Political Analysis." In *Modern Diasporas in International Politics,* edited by Gabriel Sheffer. London: Croom Helm.

Eley, Geoff, and Ronald Grigor Suny, eds. 1996. *Becoming National: A Reader.* Oxford: Oxford University Press.

Elkins, David J. 1997. "Globalization, Telecommunication, and Virtual Ethnic Communities." *International Political Science Review* 18: 139–52.

Ellen, R. F., ed. 1984. *Ethnographic Research: A Guide to General Conduct.* Research Methods in Social Anthropology Series, No. 1. London: Academic Press.

Eller, Jack David, and Reed M. Coughlan. 1993. "The Poverty of Primordialism: The Demystification of Ethnic Attachments." *Ethnic and Racial Studies* 16 (April): 183–202.

Elorza, Antonio. 1995. "Some Perspectives on the Nation-State and Autonomies in Spain." In *Spanish Cultural Studies: An Introduction, The Struggle for Modernity,* edited by Helen Graham and Jo Labanyi. Oxford: Oxford University Press.

Epstein, A. L. 1978. *Ethos and Identity: Three Studies in Ethnicity.* London: Tavistock Publications.

Erdmans, Mary Patrice. 1995. "Immigrants and Ethnics: Conflict and Identity in Chicago Polonia." *Sociological Quarterly* 36: 175–95.

Eriksen, Thomas Hylland. 1993. *Ethnicity and Nationalism: Anthropological Perspectives*. London: Pluto Press.
Escobedo Mansilla, Ronald, Ana de Zabala Beascoechea, and Oscar Alvarez Gila, eds. 1996. *Emigración y Redes Sociales de los Vascos en América*. Vitoria-Gasteiz: Servicio Editorial Universidad del País Vasco.
Esman, Milton J. 1986. "Diasporas and International Relations." In *Modern Diasporas in International Politics*, edited by Gabriel Sheffer. London: Croom Helm.
———. 1986. "The Chinese Diaspora in Southeast Asia." In *Modern Diasporas in International Politics*, edited by Gabriel Sheffer. London: Croom Helm.
———. 1995. "Ethnic Actors in International Politics." *Nationalism and Ethnic Politics* 1 (Spring): 111–25.
Esman, Milton J., and Shibley Telhami, eds. 1995. *International Organizations and Ethnic Conflict*. Ithaca: Cornell University Press.
Falcoff, Mark, and Fredrick B. Pike. 1982. *The Spanish Civil War, 1936–39: American Hemisphere Perspectives*. Lincoln: University of Nebraska Press.
Fawcett, James T. 1989. "Networks, Linkages, and Migration Systems." *International Migration Review* 23: 671–80.
Featherstone, Mike. 1995. *Undoing Culture: Globalization, Postmodernism and Identity*. London: Sage Publications.
Federación de Entidades Vasco Argentinas. 1984. Vitoria-Gasteiz: Servicio Central de Publicaciones del Gobierno Vasco.
Federal Research Division, Library of Congress. 1990. *Spain: A Country Study*, edited by Eric Solsten and Sandra W. Meditz. Washington D.C.: Library of Congress.
Felipe y Lorenzo, Emilio de. 1991. "El Real Seminario Bascongado de Vergara y sus Alumnos de Ultramar." In *América y los Vascos: Presencia Vasca en América*, edited by Jon Bilbao. Vitoria-Gasteiz: Gobierno Vasco Departamento de Cultura.
Fernandez, Alberto. 1972. *Emigración Republicana Española (1939–1945)*. Madrid: Gráficas Color.
Fernandez de Casadevante Romani, Carlos. 1985. *La Frontera Hispano-Francesa y las Relaciones de Vecindad: Especial Referencia al Sector Fronterizo del País Vasco*. Bilbao: Servicio Editorial de la Universidad del País Vasco.
Fernandez de Pinedo, Emiliano. 1993. *La Emigración Vasca a América, Siglo XIX y XX*. Gijón, Asturias: Ediciones Jucar.
Finch, Henry. 1995. "Uruguayan Migration." In *The Cambridge Survey of World Migration*, edited by Robin Cohen. Cambridge: Cambridge University Press.
Fishman, Joshua. 1989. *Language and Ethnicity in Minority Sociolinguistic Perspective*. Clevedon, Engl.: Multilingual Matters.
———. 1997. *In Praise of the Beloved Language: A Comparative View of Positive Ethnolinguistic Consciousness*. New York: Mouton de Gruyter.
Fishman, Joshua, et al., eds. 1985. *The Rise and Fall of Ethnic Revival: Perspectives on Language and Ethnicity*. New York: Mouton Publishers.
Flinspach, Susan Leigh. 1978. "The Need for Basque Language Maintenance Planning in Gipuzkoa, Spain." *Geolinguistics* 13: 89–104.

Forbes, Hugh Donald. 1997. *Ethnic Conflict: Commerce, Culture, and the Contact Hypothesis*. New Haven: Yale University Press.

Fried, C., ed. 1983. *Minorities: Community and Identity. Report of the Dahlem Workshop on Minorities: Community and Identity, Berlin, November 28–December 3, 1982*. New York: Springer-Verlag.

Galíndez, Jesús de. 1984. *Presencia Vasca en América*. Vitoria-Gasteiz: Servicio Central de Publicaciones del Gobierno Vasco.

Gans, Herbert J. 1979. "Symbolic Ethnicity: The Future of Ethnic Groups and Cultures in America." *Ethnic and Racial Studies* 2 (January): 1–20.

———. 1992. "Second Generation Decline: Scenarios for the Economic and Ethnic Futures of the Post-1965 America Immigrants." *Ethnic and Racial Studies* 15 (April): 173–92.

———. 1994. "Symbolic Ethnicity and Symbolic Religiosity: Towards a Comparison of Ethnic and Religious Acculturation." *Ethnic and Racial Studies* 17 (October): 577–89.

Garcia, Caterina. 1995. "The Autonomous Communities and External Relations." In *Democratic Spain: Reshaping External Relations in a Changing World*, edited by Richard Gillespie, Fernando Rodrigo, and Jonathon Story. London: Routledge.

García de Cortázar, Fernando, and Manuel Montero. 1980. *Historia Contemporánea del País Vasco: De las Cortes de Cádiz al Estatuto de Guernica*. San Sebastián: Editorial Txertoa.

García de Cortázar, José Angel, et al., eds. 1979. *Introducción a la Historia Medieval de Alava, Guipuzcoa, y Vizcaya en sus Textos*. San Sebastián: Editorial Txertoa.

Garmendia, Mari Karmen, and Xabier Aizpurua. 1990. "A Demolinguistic Analysis of the Basque Autonomous Community Derived from the Census of 1986." In *Minority Languages*, Vol. 2 of *Monographic Series 71, Western and Eastern European Papers. Fourth International Conference on Minority Languages*, edited by Durk Gorter et al. Clevedon, Engl.: Multilingual Matters.

Geertz, Clifford. 1973. "The Integrative Revolution: Primordial Sentiments and Civil Politics in the New States." In *The Interpretation of Cultures: Selected Essays*. New York: Basic Books.

Gellner, Ernest. 1983. *Nations and Nationalism*. Ithaca: Cornell University Press.

Giddens, Anthony. 1991. *Modernity and Self-Identity*. Cambridge: Polity Press.

Giles, Howard, and Patricia Johnson. 1987. "Ethnolinguistic Identity Theory: Social Psychological Approach to Language Maintenance." *International Journal of the Sociology of Language* 68: 69–99.

Gilmour, David. 1985. *The Transformation of Spain: From Franco to the Constitutional Monarchy*. London: Quartet Books.

Gjerde, Jon. 1997. *The Minds of the West: Ethnocultural Evolution in the Rural Middle West, 1830–1917*. Chapel Hill: University of North Carolina Press.

Glazer, Nathan, and Daniel P. Moynihan, eds. 1970. *Beyond the Melting Pot: The Negroes, Puerto Ricans, Jews, Italians, and Irish of New York City*. 2d ed. Cambridge: The MIT Press.

———. 1975. *Ethnicity: Theory and Experience*. Cambridge: Harvard University Press.

Glick Schiller, Nina, Linda Basch, and Christina Szanton Blanc. 1994. "From Migrant to Transmigrant: Theorizing Transnational Migration." *Anthropological Quarterly* 68 (January): 48–63.

Gómez Prieto, Julia. 1991. "La Emigración Vizcaina hacia América. Los Indianos de Balmaseda: Siglos XVI–XIX." In *La Emigración Española a Ultramar, 1492–1914*, edited by Antonio Eiras Roel. Madrid: Ediciones Tabapress.

Gorter, Durk, et al., eds. 1990. *Fourth International Conference on Minority Languages*. Vol. 1, *General Papers*. Monographic Series 71. Clevedon, Engl.: Multilingual Matters.

Graham, Helen, and Jo Labanyi, eds. 1995. *Spanish Cultural Studies: An Introduction, The Struggle for Modernity*. Oxford: Oxford University Press.

Greeley, Andrew M. 1974. *Ethnicity in the United States: A Preliminary Reconnaissance*. New York: John Wiley and Sons.

Greenwood, Davydd J. 1977. "Continuity in Change: Spanish Basque Ethnicity as a Historical Process." In *Ethnic Conflict in the Western World: Conference on Ethnic Pluralism and Conflict in Contemporary Western Europe and Canada,(Ithaca, N.Y. 1975)*, edited by Milton Esman. Ithaca: Cornell University Press.

Grinberg, Leon, and Rebeca Grinberg. 1989. *Psychoanalytic Perspectives on Migration and Exile*. Translated by Nancy Festinger. New Haven: Yale University Press.

Grosby, Steven. 1994. "The Verdict of History: The Inexpungeable Tie of Primordiality—A Response to Eller and Coughlan." *Ethnic and Racial Studies* 17 (January): 164–71.

Gudykunst, William B., ed. 1988. *Language and Ethnic Identity*. Clevedon, Engl.: Multilingual Matters.

Guibernau, Montserrat, and John Rex, eds. 1997. *The Ethnicity Reader: Nationalism, Multiculturalism and Migration*. Cambridge: Polity Press.

Gurr, Ted Robert. 1993. *Minorities at Risk: A Global View of Ethnopolitical Conflicts*. Washington, D.C.: United States Institute of Peace Press.

———. 1993. "Why Minorities Rebel: A Global Analysis of Communal Mobilization and Conflict Since 1945." *International Political Science Review* 14 (April): 161–201.

Haarmann, Harald. 1986. "Language in Ethnicity: A View of Basic Ecological Relations." In *Contributions to the Sociology of Language*, No. 44, edited by Joshua A. Fishman. Berlin: Mouton de Gruyter.

Hall, Stuart. 1991. "Old and New Identities, Old and New Ethnicities." In *Culture, Globalization and the World System: Contemporary Conditions for the Representation of Identity*, edited by Anthony D. King. Basingstoke, Engl.: Macmillian Education.

———. 1997. "Diaspora and Detours in Identity." In *Identity and Difference*, edited by Kathryn Woodward. London: Sage Publications.

Hall, Stuart, and Martin Jacques, eds. 1990. *New Times: The Changing Face of Politics in the 1990s*. London: Verso.

Hansen, Marcus Lee. [1937]. "Who Shall Inherit America?" In *American Immigrants and Their Generations: Studies and Commentaries on the Hansen Thesis After Fifty Years*, edited by Peter Kivisto and Dag Blanck. Urbana: University of Illinois Press, 1990.

Hardin, Russell. 1995. "Self-Interest, Group Identity." In *Nationalism and Rationality*, edited by Albert Breton et al. Cambridge: Cambridge University Press.

Harik, Iliya. 1984. "Modern Diasporas in International Politics." In *Diasporas and Communal Conflicts*, edited by Gabriel Sheffer. London: Croom Helm.

Hechter, Michael. 1978. "Group Formation and the Cultural Division of Labor." *American Journal of Sociology* 84: 293–319.

———. 1996. "Ethnicity and Rational Choice Theory." In *Ethnicity*, edited by John Hutchinson and Anthony D. Smith. Oxford: Oxford University Press.

Heiberg, Marianne. 1989. *The Making of the Basque Nation*. Cambridge: Cambridge University Press.

———. 1996. "Basques, Anti-Basques, and the Moral Community." In *Becoming National: A Reader*, edited by Geoff Eley and Ronald Grigor Suny. Oxford: Oxford University Press.

Held, David, et al. 1999. *Global Transformations: Politics, Economics and Culture*. Stanford: Stanford University Press.

Helmreich, Stefan. 1992. "Kinship, Nation, and Paul Gilroy's Concept of Diaspora." *Diaspora* 2 (Fall): 243–49.

Hertzberg, Arthur. 1996. "Israel and the Diaspora: A Relationship Reexamined." *Israel Affairs* 2 (Spring-Summer): 169–83.

Hirschman, Charles. 1983. "America's Melting Pot Reconsidered." *Annual Review of Sociology* 9: 397–423.

Hobsbawm, Eric J. 1992. *Nations and Nationalism Since 1780: Programme, Myth, Reality*. 2d ed. Cambridge: Cambridge University Press.

Hobsbawm, Eric, and Terence Ranger, eds. 1983. *The Invention of Tradition*. Cambridge: Cambridge University Press.

Hooson, David. 1994. *Geography and National Identity*. Oxford: Blackwell.

Horowitz, Donald L. 1985. *Ethnic Groups in Conflict*. Berkeley: University of California Press.

Huntington, Samuel. 1997. "The Erosion of American National Interest." *Foreign Affairs* 76 (September/October): 28–49.

Hutchinson, John, and Anthony D. Smith, eds. 1994. *Nationalism*. Oxford: Oxford University Press.

———. 1996. *Ethnicity*. Oxford: Oxford University Press.

Iberlin, Dollie, and David Romtvedt, eds. 1995. *Buffalotarrak: An Anthology of the Basque People of Buffalo, Wyoming*. Buffalo, Wyo.: Red Hills Publications.

Ignatieff, Michael. 1993. *Blood and Belonging: Journeys into the New Nationalism*. Toronto: Penguin Books.

Intxausti, Joseba. 1992. *Euskera: La Lengua de los Vascos*. San Sebastián: Elkar.

Iriani Zalakain, Marcelino. 2000. *Hacer América: Los Vascos en la Pampa Húmeda, Argentina (1840–1920)*. Leioa: Universidad del País Vasco.

Isaacs, Harold R. 1975. "Basic Group Identity: The Idols of the Tribe." In *Ethnicity: Theory and Experience*, edited by Nathaniel Glazer and Daniel Patrick Moynihan. Cambridge: Harvard University Press. Pp. 29–52.

Jacob, James E. 1985. "Politics, Ideology, and the Fueros in Vizcaya During the Initial

Phase of the Liberal Triennium (1820)." In *Basque Politics: A Case Study in Ethnic Nationalism*, edited by William A. Douglass. Reno: University of Nevada, Reno, Basque Studies Program.

———. 1994. *Hills of Conflict: Basque Nationalism in France*. Reno: University of Nevada Press.

Jacobson-Widding, Anita, ed. 1983. *Identity: Personal and Social-Cultural, A Symposium*. Atlantic Heights, N.J.: Humanities Press.

Jakobovits, Immanuel. 1991. "Israel-Diaspora Relations and Anglo-Jewish Perspective." In *Israel and Diaspora Jewry: Ideological and Political Perspectives*, edited by Eliezer Don-Yehiya. Vol. 3 of *Comparative Jewish Politics*. Jerusalem: Bar-Ilan University Press.

Jardon, Manuel. 1993. *La Normalización Linguistica, Una Anormalidad Democrática: El Caso Gallego*. Madrid: Siglo XXI de España Editores.

Jáuregui, Gurutz, José Manuel Castells, and Xabier Iriondo. 1997. *La Institucionalización Jurídica y Política de Vasconia*. San Sebastián-Donostia: Eusko Ikaskuntza.

Jáuregui Bereciartu, Gurutz. 1981. *Ideología y Estrategia Política de ETA: Análisis de Su Evolución entre 1959 y 1968*. Madrid: Siglo XXI de España Editores.

———. 1986. *Contra el Estado-Nación: En Torno al Hecho y la Cuestión Nacional*. Madrid: Siglo XXI de España Editores.

Jenkins, Richard. 1997. *Rethinking Ethnicity: Arguments and Explorations*. London: Sage Publications.

Jimenez de Aberasturi, Juan Carlos, coordinator. 1982. *Estudios de Historia Contemporánea del País Vasco*. San Sebastián: Haranburu Editor.

Johnson, Janet Buttolph, and Richard A. Joslyn. 1991. *Political Science Research Methods*. 2d ed. Washington D.C.: Congressional Quarterly.

Jupp, James, and Marie Kabala, 1993. "The Ethnic Lobby and Immigration Policy." In *The Politics of Australian Immigration*, edited by James Jupp and Marie Kabala. Canberra: Australian Government Publishing Service.

Kamen, Henry. 1983. *Spain 1469–1714: A Society of Conflict*. London: Longman Group.

Kamphoefner, Walter D. 1987. *The Westfalians: From Germany to Missouri*. Princeton: Princeton University Press.

Kecmanovic, Dusan. 1996. *Mass Psychology of Ethnonationalism*. New York: Plenum Press.

Kedourie, Elie. 1993. *Nationalism*. 4th ed. Oxford: Blackwell.

Kenny, Michael. 1976. "Twentieth Century Spanish Expatriate Ties with the Homeland: Remigration and Its Consequences." In *The Changing Faces of Rural Spain*, edited by Joseph B. Aceves and William A. Douglass. New York: John Wiley and Sons.

King, Anthony. 1991. "Introduction: Spaces of Culture, Spaces of Knowledge." In *Culture, Globalization and the World-System: Contemporary Conditions for the Representation of Identity*, edited by Anthony King. Basingstock: Macmillan Education.

King, Charles, and Neil J. Melvin, eds. 1998. *Nations Abroad: Diaspora Politics and International Relations in the Former Soviet Union*. Boulder, Colo.: Westview Press.

King, Russell, ed. 1993. *Mass Migrations in Europe: The Legacy and the Future*. London: Belhaven Press.

Kivisto, Peter. 1989. *The Ethnic Enigma: The Salience of Ethnicity for European Origin Groups*. Philadelphia: Balch Institute Press.

Kolor-Panov, Dona. 1996. "Video and the Diasporic Imagination of Self-hood: A Case Study of the Croatians in Australia." *Cultural Studies* 10 (May): 288–314.

Lacarra, José Maria. 1972. *Historia Política del Reino de Navarra: Desde sus Orígenes hasta su Incorporación a Castilla*. Vol. 1. Pamplona: Editorial Aranzadi.

Lafourcade, Maite. 1999. "Sistemas de Herencia y Transmission de la Propiedad en Iparralde bajo el Antiguo Régimen." In *Vasconia: Cuadernos de Historia-Geografía*. Donostia-San Sebastián: Eusko Ikaskuntza.

Landau, Jacob M. 1986. "Diaspora and Language." In *Modern Diasporas in International Politics*, edited by Gabriel Sheffer. London: Croom Helm.

Las Casas, Bartolomé de. 1575–1625? *Apologética Historia Sumaria. Cuanto a Las Cualidades, Dispusición, Descripción, cielo y suelo destas tierras, y condiciones naturales, policias, repúblicas, manera de vivir, e costumbres de las gentes destas Indias occidentales y meridionales cuyo imperio soberano pertenece a los Reyes de Castilla*, edited by Edmundo O'Gorman. Vols. 1 and 2. 3rd ed. Mexico City: Universidad Nacional Autónoma de México.

Lavie, Smadar, and Ted Swedenburg, eds. 1996. *Displacement, Diaspora, and Geographies of Identity*. Durham: Duke University Press.

Legarreta, Dorothy. 1984. *The Guernica Generation: Basque Refugee Children of the Spanish Civil War*. Reno: University of Nevada Press.

Leonardo, Micaela di. 1984. *The Varieties of Ethnic Experience: Kinship, Class, and Gender Among California Italian-Americans*. Ithaca: Cornell University Press.

Letamendia, Francisco. 1997. "Basque Nationalism and Cross-Border Co-operation Between the Southern and Northern Basque Countries." *Regional and Federal Studies* 7 (Summer): 25–41.

Lieberson, Stanley. 1985. "Unhyphenated Whites in the United States," *Ethnic and Racial Studies* 8 (January): 159–80.

Lieberson, Stanley, and Mary Waters. 1988. *From Many Strands: Ethnic and Racial Groups in Contemporary America*. New York: Russell Sage Foundation.

Liebkind, Karmela. 1983. "Dimensions of Identity in Multiple Group Allegiance." In *Identity: Personal and Social-Cultural, A Symposium*, edited by Anita Jacobson-Widding. Atlantic Heights, N.J.: Humanities Press.

Liebman, Charles S. 1991. "Israel in the Mind of American Jewry." In *Israel and Diaspora Jewry: Ideological and Political Perspectives*, edited by Eliezer Don-Yehiya. Vol. 3 of *Comparative Jewish Politics*. Jerusalem: Bar-Ilan University Press.

Linz, Juan J. 1985. *New Nationalisms and the Developed West: Toward Explanation*. Boston: Allen and Unwin.

———. 1986. *Conflicto en Euskadi*. Madrid: Espasa Calpe.

Livermore, Harold. 1958. *A History of Spain*. London: George Allen & Unwin.

Llera Ramo, Francisco José. 1985. *Postfranquismo y Fuerzas Políticas en Euskadi: Sociología Electoral del País Vasco*. Bilbao: Servicio Editorial Universidad del País Vasco.

———. 1994. *Los Vascos y la Política. El Proceso Político Vasco: Elecciones, Partidos,*

Opinión Pública y Legitimación en el País Vasco, 1977–1992. Bilbo: Argitarapen Zerbitzua Euskal Herriko Uniberstitatea.

Lyman, Stanford M., and William A. Douglass. 1973. "Ethnicity: Strategies of Collective and Individual Impression Management." *Social Research* 40 (Summer): 344–65.

Lynch, John. 1964. *Spain Under the Habsburgs*. Vol. 1, *Empire and Absolutism, 1516–1598*. Oxford: Basil Blackwell.

MacDonald, John S., and Leatrice D. MacDonald. 1962. "Chain Migration, Ethnic Neighbourhood Formation and Social Networks." *Social Research* 29: 433–48.

Macdonald, Nancy. 1987. *Homage to the Spanish Exiles: Voices from the Spanish Civil War*. New York: Human Sciences Press.

Madariaga, Salvador de. 1950. *Cuadro Histórico de las Indias: Introducción a Bolívar*. Buenos Aires: Editorial Sudamericana.

Malkki, Liisa H. 1995. "Refugees and Exile: From 'Refugee Studies' to the National Order of Things." In *Annual Review of Anthropology*. Palo Alto, Calif.: Annual Reviews Inc. Pp. 495–523.

Mansour, Gerda. 1993. *Multilingualism and Nation Building*. Clevedon, Engl.: Multilingual Matters.

Marenales Rossi, Marta. 1991. *La Aventura Vasca: Destino—Montevideo*. Montevideo: Centro Vasco Euskal Erria y Gobierno Vasco.

Marenales Rossi, Martha, and Juan Carlos Luzuriaga. 1990. *Vascos en el Uruguay*. Nuestras Raices, No. 4. Montevideo: Editorial Nuestra Tierra.

Mar-Molinero, Clare, and Angel Smith, eds. 1996. *Nationalism and the Nation in the Iberian Peninsula: Competing and Conflicting Identities*. Oxford: Berg.

Márques Ortiz, Reyes. 1996. "Colectividad Vasca y Asociacionismo en Argentina." In *Emigración y Redes Sociales de los Vascos en América*, edited by Ronald Escobedo Mansilla, Ana de Zabala Beascoechea, and Oscar Alvarez Gila. Vitoria-Gasteiz: Universidad del País Vasco.

Martinelli, Phylis. 1986. "A Test of the McKay and Lewins Ethnic Typology." *Ethnic and Racial Studies* 9 (April): 196–209.

Martinez-Hernandez, Eva, and Arantxa Elizondo. 1997. "Women in Politics: Are They Really Concerned About Equality? An Essay on the Basque Political System." *European Journal of Women's Studies* 4: 451–72.

Martín Rubio, Carmen. 1996. "Vascos en Potosí: Minas y Mineros según una Fuente Inédita de Arzans y Vela." In *Emigración y Redes Sociales de los Vascos en América*, edited by Ronald Escobedo Mansilla, Ana de Zabala Beascoechea, and Oscar Alvarez Gila. Vitoria-Gasteiz: Universidad del País Vasco.

Matsuo, Hisako. 1992. "Identificational Assimilation of Japanese Americans: A Reassessment of Primordial and Circumstantialism." *Sociological Perspectives* 35: 505–52.

McAllister, Ian. 1995. "Occupational Mobility Among Immigrants: The Impact of Migration on Economic Success in Australia." *International Migration Review* 29 (Summer): 441–67.

McKay, James. 1982. "An Explanatory Synthesis of Primordial and Mobilizationist Approaches to Ethnic Phenomena." *Ethnic and Racial Studies* 5 (October): 395–420.

McKay, James, and Frank Lewins. 1978. "Ethnicity and the Ethnic Group: A Conceptual Analysis and Reformulation." *Ethnic and Racial Studies* 1 (October): 412–27.

Medina, Xabier. 1997. *Los Otros Vascos: Las Emigraciones Vascas en el Siglo XX.* Madrid: Editorial Fundamentos, Colección Ciencia.

Mettler, Willy, and M. A. Leguineche. 1967. "Cortadores de Caña en Australia." *La Actualidad Española* 804 (June 1): 20–24.

Michelena, Luís. 1985. *Lengua e Historia.* Madrid: Paraninfo.

Miller, David. 1995. *On Nationality.* Oxford: Clarendon Press.

Moch, Leslie Page. 1992. *Moving Europeans: Migration in Western Europe Since 1650.* Bloomington: Indiana University Press.

Monreal Zia, Gregorio. 1989. "Annotations Regarding Basque Traditional Political Thought in the Sixteenth Century." In *Essays in Basque Social Anthropology and History,* edited by William A. Douglass. Basque Studies Program Occasional Papers Series, No. 4. Reno: University of Nevada, Reno, Basque Studies Program.

———. 1992. "Larramendi: Madurez y Crisis del Régimen Foral." In *Manuel de Larramendi: Hirugarren Mendeurrena 1690–1990,* edited by Joseba Andoni Lakarra. Andoain: Andoain Udala.

———. 1996. "La institucionalización pública y la especificidad de las Juntas Generales." *Revista Internacional de los Estudios Vascos* 41: 455–58.

———. 1999. "El Estatuto en su perspectiva histórica." *Euskonews & Media* 51 (22–29 October) (www.euskonews.com).

Montville, Joseph V., ed. 1990. *Conflict and Peacemaking in Multiethnic Societies.* Lexington, Kentucky: Lexington Books.

Moreno, Luís. 1995. "Multiple Ethnoterritorial Concurrence in Spain." *Nationalism and Ethnic Politics* 1 (Spring): 11–32.

Moya, Jose C. 1998. *Cousins and Strangers: Spanish Immigrants in Buenos Aires, 1850–1930.* Berkeley: University of California Press.

Moynihan, Daniel Patrick. 1993. *Pandemonium: Ethnicity in International Politics.* Oxford: Oxford University Press.

Murphy, Alexander, and Nancy Leeper. 1996. "Southeast Europeans in the Cities of the West: Changing Networks in a Changing World." In *The Network of Diasporas,* edited by Georges Prévélakis. Nicosia: Cyprus Research Center KYKEM.

Nagel, Joane. 1994. "Constructing Ethnicity: Creating and Recreating Ethnic Identity and Culture." *Social Problems* 41 (February): 152–76.

———. 1995. "American Indian Ethnic Renewal: Politics and the Resurgence of Identity." *American Sociological Review* 60 (December): 947–65.

Neto, Felix. 1995. "Predictors of Satisfaction with Life Among Second Generation Migrants." *Social Indicators Research: An Interdisciplinary Journal for Quality-of-Life Measurement* 35 (May): 93–116.

Newman, Saul. 1996. *Ethnoregional Conflict in Democracies: Mostly Ballots, Rarely Bullets.* Contributions in Political Science, No. 373. Westport, Conn.: Greenwood Press.

Nuñez Astrain, Luis C. 1977. *La Sociedad Vasca Actual.* San Sebastián: Editorial Txertoa.

———. 1997. *The Basques: Their Struggle for Independence*. Translated by Meic Stephens. Falmouth, Wales: Welsh Academic Press.

Nyberg Sørensen, Ninna. 1995. "Roots, Routes and Transnational Attractions: Dominican Migration, Gender and Cultural Change." In *Ethnicity, Gender and the Subversion of Nationalism*, edited by Fiona Wilson and Bodil Folke Frederiksen. London: Frank Cass.

Okamura, Jonathan Y. 1998. *Imagining the Filipino American Diaspora: Transnational Relations, Identities, and Communities*. London: Garland.

O'Leary, Brendan. 1998. "Ernest Gellner's Diagnoses of Nationalism: A Critical Overview, or, What Is Living and What Is Dead in Ernest Gellner's Philosophy of Nationalism?" In *The State of the Nation: Ernest Gellner and the Theory of Nationalism*, edited by John Hall. Cambridge: Cambridge University Press.

Olzak, Susan. 1983. "Contemporary Ethnic Mobilization." *Annual Review of Sociology* 9: 355–74.

Olzak, Suzanne, and Joane Nagel, eds. 1986. *Competitive Ethnic Relations*. Orlando: Academic Press.

Oppenheim, A. N. 1992. *Questionnaire Design, Interviewing and Attitude Measurement*. New ed. London: Pinter.

Ordaz Romay, Mari Ángeles. 1996. "El FBI y los Vascos del Exílio de 1939 en Estados Unidos." In *Emigración y Redes Sociales de los Vascos en América*, edited by Ronald Escobedo Mansilla, Ana de Zabala Beascoechea, and Oscar Alvarez Gila. Vitoria-Gasteiz: Universidad del País Vasco.

Orúe, Carlos. 1996. *Sydneyko Gure Txoko: 30 Urteurrena*. Newtown, New South Wales: El Faro Printing.

Ossa Echaburu, Rafael. 1963. *Pastores y Pelotaris Vascos en U.S.A*. Bilbao: Ediciones de la Caja de Ahorros Vizcaina.

Panossian, Razmik. 1998. "The Armenians: Conflicting Identities and the Politics of Division." In *Nations Abroad: Diaspora Politics and International Relations in the Former Soviet Union*, edited by Charles King and Neil J. Melvin. Boulder, Colo.: Westview Press.

Patterson, O. 1983. "The Nature, Causes, and Implications of Ethnic Identification." In *Minorities: Community and Identity*, edited by C. Fried. Berlin: Springer-Verlag.

Payne, Stanley G. 1975. *Basque Nationalism*. Reno: University of Nevada Press.

———. 1985. "Navarra and Basque Nationalism." In *Basque Politics: A Case Study in Ethnic Nationalism*, edited by William A. Douglass. Reno: University of Nevada, Reno, Basque Studies Program.

Peltz, Rakhmiel. 1991. "Ethnic Identity and Aging: Children of Jewish Immigrants Return to Their First Language." In *Language and Ethnicity: Focusshrift in Honor of Joshua A. Fishman*, edited by James R. Dow. Vol. 2. Amsterdam: John Benjamins Publishing Company.

Pérez-Agote, Alfonso. 1984. *La Reproducción del Nacionalismo: El Caso Vasco*. Madrid: Centro de Investigaciones Sociológicas.

———. 1986. "The Role of Religion in the Definition of a Symbolic Conflict: Religion and the Basque Problem." *Social Compass (International Review of Sociology of Religion)* 33: 419–35.

———. 1987. *El Nacionalismo Vasco a la Salida del Franquismo.* Madrid: Centro de Investigaciones Sociológicas.

———, ed. 1989. *Sociología del Nacionalismo.* Vitoria-Gasteiz: Servicio Editorial Universidad del País Vasco Gobierno Vasco

———. 1999. *La Identidad Colectiva y Su Dimensión Política.* Leioa: Facultad de Ciéncias Sociales, Universidad del País Vasco.

Pérez-Agote, Alfonso, Jesús Azcona, and Ander Gurrutxaga. 1997. *Mantener la Identidad: Los Vascos del Río Carabelas.* Bilbao: Servicio Editorial de la Universidad del País Vasco.

Pérez-Diaz, Victor. 1993. *The Return of Civil Society: The Emergence of Democratic Spain.* Cambridge: Harvard University Press.

Pérez de Arenaza Múgica, José Maria, and Javier Lasagabaster Olazábal, eds. 1991. *América y los Vascos: Presencia Vasca en América.* Gasteiz: Departamento de Cultura, Gobierno Vasco.

Petersen, William, Michael Novak, and Phillip Gleason, eds. 1982. *Concepts of Ethnicity.* Cambridge: Belknap Press of Harvard University Press.

Petrissans, Catherine M. 1991. "When Ethnic Groups Do Not Assimilate: The Case of Basque-American Resistance." *Ethnic Groups: An International Periodical of Ethnic Studies* 9: 61–81.

Phinney, Jean S., and Mary Jane Rotheram. 1987. *Children's Ethnic Socialization: Pluralism and Development.* London: Sage Publications.

Pieterse, Jan Nederveen. 1996. "Varieties of Ethnic Politics and Ethnicity Discourse." In *The Politics of Difference: Ethnic Premises in a World of Power,* edited by Edwin N. Wilmsen and Patrick McAllisten. Chicago: University of Chicago Press.

Pildain Salazar, María Pilar. 1984. *Ir a América: La Emigración Vasca a América.* San Sebastián-Donostia: Sociedad Guipuzcoana de Ediciones y Publicaciones.

Pizzorno, Alessandro. 1986. "Some Other Kinds of Otherness: A Critique of 'Rational Choice' Theories," *Development, Democracy, and the Art of Trespassing: Essays in Honor of Albert O. Hirschman,* edited by Alejandro Foxley, Michael S. McPherson, and Guillermo O'Donnell. Notre Dame, Ind.: University of Notre Dame Press.

Portes, Alejandro. 1999. "Conclusion: Towards a New World—The Origins and Effects of Transnational Activities." *Ethnic and Racial Studies* 22 (March): 463–77.

Portes, Alejandro, Luis E. Guarniza, and Patricia Landolt. 1999. "The Study of Transnationalism: Pitfalls and Promise of an Emergent Research Field." *Ethnic and Racial Studies* 22 (March): 217–37.

Portes, Alejandro, and Rubén G. Rumbaut. 1990. *Immigrant America: A Portrait.* Berkeley: University of California Press.

Preston, Paul. 1990. *The Politics of Revenge: Fascism and the Military in Twentieth-Century Spain.* London: Unwin Hyman.

———. 1994. *Franco: A Biography.* New York: Basic Books.

Prévélakis, Georges, ed. 1996. *The Network of Diasporas.* Nicosia: Cyprus Research Center KYKEM.

Querol, Javier. 1959. "Al Margen de un Congreso." *Sabado Grafico*, No. 166 (5 December).

Quijada, Mónica. 1991. *Aires de República, Aires de Cruzada: La Guerra Civil Española en Argentina*. Barcelona: Sendai Ediciones.

Quiroz Paz-Soldán, Eusebio. 1996. "Los Vascos en la Ciudad de Arequipa." In *Emigración y Redes Sociales de los Vascos en América*, edited by Ronald Escobedo Mansilla, Ana de Zabala Beascoechea, and Oscar Alvarez Gila. Vitoria-Gasteiz: Universidad del País Vasco.

Ramirez Goicoechea, Eugenia. 1991. *De Jóvenes y sus Identidades: Socioantropología de la Etnicidad de Euskadi*. Madrid: Siglo XX de España Editores, Centro de Investigaciones Sociológicas.

Rayfield, Donald. 1990. "Saving the Basque Language." *Multilingua* 9: 413–23.

Reimers, David M., and Harold Troper. 1992. "Canadian and American Immigration Policy Since 1945." In *Immigration, Language, and Ethnicity: Canada and the United States*, edited by Barry R. Chiswick. Washington D.C.: American Enterprise Institute Press.

Roldán, José Manuel. 1989. *Historia de España*. Madrid: Ediciones Eurolatinas.

Roosens, Eugene E. 1989. *Creating Ethnicity: The Process of Ethnogenesis*. Frontiers of Anthropology Series, No. 5. London: Sage Publications.

Ross, Christopher. 1997. *Contemporary Spain: A Handbook*. London: Arnold.

Ross, J. A. 1979. "Language and the Mobilization of Ethnic Identity." In *Language and Ethnic Relations*, edited by H. Giles and B. Saint-Jacques. Oxford: Pergamon Press.

Rowles, Graham, and Shularrit Reinharz. 1988. *Qualitative Gerontology*. New York: Springer.

Rubin, Joan, and Bjorn H. Jernudd, eds. 1971. *Can Language Be Planned? Sociolinguistic Theory and Practice for Developing Nations*. Honolulu: University Press of Hawaii.

Rubinstein, W. D. 1995. "Melbourne Jewry: A Diaspora Community with a Vigorous Jewish Identity." *Jewish Journal of Sociology* 37 (December): 81–99.

Ruiz de Azua, Estibaliz. 1992. *Vascongadas y América*. Madrid: Editorial MAPFRE.

Ruiz Olabuénaga, José Ignacio, et al. 1983. *La Lucha del Euskera en la Comunidad Autónoma Vasca: Una Encuesta Básica—Conocimiento, Uso, Actitudes*. Gasteiz: Servicio Central de Publicaciones del Gobierno Vasco.

Rumbaut, Ruben G. 1994. "The Crucible Within: Ethnic Identity, Self-Esteem, and Segmented Assimilation Among Children of Immigrants." *International Migration Review* 28 (Winter): 748–94.

Sachdev, Itesh, and Richard Bourhis. 1990. "Language and Social Identification." In *Social Identity Theory: Constructive and Critical Advances*, edited by Dominic Abrams and Michael A. Hogg. London: Harvester Wheatsheaf.

Safran, William. 1991. "Diasporas in Modern Societies: Myths of Homeland and Return." *Diasporas: A Journal of Transnational Studies* 1: 83–98.

———. 1995. "Nations, Ethnic Groups, States and Politics: A Preface and an Agenda." *Nationalism and Ethnic Politics* 1 (Spring): 1–10.

———. 1995. "Ethnicity and Citizenship: The Canadian Case." *Nationalism and Ethnic Politics* 1 (Autumn): 107–11.
Sanchez, Maria-José. 1992. "Les Espagnols en Belgique au XXe Siècle." In *Histoire des Étrangers et de l'Immigration en Belgique: De la Préhistoire à Nos Jours.* Brussels: Editions Vie Ouvrière, Centre Bruxellois d'Action Interculturelle.
Sánchez-Albornoz, Claudio. 1978. *El Régimen de la Tierra en el Reino Asturleonés Hace Mil Años.* Buenos Aires: Instituto de Historia de España, Universidad de Buenos Aires.
Sandberg, Neil C. 1974. *Ethnic Identity and Assimilation: The Polish-American Community.* New York: Praeger.
San Sebastián, Koldo. 1991. *The Basque Archives: Vascos en Estados Unidos (1939–1943).* Donostia-San Sebastián: Editorial Txertoa.
San Sebastián, Koldo, and Peru Ajuria. 1989. *El Exilio Vasco en Venezuela.* Vitoria-Gasteiz: Servicio Central de Publicaciones Gobierno Vasco.
Santiso González, Maria Concepción. 1991. "La Segunda Guerra Carlista y su Repercusión en la Emigración Guipuzcoana a América." In *La Emigración Española a Ultramar, 1492–1914,* edited by Antonio Eiras Roel. Madrid: Ediciones Tabapress.
Sarrailh de Ihartza, Fernando [Federico Krutwig, pseud.]. 1964. *Vasconia.* Buenos Aires: Ediciones Norbait.
Sayas Abengoechea, Juan José. 1999. "De Vascones a Romanos para volver a ser Vascones." *Revista Internacional de los Estudios Vascos* 44: 147–84.
———. 1994. *Los Vascos en la Antigüedad.* Madrid: Ediciones Cátedra.
Scott, George M., Jr. 1990. "A Resynthesis of the Primordial and Circumstantial Approaches to Ethnic Group Solidarity: Towards an Explanatory Model." *Ethnic and Racial Studies* 13 (April): 147–71.
Scott, William A., Ruth Scott, and John Stumpf. 1989. *Adaptation of Immigrants: Individual Differences and Determinants.* Oxford: Pergamon Press.
Shafir, Gershon. 1995. *Immigrants and Nationalists: Ethnic Conflict and Accommodation in Catalonia, the Basque Country, Latvia and Estonia.* Albany: State University of New York Press.
Shain, Yossi. 1989. *The Frontiers of Loyalty: Political Exiles in the Age of the Nation-State.* Middleton, Conn.: Wesleyan University Press.
———, ed. 1991. *Governments-in-Exile in the Contemporary World of Politics.* London: Routledge, Chapman and Hall.
———. 1994. "Ethnic Diasporas and U.S. Foreign Policy." *Political Science Quarterly* 109 (Winter): 811–41.
———. 1994. "Marketing the Democratic Creed Abroad: U.S. Diasporic Politics in the Era of Multiculturalism." *Diaspora: A Journal of Transnational Studies* 3 (Spring): 85–111.
Shain, Yossi, and Juan J. Linz. 1995. *Between States: Interim Governments and Democratic Transitions.* New York: Cambridge University Press.
Sheffer, Gabriel, ed. 1986. *Modern Diasporas in International Politics.* London: Croom Helm.
———. 1994. "Ethno-National Diasporas and Security." *Survival* 36 (Spring): 60–79.

———. 1996. "Whither the Study of Ethnic Diasporas? Some Theoretical, Definitional, Analytical and Comparative Considerations." In *The Network of Diasporas*, edited by Georges Prévélakis. Nicosia: Cyprus Research Center KYKEM.

Shils, Edward. 1981. *Tradition*. London: Faber and Faber.

Siegrist de Gentile, Nora, and Óscar Álvarez Gila. 1998. *De la Ría del Nervión al Río de la Plata: Estudio Histórico de un Proceso Migratorio, 1750–1850*. Pamplona: Newbook Ediciones.

Simic, Andrei. 1985. "Ethnicity as a Resource for the Aged: An Anthropological Perspective." *Journal of Applied Gerontology* 4: 6–17.

Slobin, Mark. 1994. "Music in Diaspora: The View from Euro-America." *Diaspora* 3 (Winter): 243–51.

Smith, Anthony D., ed. 1977. *Nationalist Movements*. New York: St. Martin's Press.

———. 1979. *Nationalism in the Twentieth Century*. New York: New York University Press.

———. 1981. *The Ethnic Revival*. Cambridge: Cambridge University Press.

———. 1983. *Theories of Nationalism*. 2d ed. New York: Holmes and Meier.

———. 1984. "Negotiating Ethnicity in an Uncertain Environment." *Ethnic and Racial Studies* 7: 360–72.

———. 1986. *The Ethnic Origins of Nations*. Oxford: Blackwell.

———. 1991. *National Identity*. London: Penguin Books.

———. 1994. "The Problem of National Identity: Ancient, Medieval and Modern?" *Ethnic and Racial Studies* 17 (July): 375–99.

———. 1995. *Nations and Nationalism in a Global Era*. Cambridge: Polity Press.

———. 1995. "Zionism and Diaspora Nationalism." *Israel Affairs* 2 (Winter): 1–19.

Smolicz, J. J. 1977. "Australia: From Migrant Country to Multicultural Nation." *International Migration Review* 31 (Spring): 171–86.

Snyder, Louis L. 1982. *Global Mini-Nationalisms: Autonomy or Independence*. Westport, Conn.: Greenwood Press.

———. 1984. *Macro-Nationalisms: A History of Pan Movements*. Westport, Conn.: Greenwood Press.

Soraluze, Andoni de. 1982. "¿Euskal Vida: Cuantos Vascos llegaron a la Argentina?" *Imagen Vasco: Magazine de los Negocios* 27 (February): 32.

———. 1991. "Los Vascos en Peru." *Imagen Vasco: Magazine de los Negocios* 36 (May): 76–77.

Sørensen, Ninna Nyborg. 1995. "Roots, Routes, and Transnational Attractions: Dominican Migration, Gender, and Cultural Change." In *Ethnicity, Gender, and the Subversion of Nationalism*, edited by Fiona Wilson and Bodil Folke Frederiksen. London: Frank Cass. Pp. 104–18.

Sowell, Thomas. 1981. *Ethnic America: A History*. New York: Basic Books.

———. 1996. *Migrations and Cultures: A World View*. New York: Basic Books.

Spicer, Edward. 1971. "Persistent Identity Systems." *Science* 174: 795–800.

Stack, John F., Jr., ed. 1981. *Ethnic Identities in a Transnational World*. Westport, Conn.: Greenwood Press.

Stevens, Christine A. 1995. "The Illusion of Social Inclusion: Cambodian Youth in South Australia." *Diaspora* 4: 59–75.

Stoller, Eleanor Palo. 1996. "Sauna, Sisu and Sibelius: Ethnic Identity Among Finnish Americans." *Sociological Quarterly* 37: 146–75.

Suárez Fernández, Luís. 1959. *Navegación y Comercio en el Golfo de Vizcaya: Un Estudio sobre la Política Marinera de la Casa de Trastamara*. Madrid: Consejo Superior de Investigaciones Científicas, Escuela de Estudios Medievales.

Subtelny, Orest. 1991. *Ukrainians in North America: An Illustrated History*. Toronto: University of Toronto Press.

Tajfel, Henri, ed. 1978. *Differentiation Between Social Groups: Studies in the Social Psychology of Intergroup Relations*. London: Academic Press.

———. 1981. *Human Groups and Social Categories*. Cambridge: Cambridge University Press.

———. 1982. *Social Identity and Intergroup Relations*. Cambridge: Cambridge University Press.

———, ed. 1984. *The Social Dimension: European Development in Social Psychology*. Vol. 2. Cambridge: Cambridge University Press.

Tajfel, Henri, and Turner, J. C. 1979. "An Integrative Theory of Intergroup Conflict." In *The Social Psychology of Intergroup Relations*, edited by S. Worchel and W. G. Austin. Monterey, Calif.: Brooks-Cole.

Tamayo Salaberri, Virginia. 1994. *La Autonomía Vasca Contemporánea: Foralidad y Estatutismo (1975–1979)*. San Sebastián: Instituto Vasco de Administración Pública.

Tejerina Montana, Benjamín. 1992. *Nacionalismo y Lengua: Los Procesos de Cambio Lingüístico en el País Vasco*. Madrid: Centro de Investigaciones Sociológicas, Siglo Veintiuno de Españā.

Temple, Bogusia. 1996. "Time Travels: Time, Oral Histories and British-Polish Identities." *Time and Society* 5 (February): 85–96.

"The Basques: Strongmen of the Canefields." 1967. *People*, 18 October, pp. 12–17.

Thompson, Richard H. 1989. *Theories of Ethnicity: A Critical Appraisal*. Westport, Conn.: Greenwood Press.

Tilly, Charles. 1990. "Transplanted Networks." In *Immigration Reconsidered: History, Sociology, and Politics*, edited by Virginia Yans-McLaughlin. New York: Oxford University Press.

Tollefson, James W. 1991. *Planning Language, Planning Inequality: Language Policy in the Community*. London: Longman Group.

Tölölyan, Khachig. 1996. "Rethinking Diaspora(s): Stateless Power in the Transnation Moment." *Diaspora* 5: 3–36.

Totoricagüena, Gloria. 1997. "Gabonak: Representations of a Basque Christmas in the United States." *Euskal Etxea*, No. 36, pp. 21–24.

———. 1998. "Rethinking Ethnicity: Arguments and Explorations. A Critique of Richard Jenkins." *Nations and Nationalism: Journal of the Association for the Study of Ethnicity and Nationalism* 4 (October): 237–41.

———. 1999."Los Vascos en la Argentina," coauthored with William A. Douglass. In

La Inmigración Española en la Argentina, edited by Alejandro Fernandez and Jose C. Moya. Buenos Aires: Editorial Biblos.

———. 1999. "Shrinking World, Expanding Diaspora: Globalization and Basque Diasporic Identity." In *The Basque Diaspora/La Diaspora Vasca*, edited by William A. Douglass et al. Reno: University of Nevada, Reno, Basque Studies Program and University of Nevada Press.

———. 2000. "Celebrating Basque Diasporic Identity in Ethnic Festivals: Anatomy of a Basque Community." *Revista Internacional de Estudios Vascos* 45 (Fall): 569–98.

———. 2000. "Downloading Identity in the Basque Diaspora: Utilizing the Internet to Create and Maintain Ethnic Identity." *Nevada Historical Society Quarterly* 43 (Summer): 140–54.

———. 2000. "Vascos por el Mundo: Inmigrantes genericos o diasporas?" *Euskal Etxea*, No. 45–46, pp. 36–41.

———. 2000. "Izan Zirelako Gara, Izan Garelako Izango Gara. Because of Them We Are. Because of Us They Will Be." *Eusko Etxea*, No. 47, pp. 16–23.

———. 2001. "La Identidad Contemporánea de los Vascos en la Diáspora." *Eusko Ikaskuntza Euskonews and Media Electronic Journal*, No. 121 (May) (www.euskonews.com).

———. 2001. "The North American Basque Organizations." *Eusko Ikaskuntza Euskonews and Media Electronic Journal*, No. 119 (April) (www.euskonews.com).

———. 2001. "Researching the Basque Diaspora." *Campusa* 11 (March): 32–33. Bilbao: Universidad del País Vasco.

———. 2001. "Una Aproximación al Desarrollo de la Diáspora Vasca." In *Kanpoko Etxe Berria: Emigración Vasca a América Siglos XIX–XX*. Bilbao: Museo Arqueológico, Etnográfico e Histórico Vasco.

———. 2003. *Euskal Herria visto desde la diáspora: análisis de las relaciones institucionales entre Euskal Herria y la diáspora vasca*. San Sebastián-Donostia: Eusko Ikaskuntza.

———. 2002. *The Basques of Boise: Dreamers and Doers*. Serie Urazandi. Vitoria-Gasteiz: Gobierno Vasco Servicio Editorial.

———. 2003. *The Basque of New York: A Cosmopolitan Identity*. Vitoria-Gasteiz: Gobierno Vasco Servicio Editorial.

Tovar, Antonio. 1957. *The Basque Language*. Translated by Herbert Pierrepont Houghton. Philadelphia: University of Pennsylvania Press.

Tovey, Hillary, Damian Hannan, and Hal Abramson. 1989. *Why Irish? Irish Identity and the Irish Language*. Dublin: Bord na Gaeilge.

Trost, Jan E. 1986. "Statistically Nonrepresentative Stratified Sampling: A Sampling Technique for Qualitative Studies." *Qualitative Sociology* 9: 54–57.

Tuñón de Lara, Manuel, et al. 1987. *La Guerra Civil en el País Vasco: 50 Años Después*. Bilbao: Servicio Editorial Universidad del País Vasco.

Turuzeta, Josu. 1995. *Cien Años de Nacionalismo Vasco 1895–1995*. Bilbao: Editorial Iparraguirre.

Tusell, Javier, and Alicia Alted. 1991. "The Government of the Spanish Republic in

Exile: (1939–1977)." In *Governments-in-Exile in Contemporary World Politics*, edited by Yossi Shain. London: Routledge, Chapman and Hall.
Tusell, Javier, et al., eds. 1995. *Historia de la transición y consolidación democrática en España (1975–1986)*. Vol. 1 of *International Congress: History of the Transition and the Democratic Consolidation in Spain (1975–1986)*. Department of Contemporary History, UNED and UNAM. Madrid: Pardo.
Twining, William. 1991. *Issues of Self-Determination*. Aberdeen: Aberdeen University Press.
Ugalde, M. 1979. *Conflicto Lingüístico en Euskadi*. Bilbao: Ediciones Vascos.
Ugalde Solano, Mercedes. 1993. *Mujeres y Nacionalismo Vasco: Genesis y Desarollo de Emakume Abertzale Batza. 1906–1936*. Bilbao: Servicio Editorial Universidad del País Vasco.
Ugalde Zubiri, Alexander. 1996. *La Acción Exterior del Nacionalismo Vasco (1890–1939): Historia, Pensamiento y Relaciones Internacionales*. Bilbao: Gobierno Vasco Colección Tesis Doctorales, Instituto Vasco de Administración Pública.
Untracht, Oppi. 1997. *Traditional Jewelry of India*. London: Thames and Hudson.
Urla, Jacqueline. 1988. "Ethnic Protest and Social Planning: A Look at Basque Language Revival." *Cultural Anthropology* 3 (November): 379–94.
———. 1993. "Cultural Politics in an Age of Statistics: Numbers, Nations, and the Making of Basque Identity." *American Ethnologist* 20: 818–43.
Urquijo, Iñaki Bernardo. 1993. *Galindez: La Tumba Abierta. Los Vascos y los Estados Unidos*. Vitoria-Gasteiz: Servicio Central de Publicaciones del Gobierno Vasco.
Van den Berghe, Pierre L. 1978. "Race and Ethnicity: A Sociobiological Perspective." *Ethnic and Racial Studies* 1 (October): 401–11.
———. 1981. *The Ethnic Phenomenon*. New York: Elsevier.
———. 1996. "Does Race Matter?" In *Ethnicity*, edited by John Hutchinson and Anthony D. Smith. Oxford: Oxford University Press.
Van Hear, Nicolas. 1998. *New Diasporas: The Mass Exodus, Dispersal and Regrouping of Migrant Communities*. London: UCL Press.
Van Houdenhoven, Jan Pieter, and Tineke M. Willemsen, eds. 1989. *Ethnic Minorities: Social Psychological Perspectives*. Amsterdam: Swets and Zeitlinger.
Van Knippenburg, Ad F. M. 1984. "Intergroup Differences in Group Perceptions." In *The Social Dimension: European Development in Social Psychology*, edited by Henri Tajfel. Vol. 2. Cambridge: Cambridge University Press.
Vázquez de Prada, Mercedes. 1984. *Negociaciones sobre los Fueros entre Vizcaya y el Poder Central 1839–1877*. Bilbao: Caja de Ahorros Vizcaína.
Vázques de Prada, Valentin, and Juan Bosco Amores Carredano. 1991. "La Emigración de navarros y Vascongados al Nuevo Mundo y su repercusión en las comunidades de origen." In *La Emigración Española a Ultramar, 1492–1914*, edited by A. Eires Roel. Madrid: Tabapress. Pp. 133–42.
Vázquez de Prada Vallejo, Valentín, and Jesus Mari Usunariz Garayoa. 1991. "La Emigración Navarra hacia América en el Siglo XVII." In *América y los Vascos: Presencia Vasca en América*, edited by Jon Bilbao. Gasteiz: Departamento de Cultura, Gobierno Vasco.

Vertovec, Steven. 1999. "Conceiving and Researching Transnationalism." *Ethnic and Racial Studies* 22 (March): 447–62.
Vila, Ignasi. 1986. "Bilingual Education in the Basque Country." *Journal of Multilingual and Multicultural Development* 7: 123–45.
Wardhaugh, Ronald. 1984. *Languages in Competition: Dominance, Diversity, Decline.* London: Basil Blackwell.
Waters, Mary C. 1990. *Ethnic Options: Choosing Identities in America.* Berkeley: University of California Press.
Waters, Tony. 1995. "Towards a Theory of Ethnic Identity and Migration: The Formation of Ethnic Enclaves by Migrant Germans in Russia and North America." *International Migration Review* 29 (Summer): 515–44.
Weber-Newth, Inge. 1995. "Ethnic Germans Come Home to the Fatherland." *Debatte* 1: 126–42.
Weinrich, Peter. 1986. "Identity Development in Migrant Offspring: Theory and Practice." In *Ethnic Minorities and Immigrants in a Cross-Cultural Perspective*, edited by Lars Ekstrand. Berwyn, Penn.: Swets North America.
Weinstein, Brian, ed. 1990. *Language Policy and Political Development.* Norwood, N.J.: Ablex Publishing Corporation.
Williams, Colin H. 1994. *Call Unto Liberty: On Language and Nationalism.* Clevedon, Engl.: Multilingual Matters.
Wilson, Andrew. 1998. "The Ukrainians: Engaging the Eastern Diaspora." In *Nations Abroad: Diaspora Politics and International Relations in the Former Soviet Union*, edited by Charles King and Neil J. Melvin. Boulder, Colo.: Westview Press.
Wilson, Fiona, and Bodil Folke Frederiksen, eds. 1995. *Ethnicity, Gender and the Subversion of Nationalism.* London: Frank Cass.
Winland, Daphne N. 1995. "We Are Now an Actual Nation: The Impact of National Independence on the Croatian Diaspora in Canada." *Diaspora* 4 (Spring): 3–29.
Woolard, Kathryn A. 1991. "Linkages of Language and Ethnic Identity: Changes in Barcelona, 1980–1987." In *Language and Ethnicity: Focusschrift in Honor of Joshua A. Fishman*, edited by James A. Dow. Vol. 2. Amsterdam: John Benjamins Publishing Company.
Yancey, William, Eugene Ericksen, and Richard Juliani. 1976. "Emergent Ethnicity: A Review and a Reformulation." *American Sociological Review* 41 (June): 391–403.
Yinger, Milton J. 1981. "Toward a Theory of Assimilation and Dissimilation." *Ethnic and Racial Studies* 4 (July): 249–64.
———. 1985. "Ethnicity." *Annual Review of Sociology* 11: 151–80.
Zabaleta, Iñaki. 1999. "The Basques in the International Press: Coverage by the New York Times (1950–1996)." In *Basque Politics and Nationalism on the Eve of the Millennium*, edited by William A. Douglass et al. Basque Studies Program Occasional Papers Series, No. 6. Reno: University of Nevada, Reno, Basque Studies Program.
Zirakzadeh, Cyrus Ernesto. 1991. *A Rebellious People: Basques, Protests, and Politics.* Reno: University of Nevada Press.
Zulaika, Joseba. 1998. "Tropics of Terror: From Guernica's 'Natives' to Global 'Terrorists.'" *Social Identities* 4: 93–108.

BASQUE GOVERNMENT OFFICIAL PUBLICATIONS

1986. *Basic Law of the Standardization of the Use of Basque*. Vitoria-Gasteiz: Evagraf, S. Coop.
1989. *Análisis Demolinguístico de la Comunidad Autónoma Vasca derivado del Padrón de 1986*. Vitoria-Gasteiz: Gráficas Santamaría.
1991. 1992. General Secretary for Linguistic Policy. *Comparencia, Apetición propia, de la Secretaría General de Política Linguistica ante la Comisión de Instituciones e Interior del Parlamento Vasco*. Vitoria-Gasteiz: Gobierno Vasco.
1991. *Jornadas Municipales Sobre la Normalización del Euskera*. Vitoria-Gasteiz: Gobierno Vasco.
1991. *Propuesta para una Política Linguística en al Ambito Municipal*. Vitoria-Gasteiz: Estudios Gráficos Zure.
1992. General Secretary for Linguistic Policy. *Comparencia, Apetición propia, de la Secretaría General de Política Linguistica ante la Comisión de Instituciones e Interior del Parlamento Vasco*. Vitoria-Gasteiz: Gobierno Vasco.
1992. *Descripción General da la Situación Sociolinguística da la Comunidad Autónoma del País Vasco*. Vitoria-Gasteiz: Gobierno Vasco.
1994. *Law of Relations with Basque Communities Outside the Autonomous Community of the Basque Country*. Vitoria-Gasteiz: Eusko Jaurlaritza Argitalpen Zerbitzu Nagusia.

UNPUBLISHED PAPERS AND PAMPHLETS

Arrizabalaga, Marie-Pierre. 1986. "A Statistical Study of Basque Immigration into California, Nevada, Idaho and Wyoming Between 1900 and 1910." M.A. thesis, University of Nevada, Reno, Center for Basque Studies.
Azurmendi, María José. 1993. "Hizkuntza eta Nortasun Etnosozaila Euskal Herrian." Paper presented at Conference on Language and Collective Identity, July, Euskal Herriko Unibertsitatea, Donostia-San Sebastián.
Campbell, Catherine Magda. 1992. "Identity and Gender in a Changing Society: The Social Identity of South African Township Youth." Ph.D. diss., University of Bristol.
Castelli, Joseph Roy. 1980. "Basques in the Western United States: A Functional Approach to Determination of Cultural Presence in the Geographic Landscape." Ph.D. diss. East Stroudsburg State College.
Coleman, D. 1993. "The World on the Move? International Migration in 1992." Paper presented at the European Population Conference, U.N. Commission for Europe, U.N. Population Fund, March, in Geneva, Switzerland.
Demetriou, Madeline. 1998. "Diasporic Identities, Loyalty, and the Political Process." Paper presented at Aalborg University, School of Postgraduate Interdisciplinary Research on Interculturalism and Transnationality (SPIRIT).
Edlefsen, John B. 1948. "A Sociological Study of the Basques of Southwest Idaho." Ph.D. dissertation, Washington State University, Department of Sociology.

"En Nombre de la Verdad y la Justicia Lea Este Folleto: La Verdad Siempre Prevalece." 1970. Melbourne, Australia: Basque Community of Melbourne.

Hendry, Barbara Ann. 1992. "Ethnicity and Identity in a Basque Borderland: Rioja Alavesa, Spain." Ph.D. diss., University of Florida.

Herri Batasuna, Herri Enbaxada. 1997. "Manifesto to the Public Opinion and the International Community." Pamphlet distributed to Belgian media, labor unions, and politicians. Brussels.

"Informe Sobre la Colectividad Vasca en Uruguay 1995." Report to the Basque Congress of Basque Collectivities from Basque Centers in Uruguay. Vitoria-Gasteiz.

Iztueta, Paulo. 1993. "Revisión de los Conceptos: Comunidad, Nación, Estado, Identidad en Relación con la Lengua." Paper presented to the Conference on Language and Collective Identity, July, at Euskal Herriko Unibertsitatea, Donostia-San Sebastián.

Larrañaga, Iñaki. 1993. "Comunidad Linguistica y Percepción de la Identidad Nacional." Paper presented at Conference on Language and Collective Identity, July, at Euskal Herriko Unibertsitatea, Donostia-San Sebastián.

Larumbe, Josefina, and María Fernanda Astigarraga. 1998. "Bibliotecas Existentes en Entidades Vascas de la República Argentina: Informe de Situación." Report to the Euzko Etxea of La Plata, Argentina, for the American Congress of Basque Centers.

Laurak Bat Basque Center. 1997. "El Futuro de los Centros Vascos y su Relación con el País Vasco." Paper presented to the American Congress of Basque Centers, November, Buenos Aires, Argentina.

Nelde, Peter Hans. 1993. "Contact or Conflict? Observations on the Dynamics and Vitality of European Languages." Paper presented at Conference on Language and Collective Identity, July, at Euskal Herriko Unibertsitatea, Donostia-San Sebastián.

Thursby, Jacqueline S. 1994. "Basque Women of the American West." Ph.D. diss., Bowling Green State University.

Totoricagüena, Gloria. 2000. "Comparing the Basque Diaspora: Ethnonationalism, Transnationalism, and Identity Maintenance in Argentina, Australia, Belgium, Peru, the United States of America, and Uruguay." Ph.D. diss., London School of Economics and Political Science.

Urla, Jacqueline. 1987. "Being Basque, Speaking Basque." Ph.D. diss., University of California, Berkeley.

Ybarrola, Steven. 1983. "Intermarriage, Assimilation, and Ethnicity Maintenance: A Basque-American Case Study." M.A. thesis, Brown University, Department of Anthropology.

NEWSLETTERS, NEWSPAPERS, AND JOURNALS

Basque Studies Program Newsletter. 1981–2001. University of Nevada, Reno, Basque Studies Center.

Euskal Etxeak. Newsletter of the Euzkaldunak Inc. Basque Organization. 1975–2002. Boise, Idaho.

Hitzketa. Newsletter of the North American Basque Organizations. 1992–2001. Chino Hills, Calif.
Journal of Basque Studies. 1983–1998. Indiana University of Pennsylvania, Indiana, Penn.
La Revista de los Vascos. Magazine of Haize Hegoa. June 1994–February 1995. Montevideo, Uruguay.
Society of Basque Studies in America. 1988–2002. Brooklyn, N.Y., and Naperville, Ill.
Voice of the Basques. 1974–1978. Boise, Idaho.

INTERVIEWS

NOTE: Interviewees are listed by their country of residence. The interview listing indicates the city where the interview was conducted, as well as the date of the interview. All interviews were conducted by the author. Tapes or notes of the interviews remain in the author's possession.

EXPERT INTERVIEWS

Aguirre, Aintzane. Office of Relations with the Basque Collectivities, Basque Autonomous Government. Vitoria-Gasteiz, 1995–2002.
Aguirre Arizmendi, Iñaki. Director of Relations with the Basque Communities, Basque Autonomous Government. Vitoria-Gasteiz, 1995–2001.
Alonso, Adoni. University of Extremadura. Reno, May 2002.
Aranburu Iturbe, Andoni. Euskal Irrati Telebista. Interviewed in Buenos Aires, November 1997. Various personal electronic communications, 1997–1999.
Barquin Foruria, Diana. Gernika, 1995–2002.
Douglass, William A. Director and Professor Emeritus, Center for Basque Studies, University of Nevada, Reno. Reno, 1995–2002.
Egibar Mitxelena, Mikel. Director of International Relations, Herri Batasuna. E-mail communications, September 1997.
Egurrola Albizu, Javier. Registrar of New Residents, Municipality of Gernika. Gernika, July 1999.
Esnal, Iñaki. Counselor. Vitoria-Gasteiz, October 1999.
Garmendia Lasa, Mari Karmen. Buenos Aires, November 1997.
Goitiandia, Esperanza. Gernika, July 1999.
Gurrutxaga Abad, Ander. University of the Basque Country. Leiona, July–September 2002.
Landa, Karmelo. National Directorate, Herri Batasuna. November 1996.
Legarreta, Josu. Director of Economic Development and Cooperation of the Secretariate of Foreign Action, Basque Autonomous Government. Vitoria-Gasteiz, 1995–2003.
Monreal Zia, Gregorio. Universidad Pública de Navarra, Arlegi, Nafarroa. Reno, July 1998, October 1999, August 2000, September 2002.
Oregi, Benan. Office of Relations with the Basque Collectivities, Basque Autonomous Government. Vitoria-Gasteiz, 1999–2003.

Ortuzar, Andoni. Director of the Secretariate of Foreign Action; General Manager, Euskal Irrati Telebista. Vitoria-Gasteiz, 1995–1999.
Pecharroman, Begonia. University of the Basque Country. Various communications, 1997–2002.
Perez-Agote, Alfonso. University of the Basque Country. July 1998, November 1999.
San Sebastián, Koldo. Counselor of Relations with the Basque Collectivities, Basque Autonomous Government. Vitoria-Gasteiz, October 1999.
Valverde, Lola. University of the Basque Country, Leiona. Donostia-San Sebastián, December 2001.
Vélez de Mendizábal, Jose Mari. Eusko Ikaskuntza. Donostia-San Sebastián, 1999–2002.
White, Linda. Center for Basque Studies, University of Nevada, Reno. Reno, 1997–2003.
Zabaleta, Iñaki. Professor of Media Studies and Communications, University of the Basque Country. Reno, July 1998.

PERSONAL INTERVIEWS

Argentina

Aguirre, Mikel. Rosario, November 1996.
Apesteguia, Nélida. Rosario, October 1996.
Aramburu, Enrique. Buenos Aires, October 1996.
Arozarena, Miren. Buenos Aires, September–December 1996, November, 1997; London, July 1998.
Arregui, Maria Cristina. Rosario, November 1996; Buenos Aires, November 1997.
Arribálzaga, Victor. Rosario, November 1996.
Arrondo, Cesar. Vitoria-Gasteiz, November 1999.
Baqueriza, Julio. Vitoria-Gasteiz, November 1995.
Bilbao, Carlos. Rosario, October 1996.
Blanco de Irujo, Miren Amaia. Rosario, November 1996.
Bon, Nora de. Moreno, October 1996.
Bustos, Celina. Buenos Aires, September 1996.
Castell, Adrian. Buenos Aires, October 1996, November, 1997.
Egaña, Itxaso. Buenos Aires, September 1996, November 1997.
Erquiaga, Jon Kepa. Vitoria-Gasteiz, November 1995, November 1999; Buenos Aires, September 1996.
Etxeverry, Lucia. Buenos Aires, November 1996.
Etxeverry de Irujo e Irujo, Mari Elena. Buenos Aires, October 1996.
Eyheraguibel, Felipe. Rosario, September–November 1996.
Ezkerro, Mikel. Buenos Aires, September 1996, November 1997.
Fernandez Castelli, Marianna. Buenos Aires, November 1996.
Ferrere, Emilia. Necochea, October 1996.
Gamboa, Itziar. Vitoria-Gasteiz, November 1995; Rosario, November 1996.
Goyeneche, Mauricio. Buenos Aires, November 1996.
Greaves Otxandiano, Pedro. Buenos Aires, October 1996.
Ibarrola, Juan Carlos. Buenos Aires, November 1996.

Iguain, Nicomedes. Buenos Aires, September 1996.
Irazusta, Andoni. Buenos Aires, November 1996; Bahia Blanca, November 1997.
Iriart, Michel. Buenos Aires, November 1996.
Irujo de Irujo Etcheverry, Maria Elena. Buenos Aires, 1997.
Irujo de Olaizola, Miren Amayoa. Rosario, 1996; Buenos Aires, 1997.
Landaboure, Jean. Buenos Aires, November 1996.
Landeta, Juan Ignacio. Mar del Plata, November 1996.
Landeta, Julia. Vitoria-Gasteiz, November 1999.
Legarreta, Isidro. Vitoria-Gasteiz, November 1995, November 1999; Tandil, October 1996; Buenos Aires, November 1997.
Martinez, Koldo. Mar del Plata, November 1996.
Muguerza, Emilia. Necochea, October 1996; Reno (Nev.), July 1998.
Muguerza, Felipe. Vitoria-Gasteiz, November 1995; Necochea, September 1996; Buenos Aires, November 1997; Reno (Nev.), July 1998.
Muguerza, Mila. Rosario, November 1996; Necochea, November 1996.
Muguerza, Vasco. Vitoria-Gasteiz, November 1995; Mar del Plata, November 1996.
Mujica Lizarraga, Marta. Mar del Plata, November 1996.
Olaizola, Xabier. Buenos Aires, September 1996; Vitoria-Gasteiz, November 1999.
Ordoki, Begoña. Lomas de Zamorra, October 1996.
Ordoki, Izaskun. Buenos Aires, November 1996.
Orduña, Dolores. Buenos Aires, November 1996.
Peña de San Martín, Carmele. Buenos Aires, October 1996.
Plazaola, Pedro. Mar del Plata, November 1996.
Rios de Ibarrola, Norma. Buenos Aires, November 1996.
San Martín, Jokin. Buenos Aires, October 1996, November 1997.
Soraluce, Arantza. Rosario, November 1996.
Totorikagoena, Miren de. Rosario, September 1996; Buenos Aires, November 1997.
Totorikaguena, Maria Aurela de. Villa Maria, November 1996.
Totorikaguena, Nestor. Villa Maria, November 1996.
Urquizu, Yolanda. Buenos Aires, September 1996, November 1997.
Velasco, Armando. Buenos Aires, September 1996, November, 1997.
Vicente, Miguel Angel. Mar del Plata, November 1996.
Zavaleta, Teresa. Arrecifes, October 1996; Buenos Aires, November 1997.
Zubillaga, Julio. Rosario, November 1996.

Australia

Achurra Etxebarria, Elizabeth. Ayr, April 1997.
Adarraga Elizaran, Agustín. Townsville, May 1997.
Alberdi Arkarato, Gerardo. Melbourne, April 1997.
Alberdi Elortegui, Juan. Ingham, May 1997.
Aldamizetxebarria, Fermin. Sydney, March 1997.
Alfonso Espilla, Ricardo. Ingham, May 1997.
Almirall, Maria Rosa. Townsville, May 1997.
Alonso Fernandez, Lolita. Sydney, March 1997.

Amezaga Amondo, Maria Rosa. Sydney, March 1997.
Amorebieta, Miguel. Melbourne, April 1997.
Aranas, Pedro. Ingham, May 1997.
Aranas, Peter Luis. Ingham, May 1997.
Arauco Aguirre, Maria Purificación. Ayr, April 1997.
Arrasate Cajigas, Maria Concepción. Townsville, May 1997.
Arrate Bengoa, Amayoa. Ayr, May 1997.
Arrate Bengoa, Idoya. Ayr, April 1997.
Arrate Bengoa, John. Ayr, April 1997.
Astoreka, Pilar. Sydney, March 1997.
Astorquia Jayo, Pilar. Ingham, May 1997.
Balanzategui Zemaitis, Gotzone. Ingham, May 1997.
Bañuelos, Aitor. Sydney, March 1997.
Barturen Zulueta, Juan. Ayr, April 1997.
Barueta Pujana, Martina. Melbourne, April 1997.
Belon Bilbao, Carmen. Melbourne, April 1997.
Bengoa Berreciartua, John. Ayr, April 1997.
Bengoa Berreciartua, Pedro. Ayr, April 1997.
Bengoa Berreciartua Arrate, Maryo. Ayr, April 1997.
Bengoa Martiartu, Rose Mary. Ayr, April 1997.
Bilbao, Jon Ander. Melbourne, April 1997; Vitoria-Gasteiz, November 1999.
Bilbao, Sally. Melbourne, April 1997.
Bilbao Barturen, Jone. Ayr, April 1997.
Blake Amezaga, Damien. Sydney, March 1997.
Candino, Rosarito. *See* Kandino, Nekane.
Candino, Maia. Melbourne, April 1997.
Candino, Nerea. Melbourne, April 1997.
Celaya Murelaga, Maria. Ingham, May 1997.
Domentxaurrutia, José Maria. Sydney, March 1997.
Erquiaga Farmer, David Leslie. Ayr, April 1997.
Farrell, Rhonda. Sydney, March 1997.
Fernandez Berrahondo, Maria Angeles. Ayr, April 1997.
Gabiola Anchustegui, Maria Gloria. Ingham, May 1997.
Gabiola Ibarra, José Ignacio. Ayr, April 1997.
Gabiola Laca, Elizabeth. Ayr, April 1997.
Gabiola Ronero Lock, Diana. Ayr, April 1997.
Garagarza Pérez, Miren. Melbourne, April 1997.
Garate Negugogor, Tomás. Melbourne, April 1997.
Gereka, Dolores. Melbourne, April 1997.
Goicoechea Jensen, Stephen Juan. Townsville, May 1997.
Goicoechea Ugarte, José Mari. Townsville, April–May 1997.
Goicoetxea Jensen, Maria. Townsville, April 1997.
Goikoetxea, José Mari. Sydney, March 1997.
Goñi, Iñaki. Sydney, March 1997.

Goñi, Maite. Sydney, March 1997.
Herrera, José Luis. Sydney, March 1997.
Ibañez Campos, Tómas. Ingham, May 1997.
Ibañez Fernandez, Mariasunción. Townsville, May 1997.
Illaramendi, Eusebio. Sydney, March 1997.
Iturriaga Totoricagüena, Cecilio. Ingham, May 1997.
Jayo, Miriam. Ingham, May 1997.
Jayo Celaya Wherry, Maria Victoria. Townsville, May 1997.
Jayo Murelaga, José Mari. Ingham, May 1997.
Kandino, Nekane (changed from Rosarito Candino). Melbourne, April 1997.
Laca, Jesusa Katalina. Ayr, April 1997.
Larrauri Aldamiz, Miren. Sydney, March 1997.
Larrazabal Mendiolea, Jon. Townsville, May 1997.
Lasa, Edita. Sydney, March 1997.
Lasa, Julian. Sydney, March 1997.
Laucirica, Florencio. Ingham, May 1997.
Laucirica, Joseba Loren. Ingham, May 1997.
Laucirica Yribar, Miren Begoña. Ingham, May 1997.
Malexetxebarria Intxausti, Maria Angeles. Ayr, April 1997.
Martiartu Bengoa, Maria Begoña. Ayr, April 1997.
Mendieta, David. Sydney, April 1997.
Mendiolea Etxabe, Pedro. Townsville, May 1997.
Mendiolea Uriguen, Juan (Johnny). Townsville, May 1997.
Mendiolea Uriguen Larrazabal, Dolores. Townsville, May 1997.
Monasterio Urberuaga, Pedro. Ingham, May 1997.
Morrakis Gorreki, Vanda. Telephone interview, Woolongong, May 1997.
Mugica Zozaya, Francisco. Ayr, April 1997.
Muxica, Jon. Sydney, April 1997.
Oar San Pedro Azla, Francisco. Ayr, April 1997.
Oribe, Pablo. Melbourne, April 1997.
Orúe, Carlos. Vitoria-Gasteiz, November 1995, November 1999; Sydney, March–May 1997.
Otaegui, Jon. Sydney, March 1997.
Pérez, Angel. Melbourne, April 1997.
Pérez Garagarza, Arritz. Melbourne, April 1997.
Pérez Garagarza, Lander. Melbourne, April 1997.
Reboredo Larrinaga, Ana Maria Teresa. Ayr, April 1997.
Salazar, Mari Asunción. Vitoria-Gasteiz, November 1995, November 1999; Sydney, March–May 1997.
Sanz Orúe, Miren. Sydney, March–May 1997.
Ugalde Arranguena, Juan Antonio. Melbourne, April 1997.
Ugalde Martinez, Juan Antonio. Melbourne, April 1997.
Urberuaga Bengoetxea, José Maria. Ayr, April 1997.
Urbieta, José Antonio. Vitoria-Gasteiz, November 1995; Sydney, March 1997.

Urejola, Francisca. Melbourne, April 1997.
Yribar, Begoña. Ingham, May 1997.
Zaldumbide Mooney, Wayne. Ayr, April 1997.
Zozaya Abanz, Maria Visitación. Ayr, April 1997.

Belgium

Aguirre, Martin. Antwerp, June 1997.
Aguirrezabal, Alex. Brussels, June 1997.
Alkain Gil, Miriam. Brussels, July 1997.
Baños Rodriguez Pujana, Pilar. Brussels, July 1997.
Bartolomé Guzman, Sara. Brussels, June–July 1997.
Daelemans, Bernard. Brussels, June 1997.
Egibar, Tomás. Vitoria-Gasteiz, November 1995; Brussels, June 1997.
Garcia Arranz, Raquel. Brussels, June 1997.
Madariaga Gangoiti, Leire. Brussels, July 1997.
Maoño Portillo, Cristina. Brussels, July 1997.
Mendibelzua, Ibon. Brussels, June–July 1997.
Mitxelena, Chelo. Vitoria-Gasteiz, November 1995; Brussels, July 1997.
Mitxelena, Ramon. Antwerp, June 1997.
Moreno Ramajo, Luis. Brussels, June 1997.
Pagoaga Gallastegui, Enrike. Brussels, June–July 1997.
Pardo Sanchez, Nieves. Brussels, June 1997.
Pujana Baños, Frederic. Brussels, July 1997.
Pujana Baños, Michele. Brussels, June 1997.
Pujana Zabaleta, Sabin. Brussels, July 1997.
Regidor Ugalde, Andres. Brussels, July 1997.
Sanchez, Fernando. Brussels, June 1997.
Sanchez Pardo, Doltza. Brussels, July 1997.
Sanchez Pardo, Haritz. Brussels, July 1997.
Semal Sanchez, Eric. Brussels, July 1997.
Sestao, Mario. Brussels, July 1997.
Sestao, Vicenta. Antwerp, July 1997.
Urresola Clavero, Alba. Brussels, June 1997.
Urribe-Etxebarria Olabarrieta, Mikeldi. Brussels, July 1997.
Urriz Larragan, Feliza. Brussels, July 1997.
Urtazun Abezia, Azucena. Brussels, July 1997.
Vandervinne, Juan. Brussels, July 1997.
Zamorano Crespo, Aitor. Brussels, July 1997.
Zazieta Bolinaga, Pili. Brussels, July 1997.

Mexico

Garritz, Josu. Vitoria-Gasteiz, November 1995, October 1999; Buenos Aires, November 1997.
Garritz, Julen. Vitoria-Gasteiz, October 1999.

Peru

Aguinaga, Enrique. Lima, December 1996.
Apaolaza, Féliz. Lima, December 1996.
Celaya Sagüés, Javier. Vitoria-Gasteiz, November 1995.
Elejalde Vargas, Marcelo. Lima, December 1996.
Garbizu, German. Lima, 1996.
Guarrotxena Larragán, Ion Kepa. Lima, December 1996.
Igartua, Francisco. Vitoria-Gasteiz, November 1995; Lima, December 1996.
Irisarri Isa, Mirentxu. Telephone interview, Satipo, December 1996.
Irisarri, José Miguel. Lima, December 1996.
Isa de Irisarri, María José. Lima, December 1996.
Noblecilla, Raul. Vitoria-Gasteiz, November 1995; Lima, December 1996.
Noblecilla Olaechea, Raul II. Lima, December 1996.
Ortúzar, Víctor. Vitoria-Gasteiz, November 1995; Lima, December 1996.
Zubeldia Larrea, Sabino. Lima, December 1996.

United Kingdom

Pattie, Susan. London, February 2000.

United States of America

Abadia, Margie. New York, February, December 2002.
Aberasturi, Iñaki, New York, February 2002.
Abersturi, Rose. New York, February 2002.
Achabal, Julian. Boise, September 1999.
Aguirre, Anna. New York, February 2002.
Aguirre, Irene. Brooklyn, July 1996.
Alzola, Michelle. Boise, December 1998; Algorta, November 2001.
Anacabe Franzoia, Anita. Elko, July 1998, September 1999.
Aphessetche, Xavier. Chino, February 1998.
Arana Bicandi, Mari Antonia. Boise, March 1997, September 1999.
Arbillaga, José. San Francisco, February 1998.
Arriet, Josephine. Fresno, February 1998.
Arrieta, Javier. Emmett, September 1999.
Arrubarrena Arozamena, Miren Nekane. 1995–2002.
Artiach Rementeria, Miren. Boise, 1995–2003.
Aspiazu, Steven. New York, December 2002.
Ayerza, Patricia. Portland, July 1996.
Barainca, Ray. Reno, August 1997.
Barquin Foruria, Miren. Boise, 1995–2003.
Barrinaga Mendazona, Josephine. Ontario, August 1998.
Bastida, John. Boise, October 1999.
Berhua Bilbao, Zachary. New York, 1998–2002.
Beristain, Jose Mari. Las Vegas, February 1998.

Beristain, Amaya. Las Vegas, February 1998.
Berria, Frank. Nampa, September 1999.
Berria, Helen Elgezabal. Nampa, September 1999.
Bieter Fritz, Mary. Boise, August 1998.
Bieter Garmendia, Dave. Boise, March 1999.
Bieter Garmendia, Chris. Boise, June 1999.
Bilbao Egurrola, Anita. Portland, January 1999.
Bilbao Egurrola, Josie. Portland, January 1999.
Camino, Kate. Gardnerville, July 1997; Reno, August 1997; Vitoria-Gasteiz, October 1999.
Cenarrusa, Pete T. Boise, 1995–2002.
Cengotitabengoa, José Ramon. Vitoria-Gasteiz, November 1995; San Francisco, February 1998.
Currutchet, Jean. San Francisco, February 1997.
Currutchet, Jean Louis. San Francisco, February 1997.
Donahue Overgaard, Megan. Weiser, August 1998.
Doyaga Sarriugarte, Emilia. 1995–2002.
Echeto, Isidro. Winnemucca, February 1998.
Echevarria, Christie. Boise, May 1999.
Echeverria, Candida. Chino, July 1998.
Echeverria, Cheryl. San Francisco, February 1997.
Echeverria, Cristina. Gardnerville, July 1997.
Echeverria, Diana. Boise, March 1997, September 1999.
Echeverria, Dominic. Gardnerville, July 1997.
Echeverria, Robert. Elko, July 1998, May 1999; Vitoria-Gasteiz, October 1999.
Egurrola Totoricagüena, Mari Carmen. Boise, April 1999.
Eiguren Lewis, Roy. Boise, 1995–2003.
Esain, Victor. Fresno, February 1998.
Espina Ruiz, Oscar. New York, February 2002.
Etcharren, Pierre. San Francisco, February 2002.
Etcharren Arrechea, Valerie. San Francisco, February 1998.
Etchechury, J. P. Fresno, February 1998.
Fagoaga, Catalina. Salt Lake City, February 1998.
Fagoaga, Nick. Elko, October 1999.
Flesher, Jean. Gardnerville, 2002.
Foncillas Etxebarria, Koitz. New York, February, December 2002.
Gamboa, Clarice. Elko, November 1998.
Gamboa, Ralph. Elko, November 1998.
Gaztambide, Marc. Murray, July 1997.
Gaztambide, Mary. Murray, December 1998.
Glesta, Anita. New York, December 2002.
Goicoechea, Martin. Rock Springs, October 1999.
Goitiandia, Benito. Kuna, September 1999.
Goitiandia, Sabino. Nampa, August 1998.

Goitiandia, Tomasa. Kuna, September 1999.
Goyhenetche, Noel. San Francisco, February 1998.
Griggs Totoricagüena, Carmen. Mountain Home, March 1999.
Iturralde, Karlos. New York, December 2002.
Izoco, Anita. Gardnerville, August 1997.
Kirtland, John. Boise, 1995–2003.
Kirtland Totoricagüena, Amaia. Boise, 1995–2003.
Lasuen Arrieta, Angie. Emmett, September 1999.
Lejardi, Andres. Gooding, July 1996.
Mainvil, Grace. Weiser, August 1998.
Mainvil, Johnny. Weiser, August 1998.
Mallea, Ken. Boise, December 1998.
Mendazona Totoricagüena, Enriqueta. Ontario, August 1998.
Mendive, Mary Lou. San Francisco, February 1997.
Mendive, Steve. Boise, April 1997, September 1999; Gooding, July 1998.
Miller, Patty A. Boise, 1995–2002.
Minaberry, Anne Marie. Bakersfield, February 1998.
Miral, Denise. Novato, February 1998.
Negueloua, Maurice. San Francisco, February 1998.
Oçafrain, Jean Leon. San Francisco, February 1998.
Olano, Mike. Winnemucca, February 1998.
Oleaga, Juan Manuel. Boise, 1995–2002.
Oleaga Artetxe, Sabina. Boise, 1995–2002.
Overgaard Donahue, Megan. Weiser, August 1998.
Pedeflous, Frank. Fresno, February 1998.
Pedroarena, Frances. Gardnerville, August 1997.
Pedroarena, Jesus. Gardnerville, August 1997.
Rebich Totoricagüena, Josephine. Mountain Home, March 1999.
Salegui Ostolaza, Mario. New York, December 2002.
Sarria, Justo. Boise, 1999.
Sarria Jayo, Paki. Boise, December 2001.
Totoricagüena Arana, Celestina. Boise, September 1997.
Totoricagüena Bassick, Mari Carmen Jr. Boise, February 1999.
Totoricagüena Egurrola, Mari Carmen Sr. Boise, 1995–2002.
Totoricagüena Egurrola, Rosa Mari. Boise, October 1999.
Totoricagüena Egurrola, Ted Jr. Boise, February 1998–2003.
Totoricagüena Egurrola, Teresa. Salt Lake City, February 1998.
Totoricagüena Egurrola, Tony. Boise, March 1998.
Totoricagüena Egurrola, Dolores. Boise, August 1998.
Totoricagüena Erquiaga, Teodoro. Boise, 1995–2002.
Urrutia, Jóse. Susanville, February 1998.
Uruanga, Louie. San Francisco, February 1998.
Villanueva, Manuel. Downey, February 1998.
Wilson Aldecoa, John. November 2001.

Yanci, Ricardo. Boise, March 1999.
Zugazaga, Ramon. Elko, July 1998.
Zulaika, Joseba. Reno, July 1996; Gardnerville, July 1997.
Zuluaga, Manuel. New York, December 2002.
Zuluaga-Papp, Vivian. New York, December 2002.

Uruguay

Aguirre, Fernando. Montevideo, November 1996.
Ahuntchain, Dely. Rosario, November 1996; Vitoria-Gasteiz, October 1999.
Alzueta, Luis. Carmelo, December 1996.
Arin, Jorge. Montevideo, November 1996.
Arin, Juan Pedro. Montevideo, November 1996.
Arin, Roberto. Montevideo, November 1996.
Aristeguy, Juan Carlos. Vitoria-Gasteiz, November 1995, November 1999; Montevideo, November 1996.
Ariztia, Julio. Carmelo, December 1996.
Arribillaga, Graciela. Carmelo, December 1996.
Arribillaga, Susana. Carmelo, December 1996.
Aznarez, Eloisa. Carmelo, December 1996.
Balberde Tolosa, Martín. Rosario, November 1996.
Balzamo, Beatriz. Durazno, December 1996.
Bengoa, Maite. Montevideo, December 1996; Vitoria-Gasteiz, October 1999.
Bermudez Iturbura, Fernando. Carmelo, December 1996.
Bessonart, Celia. Trinidad, December 1996.
Bessonart, Polo. Trinidad, December 1996.
Betartea, Mario. Rosario, November 1996.
Bidart, Graciela. Rosario, November 1996.
Cabrera, Francisco. Durazno, December 1996.
Cabrera Heguaburu, Maria Gracia. Durazno, December 1996.
Castells, Elisa. Durazno, December 1996.
Castells, Felipe. Durazno, December 1996.
Couture, Mario. Salto, December 1996.
Couture, Mario II. Salto, December 1996.
Curutchague, Juan. Montevideo, November 1996.
Demarco, Monica. Montevideo, November 1996.
Echeverria, Rosa. Carmelo, December 1996.
Elizarzu, Felix. Rosario, November 1996.
Gabarot, Alvaro. Carmelo, December 1996.
Heguaburu, Cristina. Durazno, December 1996.
Heguaburu, Susana. Durazno, December 1996.
Hernandez, Carlos. Rosario, November 1996.
Hernandez Gabiola, Ramon. Montevideo, December 1996.
Hitta, Juan Federico. Rosario, November 1996.
Iguain, Gurutz. Montevideo, November 1996.

Irigoyen, Alberto. Vitoria-Gasteiz, November 1995, October 1999; Durazno, December 1996; Reno (Nev.), July 1998.
Irigoyen, Adriana de. Durazno, December 1996; Reno (Nev.), July 1998; Vitoria-Gasteiz, October 1999.
Isoco, Mirta. Carmelo, December 1996.
Jorajudia, Nybia. Carmelo, December 1996.
Juanicotenea, Federico. Salto, December 1996.
Karageta, Angela. Carmelo, November 1996.
Landechea, Alcides. Carmelo, December 1996.
Leiza, Elena. Carmelo, December 1996.
Marenales, Marta. Montevideo, November 1996.
Mariezkurrena, Ana Maria. Montevideo, December 1996.
Maytia, Danilo. Vitoria-Gasteiz, November 1995; Montevideo, November 1996.
Otegui, Raúl. Durazno, December 1996.
Oyarbide, Carlota. Montevideo, November 1996.
Palacios de Echeberrito, Susana. Durazno, December 1996.
Poiuttevein, Enrique. Montevideo, November 1996.
Querejeta, Rosa Ana. Carmelo, December 1996.
Salaberry, Cecilia. Durazno, December 1996.
Salaberry, Juan Miguel. Rosario, November 1996.
Sanchez, Irma. Rosario, November 1996.
Sarazola, Juan. Montevideo, November 1996.
Scheitter, Andrea. Montevideo, November 1996.
Wolcan de Betartea, Alejandra. Rosario, November 1996.
Zaldua, Hugo. Salto, December 1996.
Zuazola, Gloria. Montevideo, November 1996; Buenos Aires, November 1997.
Zuazola, Mikel. Montevideo, November 1996.

Index

Note: Italic page numbers refer to illustrations.

Aberri Eguna (Day of the Homeland) festival, 12, 77, *following p. 80*, 83–84, 97
abertzale (patriot), 37, 47, 52–53, 82, 84
Acción Vasca (Basque Action), 94
acculturation, 5–8. *See also* ethnic identity and ethnicity
Achabal, Julian, 90
Advisory Council for Relations with Basque Communities, 62, 159, 166–69, 172
African diaspora, 14
age groupings: Basque ethnic-identity definitions, 12–13, 109; Basque language, 112; Basque language maintenance, 135; Catholicism, 145; diaspora hopes for homeland's future, 106; Franco dictatorship, 117; music, 127; political participation, 101; return to homeland, 114
agriculture, 65, 66, 67, 72, 74
Aguirre, Iñaki, 175
Aguirre y Lecube, José Antonio de, 40, 71, 82, 87, 156
Aguirrezabal, Alex, 95
Aiztan Artean, 146
Alava. *See* Araba (Avala)
Alba, Richard D., 200
Alberdi, Juan Bautista, 64
Aldsoro, Ramón, 86
Alfonso VIII of Castile, 23
Álvarez Emparanza, José Luis (Txillardegui), 44, 46
Amaia, 212 n. 1
American Basque Foundation, 184

American Congress of Basque Centers, 131, 175–76, 188, 205
Anaiak Danok (Brothers All), 87, 88
Anderson, Benedict, 11, 17, 176, 192
antiterrorism pact, 51
Araba (Avala): autonomy of, 9, 20, 33, 40, 50–51, 155; Basque nationalism in, 68; choice of terminology and spelling for, xix; *fueros* (local laws) of, 25; history of, 23–27, 33; map of, 21; and Spanish Civil War, 39. *See also* Euskadi (Basque Autonomous Government)
Arana y Goiri, Luis, 34, 37, 40
Arana y Goiri, Sabino, xvii, 30–31, 34–37, 45, 53, 54, 79, 82, 83, 84, 118, 134, 193, 203
Ardanza, José Antonio Garro, 98–99, 157, 171
Argentina: Aberri Eguna celebrated in, 83–84, 97; anti-Franco feelings in, 44, 73, 76; Association of Patriotic Women in, 38; Basque emigrants to, in nineteenth century, 62, 63, 64–65; Basque emigrants to, in twentieth century, 38, 71–72, 82, 83, 85; Basque ethnic identity in, 10, 109–17, 181, 196; Basque government official's visit to, 171; and Basque government-in-exile, 85–86; Basque language maintenance in, 112, 113, 133–36; Basque nationalism in, 68, 83–85, 87; Basque organizations in, xiii, 6, 68–69, 71, 84, 117, 122, 124, 130–32, 145–46, 160–61; business and economic foundations and institutes

255

in, 184–86; Catholicism in, 65–66, 126, 145; colonial diaspora in, 60, 63–64; commercial codes of, 64; and Congress of Basque Collectivities, xiii, 88–89, 139; constitution of, 64; and cultural exchange, 159; dictatorial regime in, 77; "Disappeared" in, 77; and economic and personal ties to Basque Country, 137; economy of, 169; and election coverage from Basque Country in, 14, 80; federation of Basque centers in, 94, 158, 160–61, 175–76, 185; financial support from Basque government to, 164, 165, 180; independence for, 64; and Jaialdi International Festival, 15; labor specialties and businesses of Basques in, 3, 65, 66; Laurac/Laurak Bat in, 20, 68, *following p. 80*, 84, 85, 161; low-interest loans for Basque centers in, 181; magazines and newspapers in, 69, 73, 83, 84–85, 137; marriage patterns in, 67; music in, 127–28; National Basque Festival in, 159; Navarrese center in, 57; photographs of, *following p. 80*; political and partisan activities of Basques in, 93, 94, 100–105; preservation of Basque traditions and culture in, 128–32; prestige and positive social identity of Basques in, 9, 12–13, 63, 64–65, 150–52, 202; pro-Franco feelings in, 70, 73; reactions to Basque homeland violence in, 76–77, 107–8; registered Basque centers in, 158; registered voters in for Basque homeland elections, 93; sixth-generation Basques in, 10; and Spanish Civil War, 39, 71, 82; statistics on immigration to, 65, 69, 71, 72; television and radio in, 14, 73, 80, 138, 178; travel to Basque Country from, 138

Armenia and Armenian diaspora, xvi, 7, 114, 117, 118, 124, 126, 203, 204, 212 n. 2

arrebak, 142

Askúe, 37

assassinations, 47–48, 76. *See also* violence

assimilation, 5–8, 10, 201, 206. *See also* ethnic identity and ethnicity

Association of Patriotic Women (EAB), 38

associations. *See* organizations and Basque centers

athletics. *See* sports and athletics

attitudes. *See* political attitudes

Australia: Aberri Eguna celebrated in, 97; Aboriginal peoples in, 77; anti-Franco feelings in, 73, 76, 91–92; Basque emigrants to, 42, 72, 74, 91; Basque ethnic identity in, 109–17, 196; Basque experts needed in, 168; and Basque government-in-exile, 85; Basque language maintenance in, 112, 113, 133–36; Basque names in, 141–42; Basque nationalism in, 91–92; Basque organizations in, 6, 122, 130–31, 161; Catholicism in, 126, 145; and Congress of Basque Collectivities, 88–89; democratic government of, 4–5, 17; and economic and personal ties to Basque Country, 137; and economic networks, 184; financial support from Basque government to, 180; immigration policies of, 72, 74; and Jaialdi International Festival, 15, 159–60; labor strike in, 76, 91–92; music in, 127–28; photographs, *following p. 80*; political and partisan activities of Basques in, 5, 74, 81, 91–92, 94, 97, 100–105; preservation of Basque traditions and culture in, 128–32; prestige and positive social identity of Basques in, 9, 150–52; pro-Franco feelings in, 70, 210 n. 4; reactions to Basque homeland violence, 76–77, 107–8; registered Basque centers in, 158; registered voters in for Basque homeland elections, 93, 188; sugar-cane

industry in, 72, 74, *following p. 80;* television in, 137; travel to Basque Country from, 138, 149; women immigrants in, 143–44, 210 n. 3 autonomy statutes for Basque Country, 9, 20, 33, 38, 40, 50–51, 155
Avala. *See* Araba (Avala)
Aznar, José María, 77
Azua Mendia, Jon, 171–72

Bakalian, Anny, 7
banal nationalism, 140
Barth, Fredrik, 1
Baskonia, La, 69, 84
Basque Association of Navarre, 33
Basque Autonomous Government. *See* Euskadi (Basque Autonomous Government)
Basque centers. *See* organizations and Basque centers
Basque Consultative Council, 42
Basque Country (Euskal Herria): agriculture in, 67; and autonomy statute, 9, 20, 33, 38, 40, 50–51, 155, 169; citizenship of, 170; and collective nobility, 25, 29; connections between diaspora and, 136–39; definition of, xix; definition of Basqueness in, 82, 166, 193–94; development of Basque nationalism, 30–38; diaspora aid to, 70–72, 86, 87, 165, 204; diaspora hopes for future of, 104–8; economic and personal ties between diaspora and, 137; and emergence of Spain, 23–27; employment in, 125; and Franco, 20, 41–44; *fueros* (local laws) of, 23–26, 28–30, 32, 33, 64, 67, 68, 69, 81, 194, 209 n. 2; government of, 50–51; history of, 19–50, 194–95; institutional connections between diaspora and, 138–39; and Jaialdi International Festival, 15, 160; and Lizarra-Garazi Agreement, 89, 210–11 n. 3; map of, 21; negative media images of, 176–77; "North" and "South" of, 20, 21, 27–28; physical borders of, 19; police force for, 50, 51; political parties and elections in, 14, 51, 80, 86; population of, 19; primogeniture inheritance in, 66–67; provinces of, 20, 21; return migration to, 78, 114, 164, 171, 174, 195, 210 n. 6; and Spanish Civil War, 39–41; Spanish language used in, 52; travel from diaspora to, 138–39, 148–49, 174, 186, 195; U.S. Senator Church's visit to, 88; violence in, 46–50, 75–78. *See also* Euskadi (Basque Autonomous Government)
Basque diaspora: aid to homeland from, 70–72, 86, 87, 165, 204; Basque language maintenance in, 52, 112, 113, 133–36; and Basque nationalism, 68–69, 74–78; book series on histories of, 181; and business and economic *fundaciones* and *institutos,* 183–86, 194, 203, 204; categorizing Basque communities as, 194–97; and chain-migration theory, 16, 59, 63, 79–80, 110, 122, 125, 195, 205; citizenship rights and voting in Basque Autonomous Government elections, 93–96, 170, 187–90, 204; and Cohen's definition of diaspora, xvi, 10–13, 15, 114–15, 192, 196, 207; in colonial period, 56–61; confusions of on homeland nationalist movement, 74–75; and cultural adaptation, 122–26; current homeland partisan representation in, 93–100; definitions of "Basqueness" in, 54, 79–80, 109–19, 193–94; and diaspora identity, 147–48, 192–94, 199; economic and personal ties between homeland and, 137; and ETA, 74, 75, 77, 82, 87, 88, 92, 98–99, 100, 106–7; and ethnic identity, 11, 15–17, 56–61, 78–79, 92–94, 109–54, 192–94, 199, 200–202; ethnonationalism in, 11, 68–69, 81–100, 203; Euskadi

government policy formulation for, xiii, 165–72, 205; Euskadi's commitment to, 180–87; factors contributing to Basque emigration, 55, 63–66, 79; financial aid from Euskadi to, 90–91, 98, 155, 160, 161, 162, 164–65, 171, 173, 174, 180–83, 204–5, 211 n. 6; and Franco's political repression, 72–75; future study of, 205–8; and Gaztemundu (World of Youth), 186–87; and Herri Batasuna, 92–101, 104, 107, 211 n. 8; home decoration in, 139–40; and homeland connections, 17, 136–39, 203; hopes of for homeland's future, 104–8; individual and group choice for identification with, 12; institutional connections between homeland and, 138–39; and Internet, 78–79, 90, 136, 138, 148, 149, 153, 172, 175, 177–78, 188, 195, 197–98, 202–3; as interstate society, 14; jewelry and personal adornment in, 140–41, 153; and Law of Relations with the Basque Collectivities in the Exterior (*Ley 8/1994*), xviii, 157–67, 171, 172–73, 180, 190–91, 203; and loyalty of Basques to host countries, 116; music in, 126–28; naming of children in, 139, 141–42; newspapers and magazines, 17; in nineteenth century, 61–69; nonpoliticized nature of, 202–5; oral histories of, 182; phases of Basque emigration, 55–56; photographs of, *following p. 80*; and PNV, 75, 77, 86, 93, 94, 98, 100, 101, 104, 107, 160–61, 171–72, 186, 189; political attitudes in, 100–108; political participation in, 17–18, 100–105; and political parties generally, 93–96, 100, 103; and political transitions as influences on end to emigration, 78–80; preservation of traditions and culture in, 128–32; prestige and positive social identity of Basques in, 9, 12–13, 63, 150–52; and reactions to homeland violence, 75–78, 89, 107–8; relations between Euskadi (Basque Autonomous Government) and, 155–91; rights and benefits for members of Basque organizations in, 163–65; and search for lost relatives, 179; social, educational, and cultural functions of Basque institutions in, 121–32; and Spanish Civil War, 69–72, 70–72; statistics on immigration, 61, 62, 63, 69, 71, 72; television transmission from Basque Country to, 137, 138; and transnationalism and globalization, 11–15, 78–79, 115–16, 146–53, 165, 197–99, 205, 207–8; travel to homeland from, 138–39, 148–49, 174, 186, 195; triadic relationship among homeland, host country, and, 17, 203; typical male immigrant in nineteenth century, 67; and women as immigrants, 67–68, 210 n. 3; women's migration experiences, 142–46. *See also* organizations and Basque centers; *and specific countries*

Basque ethnic identity. *See* ethnic identity and ethnicity

Basque General Council, 49

Basque government-in-exile, xv, 71, 82, 85–87, 176

Basque Homeland and Liberty. *See* Euskadi eta Asktasuna (ETA-Basque Homeland and Liberty)

Basque nationalism: Arana y Goiri and traditionalist approach to, xvii, 30–31, 34–37, 54, 79, 82, 83, 84, 118, 134, 193, 203; and armed struggle against Franco, 47–50; and banal nationalism, 140; building nationalist coalitions, 37–38; and Catholicism, 34–35, 37, 38, 40, 47, 82; confusions of diaspora on homeland nationalist movement, 74–78; development of, 30–38, 53–54; diaspora nationalism, 11, 68–69,

81–100; e-mail nationalism, 11; and ethnonationalism, 11, 30–34, 68–69, 81–100, 203; and Euskadi eta Asktasuna (ETA), xvii, 17, 44–49, 51, 74, 75, 77, 82, 87, 88, 98–99, 100, 106–7, 209–10 n. 6; and Franco, 38–50; and Herri Batasuna (HB), 49, 50, 92–99, 100–101, 104, 211 n. 7; and KAS Alternative, 49–50; and print media, 17, 83, 84–85, 138, 176–77; and socialism, 47; and Spanish Civil War, 38–41; and underground resistance to Franco, 43–44; women's organization of, 71

Basque Nationalist Party (PNV): and autonomy statute, 50; and Basque diaspora, 38, 75, 77, 85, 86, 93, 94, 98, 100, 101, 104, 107, 160–61, 171–72, 186, 189; and Basque Homeland and Liberty (ETA), 44–46, 75, 77; Basque Resistance Committee of, 42; dissociation from nationalist movements in Iparralde, 43; and Ekin, 44; in election of 1998, 93; in election of 2001, 51, 71, 80, 93–94; and e-mail communication, 11; establishment of, xvii; first PNV Center, 35; and Herri Batasuna, 94; as party of middle class, 43; platform of, 34; and preservation of Euskera, 44; registered voters in, 189; and Spanish Civil War, 39–40; working-class support for, 37

Basque Resistance Committee, 42

Basque Society for the Promotion and Reconversion of Industry (SPRI), 184

Basque Solidarity Party (Eusko Alkartasuna), 51

Basqueness: and *abertzale* (patriot) identity, 52–53, 82; Aranist and traditional Basqueness, 35–36, 52–53, 82, 109–13, 193, 203; as defined in diaspora, xvi, 54, 79–80, 109–19, 193–94; development of diasporic consciousness and specific diasporic Basque identity, 113–17; homeland definitions of, 82, 166, 193–94; inclusive civic definition of, 166, 203. *See also* Basque Country (Euskal Herria); Basque diaspora; ethnic identity and ethnicity

Batua language, 52. *See also* language

Behe Nafarroa, 156

Belgium: anti-Franco feelings in, 76, 97; Basque children evacuated to during Spanish Civil War, 40, 70, 72, 93, 209 n. 5; Basque civil servants in EU employment in, 12, 95, 110; Basque delegation to European Union in, *following p. 80*, 95–96, 97, 125, 170, 184; Basque ethnic identity in, 11, 109–17, 194, 195–96, 205; and Basque government-in-exile, 85; Basque language maintenance in, 112, 113, 133–36; Basque nationalism in, 92–93; Basque organizations in, 6, 94–97, 130–31, 169; Catholicism in, 145; and Congress of Basque Collectivities, 88–89; democratic government of, 4–5, 17; distrust of Spanish government by Basques in, 9; economic and personal ties to Basque Country, 137; financial support from Basque government to, 180; and Herri Batasuna, 94–96, 97; Herri Enbaxada in, 94–95, 96, 97; magazines and newspapers in, 137; marriage in, 110; multiculturalism in, 77; music in, 127–28; political and partisan activities of Basques in, 5, 81, 92–97, 100–105; political exiles in, 46, 48, 95, 100; preservation of Basque traditions and culture in, 128–32; prestige and positive social identity of Basques in, 9, 150–52; reactions to Basque homeland violence in, 107–8; registered Basque center in, 158; registered diaspora voters in for Basque homeland elections, 93; travel to Basque Country from, 169; Txalaparta Basque Center in, 96–97, 117

Belon, Carmen "Mentxu," 92

Belón Bilbao, Carmen, 210 n. 4
Bernard, 4
Bieter, David, 89
Bilbao, Jon Ander, *following p. 80*
Bilbao, Juan M., 71
Bilbao, Julio, 211 n. 1
bilingualism, 51–53, 133. *See also* language
Billig, Michael, 140
Bizkaia: autonomy of, 9, 20, 33, 40, 50–51, 155; and Basque nationalism, 34–35, 38, 68; choice of terminology and spelling for, xix; and colonial diaspora, 57, 60; under Franco dictatorship, 41; *fueros* (local laws) of, 25, 28, 59; history of, 23–27, 33; industry in, 28, 33, 34, 35; population of, 35; and Spanish Civil War, 40–41; and trade, 56. *See also* Euskadi (Basque Autonomous Government)
Bizkaianism, 34–35
boardinghouses, 122, 200
Bolivia, 57, 59
Brass, Paul, 2
Brazil, 158
briska, 129
Britain/United Kingdom, 39, 40, 42, 54, 72, 73, 85, 158, 181
Brunn, Stanley, 197
bumpy-line theory of acculturation and assimilation, 5–6
Burgos Trials, 17, 48, 76, 80, 91, 206
business *fundaciones* and *institutos*, 183–86, 194, 203, 204

Cachenaut, Father Jean Pierre, *following p. 80*
California, 66, 69, 87, 88, 126, 161. *See also* United States
California'ko Euskal Herria, 69
Campión, 37
Canada, xiii, 15, 158, 160, 212 n. 1
card playing, *following p. 80*, 129, 138
Caribbean diaspora, 204

Carlist Wars, xviii, 31–33, 55, 62, 68, 194
Carlos, 32
Carlos IV, 26
Caro Baroja, Julio, 66–67
Carrero Blanco, Luís, 48
Castells, Manuel, 16–17, 146–47, 198–99
Castile, Kingdom of, 23–25
Castro, Fidel, 11
Catalonia and Catalans, 9, 34, 36, 54, 61, 170, 193, 206, 209 n. 3
Catholicism: in Argentina, 65–66; and Basque nationalism, 34–35, 37, 38, 40, 47, 82, 176; and Basque women, 109–10, 145, 210 n. 3; and colonization, 57, 58; and ethnic identity, 109, 145, 198; and Franco, 41, 70, 110, 210 n. 4; photographs of, *following p. 80*; in Poland, 181; and Spanish Civil War, 110; and Spanish nationalists, 40; in United States, 126, 145, 196, 200
cattle industry, 65, 66
Cenarrusa, Pete, *following p. 80*, 88, 89
censorship, 73, 97
Chaho, Joseph Augustín, 32, 37
chain migration, 16, 59, 63, 79–80, 110, 122, 125, 195, 205
Champlain, Samuel, 210 n. 1 (chapter 3)
Chile: and Advisory Council for Relations with Basque Communities, 168; Basque cooking in, 129; Basque emigrants to, 38, 62; Basque government official's visit to, 171; and Basque government-in-exile, 71, 85; business and economic foundations and institutes in, 184–86; colonization of, 58–59, 60; registered Basque centers in, 158; television in, 178
Chinese diaspora, 126
Church, Frank, 87–88
circumstantialist approach to ethnicity, 3–5, 9
citizenship, 93–96, 170, 204
Cohen, Robin, xvi, 10–11, 15, 114, 192, 196, 199, 207

College of the Vizcayans, 58
Colombia, 60, 85
colonization of New World, xviii, 25, 26, 30, 54, 55–61
Columbus, Christopher, 57
Comité Pro Inmigración (Committee for Basque Immigration), 71
Communist party, 47, 70, 100, 210 n. 4
Confraternity of Aránzazu, 21, 59
Congress of American Basque Centers, 131, 175–76, 188, 205
Congress of Basque Collectivities, xiii, 11, 51, *following p. 80*, 88–89, 130, 139, 159, 162, 166–67, 169, 172–76, 191, 203, 205
Connor, Walker, 2
cooking, *following p. 80*, 128–29, 144, 146, 172, 193
Craig, Larry, 89
Cranson, Alan, 88
Croatia and Croatian diaspora, 117, 118, 181, 195, 204
Cuba: Basque emigrants to, 40; Basque government official's visit to, 171; and Basque government-in-exile, 71, 85, 87; colonization of, 57, 60; registered Basque center in, 158; and U.S. anti-Castro feelings, 11
cultural adaptation, 122–26
cultural exchanges, 159, 163, 172

Da Silva, Milton M., 2
dance, *following p. 80*, 128, 130, 138, 159, 172, 181
De la Cosa, Juan, 57
De la Sota, Ramón, 71
Del Valle, Teresa, 193
Denmark, 40
"deterritorialized" nations, 203
diaspora identity, 11, 147–48, 192–94, 199. *See also* Basque diaspora; ethnic identity and ethnicity
diasporas: definition and characteristics of, xvi, 10–11, 114–15, 194, 207; and ethnic institutions, 120; and globalization, 197; questions on, 9–10; Salman Rushdie on, 15; and transnationalism, 207; triadic relationship among homeland, host country, and, 17, 203. *See also* Basque diaspora; *and specific countries*
diglossia, 133
Diputationes (executive branches), 51
Dominican Republic, 158
Douglas, Mary, 153–54
Douglass, William A., 3

EA. *See* Eusko Alkartasuna (EA-Basque Solidarity Party)
EAB. *See* Emakume Abertzale Batza (EAB)
Echave, Baltasar de, 31, 58
economic *fundaciones* and *institutos*, 183–86, 194, 203, 204
education: in Argentina, 69, 122; Basque language removed from schools, 41; Basque-language programs in diaspora, *following p. 80*, 136, 162, 163, 173; in colonies, 58; ethnic identity and educational level, 153; Euskera and Batua language in schools, 51–52; and host-country language, 133; *ikastola* (Basque-language school) movement, 38, 43, 136; University of the Basque Country, 163–65, 174; University Studies Abroad Consortium (USAC), 156
EITB (Euskal Irrati Telebista), 173, 177, 178, 196, 198, 202, 203
Ekin, 44
El Salvador, 158
elderly, 69, 122, 164, 165
elections in Basque Country, 14, 51, 71, 80, 93–96, 187–90, 212 n. 3
Elkins, David J., 13, 149
e-mail, 11, 15, 149, 177
Emakume Abertzale Batza (EAB), 38, 71, *following p. 80*, 85, 94, 145–46
emigration. *See* Basque diaspora

employment: in Basque Country (Euskal Herria), 125; and Basque identity, 150–52; in European Union, 12, 95, 110, 125; and host-country language, 13, 133; labor specialties and businesses of Basques, 3, 65–66
endogamy, 67–68, 110
England. *See* Britain/United Kingdom
Eriksen, T. H., 121, 151, 153
Erquiaga, Albert, 211–12 n. 1
Ertzaintza (Basque police), 50, 51
Esman, Milton, 18, 207
españolistas, 47, 84
Espartero, General, 32
ETA. *See* Euskadi eta Asktasuna (ETA-Basque Homeland and Liberty)
ethnic anomalies, 153–54
ethnic identity and ethnicity: and acculturation, 5–8; and assimilation, 5–8, 10, 201, 206; and Catholicism, 109, 145, 198, 200; circumstantialist approach to, 3–5, 9; in colonial diaspora, 56–61; and connections between homeland and diaspora, 136–39; in contemporary Euskal Herria, 50–53; and cultural adaptation, 122–26; in current diaspora, 78–79, 109–54, 192–94, 199, 200–202; definition of, 1; definitions of "Basqueness," xiv, 35–36, 52–53, 54, 79–80, 82, 109–19, 166, 193–94; and diaspora identity, 11, 147–48, 192–94, 199; and food, 128–29, 144, 146; and globalization, 78–79, 115–16, 146–53; and home decoration, 139–40; instrumentalist approach to, 3–5; and jewelry and personal adornment, 140–41, 153; and language, 12, 20, 27, 35, 36–37, 41, 51–53, 58, 82, 113, 133–36; and marriage, 110; mobilizationist approach to, 3–5; and music, 126–28; and naming of children, 139, 141–42; oppositional approach to, 9; optional ethnicity, 200; persistence of, 5–9; as plural and partial, 15–17; and political participation, 104; and preservation of traditions and culture, 128–32; prestige and positive social identity of Basques in diaspora, 9, 12–13, 63, 150–52, 193; primordialism hypothesis of, 1–3, 9; questions on, xiii–xiv, xvi, 1; and self-interest, 4; and social-identity theory, 8–9, 149, 193, 202; symbolic ethnicity, 5–9; theories of, 1–5; third-generation return hypothesis of, 7
ethnomusicology, 126–28
ethnonationalism, 11, 30–34, 68–69, 81–100, 203. *See also* Basque nationalism
European Union, 78, *following p. 80*, 93, 95–96, 103, 125, 170, 184
Euscaldun Gazeta, 69
Euskadi (Basque Autonomous Government): autonomy of, xix, 9, 20, 33, 50–51, 155, 169; and business and economic *fundaciones* and *institutos*, 183–86, 194, 203, 204; citizenship rights and qualified voters in diaspora, 93–96, 170, 187–90, 204; commitment of, to diaspora, 180–87; Communist and Socialist parties in, 47; and Congress of Basque Collectivities, xiii; contemporary Basque identity in, 50–53; definition of, xix; diaspora hopes for future of, 104–7; diaspora organizations and Basque centers registered with, 6, 90–91, 211 n. 6; economic goals of, 17, 160, 204; and ETA, 98–99; European Union delegation from, *following p. 80*, 95–96, 125, 170, 184; and federal democracy of Spain, 78; financial aid from, to Basque diaspora, 90–91, 98, 155, 160, 161, 162, 164–65, 171, 173, 174, 180–83, 204–5, 211 n. 6; and Gaztemundu (World of Youth), 186–87; government of, 50–51; and Internet, 138, 148, 172, 175, 177–78, 198; and Law of Relations

with the Basque Collectivities in the Exterior (*Ley 8/1994*), xviii, 157–67, 171, 172–73, 180, 190–91, 203; legal framework of foreign policy of, 169–72; map of, 21; parliamentary-election results from, 14; and policy formulation for diaspora, xiii, 165–72, 205; political parties in, 86; provinces of, 20; relations between diaspora and, 155–91; relationship between host countries and, 17–18; representatives of, in U.S., 88; survey of definitions of Basqueness by, 82, 111; and telecommunications, 176–80; and visits to diaspora organizations and Basque centers, 156; voter turnout in, 93, 212 n. 3. *See also* Araba (Avala); Basque Country (Euskal Herria); Bizkaia; Gipuzkoa

Euskadi eta Asktasuna (ETA-Basque Homeland and Liberty): annual assemblies of, 209–10 n. 6; and Belgium, 46, 95; and Burgos Trials, 17, 48, 76, 80, 91; and cease-fire in 1998, 88–89, 107, 177, 188; and diaspora, 74–75, 77, 82, 87, 88, 92, 98–99, 100, 106–7; and elections in 2001, 51; establishment of, xvii, 44; fragmentation of, 46, 74–75; and PNV, 44–46, 75, 77; Spanish trials and executions of ETA militants in 1975, 88; structure and membership of, 44–46; Uruguay's extradition of ETA sympathizers and activists, 82, 98–99, 100; and violence, 46–49, 99

Euskadiko Ezkerra (Basque Left), 50, 98

Euskadiren Ordezkaritza Bruselan (delegation to European Union), *following p. 80*, 95–96, 97, 170, 184

Euskal Erria Center, 98–99

Euskal Etxeak journal, 17, 138, 144, 162, 178–80, 188, 191, 203

Euskal Herria. *See* Basque Country (Euskal Herria)

Euskal Herritarrok Party, 11, 51, 189, 211 n. 6. *See also* Herri Batasuna (HB-One United People/One United Land)

Euskal Irrati Telebista (EITB), 173, 177, 178, 196, 198, 202, 203

Euskaldunak (speakers of Euskera), 20

Euskaro center, 98

Euskera (Basque language), 20, 22, 27, 35, 36–37, 38, 41, 44, 51–53, 73, 82, 112, 113, 133–36. *See also* language

Eusko Alkartasuna (EA-Basque Solidarity Party), 51, 98, 172, 189

Euzkadi (Euskadi), 35

Euzkotarra, 85

Fanon, Franz, 46

FBI investigations, 87

Federación de Instituciones Vascas de Uruguay (FIVU), 158, 160–61

Federation of Basque Entities in Argentina (FEVA), 94, 158, 160–61, 175–76, 185

Federations of Basque centers, 158, 160–62

Felipe V, King of Spain, 25–26

Fernando VII, 26, 31–32

festivals, 12, 15, 77, *following p. 80*, 83–84, 97, 159–60, 182

FEVA (Federation of Basque Entities in Argentina), 94, 158, 160–61, 175–76, 185

Filipino diaspora. *See* Philippines and Filipino diaspora

financial needs of individuals, 164, 171, 174–75

FIVU (Federación de Instituciones Vascas de Uruguay), 158, 160–61

folk dance, 30, *following p. 80*, 128, 138, 159, 172, 181

folk music, *following p. 80*, 126–28, 146, 172, 181

food, *following p. 80*, 128–29, 144, 146, 172, 193

Foral Community of Nafarroa, 50, 78, 156, 159. *See also* Nafarroa (Navarre)
foral laws. See *fueros* (local laws)
Four-Year Plan for Institutional Action, 166, 167, 172, 190, 203
France: anti-Franco activities in, 42; Basque children evacuated to during Spanish Civil War, 40; and Basque government-in-exile, 85; and Basque nationalism, 49; Basque radicals' exile to, in 1970s, 48; Basque region of, 27, 28, 29–30, 42; citizenship in, 170; colonization by, 56, 60–61; ETA members in exile in, 46; and French Revolution, 30, 61–62; and *fueros* (local laws) of Basques, 29–30, 209 n. 2; history of, 26, 27, 29–30; registered Basque centers in, 158, 169; and Spanish Civil War, 39; statistics on immigrants from, 62; travel to Basque Country from, 169. *See also* Iparralde
Franco, Francisco: anti-Franco feelings in diaspora, 9, 17–18, 44, 72–76, 80, 82, 84, 91–92, 97, 117; armed struggle against, 47–50; and Basque Country, 20, 41–44, 55; Basque government-in-exile during dictatorship of, xv; and Basque nationalism, 38–50; Basque response to political repression by, 72–75; and Burgos Trials, 17; and Catholicism, 41, 70, 110, 210 n. 4; censorship of speech and the press by, 73; death of, 11, 49, 78, 88, 195, 206; Law on Political Responsibilities under, 42; pro-Franco feelings in host countries of diaspora, 70, 73, 210 n. 4; prohibition of Basque language under, 20, 41, 52, 113, 134; public silence on protest against, 107; Spanish nation-building by, 41–43, 70; underground resistance to, 43–44. *See also* Spanish Civil War
Franks, 23
French language, 73, 133, 134

French Revolution, 30, 61–62
Fueros (local laws), 23–26, 28–30, 32, 33, 59, 64, 67, 68, 69, 81, 194
funerals, 211 n. 4 (chapter 5)

Galicia and Galicians, 54, 61, 187, 204, 206
Gallastegui, Elias, 37, 45
Gans, Herbert J., 5–8
Garagarza Perez, Miren, *following p. 80*
Garay, Juan de, 63–64
Gaztemundu (World of Youth), *following p. 80*, 163, 186–87
Geertz, Clifford, 2
Gellner, Ernest, 17, 121, 176
gender: and Basque ethnic-identity definitions, 93, 109–10, 112, 118–19; and Basque language, 112; and Catholicism, 109–10, 145; and cultural adaptation, 126; and *haizpak* (sisterhood), 142–46; and marriage patterns, 67–68; and myth of Basque matriarchy, 193; and political participation, 101, 102; and political parties in Euskadi, 86, 101; and political violence as effective for autonomy of Basque Country, 107; typical male emigrants, 67; women's migration experiences, 67–68, 142–46, 193, 196, 210 n. 3. *See also* women
generational comparisons: Basque language maintenance, 133–34; diaspora hopes for homeland's future, 106; ethnicity, 154; *haizpak* (sisterhood), 146; homeland-diaspora connections, 136; political participation, 101, 102; preservation of Basque traditions and culture, 130; roles of Basque centers, 200–201
Germanic kingdoms, 22–23
Germany, 39, 40, 42, 170
Ghandi, Mahatma, 45
Gipuzkoa: autonomy of, 9, 20, 33, 40, 50–51, 155; Basque ethnic-identity

definitions in, 53; and Basque nationalism, 38, 68; choice of terminology and spelling for, xix; under Franco dictatorship, 41; *fueros* (local laws) of, 25; history of, 23–27, 33; industry in, 28, 33; and trade, 56. *See also* Euskadi (Basque Autonomous Government)
Gipuzkoan Company, 26
Glazer, Nathan, 4
Glick Schiller, Nina, 147, 199
globalization: *aterritorial* nature of, 15; and Basque diaspora, 11–15, 78–79, 115–16, 136, 146–54, 197–99; and Basque organizations and Basque centers, 6–7; and connections between diaspora and homeland, 136, 138, 148, 149; definition of, 13, 14, 198; and diaspora identity, 147–48, 192–94, 199; and e-mail, 11, 15, 149, 177; and ethnic identity of Basques, 78–79, 115–16, 146–53; and Internet, xvi–xvii, xviii, 75, 78–79, 90, 93, 136, 138, 148, 149, 153, 172, 177–78, 188, 195, 197–98, 202–3; and transnationalism, 11–15, 147–48, 165, 197, 198–99, 205, 207–8
González, Felipe, 77
Gore, Al, 171, 184
Great Britain. *See* Britain/United Kingdom
Greek diaspora, xvi, 114
Greeley, Andrew M., 2
Guaresti, Juan José, 64
Guatemala, 58
Guernica (Picasso), 40
Guevara, Ernesto "Che," 46, 98
Guggenheim Museum, 77

Haiti, 187, 204
Haizpak (sisterhood), 142–46
Hansen, Marcus Lee, 7
HB. *See* Herri Batasuna (HB-One United People/One United Land)
health care, 164, 174, 176

Hegoalde, 20, 27, 28. *See also* Bizkaia; Gipuzkoa
Held, David, 14, 15
Herri Batasuna (HB-One United People/One United Land): and autonomy statute for Basque provinces, 50; and Basque diaspora, 92–101, 104, 107, 211 n 8; establishment and purpose of, 49; Herri Enbaxada in Belgium, 94–95, 96, 97; imprisonment of National Directorate of, 188; name change for, 51, 211 n. 7; and PNV, 94; registered voters in, 189; and violence, 92, 107. *See also* Euskal Herritarrok Party
Herri Enbaxada, 94–95, 96, 97
Hispaniola, 57
Hitler, Adolf, 70
home decoration, 139–40
Hoover, J. Edgar, 87

Ibarne, Fraga, 187
Ibarra, Francisco, 57–58
Ibarrexte Markuartu, Juan José, *following p. 80*, 169
Idaho, 15, 66, 68, 70, 71, 73, 76, 80, *following p. 80*, 87–89, 94, 126, 159–61, 210 n. 4. *See also* United States
identity. *See* ethnic identity and ethnicity
Igartua, Francisco, 97
Iguain, Gurutz, 98–99
Ikastola (Basque-language school), 38, 43, 136
ikurriña (Basque flag), 35, 98, 140, 141
Imaginary Homelands (Rushdie), 15
immigration. *See* Basque diaspora; diasporas; *and specific countries*
income assistance, 164, 171, 174–75
Inda, Nere, *following p. 80*
Independent Order of Spanish-Basque Speaking People of Idaho, 210 n. 4
India, 140
industrialization, 28, 33, 34, 35, 54, 65, 68

inheritance system. *See* primogeniture inheritance system
instrumentalist approach to ethnicity, 3–5
integration versus assimilation, 5
interest groups, 4
International Association of Basque Sports, 173
International Association of Friends of the Basques, 174
International Day of the Basque Language, 173
Internet, xvi–xvii, xviii, 78–79, 90, 93, 95, 136, 138, 148, 149, 153, 172, 175, 177–78, 188, 197–98, 202–3
Intxausti, Jokin, 156
Iparralde: and Advisory Council for Relations with Basque Communities, 159; aid from American Basques to, 87; anti-Franco activities in, 42; and Basque centers in diaspora, 156; and colonial diaspora, 60, 62; diaspora hopes for future of, 104–7; emigrants from, 93; map of, 21; nationalist movements in, 43; as "North," 20, 27, 28; radio in, 73; and Spanish Civil War, 40, 42, 70, 72, 210 n. 5
Irala e Irala, Antonio de, 71, 87
Ireland and Irish diaspora, 9, 54, 84, 114, 124, 187
Irrintzi, 69, 83, 84
Isaacs, Harold R., 2
Isabel, Princess, 32
Israel, 187, 195
Italy and Italian diaspora, 39, 40, 124
IU. *See* Izquierda Unida (IU)
Izquierda Unida (IU), 189

Jacob, James E., 30
Jai alai, 131, 173
Jaialdi International Festival, 15, 159–60
Jakobovitz, Immanuel, 205
Jáuregui Bereciartu, Gurutz, 16
jewelry, 140–41, 153

Jews and Jewish diaspora, xvi, 9, 11, 114, 117, 118, 124, 126, 196, 203, 205
journals. *See* magazines and newspapers
Juan Carlos, King, 99

Kandino, Nekane, 141
KAS Alternative (Democratic Alternative for the Basque Country), 49–50
Krutwig, Frederico, 46, 48, 75

labor unions, 37, 43, 45, 46, 49, 75, 76, 91–92, 98
Labourd. *See* Lapurdi (Labourd)
Landa Mendive, Karmelo, 94, 99
language: and Basque diaspora, 112, 113, 133–36; Basque-language programs in diaspora, *following p. 80*, 136, 162, 163, 173; Batua language, 52; dialects of Basque, 51–52; and diglossia, 133; and ethnic identity, 20, 27, 35, 36–37, 41, 51–53, 58, 82, 112, 113, 133–36; Euskera (Basque language), 20, 22, 27, 35, 36–37, 38, 41, 44, 51–53, 73, 82, 112, 113, 133–36; French language, 73, 133, 134; host-country language needed for employment in host countries, 13; International Day of the Basque Language, 173; knowledge versus use of Basque language, 135–36; newspaper in Catalan language, 34; prohibition of Basque language under Franco, 20, 41, 52, 113, 134; relationships between Basque and other languages, 20; Spanish language, 36, 41, 51, 52, 58, 61, 73, 133, 134
Lapurdi (Labourd), 29–30, 104, 156
Larramendi, Manuel de, 31
Lasagabaster Olazábal, Javier, 63
Lasarte Arana, José María, 87
Latin America: immigration policies of, 72; independentist movements in, 55, 61; right-wing politics in, 71; Spanish colonization of, xviii, 25, 26, 30, 54, 55–61. *See also specific countries*

lauburu, 141, 153, 211 n. 5 (chapter 5)
Laurac Bat/Laurak Bat, 20, 68, *following p. 80*, 84, 85, 161
law. See *fueros* (local laws)
Law of Relations with the Basque Collectivities in the Exterior (*Ley 8/1994*), xviii, 157–67, 171, 172–73, 180, 190–91, 203
Laxalt, Paul, 87
Leeper, Nancy, 120
Legarreta, Dorothy, 209 n. 5
Legarreta, Josu, 156, 163, 180
Ley 8/1994, xviii, 157–67, 171, 172–73, 180, 190–91, 203
Lhande, Pierre, 69
libraries, 131–32, 169
literacy. See education; magazines and newspapers
literature, 37, 53, 212 n. 1
Lizarra-Garazi Agreement, 89, 210–11 n. 3
Louisiana, 85. See also United States
Lyman, Stanford M., 3
Lynch, John, 60

Madariaga, Julen, 45, 59
Maeztu, 37
magazines and newspapers: of Basque diaspora, 69, 73, 83, 84–85, 97, 132; in Batua language, 52; in Catalan language, 34; censorship of, 41, 73, 97; and connections between homeland and diaspora, 137, 138, 144, 162; *Euskal Etxeak* journal, 17, 138, 144, 162, 178–80, 188, 191, 203; and nationalism, 17; negative images of Basque Country in, 176–77; newsletters of Basque diaspora associations, 132
Malvinas/Falkland Islands War, 181
Manzanas, Melitón, 47, 48, 76
Mao Tse-tung, 46
Marcos, Ferdinand, 11
Maroto, General, 32

marriage, 67–68, 78, 110
Martínez de Landecho, Juan, 58
matriarchy, myth of, 193
Maya, 9
Mayor Oreja, Jaime, 93
media. See magazines and newspapers; radio; television
men. See gender
Mendibil, Intxaurraga, 172
Mendieta, Francisco de, 209 n. 2
Mendiolea, Teresa, 72
Mexico: Basque cooking in, 129; Basque emigrants to, 38, 40, 72; Basque government official's visit to, 171; and Basque government-in-exile, 71, 85; Basque nationalism in, 42, 44, 85; business and economic foundations and institutes in, 184–86; colonization of, 57, 58, 60, 63; and Jaialdi International Festival, 15, 159–60; low-interest loans for Basque centers in, 181; magazines and newspapers in, 73, 85; music in, 127; and NABO, 212 n. 1; registered Basque centers in, 158; television in, 138, 178
migration. See Basque diaspora; diasporas
miqueletes (security forces), 41
mobilizationist approach to ethnicity, 3–5
Mola, General, 39–40
Monreal Zia, Gregorio, 31
Moynihan, Daniel P., 4
Murphy, Alexander, 120
mus (card game), *following p. 80*, 129, 138
music, *following p. 80*, 126–28, 138, 146, 161, 172, 181
Muslims, 23
Mussolini, Benito, 39, 70
mutual-aid organizations. See organizations and Basque centers

NABO (North American Basque Organization), 90, 159, 160–62, 185, 211–12 n. 1

Nafarroa (Navarre): and Advisory Council for Relations with Basque Communities, 159; autonomy of, 9, 20, 33, 50, 155; and Basque centers in diaspora, 156–57; Basque nationalism in, 68; definition of, xix; diaspora hopes for future of, 104–7; emigrants from, 93; and federal democracy of Spain, 78; history of, 33; inheritance patterns in, 67; map of, 21; and Spanish Civil War, 39–40
names, of children, 139, 141–42
Napoleon, 26, 55, 62
nationalism. *See* Basque nationalism
Nationalist Communion of the Republic of Argentina, 83
Navajo, 9
Navarre. *See* Nafarroa (Navarre)
Navarre, Kingdom of, 23, 25, 26, 27
networks. *See* organizations and Basque centers
Nevada, 66, 71, 76, 87, 126. *See also* United States
New York, 70–71, 87. *See also* United States
Newfoundland, 56, 210 n. 1
newsletters of Basque diaspora associations, 132
newspapers. *See* magazines and newspapers
Niña (ship), 57
North American Basque Organization (NABO), 90, 159, 160–62, 185, 211–12 n. 1
Northern Ireland, 54. *See also* Ireland and Irish diaspora
Norwegian immigrants, 181

Office of Relations with the Basque Diaspora Communities, 182, 183, 204–5
Oñate, Cristobal de, 57
Oñate, Juan de, 57
One United People/One United Land (HB). *See* Herri Batasuna (HB-One United People/One United Land)
oppositional approach to ethnicity, 9
oral histories of Basque immigrants, 182
"Ordinance of Bilbao," 64
Oregon, 76, 87. *See also* United States
Organization of Basque Intelligence, 87
organizations and Basque centers: as ambassadors for Basque Country, 175, 184–185, 190; in Argentina, xiii, 6, 17, 68–69, 71, 122, 124, 130–32, 145–46, 160–61; in Australia, 6, 122, 130–31, 161; and Basque language maintenance, 133–36; benefits of Basque government recognition of, 138, 148, 157, 159, 160–65; and business and economic *fundaciones* and *institutos*, 184–85; changing roles of, 154; and cooking, 128–29; and cultural adaptation, 122–26; and diasporas generally, 120; federations of Basque centers, 158, 160–62; financial support from Euskadi to, 90–91, 98, 155, 160, 161, 162, 164–65, 173, 180–83, 204–5, 211 n. 6; and Gaztemundu (World of Youth), 186–87; and International Association of Friends of the Basques, 174; Internet access for, 138, 148, 177, 198; and libraries, 131–32; low-interest loans for, 181; map of registered Basque centers in diaspora, 158; and meetings between Basque and host-country government officials, 170–71; and music, 126–28; mutual-aid societies, 69, 121–22; newsletters of, 132; nonpolitical and cultural nature of in diaspora, 75, 81, 83, 85, 99–100, 117–18, 202–5; in Peru, 68, 121–22, 130–31, 146, 149, 211 n. 6; political nature of, in diaspora, 83–93; and preservation of traditions and culture, 128–32; and Registry of Basque Centers, 6, 90–91, 157–59, 211 n. 6; social, educational, and cultural

functions of, 121–32, 193, 200–201; and sports, 131; statistics on, 6, 130, 181, 190; and third-generation return hypothesis, 7; in United States, 6, 60–61, 68, 122, 124, 130–31, 146; in Uruguay, 6, 68, 117, 122, 130–31, 146, 160–61; volunteers at, 123, 164, 185, 201, 212 n. 2; women leaders in, 146; women's political organizations, 38, 71, 85, 94. See also *specific organizations*
Oribe, Pablo, 92, 210 n. 4
orphans, 69, 72, 93
Ortiz de Uruela, Telesforo Monzón, 87
Ortíz Lizardi, Roberto, 71, 82
Otaegi, Angel, 88

Pacto de Ajuria Enea, El, 51
Palestinians, 114
Paraguay, 60, 158
Paredes Manot, Juan, 88
Partido Comunista de España (PCE-Communist Party of Spain), 100
Partido Nacionalista Vasco. *See* Basque Nationalist Party (PNV)
Partido Popular (PP-Popular Party), 93, 100, 189
Partido Socialista Obrero Español (PSOE), 189
PCE. *See* Partido Comunista de España (PCE-Communist Party of Spain)
pelota (handball), *following p. 80*, 130, 131, 159, 161, 173
Pérez de Arenaza Múgica, José Maria, 63
Pérez-Agote, Alfonso, 64–65, 109
periodicals. *See* magazines and newspapers
Peru: Aberri Eguna celebrated in, 97; anti-Franco feelings in, 97; Basque ethnic identity in, 63, 109–17, 196, 205; and Basque government-in-exile, 85; Basque language maintenance in, 112, 113, 133–36; Basque organizations in, 68, 121–22, 130–31, 146, 149, 196, 211 n. 6; colonial diaspora in, 57, 59, 60, 63; and Congress of Basque Collectivities, 88–89; economic and personal ties to Basque Country, 137; economy of, 169; ethnic conflict in during colonial period, 59; financial support from Basque government to, 180; government of, 17, 97; and Jaialdi International Festival, 15, 159–60; magazines and newspapers in, 97, 137; music in, 127–28; photographs of, *following p. 80*; political and partisan activities of Basques in, 8, 97, 100–105; preservation of Basque traditions and culture in, 128–32; prestige and positive social identity of Basques in, 9, 63, 150–52; pro-Franco feelings in, 70; reactions to Basque homeland violence in, 77, 107–8; refusal of to accept Basque political exiles, 80; registered Basque center in, 158; registered diaspora voters in for Basque homeland elections, 93, 188; Sendero Luminoso movement in, 107; television in, 178; travel to Basque Country from, 138
Philippines and Filipino diaspora, 11, 42, 55, 56, 86, 187, 203, 204
physiology, of Basques, 20, 22, 176
Picasso, Pablo, 40
Pío Baroja, 37
Plaza Euskara, 69
PNV. *See* Basque Nationalist Party (PNV)
Poland and Polish diaspora, 124, 181, 195, 201, 203
police, 50, 51, 100, 211 n. 8
political attitudes: in Basque diaspora, 100–108; diaspora hopes for homeland's future, 104–8; and political participation, 100–105; on political parties in Euskadi, 86; political violence as effective for autonomy of Basque Country, 75–78, 89, 107–8

political participation, 100–105. See also voting and elections
political parties, 51, 83, 86, 93–96, 100–101, 103, 189, 204. See also Basque Nationalist Party (PNV)
Popular Party. See Partido Popular (PP-Popular Party)
Portugal, 25
"potato principle," 121
PP. See Partido Popular (PP-Popular Party)
Primo de Rivera, Miguel, 38
primogeniture inheritance system, xviii, 55, 66–67
primordialism, 1–3, 9
print media. See magazines and newspapers
Program for Relations with the Basque Centers, 165–66
PSOE. See Partido Socialista Obrero Español (PSOE)
Puerto Rico, 158, 204

race, 35–36. See also ethnic identity and ethnicity
radio, 41, 42–43, 52, 73, 162, 173, 177
Ramirez Goicoechea, Eugenia, 53
Real Sociedad Bascongada de los Amigos del País (Royal Basque Society of the Friends of the Basque Country), 26, 31
Reconquista, 23
Registry of Basque Centers, 6, 90–91, 157–59, 211 n. 6
religious medals, 140–41
Rementeria Artiach, Miren, 211 n. 1
return migration, 78, 114, 164, 171, 174, 195, 210 n. 6
Roca, Julio Argentino, 64
Roman Empire, 22
Royal Basque Society of the Friends of the Basque Country. See Real Sociédad Bascongada de los Amigos del País

Rushdie, Salman, 15
Russia. See Soviet Union

Safran, William, 207
Sagarminaga y Epalza, Fidel de, 33
Salaberry, Juan Miguel, 141
Salcedo, Francisco de, 59
Sandberg, Neil C., 5
Santa María (ship), 57
Santo Domingo, 57, 60
Sanz, President, 157
Sarrailh de Ihartza, Fernando. See Krutwig, Frederico
schools. See education
Scotland, 54
Scott, George M., Jr., 3
Scott, Ruth, 126
Scott, William A., 126
self-interest and Basque ethnic identity, 4
Sendero Luminoso movement, 107
Service for Relations with Basque Centers, 156
sheep industry, 65, 66, following p. 80
Sheffer, Gabriel, 186
Shils, Edward, 1–2
social-identity theory, 8–9, 149, 193, 202
Socialist party, 47, 77, 189
social-security benefits, 174
Sociedad de Socorros Mútuos, 68
Society of Mutual Aid (Argentina), 69
socorros mútuos (mutual-aid societies), 122, 200
Sofia, Queen, 99
Soule. See Zuberoa (Soule)
South America. See specific countries
Soviet Union, 39, 40, 72, 97, 172
Spain: Burgos Trials in, 17, 48, 76, 80, 91, 206; and Carlist Wars, xviii, 31–33, 55, 62, 68, 194; colonization of New World by, xviii, 25, 26, 30, 54, 55–61; Constitution of 1978 in, 20, 50–52, 55, 171; distrust of in Basque diaspora, 9; emigration restrictions of, 60–61, 64; in European Community, 78; federal

democracy in, 9, 78, 83, 118, 125; and *fueros* (local laws) of Basques, 28–29; history of, 23–27, 31–33, 37–41, 61–62; industry in, 28; Law on Political Responsibilities under Franco, 42; and *Reconquista*, 23; registered Basque centers in, 158; and Spanish-American War, 30, 55; statistics on immigrants from, 61, 63, 71, 72; Suárez government of, 49, 50; and World War I, 37. *See also* Franco, Francisco; Spanish Civil War
Spanish-American War, 30, 55
Spanish Civil War, xv, xviii, 9, 17, 28, 38–41, 55, 65, 69–74, 80, 82, 84, 87, 92, 93, 97, 110, 132, 163, 176, 206. *See also* Franco, Francisco
Spanish language, 36, 41, 51, 52, 58, 61, 73, 133, 134
Spicer, Edward, 2–3, 9
spiral theory of violence, 46, 48–49
sports and athletics, 69, 130, 131, 138, 172, 173, 181
SPRI. *See* Basque Society for the Promotion and Reconversion of Industry (SPRI)
straight-line theory of acculturation assimilation, 5
Strickon, Arnold, 181
Suárez, Adolfo, 49, 50
sugarcane industry, 72, 74, *following p. 80*
Switzerland, 40
symbolic ethnicity, 5–9

Tajfel, Henri, 8, 149, 193, 202
tattoos, 141
telecommunications technology. *See* globalization; Internet; radio; television
television, 14, 52, 80, 93, 137, 138, 162, 173, 177, 178, 196, 198, 202, 203
terrorism, 46–50, 89, 92. *See also* violence
Thayer y Ojeda, 58–59
third-generation return hypothesis, 7
Tölölyan, Khachig, 136–37, 206–7

Tolosa, Juan de, 57
torture, 47, 48. *See also* violence
tourism. *See* travel and tourism to Basque homeland
trade diaspora, 55, 56, 60
traditionalism and nationalism, xvii, 30–31, 34–37
transnationalism, 11–15, 147–48, 165, 197, 198–99, 205, 207–8. *See also* globalization
travel and tourism to Basque homeland, 138–39, 148–49, 169, 174, 186, 195
Tree of Gernika, 40, 127, 140, 209 n. 2
triadic relationship, 17, 203
Trueba, 37
Tupamaros, 77, 83, 107
Txalaparta Basque Center, 96–97, 117
txapela (beret), 141
Txillardegui, 44, 46
txistu (Basque flute), 128
txistularis (players of Basque flute), *following p. 80*, 128, 140
txokos (private kitchens), 128

Udalbiltza organization of municipal mayors, 11
Ukraine, 195, 204
Unamuno, 37
United Kingdom. *See* Britain/United Kingdom
United Nationalist Women (EAB), 71, 85, 94
United Nations, 70
United Nations Research Institute for Social Development, 198
United Patriotic Women (Emakume Abertzale Batza), 71
United States: Aberri Eguna celebrated in, 97; aid to Basque homeland from, 86, 87; anti-Franco feelings in, 76; and antiterrorism pact, 51; Basque emigrants to, 66, 72; Basque ethnic-identity definitions in, 109–17; Basque experts needed in, 168; Basque

government official's visit to, 171; and Basque government-in-exile, 85, 86–87; Basque language maintenance in, 112, 113, 133–36; Basque names in, 141–42; Basque nationalism in, 85, 86–91; Basque organizations in, 6, 68, 122, 124, 130–31, 146, 160–61; business and economic foundations and institutes in, 184–86; Catholicism in, 126, 145, 196, 200; citizenship in, 170, 204; civil rights movement in, 77; and cultural exchange, 159; democratic government of, 4–5, 17, 209 n. 1; distrust of Spanish government by Basques in, 9; economic and personal ties to Basque Country, 137; ethnic identity and educational level in, 153; FBI investigations in, 87; federation of Basque centers in, 158, 160–62; financial support from Basque government to, 180; gold discovery in, 66; and Herri Batasuna, 94; immigration policies of, 72; and Jaialdi International Festival, 15, 159–60; labor specialties of Basques in, 3; magazines and newspapers in, 69, 85, 137, 177; marriage patterns in, 67; music in, 127–28; political and partisan activities of Basques in, 5, 11, 81, 83, 87–90, 94, 97, 100–105, 209 n. 1; preservation of Basque traditions and culture in, 128–32; prestige and positive social identity of Basques in, 9, 12, 150–52, 202; pro-Franco feelings in, 70; reactions to Basque homeland violence in, 89, 107–8; registered Basque centers in, 158; registered voters in for Basque homeland elections, 188; and Spanish Civil War, 39, 70–71; television in, 178; travel to Basque Country from, 138, 149; women immigrants in, 142–46

University of the Basque Country, 163–65, 166, 174

University Studies Abroad Consortium (USAC), 156

Uruguay: Aberri Eguna celebrated in, 83–84, 97; agriculture in, 65, 66; anti-Franco feelings in, 44, 73, 76, 82; and antiterrorism pact, 51; Basque emigrants to in nineteenth century, 62, 63, 64, 65, 210 n. 2; Basque ethnic identity in, 10, 53, 109–17, 196, 205; Basque government official's visit to, 171; and Basque government-in-exile, 85; Basque language maintenance in, 112, 113, 133–36; Basque nationalism in, 38, 83–84, 85; Basque organizations in, 6, 68, 98, 117, 122, 130–31, 146, 160–61; Catholicism in, 145; colonial diaspora in, 60; and Congress of Basque Collectivities, xiii, 88–89; dictatorial regime in, 77; distrust of Spanish government by Basques in, 9; and economic and personal ties to Basque Country, 137; economy of, 169; extradition of ETA sympathizers and activists by, 82, 98–99, 100; federation of Basque centers in, 160–61; financial support from Basque government to, 180; foreign policy of, 82–83; Grand War in, 210 n. 2; Herri Batasuna (HB) in, 98, 211 n. 8; and Jaialdi International Festival, 15, 159–60; labor specialties and businesses of Basques in, 3, 65, 66; low-interest loans for Basque centers in, 181; magazines and newspapers in, 85, 137; marriage patterns in, 67; music in, 127–28; photographs of, *following p. 80*; police in, 211 n. 8; political and partisan activities of Basques in, 81, 93, 97, 98–100, 100–105; preservation of Basque traditions and culture in, 128–32; prestige and positive social identity of Basques in, 9, 63, 64, 65, 150–52, 202; pro-Franco feelings in, 70, 73; reactions to Basque homeland violence, 76–77,

107–8; registered Basque centers in, 158; registered diaspora voters in for Basque homeland elections, 93, 188; sixth-generation Basques in, 10, 196; and Spanish Civil War, 39, 71; statistics on immigration to, 69; television and radio in, 73, 138, 178; travel to Basque Country from, 138; Tupamaros in, 77, 83, 107; women immigrants in, 143
USAC. *See* University Studies Abroad Consortium (USAC)
Utah, 87. *See also* United States

Van den Berghe, Pierre, 2, 4
Van Hear, Nicolas, 121–36, 207
Vasconia, 46
Venezuela: Basque cooking in, 129; Basque emigrants to, 38, 48, 72; and Basque government-in-exile, 71, 85; Basque nationalism in, 42–43, 44, 85; business and economic foundations and institutes in, 184–86; colonization of, 26, 57, 60, 63; and cultural exchange, 159; and ETA, 48; magazines and newspapers in, 85; registered Basque centers in, 158; television and radio in, 73, 138, 178
violence: assassinations, 47–48, 76; attitude on in diaspora, 107–8; in Basque Country, 46–50, 75–78; in colonies, 59; diaspora reactions to homeland violence, 75–78, 89; and ETA, 46–49, 99; and Herri Batasuna (HB), 92, 107; spiral theory of, 46, 48–49; torture, 47, 48. *See also* terrorism

Visigoths, 23
voting and elections, 14, 51, 71, 80, 93–96, 187–90, 204, 212 n. 3

Waters, Mary C., 3
women: and Catholicism, 109–10, 145; and cultural preservation, 144–45; and *haizpak* (sisterhood), 142–46; in leadership positions in Basque diaspora centers, 146; marriage of, 67–68; migration experiences of, 67–68, 142–46, 193, 196, 210 n. 3; and myth of Basque matriarchy, 193; names of married women, 142; political organizations of, 38, 71, 85, 94. *See also* gender
World Congress of Basque Collectivities. *See* Congress of Basque Collectivities
World War I, 37
World War II, 42, 70, 87
Wretched of the Earth, The (Fanon), 46
Wyoming, 73, 87. *See also* United States

youth program. *See* Gaztemundu (World of Youth)
Yparraguirre, 37
Yugoslavia, 181

Zabala, Lorenzo, 48
Zabaleta, Iñaki, 176–77
Zuberoa (Soule), 29–30, 32, 156
Zumarraga, Juan de, 57
Zutik (Arise), 46